Belfast Naturalists' Field Club

Annual Reports and Proceedings of the Belfast Naturalists' Field Club

Vol. 1

Belfast Naturalists' Field Club

Annual Reports and Proceedings of the Belfast Naturalists' Field Club
Vol. 1

ISBN/EAN: 9783337429690

Printed in Europe, USA, Canada, Australia, Japan

Cover: Foto ©Suzi / pixelio.de

More available books at **www.hansebooks.com**

ANNUAL REPORTS

AND

PROCEEDINGS

OF THE

BELFAST NATURALISTS' FIELD CLUB.

New Series.

VOLUME I. 1873-80.

BELFAST:
PRINTED FOR THE CLUB.

1881.

INDEX.

	PAGE
Abbeys—in County Down	118
Abbeys—Monkstown	13
Altfrakyn	227
Annual Meetings	52, 125, 200, 267, 319, 361, 429
Antrim	155
Antrim Coast Road	165, 392
Arboe	21
Archæological Association of Ireland	71, 96
Ardglass	299
Armagh	230
Aurora Borealis, Notes on, Dr. T. H. Keown	49
Avicula contorta Beds	241
Ballintoy, Bannmouth, Bushfoot	265
Ballycarry	225
Ballygally Castle	75
Ballygally Head	166, 265, 269
Ballyholme	265
Ballynahinch	163
Ballynure	80, 162
Ballymena	229
Ballyoran	303
Ballyruther	166
Banagher	238
Bann River	77, 400
Bauxite in County Antrim	359
Beginnings of Life	181
Belfast Naturalists' Field Club—Origin of	93
Birds of Lough Neagh	183
Black Mountain	75, 251, 402
Boulder Clay	101, 106, 390, 428
Bristow, Rev. John, on Practical Hints to Collectors of Lepidoptera	185
British Association	5, 23, 70, 82, 95, 96, 127, 174, 310, 343

	PAGE
Broughshane	15
Browne (John), Origin and Progress of Coinage	249
Browne (John), British War-Medals	417
Browne (W. J.), Beginnings of Life	181
Butterflies	185, 188, 391
Cairn Hill	80
Calamagrostis Hookeri	298
Camus	78
Carlingford	329
Carncastle	75, 393
Carncarney Mountain	158
Carnlough	394, 265
Carnmoney	12, 336, 353
Carrickfergus	79, 265, 295
Castle-Espie	102
Castle-Robin	240
Chalk Foraminifera	46, 95
Cinerary Urns	430
Cistercian Remains in County Down	117, 296
Coalisland	8
Coinage—its Origin and Progress	249
Coast Road (Antrim)	165, 392
Coleraine	77
Colin Glen	240, 255, 270
Comber Abbey	119
Committee's Reports	3, 69, 149, 219, 289, 321, 381
Conversaziones	130, 305, 339, 407
Court, The	388
Crannogs—Irish	47
Creenagh Colliery	10
Cretaceous Fossil Patellidæ	320
Cretaceous Microzoa	46, 95, 221
Cretaceous Rocks	22, 241, 251, 294, 333, 336, 390, 394, 402, 428
Cromlechs	20, 21, 229, 296, 303, 328, 351, 404
Crosses of Camus	78
Crow Glen	333
Crumlin	336
Cryptogams	113
Ouil Rathen	78
Cup-marked Stones	398, 427
Cushendall	15, 167, 392

Index.

	PAGE
Darragh (Thomas), Parasites in Water-hen	267
Darragh (Thomas), Notes on Birds	319
Day (Robert), On Old Finger-Rings	315
Doagh	79
Donegal—North	69
Downpatrick	299
Downpatrick Abbey	119
Dredging in Belfast Bay, &c.	200, 268, 306
Do. Strangford Lough	244
Drumbo	387
Drumglass Colliery	10
Dufferin (Earl of), Vote of Thanks to	199
Duncrue	294
Dun-da-Bheann	79
Dundonald	296, 301
Dundrum	265, 328
Dungannon	8
Dungiven	296
Dunledy Glen	302
Eas Creibh	79
Elephas primigenius	167
Emania	231
Eskers—Origin of	100
Estuarine Clays	95, 428
Exchange of Proceedings	54, 134, 203, 272, 363, 438
Farrell's Fort	389
Ferns and Fern Collecting	357
Finger Rings—Old	315
Flints and their Microzoa	46
Flint Flakes	109, 265
Flint Scrapers	112, 265
Foraminifera—Recent	177, 200, 268, 306, 312, 323, 349, 428
Foraminifera—Irish Chalk	46, 95, 221
Foraminifera—Irish Liassic	95, 269
Fossil Plants	170
Garron Point	20, 167, 394
Gault (Wm.), Geology of the Black Mountain	251
Gault (Wm.), Irish Cretaceous Strata	428
Gault (Wm.), Occurrence and Origin of Hullite	353

Giants' Graves	337
Giant's Ring	387
Glacial Drift	105
Glacial Periods	101, 104, 105, 423
Glenariffe	168, 396
Glenarm	335, 394, 400
Glenavy	170
Glendun	20, 169, 396
Glenoe	162
Glenravel	15
Glenwherry	229
Glens of Antrim	165
Glynn and Glenoe	160
Gobbins	21, 389
Graptolites	306
Graptolites of Co. Down	115
Gray (Wm.), on the British Association	23
Gray (Wm.), Rudely Worked Flints of Down and Antrim	108
Gray (Wm.), Hunting in the Sand-dunes	264
Gray (Wm.), Our Northern Rocks	319
Gray (Wm.), Vice-President's Address, 1878	343
Gray (Wm.), Occurrence of Bauxite in County Antrim	359
Gray (Wm.), Presidential Address, 1879	411
Gray (Wm.), Cup Marked Stones	427
Groyabbey	118, 295
Guide to Belfast and adjacent Counties	5, 70, 127, 128, 177, 344
Harbison (Mann), Origin of Eskers	100
Harbison (Mann), Tour through Switzerland	420
Hillhall	387
Historical and Archæological Society of Ireland	5, 71, 96
Holywood	265
Honey Bee, On the	425
Hullite	337, 353
Inch Abbey	118
Irish Antiquities, Exhibition of	71, 96, 127, 292
Irish Hill	80
Iron Ores, Antrim	18
Islandmagee	21
Jones (T. Rupert), Vote of Thanks to	202

Kempe Stone, the	303, 404
Keown (Dr. T. H.), on the Aurora	49
Kildare Round Tower and Cathedral	360
Kilroot	265
Killyleagh	243, 268
Kistvaens	337
Knight (Henry), Lower Forms of Vegetable Life	113
Knockagh	171
Knowles (W. J.), Prehistoric Remains at Portstewart	100
Lagan Canal	13
Langtry (George), Progressive Development	24
Larne	74, 166, 229, 393, 265
Lava-rearing	196
Legainaddy	299
Leistono	265
Lepidoptera	270
Lepidoptera, Hints to Collectors	185
Liassic Foraminifera	254, 269
Liassic Rocks	22, 46, 241, 333, 335, 390, 393
Lignites	170
Liguapeiste	236
Limavady	236
Lockwood (F. W.), Round Tower and Cathedral of Kildare	360
Lockwood (F. W.), On Round Towers	423
Lough Beg	401
Loughgall	297
Lough Neagh	103, 297
Lough Neagh, Birds of	183
Lurigethan	262
Madman's Window, the	339
Maghery	298
Magheralin, Cinerary Urns at	430
Members, Lists of	58, 138, 208, 277, 369, 442
Microscopes, Exhibition of	27
Miller (Wm.), Antiquarian Remains on Lurigethan	262
Miller (Wm.), Rude Stone Monuments in Antrim	351
Miocene Plants	170
Moneymore	21
Monkstown Abbey	13
Montalto	164

	PAGE
Mosses	113, 117, 177, 269
Moths	185
Mountstewart	296
Museum Natural History Collections	221
M'Clure (Rev. Edmond)—Surnames in County Antrim	28
Mac Ilwaine (Rev. Dr.)—Presidential Address, 1874	81
Mac Ilwaine (Rev. Dr.)—Presidential Address, 1875	174
Mac Ilwaine (Rev. Dr.)—Presidential Address, 1876	246
Mac Ilwaine (Rev Canon)—Presidential Address, 1877	310
Navan Fort	230
Newcastle	328
Newry Abbey	118
Newtownards	403
North Donegal	69
Ogham Stone	49
Origin of Belfast Naturalists' Field Club	93
Origin of Eskers	100
Orthotrichum Sprucei	320, 388
Ossian's Grave	20
Peat—Submerged	107
Phillips (James J.), Architectural Remains of the Cistercians in Co. Down	117
Phillips (W. H.), Ferns and Fern Collecting	357
Pliocene Clays of Lough Neagh	348
Portrush	100, 265
Portstewart	100
Prehistoric Remains at Portstewart	100
Presidents' Addresses	23, 81, 174, 246, 310, 343, 411
Prizes, Awarded	5, 72, 151, 222, 270, 292, 305, 323, 383
Prizes, Offered	65, 145, 215, 286, 378, 436
Prizes, at Excursions	76, 163, 165
Prizes, Special	6, 67, 147, 217, 288, 308, 323, 362, 380, 384, 446
Proceedings, Exchanges of	54, 134, 203, 272, 363, 438
Progressive Development	24
Pupa Digging	198
Raised Beaches	266
Rademon	243
Radloy (Joseph), on Woodpeckers and Kingfishers	262
Ram's Island	170

Index.

	PAGE
Red Bay	18, 167, 395
Redhall	225
Reports of Committee	3, 69, 149, 219, 289, 321, 381
Robinson (Rev. George), Birds of Lough Neagh	183
Robinson, (J. R.), Water as an Agent of Denudation	312
Roughfort	336
Round Towers	423
Round Tower of Antrim	156
Round Tower of Kildare	360
Royal Hist. and Archæol. Society of Ireland	5, 71, 96
Rudely Worked Flints of Down and Antrim	108
Rules of the Club	62, 142, 212, 282, 374, 432
Russell (Charles C.), on the Honey Bee	425
Sallagh Braes	53, 74
Sand-dunes, Hunting in	264
Scawdey Island	298
Scott (Dr. J. M. J.), Vegetable Parasites of the Human Body	177
Scrabo	403
Shane's Hill	74, 229
Silicified Wood	170, 350
Silurian Rocks of County Down	262, 296, 312, 328
Souterrains	334, 351
Speers (Adam), Water and its Effects in Nature	178
Standing Stones Hill	75
Stewart (S. A.), Mosses of the District	117
Stewart (S. A.), A Trip from Galway to Dingle	352
Stone Circle	299
Straid	80
Strangford Lough	243
Submerged Peat	107
Surnames in County Antrim	28
Swanston (Wm.), Graptolites in County Down	115
Swanston (Wm.), Correlation of the Silurian Rocks of Co. Down	262
Swanston (Wm.), Supposed Pliocene Fossiliferous Clays of Lough Neagh	348
Switzerland, Tour Through	420
Tardree	155
Tartaraghan	297
Templecorran Old Church	225
Toome Bridge	400
Torr Head	265, 399

Treasurer's Statements	7, 73, 154, 224, 293, 326, 386
Tullyard	388
Vegetable Parasites of the Human Body	177
Vicia orobus	53
Vitrified Fort	388
Wakeman (W. F.),—Irish Crannogs	47
War-Medals, British	417
Water-Hen, Parasites in	267
Water and its Effects in Nature	178
Water as an Agent of Denudation	312
Water Supply	344
Whitewell Quarries	336
Wiley's Fort	80
Woodburn	294, 428
Woodpeckers and Kingfishers	262
Worked Flints of Down and Antrim	108
Wright (Joseph), Flints, and the Foraminifera, Entomostraca, etc., contained in them	46
Wright (Joseph), Dredging in Belfast Bay	200, 268
Wright (Joseph), Post-tertiary Foraminifera	428

LIST OF DRAWINGS, PHOTOGRAPHS, &c.,

In the Club's Album.

NATURAL HISTORY.

	PAGE
Large Cork Tree, near Cork	4
Ribbon Fish found at Bundoran	11

ANTIQUITIES.

ABBEYS AND CHURCHES:

	PAGE
Bonamargey Abbey, Ballycastle	5
Cranfield Church, Co. Antrim	45
Greyabbey, Co. Down	7, 10
Doorway, Maghera Old Church (the Crucifixion)	38
Do. Newtownards Old Church	20
Old Church, Church Island, Lough Beg, Co. Antrim	45

ROUND TOWERS:

Antrim	42
Do.	42
Kildare (Doorway)	39

CASTLES:

Audley, Strangford	30
Ballygally	14, 15
Benburb	46
Buncrana (the Keep)	47
Castleward, Strangford	30
The Court, Lisburn	40
Kilclief, Strangford	28
Kirkistown,	21
Olderfleet, Larne	47
Strangford	29

CROMLECHS, &C.

Broadstone, Craigs, Co. Antrim	44
Clontum Cromlech, Co. Armagh	44
Dundonald, the Kempe Stone	6
Islandmagee	35

CROMLECHS, &c.—*Continued.*

	PAGE
County Monaghan, near Lord Cremorne's	6
Giant's Grave, Dunteige, Glenarm	36
Giant's Grave, Cairnaseggart, Glenarm	36

CROSSES :

Donoughmore, Co. Down	41
Innispollen, Cushendun	41

MISCELLANEOUS :

Armlet (Silver) found at Downpatrick	16
Casket (Soiscel Molaise) in R. I. Academy	25
Casket (Domnach Airgid) do.	26
Fibula (Silver) found at Ballymoney	16
Bronze Hook found near Belfast	17
Bronze Trumpet found at Kilrauts, Co. Antrim	18
Bronze Instrument found at Bog near Ballymoney	19
Necklace and Rings (Roman ?), Donaghadee	17
Tara Brooch, in R. I. Academy	27
Stone Implements, E. Benn, Esq., Glenravel	37

GEOLOGICAL.

Cultra, Distorted Permian and Carboniferous Strata	23
Galboley, Fault and Iron Ore Beds	35
Garron Point	34
Iron Ore Workings, Kilwaughter, Larne	37
Slate Quarries, Wales, Distorted Strata	12
Slate Quarries, Wales, Ripple Marks	13
Trap Dykes, Squires' Hill (two)	1
Do. Cave Hill (two)	2
Do. Scrabo	2
Do. Squires' Hill	3
Do. Cave Hill	3
Do. Knock Dhu, Co. Antrim	22
Do. Causeway and Fair Head	31
Cave of "Seven Arches," Lough Swilly	43

ANNUAL REPORT

AND

PROCEEDINGS

OF THE

Belfast Naturalists' Field Club.

1873-1874.

SERIES II.

Volume I.   Part I.

PRINTED FOR MEMBERS ONLY.

AND

PROCEEDINGS

OF THE

Belfast Naturalists' Field Club,

FOR THE

YEAR ENDING 31ST MARCH, 1874.

(ELEVENTH YEAR.)

NEW SERIES.

VOLUME I.   PART I.

BELFAST:
PRINTED FOR THE CLUB,
AT THE "BELFAST NEWS-LETTER" STEAM-PRINTING HOUSE,
55, 57, & 59, DONEGALL STREET.

1875.

REPORT

OF THE

Belfast Naturalists' Field Club,

FOR THE YEAR 1873-74.

T the close of the eleventh year of the Club's existence, your Committee have the gratification of being able to report that the financial position and prospects of the Society were never more encouraging. The number of members enrolled continues to increase, amongst whom are many well-known students of natural science. The Excursions during the Summer Session were conducted as usual, and the following places were visited :—

      17th May. Dungannon and Coalisland.
      7th June. Carnmoney.
      28th June. Lagan Canal.
  16th, 17th, and 18th July. Glenravel and Cushendall.
      16th August. Moneymore and Arboe.
      6th September. Islandmagee and the Gobbins.

During the Winter Session the following papers were read (abstracts of which are appended) :—

1873.
19th Nov. "On the British Association: its Aims and Objects." By Mr. William Gray, M.R.I.A.
10th Dec. "On Progressive Development." By Mr. George Langtry.
1874.
15th Jan. This Meeting was devoted to the exhibition of Microscopes and Microscopic Objects.
28th Jan. "On the Surnames of the Inhabitants of the County Antrim, and their Indications." By Rev. Edmund M'Clure, A.M., M.R.I.A.
18th Feb. "On Flints, and the Foraminifera, Entomostraca, &c., contained in them." By Mr. Joseph Wright, F.G.S., &c.
11th March. "Irish Cranoges and their Contents." By Mr. W. F. Wakeman.
15th April. "Notes on the Aurora Borealis, taken in Belfast in the years 1870-71, with suggestions as to its source, and that of the Earth's Magnetism and Magnetic Currents." By Dr. T. H. Keown, R.N.

The Sub-Committee continue the work of re-arranging the valuable collections in the Museum of the Natural History and Philosophical Society, and for this purpose have attended at the Museum every week, without intermission, since last session. The result is that the Herbarium of Flowering Plants is now nearly complete, and considerable progress has been made with that of the Mosses, and in the mounting of the collections of Foreign Shells—the latter are very numerous, and promise to make a very effective display.

In anticipation of the meeting of the British Association, to be held in Belfast next August, your Committee sent a deputation to the Bradford meeting, with instructions to endeavour to obtain such information as would enable the Club to render effective assistance in preparing for the forthcoming meeting in Belfast.

The deputation also visited several museums, and obtained hints that will not be lost sight of in the work of re-arranging our local Museum.

Your Committee, believing that a "Naturalists' Guide" to Belfast and the adjacent counties would be acceptable to the members of the British Association and other visitors to the North of Ireland, resolved to prepare and publish such a "Guide." It is intended that the "Guide" shall contain about two hundred pages, and be illustrated by a map and sketches, and will contain chapters on the Topography, Geology. Botany, Zoology, Ethnology, and Antiquities of the district; together with observations on the Trade, Commerce, and Agriculture of the North of Ireland. Such an undertaking will involve considerable expense; your Committee, therefore, hope that the appeal for aid about to be made to the members of the Club and the public generally, will meet with an encouraging response, so that the promoters may be enabled to go to press in proper time.

Your Committee propose also, in conjunction with the Council of the Royal Historical and Archæological Society of Ireland, to have an Exhibition of Irish Antiquities in Belfast, during the meeting of the British Association. Arrangements are already in progress, and many valuable contributions are promised, and there is every prospect of having a very creditable Exhibition. This result can only be secured by the kindly assistance of all who are interested in our national antiquities.

In consequence of the amount of labour involved by the preparations in progress for the approaching meeting of the British Association, together with the difficulties arising from the rearrangement of the Museum, your Committee have reluctantly resolved to abandon the Conversazione for this year.

Your Committee continue to exchange "Transactions" with other Societies in various parts of the world. The names of these Societies, and the contributions received from them, are appended.

The following gentlemen were requested by your Committee to act as judges in awarding the prizes offered by the Club :—Dr. James Moore, H.R.H.A., Mr. Robert Young, C.E., Mr. William Swanston, and Mr. Greer Malcomson.

The following are declared to be the successful competitors :—
For best collection of Ferns—Mr. S. A. Stewart.
For best collection of Cretaceous Fossils—Mr. Geo. Donaldson.
For best collection of Liassic Fossils—Mr. Geo. Donaldson.

For best collection of Geological Specimens, illustrative of the mineral resources of Ulster—Mr. William Gray.

The President's Prize, for the best Original Measured Drawing, and details of some ruined building in Ireland, of not later date than the 15th century—Mr. F. W. Lockwood.

For the best six Field Sketches, appertaining to Geology, Archæology, or Natural History—Mr. William Gray.

WILLIAM GRAY, } *Hon. Secs.*
HUGH ROBINSON,

Dr. *Belfast Naturalists' Field Club in Account with Treasurer.* **Cr.**

	£ s. d.		£ s. d.
To Balance from 1872-73	34 13 0	By Expenses of Conversazione	9 3 0
,, Subscriptions	50 5 0	,, Printing Annual Report	16 6 0
,, Arrears of Subscriptions	3 0 0	,, Advertising, Printing, Stationery, &c...	14 5 1
,, Conversazione Tickets sold	3 15 0	,, Delivery of Circulars	1 10 0
		,, Postages	3 17 9
		,, Prizes	3 0 0
		,, Rent of Museum	5 0 0
		,, Curator	3 0 0
		,, Loss on Excursions	0 0 6
		,, Subscription to Palæontographical Society	3 3 0
		,, Expenses of Deputation to Bradford Meeting of British Association	17 14 6
		,, Balance on hands	14 13 2
	£91 13 0		£91 13 0

Audited and found correct,

HUGH ROBINSON.

GREER MALCOMSON, *Treasurer.*

SUMMER SESSION.

The following Excursions were made during the Summer Session:

On Saturday, 17th May, to

DUNGANNON AND COALISLAND.

The Tyrone coal-field has been the subject of many elaborate reports, forming no small share of the scientific literature of the North of Ireland. Sir Richard Griffith, in his capacity as mining engineer to the Royal Dublin Society, was the first to deal with the subject in a proper manner. Sir Robert Kane, too, enlarged on the same theme; and Col. Portlock, of the Royal Engineers, when conducting the geological branch of the Ordnance Survey of Ireland, gave a summary of all that was then known, and added the result of his own observations and inquiries in his report of the geology of Londonderry, &c. Since then occasional papers have been published by others interested in the matter; but the most valuable of all other publications must be the memoir in course of publication by the Government Geological Surveyors, under the direction of Professor Hull, F.R.S. Indeed, Professor Hull has already given his opinion regarding the nature and extent of the field in his report to the Commissioners appointed in 1870 to ascertain the probable duration of British coal-fields; and E. T.

Hardman, Esq., one of Professor Hull's staff, who has been surveying the district for a considerable period, has, in anticipation of the official memoir, published his views in a valuable paper read before the Royal Dublin Society.

This mass of undisputed testimony demonstrates that the Tyrone coal-field contains nine or ten beds of true coal, varying in thickness from two to nine feet! and so distributed over an area of about six or seven thousand acres as to be capable of yielding something like thirty-two million tons of coal—no mere substitute, but genuine coal—which, as to origin, geological age, or mineral character, is identical with the coals of Scotland or England.

On arrival of the members of the Club at Dungannon they were met by Thos. A. Dixon, Esq., M.P., who most courteously entertained the party, and accompanied them on their trip, giving them the fullest information in relation to the nature and extent of the collieries, and explaining the contemplated improvements.

The coal-field extends from near Dungannon to some distance beyond Coalisland, the coal-beds being here interstratified with beds of shale, fire-clay, and sandstone, which unite to make up a thickness of, say, 1,000 feet, constituting the "coal measures;" filling a depression in the limestone, and dipping towards the north-east, where they are covered by the new red sandstone.

Unfortunately, the extraction of the coal is rendered difficult and costly from the disturbed nature of the strata. If the beds lay one over another in continuous sheets for the whole extent of the field, their being tilted would facilitate the working of the coal; but the area they occupy is cut up by faults, dislocations, and other disturbances, so that continuity of the coal is frequently broken. Many coal seams run up near the surface, and these offer tempting opportunities for *shallow-workings—a grievous evil in Tyrone.* From these shallow and often extremely rude workings, millions of tons of coal have been removed by the colliers from time to time for the last 100 years; their history being one of bungling mismanagement, and consequent failure, notwithstanding the engineering skill of Ducart, his superior pits and canals, or the patronage and support of the Irish Parliament, the enterprise and ample expenditure of the Hibernian Mining Company, or the scientific knowledge applied under Mr. Griffith's management.

The members of the Field Club visited one of these shallow pits—say, thirty yards deep. It was worked by a common winch, such as a pump-sinker would use. The party were let down the pit, one by one in a bucket, or rather they held on by the rope, had one foot in a bucket and the other out, spinning round as the rope descended, and dangling from side to side. Now and then the bucket caught on the projections from the pit's sides and turned over as if to give the visitor a quicker passage to the bottom. A little care prevented such an issue, but did not prevent the bucket from coming with a bump at the bottom; then, completely turning over, pitched out the visitor at a square hole, like the mouth of a sewer, and, leaving him sprawling, went aloft for his companions. This was a new pit in Drumglass field. The cuttings, props, and all were rough, but tolerably dry and firm, although the supporting timbers gave evidence in many cases of the yielding character of the roof. After traversing the colliery underground, the members of the club were brought to the surface up another shaft in a bucket similar to that by which they were let down.

They then visited the Creenagh colliery, where all is wrought by steam-power. The large quantity of water thrown out by the pumps was not an agreeable subject to contemplate by those who were preparing to descend. However, several of the party entered the cage, adjusted their lamps, gave the signal, and were shot down some fifty yards deep. In the descent, the water from the sides of the shaft increased from a pleasant spray to a perfect shower bath, which fell thick at the bottom, and drove the visitors into the dark chambers of the mine. The slovenly, rude, and unskilful manner of working the colliery was very soon apparent. The passages were small, irregular, wet, and dirty. There were no rails for the coal hutches to run on, but they were dragged over the irregular up-and-down floor by the unfortunate, half-naked, but merry "putters," who progressed in a crouching attitude, with a swaying motion, like the ungainly movement of an antediluvian reptile, the ruts cut by the rough-shod bottom of the coal-laden hutch answering for the mud-track of the monster's tail. And thus they dragged their heavy load over the rock floor of undulating levels, or pushed them down the steep adits from the rise, with wet dropping from the low roof, and coal-dust and rubbish ground into thick mud by the traffic, and forming a continuous stream along the passages to the lower levels. Having traversed several dozen yards in this manner through these dreary workings, the members of the Field Club returned to the surface, where they could scarcely recognise each other, so transformed were they by being blackened with mud and smeared with dirt. The "Torrent" river, however, soon restored them to their normal condition, and they left the Creenagh colliery with no very exalted notion of the skill displayed in its working.

It is this Creenagh colliery that yields the very best coal in Tyrone, if not in Ireland, and the largest price is obtained for it. There is here a seam of "cannel," or gas coal, proved by reliable analysis to be equal to the *best samples* of Lismahagow cannel. This seam, however, is limited in quantity and exceptional in quality; as a rule, the product of the Tyrone collieries is by no means a superior coal, it has a tendency to be sulphurous, yields a large per centage of ash, and contains a great proportion of small coal or slack, and cannot compete with the better qualities of imported coal. It would be extremely useful for steam purposes generally, and for domestic use when the consumer wishes to be economical at the cost of a little inconvenience from dust, &c. For the latter purpose large quantities could be disposed of. Hitherto the quantity produced at the collieries entirely failed to supply even the local demand, and therefore never affected the market price of coal—*the point in which the public is most interested*. It has been demonstrated on undoubted authority that this field contains large quantities of coal sufficient for the consumption of the North of Ireland for many years to come. The collieries in former years yielded from 1,000 to 10,000 tons per annum, but they are capable of yielding a very much larger quantity. For this purpose a new company has been recently formed, and guided by the best authorities and supported by ample means, they will avail themselves of the highest skill, and adopt the most approved modern appliances, which, with their large resources, will enable them to work the collieries more extensively than has hitherto been attempted. Time alone will tell how far they may succeed; at all events, the spirit of enterprise that prompted the undertaking deserves the sympathy and hearty support of all who love their country, and are interested in the development of its mineral resources, and the advancement of its native industries. It is to be hoped that the next time the Belfast Naturalists' Field Club visit the collieries of Tyrone, the works of the several companies will be in a most flourishing condition.

On Saturday, 7th June, to

CARNMONEY, &c.

A goodly number of members assembled at the appointed rendezvous—The Ulster Hall—and on suitable vehicles left town by the Antrim Road. The first halt was called near the Whitewell, where the whole party examined the interesting geological features of the place. The road is here very unstable and shifting, having been originally formed on a talus slipped down from the cliffs above, over the surface of the Lias and New Red Marls, and the pressure of the vast masses of tumbled-over chalk and trap taxes the skill of the "surface men" to keep the road in tolerable order. After a ramble through the fields the party met at the parish church, and went off together to the adjoining quarry, where there occurs a peculiar scoriaceous form of trap with chalcedony and iron pyrites, and several good samples were secured.

Ascending the hill the party next scrambled up to Dunanney

Fort, a very fine example of the ancient Irish fortified residences, commanding a grand view of Belfast Lough and the country at both sides. The fatigue of the trip, so far, was very pleasantly relieved by the timely consideration of the very excellent rector of the parish, the Rev. Geo. C. Smythe, A.M., who most generously entertained the entire party on the beautiful lawn in front of Coole Glebe, where a number of distinguished visitors awaited the arrival of the Club.

Thus renewed, the party set off with fresh vigour for Monkstown Abbey, on the south-western slope of the Knockagh. The fragment of this abbey now remaining is so small it was with some difficulty found, and consists of a mere boss of rude rubble masonry covered with foliage, and almost hidden from view. The original structure measured about 63 feet by 17 feet. It was here King Fergus, from whom Carrickfergus derived its name, was buried. " This Fergus, the son of Erc, was the first of the Dalriadic kings of Scotland. He was descended through Cairbre Riada, from Conaire, monarch of Ireland, who died in the year 220. At the commencement of the sixth century, Fergus Mac Erc, accompanied by his two brothers, Loarn and Angus, led an expedition into Alba (Scotland), and took possession of all the north-western coast and the adjoining islands. Fergus became the first king of the territory thus occupied by the colonists from the Irish shores, and was succeeded in this sovereignty by a long line of sixty Dalriadic rulers, the last of whom being Alexander III., who died in the year 1286." *(See note to the Montgomery Manuscripts, by Rev. G. Hill, p. 427.)*

Leaving Monkstown Abbey, the party returned to town by the lower road, which afforded them an opportunity of exploring the ivy-clad ruins of Whiteabbey, &c.

On Saturday, 28th June, 1873, to

LAGAN CANAL.

Where shall we go for a day's outing? is oftener asked in Belfast than practically answered, mainly because places within reach, and capable of affording a day's pleasure, seem quite unknown. The Belfast Naturalists' Field Club are never at a loss in selecting suitable trips. They have had six excursions every year for the last ten years, and yet they can still fill their programme with new places of interest, and seldom traverse the same ground twice. The last trip was on the Lagan Canal, and it proved one of the pleasantest excursions enjoyed for a long time. It was a thorough naturalists' excursion, involving no fatigue, while it afforded ample opportunity for botanical rambles, sketching, dredging, and collecting specimens for cabinets at home. The party left town by train for Moira. Here a well-appointed barge awaited them, kindly lent for the occasion by the directors of the Lagan Navigation Company. It was capable of comfortably accommodating sixteen or eighteen passengers, and was drawn over the canal at a rapid rate by a horse travelling along the bank. This mode of locomotion was as agreeable as it was novel; and, being quite under the control of the skipper, a halt was made whenever the party wished to land on either side of the canal. Such stoppages were frequent, as they afforded opportunity for collecting the plants fringing the canal, which could not be secured by other means, and the dredging operations for freshwater shells and sponges were enjoyed without the disagreeable effects of similar operations at sea, or even in the harbour. For the greater portion of the distance between Moira and Lisburn, the canal is unbroken by locks, but from Lisburn to Belfast the locks are very frequent, and the canal more tortuous in its course; but the physical features of the country that necessitate these appliances add very much to the beauty of the scenery on each side. The upper portion of the canal lies in a comparatively tame country, but the lower part is through a succession of diversified plantations, many spots being exceedingly picturesque and beautiful, reminding us very much of the charming paintings we so often see of views "on the Thames." Gliding through a succession of such scenes along the Lagan on a calm summer evening is exceedingly agreeable. On this occasion its particularly soothing effect tempered the zeal of our naturalists, who, laying aside dredge, and net, and vasculum, abandoned themselves to the quiet enjoyment of the surrounding beauty, ploughing their way through the calm waters on their rapid homeward course. The botanical wealth of the locality visited is very considerable, and specimens were collected of several rare plants. The sweet flag (*Acorus Calamus*) was found in abundance on both banks of the canal between Moira and Lisburn. The history of this plant is interesting. It grows nowhere else in Ireland, but was known to occur in Co. Down in 1788. Subsequently it was lost sight of until 1866, when it was re-discovered by members of the Belfast Naturalists' Field Club. The sweet flag may not be entitled to rank in the strictest sense as an indigenous plant; nevertheless, the fact of its having occupied a position in the country for nearly a hundred years makes it an old-established denizen. Another rare plant, the bitter cress *(Cardamine amara)*, was found growing in very small quantity on the canal banks. Several species of pondweed are abundant, the rarest of which is *Potamageton prælongus*—quite a scarce plant. The pretty little lily-like plant *Villarisa nymphæoides* is also found in the canal, and the flowering rush adorns the banks with its umbels of showy flowers. The gipsy wort *(Lycopus europæus)* occurs, with many others deserving of notice. The water thyme *(Anacharis Alsinastrum)*, an unwelcome immigrant, extends itself in dense masses all through the canal; indeed it was known here years before it was noted as occurring in the sister kingdom.

On 16th, 17th, and 18th July, to

GLENRAVEL AND CUSHENDALL.

The party went by train to Ballymena, and there a large van awaited to convey them to Glenravel and Cushendall. Driving first to Broughshane, they visited Dr. Grainger, the rector of the parish, who kindly exhibited his very fine collection of archæological, geological, and natural history objects. The valley of The Braid, associated with the history of St. Patrick, is a rich field for the archæologist; and Dr. Grainger has a valuable collection of bronze and stone tools, implements, and personal ornaments, found within the limits of his parish, one of the largest in the county; indeed, his collection would form in itself a very respectable museum.

From Broughshane the party went to Ballycloghan, so-called, "freestone" quarry. The stone of this quarry was supposed to be a freestone, or sandstone, and, as such, connected with the coal measures; and for a long time past the people of this locality believed that the coal existed there not far from the surface. This opinion was confirmed by a mining engineer, who predicted that several beds of coal would be found at certain depths; he even gave the thickness of the beds supposed to occur within 400 feet. These favourable prospects cheered the whole country, and the farmers of Carncoa told how they frequently raised coal in their lands when turning up the soil for farming purposes, &c. When this information was published here, a member of the Naturalists' Field Club stated point-blank the whole affair was a mistake; that no coal was ever found in the locality, or ever would be found; that the supposed "freestone" was not freestone, but a variety of porphyry, and that if a boring was made the borer would only find what could be found on the top of Cave Hill. Here was a most direct conflict of opinion. The mining engineer positively asserted coal would be found; the amateur geologist as decidedly stated it would not. Now for the test. Lord O'Neill, on whose property the supposed freestone quarry occurs, generously agreed to have a boring at his cost, and engaged the services of the Diamond Boring Company, who came on the ground at once and commenced operations, which were not suspended until they reached a depth of 550 feet, or over 200 feet below the level of the sea! But no coal was touched; nothing, in fact, but what could be had on the Cave Hill—common trap rock; and thus, at an expenditure of hundreds of pounds, the predictions of the mining engineer were proved unfounded, and the opinion of the member of the Belfast Naturalists' Field Club demonstrated to be correct. It is only to be regretted now that the landlord's liberality and the boring company's most efficient apparatus did not secure better results. This was the first boring made by this company in Ireland, and probably the severest test the apparatus was ever put to, inasmuch as it had to bore through solid trap rock for the entire depth; yet it went down steadily, often thirty feet per day, and brought to the surface from all depths, even to 558 feet, not muddy *debris*, like the ordinary jumper, but solid cores of the rock passed through; so that by this wonderful apparatus a boring can now be made in as many days as it took months before, while the resulting cores give actual samples of the several strata passed through, whether soft as clay or as hard as granite. Having obtained specimens of the cores of trap rock brought up by the borer, and expressed their regret at the failure of the undertaking, the party left for Glenravel. The country all around looked in its very best attire, meadows and corn-fields smiling with the happy indication of abundant crops; even the potato fields bloomed with their long line of variegated blossoms, now in their very best condition, rivalling the choicest tints of the garden, and claiming admiration as the poor man's friend.

A halt was made at Glenravel House, the residence of E. Benn, Esq., who very kindly showed the party his extensive and valuable collection of Irish Antiquities; extensive, because it is the accumulation of many years, and valuable, as all the specimens have been found around Mr. Benn's estate. They consist of all kinds of objects in pottery, stone, bronze, and iron, including a great variety of cinerary urns, stone celts, hammers, arrow heads, spears, &c.; also bronze celts, plain and ornamented; spear heads of all patterns, enamelled fibulæ, and gold ornaments, and beads of pottery, stone, glass, and enamel. Mr. Benn has done good service in thus securing this very fine collection, and preventing so many interesting objects from being scattered. It is to be regretted that we have not in Belfast anything like so good a collection, and no available means of securing for our Museum the most valuable objects of ancient art found in the North of Ireland; while Antrim alone is the great collecting-ground for English antiquarians, and furnishes the very choicest specimens of Irish antiquities in almost every good collection; indeed, the earnestness with which they are sought for, and the high prices they command, has created a regular trade in forged objects, many of which are purchased as rapidly as genuine articles by those who do not know better. Valuable collections like Mr. Benn's are not made in a day, and should have a permanent place in one of our museums, where they could be referred to with interest and profit. In addition to making this collection, Mr. Benn has done no small service in developing the mineral resources of his locality, particularly the iron mines, daily growing in importance, and changing the aspect of the country.

The Antrim iron ores were well known to writers for a very long time, but no steps were taken to apply that knowledge to any practical purpose until a very few years ago. Indications of iron were common on the slopes of the hills around Glenravel; but as it required the investment of some capital to open up the beds and show their nature and extent, speculators were deterred, until Mr. Benn proved the mines by an outlay of six shillings! The result was very promising, and Mr. Benn—fortunately becoming acquainted with Mr. Fisher, who had a practical knowledge of iron mining— granted that gentleman permission to work the mines for a short period, after November, 1866, at a nominal rent of £10. This was the modest commencement of the iron mines of the Glenravel district, which at this moment yield large revenues to the fortunate landlords, and engage the energies of several mining companies, who are spending thousands of pounds in the locality, and giving constant employment at remunerative wages to several hundred miners; and hence, the mountain slopes from Glenravel to Red Bay, formerly seldom visited except by the sportsman, are now burrowed with mines, and alive with busy groups of industrious workmen; trams, waggons, and machinery are active on every side, and vast quantities of the red ore is transported daily to the shipping port at Red Bay. On the hills new pits are open, along the valleys new railways are being laid down, and at the shore new piers are being constructed. The beauty of the scenery has been invaded by greasy fitters and an army of red-stained miners, and the romance of the glens has been well nigh annihilated by the steady march of practical utility.

Interesting as all these works are, the wire tramway, from its very novelty, attracts the first attention. This very ingenious mode of transporting the produce of the mines is wholly different from any ordinary tramway, the material being carried *in the air* by buckets suspended from an endless wire rope, instead of along the ground by rails. The tramway is made up of sections, each having a separate loop of wire rope, revolving around a horizontal wheel at each end, and carried over wheels on tressels placed along the line at about the same distance apart as telegraph poles, the wire rope being about the same distance above the ground as the telegraph wire. The rope passes round a large wheel at one end, and over small wheels—one at each side of the series of tressels— and is kept continually revolving by steam power. The buckets are suspended to this rope; the full ones come down one side, and the empty are carried back at the other side, as the rope revolves, looking like a double line of telegraph poles, with buckets suspended from the wires, and travelling along them at the rate of about four miles an hour. Thus the wire tramway traverses the county for a length of eight miles, accommodating itself to the undulations of the surface, and transporting about 200 tons of ore per day. Besides the tramway, a regular railway is being laid down along the south side of Glenariff, and another railway is being made from Glenravel to Ballymena.

Mr. Powell, the engineer of the tramway, was very attentive to the members of the Naturalists' Field Club during their visit, and explained all the details of its working machinery. Mr. Fisher, too, gave them every facility for seeing his iron mines, and his efficient manager conducted the party through them. This courtesy was not granted by the Antrim Iron Ore Company. The Club's application was not even answered, although members of the Naturalists' Field Club were the first to publish any description of the iron ores of Antrim, and direct attention to their importance.

During the sojourn in the locality the party were well-cared for by the courteous and obliging manager of The Glens of Antrim Hotel, Cushendall, and he was ably seconded by his efficient staff, who left nothing undone that was necessary to secure the homely comfort and real pleasure of their numerous visitors.

The second day was spent in a walking excursion from Cushendall to Cushendun caves, by the old church of Layd parish; from thence to the splendid valley of Glendun, and then to the curious and interesting group of stones known as "Ossian's grave." This megalitic structure consists of about thirty-four stones, forming a semi-circle of about 10 feet in diameter, and three or four chambers at the north end. It is situated about one and a half miles directly west of Cushendall, and half-way between the two mountain roads that lead to the slope of Trostan mountain. The central axis of the group is in the direction of Garron Point from Ossian's grave. The party visited two other remains of ancient Irish cromlechs that occur still further west and higher up the hill. From this to the hotel, a distance of about two miles, completed the day's walk of about twelve miles, and prepared the party for the enjoyment of their dinner, which Mrs. Hall had ready to serve on their arrival. After an early bath and a good breakfast the party regretfully left the hotel for Belfast, spending the whole day on the well-known coast road, often described, but ever new, and always interesting to those who can appreciate the sublimity and beauty of Nature.

Frequent halts were made along the road, none more enjoyable than the visit to Garron Tower, where Mr. Porteous, the gardener, has a most magnificent display of flowers, while the castle itself is a perfect museum of curiosities, and a very model of neatness and order. With the grand scenery of Glenariff and the coast cliffs, the attractions of Garron Tower, the excellent accommodation of Carnlough Hotel, and the beautiful park at Glenarm, it is surprising that the coast road is not more frequently visited, particularly as the railway and car arrangements would enable tourists from Belfast to travel the whole line and return on the same day.

On Saturday, 16th August, to

MONEYMORE AND ARBOE.

It is to be regretted that this excursion was so very badly attended. The few members who made up the party spent a very pleasant day on the road from Moneymore to Arboe, and visited Tamlaght cromlech, Coagh standing-stone, and Arboe sculptured cross. The cromlech is a very fine example of the ancient Irish megalithic structures, and stands by the side of the road near Coagh, forming a portion of the boundary wall. The standing-stone is in a field by the side of the river, near to the village of Coagh. The cross of Arboe is one of the very best examples of Irish sculptured crosses. It stands near the ruins of an old church on the shore of Lough Neagh. Independent of the geological and botanical features of this trip, the three ancient monuments referred to would well repay the visit of a larger party.

On Saturday, 6th September, to

ISLANDMAGEE AND THE GOBBINS.

A large party met at the Northern Counties Railway Station, and proceeded by the 9-30 train to Ballycarry Station. They then walked on to the east shore of Islandmagee, and spent the entire day exploring the coast line from Blackhead to the mural cliffs of the Gobbins. The several exposures of the Tertiary clays, Chalk, Greensand, and Lias, afforded the geologists an opportunity of collecting the characteristic fossils of the respective formations, and a large number of the common species were secured. The Lias particularly yielded a good number. The weather was exceedingly fine, which, with the diversified character of the coast scenery along the shore, gave a day's thorough enjoyment to the whole party.

WINTER SESSION.

NOTE.—The Authors of the various papers, of which abstracts are here appended, are alone responsible for the views expressed in them.

THE opening meeting of the Session was held on 19th November, when Mr. WILLIAM GRAY delivered an address on "The British Association."

Mr. Gray's address was mainly a report of the deputation sent to the Bradford meeting, with a view of obtaining such information as would enable the Club to render more active assistance in promoting the success of the meeting in Belfast.

Mr. Gray referred to the early history of the Association, and explained its aim and objects, and gave a detailed account of the financial and other arrangements made for carrying out the objects of the Association. He then gave an interesting account of the Bradford meeting, describing the several sectional meetings, the public lectures, and the numerous excursions arranged for the members. Mr. Gray referred particularly to the marked attention and generous hospitality extended to all the members from Belfast. He drew a comparison between Belfast and Bradford, both being remarkable for their active industry and healthy progress; and, from his observation in Bradford, explained how the meeting would probably be conducted in Belfast, and what the town should do in order to emulate Bradford, and secure a meeting here that will be creditable to our commercial wealth and national hospitality. Mr. Gray also reported his visits to several museums in Bradford, Leeds, York, Whitby, Richmond, and Scarborough, and detailed the hints he received for the improvement of our local Museum.

On the 10th December, a paper was contributed by Mr. GEORGE LANGTRY, entitled "Thoughts on Progressive Development," which, owing to the unavoidable absence of the writer, was read by Mr. Wm. Hancock.

After some preliminary remarks, the writer proceeded to show the great care which should be exercised in drawing correct conclusions from observed facts. He proved how often incorrect, analogical reasoning is; and quoted the very forcible remark of Mr. Johnston :—" He who will determine against that which he knows, because there may be something which he knows not ; he who can set hypothetic possibility against acknowledged certainty; is not to be admitted amongst reasonable beings."

He then went on to say :—I must freely confess that were I similarly situated with Mr. Darwin, I should have no hesitation in believing and holding the same opinions as he does ; but, although I have for several years given his theory my careful and thoughtful consideration, yet I am not, on the evidence already adduced, prepared to accept it *in globo*. Be it understood, I do not refuse it credence on account of its seeming antipathy to scripture, for I do not believe such really exists. I will take, what Mr. Darwin admits, a Creator—necessarily a divine one (which no one, I think, who is acquainted with the latest investigations of Beale, Schwann, and others, will deny), and I say, once we admit the existence of this Creator, it matters not whether creation has been carried on by evolution, or by separate and distinct creative acts. Yea, I rather consider the evolution theory the most wonderful of the two, and it would bring about, what we generally see in nature, a smooth and equally adjusted movement. For as we now find, at least so astronomers say, the world hastening towards that time when it shall approach the sun so nearly and rapidly that fusion will take place—and all this going on without anything unusual being perceptible to ordinary observers—so, I think, might creation have culminated by gradual development, without any vast hiatus or gap having occurred. I shall briefly explain what I mean. We are told, in the "Book of Genesis," that on the third day were created grass, trees, herbage, &c., whilst it was not until the fifth day that animated nature made its appearance. Now it has generally been admitted of late years that the word which has been translated *day* in reality means a period of time; in fact, it may be that it comprises a cycle of years, or periods so vast that the human mind refuses to grasp their immensity. Now it is also a fact, well known to naturalists, that very little difference exists between the lowest forms of animal and some low forms of vegetable life; and I think it would be as wonderful, yea, as I said before, more wonderful, if the one had been resolved from the other than if they had been separately created; and I am of the opinion, if this work of evolution were completed in the period which is comprehended in the *fifth day*, it is only on that day that it can be said that special creation has taken place. Just as in the case of an artizan; he makes the wheels and springs of a watch, but it is only when all these parts are in proper relation to each other, and it can be contemplated as a perfect whole, that the term *watch* can be applied. Again, the flying reptiles and gliding animals are very little removed from others which have not a membraneous cuticle adapted as a wing, and I think it is quite possible that this cuticle—as in the Lemuridæ—may have arisen from such causes as Mr. Darwin terms "natural selection." But I deny that the creature knowingly of itself exerted any influence in this selection; and herein I differ from Mr. Darwin. However, I may briefly state, that I believe those who say creation was done and could only have been done in this way or that, without having due and very weighty reasons for doing so, are likely to be in error, and I consider by so doing they are limiting the power and adapting the infinite wisdom of the Creator to that of our finite understandings.

He next reviewed Dr. Bastian's experiments in regard to spontaneous generation. He said the testimony was very conflicting, and as yet we should consider the weight of evidence against this theory. He did not believe that inanimate existence could create animate life; in other words, that a thing could be before it existed—a manifest absurdity.

He next examined some of Dr. Darwin's hypotheses, and pointed out the reasons why he considered many of them untenable, and which, in his opinion, would militate against their general acceptance. He said that development must have been very slow and gradual, and showed, from Sir Charles Lyell's works, that man's outward form has not altered since the days of the Pharaohs. He then asked—" Has his mental capacity improved since the days of Socrates or Homer? I own," he said, "it is not right to compare a nation or nations at large with two such bright and shining lights. We may say England has produced but one Shakespeare, Rome one Virgil, and Greece only one Homer. Yet had Shakespeare —rollicking Will—lived in Homer's time, it is questionable if the world would have been enriched with the matchless efforts of his genius. But, even should England sink quietly into the lap of luxury—as did Greece, Rome, and the nations of antiquity—it will not long be a question whether she, too, shall not fall a prey to a less intellectual, but, at the same time, a more vigorous, hardier, and less sensual people than they. Of course, their works may remain, but these will only be vestiges of former greatness; not that greatness itself."

He pointed out the causes which tended to restrict a diversification of type, viz., reversion, sterility, degeneracy, &c., and said that, taking into account how slow and gradual all these changes must necessarily have been, he did not consider 200,000,000 years (the maximum time allowed by Sir Wm. Thompson for the existence of the earth since its cooling), sufficient for the theory of the evolutionist; and if the maximum be not sufficient, how much less the minimum of 20,000,000 years. "I am, therefore, of opinion," the essayist proceeded to say, "that there must have been several centres—not local but animated centres—from which, and by which, all the world was peopled, or stocked, with all life; and I believe that these centres were presided over by one supreme, omnipotent, and omnipresent Creator. But if asked to define one of these centres, I at once admit my inability to do so. It is even yet with difficulty that naturalists resolve or place animals in their proper orders; and this is especially the case in regard to invertebrates. I believe the 'Book of Nature' will never be disclosed and laid open before us, so that we can say, Lo! here is the commencement of life; from this germ, or such as this, sprang such and such organisms and forms. Yet I consider the theory which I have advanced is the one most in accordance with revealed truth—geological and otherwise—and, I say it with due reverence, also with what I conceive to be the intelligence of a divine Creator."

On 15th January, the meeting was devoted to the

EXHIBITION OF MICROSCOPES AND MICROSCOPIC OBJECTS.

The meeting was largely attended, and a considerable number of the members exhibited their collections of microscopic preparations. A great variety of the more common objects were on view, and, in addition, a series of chemical preparations, and a large number of the recently-discovered microzoa from the Chalk flints. A spectroscope was also exhibited by Dr. Henry Burden, giving those present an opportunity of observing the spectra of the various metals, &c., and comparing the characteristic bands shown during the combustion of each.

On 28th January, a paper was read by the Rev. EDMUND M'CLURE, A.M., on "The Surnames of the Inhabitants of the County Antrim, and their Indications."*

The County Antrim has of late years, at least, furnished a fair field for the labours of the archæologist and historian—rich as it is in materials to incite and encourage their researches. The last contribution to its annals, from the scholarly and industrious pen of the Rev. George Hill, exhibits something of the rich harvest which may be gathered in this domain by accurate observation and patient labour. The extremely favourable reception which that valuable book has received, not only from the intelligent public of this county, but from all who are interested in our national history everywhere—while it must be very gratifying to the author—is, at the same time, a fair warrant that any further investigation in the same direction will not be thrown away. I feel, therefore, that I have not undertaken a useless or superfluous task in endeavouring, in ever so little a measure, to further elucidate the history of my native county, and that from a source which has never been employed, as it ought, for this purpose.

The family names in the county, when treated in a philosophic spirit, are capable of furnishing a great deal of material towards its history, as I hope to show you to-night. Surnames, which are tolerably permanent amid the vicissitudes occasioned by immigration or conquest, bear very clear and unmistakable testimony to the various elements of the population in any place; and this county, which has been subject to the inroads of many peoples, affords very abundant evidence in its existing surnames of the nature and extent of the mixture of population thus brought about. If we could procure a reliable list of all the family names existing in the county, giving also their relative distribution, we should have a very fair means for determining the various elements in the population, and for arriving thus at the origin of the inhabitants.

* In accordance with a special resolution of the Club, this paper is published *in extenso.*

Such a complete list does not exist; but we have something almost as good—the County Electoral Roll. This, it is true, contains the names of those only whose tenements are valued above £12 per annum—a very small proportion of the entire inhabitants; but then it is selective, and represents fairly enough the number of names and their relative distribution in the county. From private inquiries made through clerical friends and others, I have found that the number of names in the county omitted from this list is not very great, and that the names which do not appear in it are confined to one or two localities, where the inhabitants are too poor to be enrolled as voters. This is the fact chiefly with the old native population, which, like the oldest fauna and flora of a country, are to be found generally in its mountainous and inhospitable parts.

The Electoral Roll gives the names of the voters as they appear in the twenty-one electoral districts recently laid down. I found it necessary, in the first place, to make from this an alphabetical list of the names of all the electors in the county, and to place opposite each name the particular district and the number of times in which it appears. If each surname bore upon its face the history of its origin, one could readily determine from such a table the various elements and their relative distribution in the county. But this is not always the case. Very often, indeed, it is no easy matter to find out the indication and origin of a name. Names suffer from time and wear as everything else, and become so metamorphosed in the process of years that their original owners would hardly recognise them. Indeed, a tedious preparation is necessary in order to arrive at anything like correct results. It is needful, in the first place, to study carefully the different modes of name-giving among the various races of the west, and the changes to which they are liable, before one can proceed to determine from surnames alone the mixed elements in such a heterogenous population as we find in this country. It will not be out of place here to give a short sketch of these different methods of nomenclature. You must know, in the first place, that surnames are of comparatively recent origin. People in ancient times were distinguished by but a single name. The persons we meet with in the Bible, for instance—one of the oldest of books—are, with a few exceptions, thus noted. Abraham, Samuel, David, Solomon, and John are instances of this. The Greeks used the same method—putting after the single name, where an ambiguity might arise, the name of the father, in the genitive case. The Romans had a much better system—more perfect, indeed, than any existing mode of nomenclature. Every Roman in the days of the Republic had at least two, and nearly always three, names—(1) a forename *(præ-nomen)*, (2) a name *(nomen)*, and (3) an additional name *(cognomen)*. The first corresponded with our Christian name, the middle name noted the kin *(gens)* or clan to which the individual belonged; the *cognomen* indicated the branch or family of the clan. Thus, in Caius Julius Cæsar, we understand that the person so called was of the Julian clan—the Cæsar branch of it—and that he was distinguished from other members of this branch by the name Caius. The Gothic races and Celts had anciently but a single name system, except, indeed, where a nickname was added, which was not unfrequently the case: *e.g.*, Brian *Boru*—*i.e.*, of the tribute; Malcolm *Canmore*—*i.e.*, of the large head; Frederick *Barbarossa* —*i.e.*, of the red beard; Harold *Harfagr*—*i.e.*, of the fair hair; Rhys *Gethin*—*i.e.*, of the squint. Things continued in this condition in Western Europe until about the 11th century, and in some places until a much later period. The confusion finally became so great through this method that, as a remedy, the plan of having a family name which should descend from father to son was adopted, every one having a baptismal name besides. This fixed name became the *sur* or additional name. It was formed in a variety of ways, but generally from existing names, by putting some prefix or affix, which indicated sonship. The designations employed before surnames came into use became thus fixed. These were formed in ancient times in Ireland in a variety of ways.

I can note but a few of these modes of name-giving. In the first place we find many personal designations in common use in ancient times which were based upon natural distinctions in stature, colour, or other physical characteristics; such for instance are the following names formed from adjectives denoting colour. Thus the common personal name Banan was formed from *Ban*, white; Corcran from *Corcair*, ruddy; Ciaran from *Ciar*, black; Cronan and Croinin from *Cron*, dark; Donnan from *Donn*, brown; Deargan from *Dearg*, red; Dubhan from *Dubh*, black; Fionnan and Fionnagan from *Fionn*, fair. There are some early Irish names which seem to belong to this class, but another explanation must be sought for them. Thus we have such designations as *Leath dhearg* (*i.e.* half-red), *Sriabh dhearg* (red-circles), *Dubh-da-leath* (both sides black), &c., which would seem to indicate that the persons bearing these names were so called from artificial rather than natural distinctions. It has been suggested that these names were used to designate individuals who had stained their bodies in this fashion, and the fact of one section of the Celts, the Picts, doing so, renders this suggestion not impossible.

Another class of names includes all those derived from moral or mental qualities—such as Hanratty, anciently *Inreachtach* (worthy of honour), Coffey, anciently *Cobhtach* (worthy of victory), Connor, anciently *Concobhar* (strong victor); names compounded of *gal* valour, and *gus*, virtue, belong to this class, *e.g.*, Ferghal (now Farrel), Fergus, &c. Another class contains those names which were given on account of occupation, *e.g.*, MacGowan (*i.e.*, Gobhan, a smith). In the Highlands of Scotland we have many such names, such as MacGreusich, the son of the shoemaker; MacChruiter, the son of the harper (otherwise Harperson).

Another class embraces names derived from nationality or locality, *e.g.*, Brannagh (*i.e.*, Breatnach, a Briton or Welshman), Davoren (*i.e.*, Dubh da Bhoireann, the black man of the two rocks), &c., &c. The prefix *Cu*, meaning hound or champion, was often prefixed to names of locality, such as Cumaighe (now Cooey), meaning the hound of the plain.

Another class was formed by prefixing Gilla (a servant), Mael (tonsured), and Ceile (a companion), to the name of God or some saint; *e.g.*, Gilla-De, the servant of God ; Gilla-Cholum, the servant of S. Columba ; Gilla-Brighde, servant of S. Bridget ; Mael-Patraic, one tonsured in the name of S. Patrick ; Mael-Eoin (now Malone), one tonsured in the name of S. John ; Ceile-De (hence the Culdees); Ceile-Petair, the vassal of S. Peter. In addition to the names of this class, the Irish had adopted at this time several names from the Norse invaders of the country. Dr. O'Donovan notes among these the following:—Tomar and Tomrair (now Toner); Maghnus (in M'Manus); Raghnall (now Reynolds); Amhlaeibh (now Awley in MacAwley, and Auliffe); Imhar (in M'Ivor or M'Keever). About the 11th century the Irish began to use permanent surnames, each family fixing for that purpose on one of its distinguished ancestors—near or remote—and prefixing to his name the word Ua (O), meaning descendant, or the word Mac, meaning son. These prefixes, in accordance with the structure of the Celtic language, modified often the initial consonant of the name following, so as to give it in its new combination quite an altered appearance. Thus, a branch of the O'Kanes of Ulster took at the introduction of surnames their appellation from a certain Bloscadh O'Kane, who flourished in the 13th century. The "Mac" which was prefixed to this Bloscadh aspirated the initial consonant, and thus gave it the sound of a "w" nearly ; the new composition being pronounced as if written MacCloskey. This is the form in which it now exists. In the same manner, MacDonnel became MacDhonnel, pronounced MacConnell (to be distinguished from another MacConnell—MacChongal); MacDonnaghy, MacConnaghy, or MacConkey, &c. In this way, too, the Ua or O Flynn became O'Lynn ; O'Flannagan, O'Lannegan.

The Celtic names in the Highlands of Scotland are formed very much after the same model as those in Ireland. Indeed, from the current names on both sides of the North Channel, one would argue a very close connection between the inhabitants, even without testimony of history, which shows them to be of the same stock. The same names which became the great leading surnames in the north of Ireland, and especially in the parts adjacent to the

North Channel, are to be found abundantly in Argyle and the Western Isles. Thus we find MacRorys, MacNeills, MacConnells, MacLochlanns, MacEvins, MacAuleys, Doughall or Doyle, and so forth, both in the Western Highlands and the same names current among the septs of Ulster. The Dalriadic invasion of Scotland in the 5th century is thus borne witness to in a marked manner, and the Highland immigrants who, under the leadership of the Mac Donnells, found at various times permanent homes in the glens and along the shores of Antrim, brought to Ireland with them, not only a language, but also surnames which proved them kin to the former possessors of the very soil they came to occupy.

Some of the Christian names which they imported, such as Torquil, Somerled, Ranald, prove them to have been subjected to a strong Danish influence while resident in the Isles and in the Argyleshire Highlands. There is the same tendency to confusion in these names, from the laws of the language, as we find among those of Ireland. The prefix Mac modifies the initial consonants in a similar manner, and we have thus from a few original names a great many apparently different ones. Thus the name Finnon (fair) becomes, with Mac, MacKinnon, the F becoming silent and the K sound belonging to the C in Mac; the same is the case with MacFinlay, which becomes MacKinlay; MacPhillip, which becomes MacKillop; MacParlan, MacPharlan; MacPeter, Mac Pheters; MacPaul, MacFaul; MacDonnaghie, MacConnaghie, or M'Conkey; MacDuffie, MacAfee and Mehaffey; MacGillean, MacClean and MacAlinn, M'Killen, and even Gillen and Killen; MacGilvain, MacIlwaine; MacGilpatrick, MacIlfatrick; MacGilgorm, MacIlgorm; MacGilroy, MacIlroy; MacGilmurray into M'Ilmurray and MacMurray; MacGilbride, into MacIlbride, and finally MacBride; &c.

I shall notice only one other branch of the Celtic family with regard to their name system, viz., the Welsh. Here, as among the Irish and Scoto-Irish, terms which were used at first simply as marks of office or physical appearance, became, at the time of the adoption of fixed surnames, the distinguishing and permanent

C

names of the people. Thus Gogh, which means red, became the common name Gough; Vaghan, which means little, became the common name Vaughan; Tew, which means fat, still exists in Tew and Tow as a surname; Gwyn or Wynne, meaning white, are well known existing names, and all these and many more Welsh names are to be found at present in this county.

Fixed surnames were not introduced into Wales until comparatively late times. In Henry the Seventh's time they were a rare exception. Lower quotes from a play, printed as late as 1600, an instance of Welsh nomenclature, which is very amusing:—

Judge. What bail? What sureties?
Davy. Her Cozen ap Rice ap Evan ap Morice ap Morgan ap Llewellyn ap Madoc ap Meredith ap Griffin ap Davis ap Owen ap Shinken Jones.
Judge. Two of the most sufficient are enow.
Sheriff. An't please your lordship these are all *but one.*

The Ap, which was originally *Map*, is the Welsh form of *Mac*. The P in Welsh being represented, strangely enough, very often by the Irish C. This prefix causes frequently a modification of the name before which it comes by combining with it, thus forming an apparently entirely new name. In this manner, Ap Owen has become Bowen; Ap Ithel, Bithel and Bethel; Ap Evan, Bevan; Ap Howel, Powel; Ap Harry, Parry; Ap Richard, Prichard and Uprichard; Ap Hugh, Pugh; Ap Rys, Price; Ap Rosser, Prosser; Ap Einion, Beinion; Ap Heilyn, Peilyn; Ap Oyskin, Poyskin. The genitive case in "S" is another later mode used among the Welsh to designate the descendants of any given name. Thus, Richards, Jones, Owens, Williams, are very common Welsh surnames.

It now remains to notice the mode of name-giving employed by the non-Celtic people who dwelt within an accessible distance of this island. The earliest form of surname in use among the Saxons of England (to begin with them), and still to be found in Friesland, was the father's name with the addition of the syllable *ing* to express son; thus Ceonred Ceolwalding, Conrad the son of Ceolwald; Ceolwald Cuthwinning, *i.e.*, Ceolwald the son of Cuthwin. We find this form abundantly in the names of places in England, and especially in those parts occupied by the Saxons. Thus Bevington, Ellington, Bellingham, &c., are names of places formed from the names of their ancient occupants, names of places which furnished afterwards new appellations to other inhabitants.

Another mode was that by which descent from an ancestor was indicated by the termination "son." This method was that which prevailed amongst the Northmen, the Dutch, and those invaders of England in the 5th century who came from the North of Germany.* The Angles, who were of this class, and who formed settlements in the north of England, probably used this form of surname most frequently. Among the Saxons of the south it was rare, if used at all. In a list of captains of merchant vessels trading in the year 1417, between the south-east coast of England and Normandy, I find, among over ninety names, but two ending in "son," the majority of the remainder are formed either from the names of places or from occupations; e.g., Mountfort, Multon, Stanley, Wyllaby, Leycestre, Dalton, &c.; Miller, Clerk, Fauconer, Taillour, Wryght, Baker, Osteler, Beermann, Fyssher, &c.

In a list of about 120 Dutch captains of the same period, over three-fourths have the termination in "son." Another termination in use among the Low-German invaders of England was "man," e.g., Freeman, Richeman, Bowman, &c., this form of name is abundant still in Friesland. The Normans, who seem to have originated surnames in England, had a large influence upon the form of those which became prevalent. Territorial names or designations from the paternal estate were first used by them, and soon became very common among the Anglo-Saxons. Names formed from trades and offices with the prefix "le" seemed to have been first used by the Norman invaders in the 11th century. Camden remarks that there is not a single village in Normandy that has

---

* Worsaae says that the termination "son" is peculiar to the Scandinavians, and it is probable that this termination, in the north and east of England, is to be traced entirely to their influence.

not surnamed some family in England ; Percy, Warren, Devereux, Neville, Tracy, Montfort, Montgomery, St. Maure (corrupted into Seymour), are a few of the many examples. The English landowners were not slow in adopting this mode of distinguishing themselves, introducing the French preposition "de" before their manors, and thus forming many new surnames. The prefix "*de*" seems, however, to have been generally dropped about the reign of Henry VI. This accounts for the many existing surnames formed from places. Owing to the prevalence of surnames of this class in the 13th century in England, it was proverbially said :—

"In Ford, in Ham, in Ley, and Ton,
The most of·English surnames run."

To these may be added, field, hurst, wood, wick, sted, &c.

There were others derived not from possession of property but simply from locality. If a man dwelt at a wood, he was called Atte wood (Atwood); at a well, he was named Atte well (Atwell), at a moor, Atte moore. These forms further shortened have given rise to many surnames, such as Gate, Hill, Greene, Dyke, Dale, Dean, Brooke, &c. The plural Atten was used with plural nouns—*e.g.*, Atten oaks, afterwards shortened into Nokes and Oakes. Surnames from occupation form a very numerous class; the Le Botelers, Le Stewards, and others of this class, played an important part in the history of these countries. A host of instances of this form will occur to all of you. There are some occupations no longer practised, expressed in obsolete words, which have still their representatives in existing surnames ; such are the Cappers (Capmakers), Lorimers (makers of iron work for saddles), Pointers (makers of ties, once used instead of buttons), Chaucer (shoemaker), Leech (a medical man), Latimer (a writer in Latin), Barker (a tanner), Jenner (a joiner), Pilcher (a maker of pilches—a warm upper garment—the great coat of the 14th century), Arkwright (a maker of meal chests), Fletcher (an arrowsmith, maker of arrows), Walker (a fuller), &c. These lowly names are often now found in high places. The names of Collier and Salter for instance, are or have been in the British peerage, although those occupations were in the middle ages considered so vile and menial that none but bondsmen or slaves would follow them.

What I have said about English surnames applies in the main to those of the Lowlands of Scotland. It is well to take note of this, for the Scottish Lowlands have furnished a very large proportion of the inhabitants of this county. The names of places here predominate as surnames. As these names are often significant—indicating at least the race of those who first imposed them—it might be well to give a short account of their origin. We find in the Lowlands, for instance, local names which must have been imposed by men speaking the language of ancient Ireland; others which must have originated from the mouths of people akin to the modern Welsh; others which have been imposed by the Norsemen, and by the Angles and Saxons of the south.

Thus these local names, or the surnames formed from them, embrace within them indications of the vicissitudes of conquest to which the Lowlands of Scotland have been subjected. Authentic history tells us, and existing local names confirm it, that the Lowlands, from the Firth of Clyde and the Perthshire hills to Northumbria, were in early times the seat of a people akin to the modern Welsh. This constituted, as it has been argued, the ancient Pictish kingdom of Scotland. Beyond them to the north were the Scots, descendants of the Dalriadic and other invaders from Ireland in the 5th and 6th centuries. About the year 842, the Scots and Picts were united under one king, Kenneth MacAlpin, and thenceforward the name of Picts as a nation disappears, still leaving, however, a testimony of their presence and language, it is contended, in the names of places they inhabited. The words Pen—*e.g.*, Pentland hills, Penwally; Aber (as in Abernethy, Aberbrothick); Uchel (high), as in Ochiltree; Pol, Trefe, Frostre, Llan, &c., all bear testimony to a former Cymric or Welsh population. To the north, the Cymric Pen becomes the Gaelic Ben or Cen; the Cymric Aber, the Gaelic Inver; the Cymric Llan, the Gaelic Kil, &c. The Norsemen, who have left their mark on every country in

Europe, from Constantinople to the Shannon, and from Gibraltar to Archangel, have left no insignificant token of their presence in the Lowlands, as well as along the shores and in the isles of Scotland. Putting Sutherland and the Orkneys out of the question, which were almost entirely Norwegian, we find abundant evidence of the Norsemen, both on the coast and in the interior of the country. In Dumfrieshire, for instance, and in Kirkcudbright and Wigton, we find a considerable number of names ending in the Norse suffixes, *by, garth, beck, thwaite;* we have also the usual insular coast terminations and affixes in *ey, ness, scar,* &c. The places called Bore, Boreland (a common surname in this county), Tungland, and Tinwald, are all pure Norse.

The Norse influence on the nomenclature was, perhaps, equalled by their influence on the population. The Norse personal names in use among the ancient inhabitants would seem to express a mixture of blood. The Saxon and Norman names in the Lowlands are to be accounted for by immigrations from the south.

Malcolm III. (1093), or Malcolm Canmore, as he was called, who had married a daughter of Edward the Confessor, had strong English leanings, and invited many of the discontented Saxon nobles at the time of the Norman conquest, to take up their residence in his kingdom, giving them a home and lands. His successors, some of them brought up at the English court, or connected with it by marriage, favoured in like manner the settlement of Anglo-Normans in Scotland; all the high officers of state at this time, as we learn from old chartularies, were southern strangers. Hence the Saxon and Norman names of places, which afterwards in several instances gave rise to distinguished surnames; *e.g.,* Maxwell, written in ancient records Maccusville, Maccuston; Richardtun (called after a Richard Waleys (or foreigner), an ancestor of the great Wallace); Maleville, or Melville, in Lothian, called after the Norman ancestor of the Maule family; Seton, from a Norman adventurer Say; Tankerton in Clydesdale was the fief of Tancard, a Fleming who came into Scotland in the reign of Malcolm IV.; and a few village names like Ingleston, Normanton, and Flemington, afford further evidence of the immigration of foreign adventurers, encouraged by the Scottish kings.

The current Scottish names of Sinclair, Mowatt (from Robert de Montalt), Baliol, Grant, Hay, Fleming, Boyle, Bruce, Bisset, Cumin (Cuming, Comyn), Corbet, Cheyne, Charteris, Montgomery, Mortimer, Muschet, Russell, Norvel, Veitch (de Vesci), Weir (de Vere), are, according to Cosmo Innes, all of continental ancestry.

The Berkelais (Barclay), Hamiltons, Moubrays, were als) Anglo-Norman families. There is a host of pure Anglo-Saxon names of places which also gave rise to surnames; *e.g.*, Blackburn, Braidwood, Brounlie, Brunton, Burton, Burn (or Burns), Chisholme, Copland, Crauford, Cunninghame, Denham (Denholm), Edmondston, Elphinston, and Edelston, Greenlies, Halkerston, Hepburn, Houston, Levingston, Maisterton, Preston, Schaw, Whyteford, Skelton, Trail, Waddell, &c. This would show that the original Celtic population of the Lowlands was subjected to a strong infusion of Norman and Saxon blood. The counties of the west of Scotland, except the west of Wigton, or Galloway, seem to have experienced this foreign influence very much, and these were the counties which, as we shall see, contributed most to the Scottish element in the population of Antrim. Galloway, which also furnished a large quota both to this county and that of Down, was more purely Celtic. So late as 1672, as we learn, the Gaelic was commonly spoken in Galloway (*p. 12, Patterson's Lands and their Owners in Galloway*).

I have now gone over in a cursory way the various modes of naming employed among the people who at various times formed settlements in this country, and especially in this county. It now remains to apply the information thus obtained to the list of names furnished by the County Electoral Roll.

In the 1,357 names of the Roll, I find that 565 are Lowland Scotch, 18 of which are Norman names. There are 234 Highland names. There are in all 181 Irish names, and 16 Anglo-Norman of the time of the conquest. The English names amount to 251. The Welsh to 7. The Huguenots to 6. The remaining names, about 100, are those of a few foreigners and those which I have left as undetermined. This shows simply the relative position of the names on the Roll. The number of Lowland Scotch I find represented by the 565 names amounts to 5,682, or about 55·80 per cent. of the entire Roll. Of Scotch of foreign origin, there is a per centage of 1·48.

The Scottish Celts represented by the 234 names exhibit a proportion of 23·68 per cent. of the Roll. The number of Irish names (181) represents only 824 of a native population, or about 8·09 per cent. Here the results, from an examination of the Electoral Roll, seem to vary from those obtained from other sources. To represent the proportion of the native Irish in the county, we should have to add 3 per cent., or even a little more, to this per centage of 8·09. For I find that the native population, as a rule, are much poorer than their neighbours, so that a far less proportion of them have the qualifications of county voters, that is holdings valued at £12 per annum. By private enquiry in the districts in which the native population is large, I find this to be the case, and that many of their names do not figure on the Roll at all. I think, however, that the per centage over the entire county is not over 12 per cent. The English represented by the 251 names amount to 783. Those of long settlement in the county—*i.e.*, who came centuries before the Plantation—number 40 in addition. The Welsh names represent 28. All these taken together make 851, or show a per centage of 8·35 of the entire Roll. Foreigners, Huguenots and Germans, are represented by 21 people on the list. The undetermined names represent 243 on the list, or about 2·38 per cent. of the Roll.

The native population is descended in the main from well known Irish tribes, who dwelt in this part of the country before the wars of Essex (Queen Elizabeth's time). The O'Neils of the clan of Aodh Boy (Yellow Hugh, as he is improperly called), had then been settled in the districts of North and South Clannaboy for over 200 years. The descendants are still very numerous in North Clannaboy. There are 44 O'Neils alone on the Electoral Roll of the county, all living about this district. The M'Canns and O'Larkens (now Larken), of Clann Breasil, and the O'Cahans, of Keenaght, Co. Derry, are, too, found not far away from their ancient sites. The O'Boyles, probably those of Donegal, are still numerous, and the ancient Ui Tuirtre and Fir Li, of whom *O'Fhloinn* (O'Lyn), a descendant of Colla Uais, was king in 1177, and held then all Dalriada, are still to be found in their ancient locality. In S. Patrick's time they dwelt on the west side of the Bann, but, as Dr. O'Donovan shows, they were certainly on the east side of it when Sir John de Courcy invaded Ulster, having in all probability driven out the posterity of Cairbre Riada, the ancient possessors of the soil.

The townland names which I am examining at present, both the early lists preserved in the Inquisitions and in other documents, and those still in use, show that many of the native names still current are to be found near their ancient localities. The various *Duns* throughout the county are generally made of this word and the name of some ancient families; Bally and Lis and other words are not unfrequently compounded in the same way. Thus we have a Carrive Murphy where Murpheys are still numerous. There is a Knock, and a Lis Macolusky, where MacCluskeys (a sept, as I have said, of the O'Cahans), are still to be found. We have Ballyscullion (*cf.* Ti Scullen), and many of that name still living there. We have Dun-gonnel, Tully-bally-donnel, &c., all pointing to O'Donnels or MacDonnels of other times. Straidhavern (street, as Joyce has it—more probably Scotch *Strath*, a valley), contains the name of a native stock not dwelling at present far from their former abode. Duneany probably contains the name of a sept called the O'Heaneys (formerly of Clann Kearny), still to be found not far away from this ancient fort. Straidnahanna, and Hannahstown, and perhaps Dunanney, all near each other, are significant of the locality occupied by the ancestors of the Hannahs (not the Scotch family of that name), still living in the county. The Murrigan, contained in Muinter Murrigan and Listy-murrigan, are, perhaps, now represented by Morgans.

Dunmurry, or as it appears in the old Inquisitions Dun-y-morie (alongside a Bally-o-morie), contains the name of Murrays, who still cling round their probably ancestral dwelling place. Lis Murnaghan, Dunarragan, Dunyvadden, Lisselinchy, Bally-Mac-Ilhoyle, Ardtiferral, Ardtihannon, Ballykelly, and Islandkelly and Donakelly (*see Dubourdieu, p. 627, Clan Breasail*), Lisnataylor (alias in Inquisitions Lis-ne-Daley), and many more which I have not time to note, involve probably the names of former inhabitants of whom descendants may still exist.

The Inquisition made 1600 to 1635, shows that O'Gneeves (now corrupted to Agnews), Hamills, O'Dreans, O'Dowds, M'Enultys, Magees, O'Haras, Maduffies, M'Lewarties, and Mulhollands, were common names in the county.

These townland names contain also many indications of the ancient Highland settlements in the north of the county; *e.g.*, Eilan MacAllen, Dun Mackelter, Farran MacArter, and Farran Mac Alister, Narran MacAllen (*i.e.*, an Fharran MacAllen), Fal Mac Rilly, Carnalbanagh, Highlandtown, are all significant of former Highland proprietors. They bear no less certain testimony to former English and Scotch settlers; *e.g.*, Ballyhacket, B. Edward, B. Hampton, B. Savage, B. Vesey, B. Henry, B. Hone, B. Jordan, Dobbsland, Englishtown; *e.g.*, of Lowland Scotch, these are chiefly on the coast, Crawfordsland, Doughlasland, Duncansland, M'Vickersland, Maxwell's Walls, Potter's Walls, Ballymartin, Tatesfort, Moore Lodge, Dickeystown, &c. The Highland inhabitants in the county have all come from Argyleshire and the Isles—in most instances as followers of the M'Donnels. Thus we have Highland names in the county of septs which derive their origin from the M'Donnels; *e.g.*, MacAlisters, MacNabs (MacNabenies in Donegal, says Buchanan, p. 76), MacIntyres, MacDuffies or Mac Afees, MacKeachairn, and MacKechnie; and of some subordinate septs of the same family; *e.g.*, MacKenricks. We have also of the same race as the M'Donnels, the MacDowells and the MacRorys. The MacNeills are said to be an offshoot of the O'Neills of Tyrone, who went to Scotland early.

Of the MacCleans of the great Clann Gillean we have many representatives, somewhat disguised in name in many cases; *e.g.*, MacAlinn, MacKillen, Gillen, Killen. The Campbells appear amongst us both under the clan name of Campbell and also as MacCollum, McCallum, MacAllin, M'Callin, M'Callion, also, McCaillean, from the name of the MacCaillean More.

MacLeods, in the form of MacCloy, are also amongst us; and MacIntoshes and M'Cosh, which signify the same thing (the sons of the Tosach or Chief). There are also MacKinlays, descendants of the Highland chief Finlay Moir—MacFarlans, MacEoins, MacRobbs (often changed to Robinson), MacPhails, MacLachlans, MacNauchtans, and MacLamonds (asserted to be descended from Lawmon O'Neill, son of the great O'Neill, provincial king of Ulster), MacInturners (or Turners), MacIlwhorrys, MacKays, and MacAulays; and Mewhinneys, or Buchanans.

The Lowland settlers in this county can all be traced pretty clearly to their former dwelling places in Scotland by their names. For it so happens, as I mentioned before, that surnames were there formed from local names—either from landed property, or simply from locality.

Thus we have in Renfrew and Lanark the following places, giving names to people abundantly scattered over Antrim :— Houston, Cathcart (a castle on the Cart), Calder (a river), Killèlan (a parish; *cf.* Gillelan), Erskine parish, Renfrew parish, Mearns, Neilston, Blackhall, Caldwell, Cochran, Knock (Ranfurley), Waterstown, Kilpatrick, Park (whence Park of that ilk), Johnstone, Pollok, Ralstoun, Whiteford, Walkenshaw. We have also common Renfrew family names formed in otherwise—Alexander, Hall, Brown, Hutcheson, Hyndman, King, M'Gilchrist, M'Dowell, Napier, Paterson, Stewart, Wallace.

The following names of places in Ayr have given rise to many surnames in Antrim :—Ayr, Barr, Barbour, Burns, Berryhill, Bigert, Bog (Boig), Bowie, Bowland, Braidshaw, Brownley, Burnsyde, Busbie, Cairns, Carrith, Colvil, Corsbie, Coulstoun, Craig, Cruicks, Cunninghame, Currie, Dalrymple, Dularg, Dunlop, Fairlie, Fenton,

Fullartoun, Fulltoun, Giffan, Gill, Girvan, Glen, Greenlees, Greenhill, &c. Wigton has contributed from names of places the surnames of Logan, Clugston, and Sorbie.

There are many other names of places to be found in the counties of Scotland on the North Channel, and even considerably toward the interior, which have furnished surnames. Aud even places more remote, such as Fife and Coupar, Eccles (in Berwick), Blair (as in Blair-Athol, Blairgowrie, Ard-Blair, &c.), Sutherland (in the north), &c. I have time to refer to a few only:— Ayrshire, &c. : Underwood, Uchiltree, Kirkwood, Allardice, Blackadder, Barnet, Carmichael (not as Mr. O'Donovan says, from Cara, friend of Michael), Kyle, Lamberton, Lilburn, Lyndsay, Meak, Munfode, Muir, Parkhill, Sands, Snodgrass, Stanelea, Symington, Thom, Thorndyke, Thornton, Ward, Wardlaw, Waterland, Wellwood, Woodsyde, Reside, Gourlay, Dunseath, Hume, Hannay, Cokburne, Reidpath, Maitland, Ballyntine, Colquhoun, Dreghorn, Drummond, Lennox, Lyttle, Sempill, Peebles, Darroch, Glenny.

The names of people in the same counties formed in other ways, appear in the *Rotulo Scotiæ* as very like a list of the inhabitants of Antrim and Down. There are Boyds, Fergusons, Hunters, Kennedys, of which this part of Scotland was one time so full as to give rise to this rhyme—

> 'Twixt Wigtown and the town of Ayr,
> And laigh down by the cruves of Cree,
> Ye shall not get a lodging there
> Except ye court a Kennedy.

There are also Chalmers, Forresters (Fosters), Grahams, Hamiltons, Hays, Inglis, M'Crea, M'Gill, McKie, Stewart, Neilson, Weir, Young, M'Calmont, M'Grane, Alexanders, Baxters, Browns.

The great abundance of Scotch names in this county is somewhat astonishing, when we consider that there was no regular plantation, as in the other parts of Ulster which had been escheated by the Crown. Any plantation carried out in this county was that made in the barony of Upper Massareene and

Lower Belfast, by Sir Fulke Conway and Sir Arthur Chichester respectively. But this plantation was effected by the introduction of English and Welsh families chiefly, and not by Scotch. The Scotch seemed to have arrived here at intervals, but chiefly during the time that the rest of Ulster was portioned out to their countrymen. I shall give you here two extracts from Mr. Hill's book, which throw considerable light upon this immigration.

[The lecturer here read some passages from "The MacDonnells of Antrim."]

It remains to say a few words about the English settlement in the county. This was carried out, as I said, by Sir F. Conway and Sir A. Chichester early in the 17th century. But long before this, Carrickfergus and the adjacent coast-line—as testified by the existing townland names—had been an English settlement. I see in the Electoral Roll several names which indicate descent from these early settlers. There are Taaf, Plunkett, Dobbin, Hackett, Power, Cusack, Copeland, Burke, Pearson, Baret, Brett, Seymour, Russel, and Phillips; many bearing the two latter names being also Scotch, and of much later date in the county.

These names carry us back for the most part to the time of the Anglo-Norman conquest of the country. At one time—in the reign of King John especially—English influence and English settlers were very strong in this country. But at the time of the plantation of Ulster it was very inconsiderable indeed, being chiefly confined to Carrickfergus and neighbourhood. Co-incident with the plantation, Sir Moyses Hill, Sir Arthur Chichester, Sir Fulke Conway, and others, brought in Welsh and English settlers, some of whose descendants are still to be found on the estates possessed by the heirs of these noblemen. Indeed, the English element in the county may almost entirely be traced to this source.

On the 18th February, Mr. JOSEPH WRIGHT, F.G.S., read a paper on "Flints, and the Foraminifera, Entomostraca, &c., contained in them."

Mr. Wright stated that previous to 1870 only two species of these minute fossils were known as occurring in the Mesozoic rocks of this district, viz., *Dentalina obliquaa*, from our Lias shales, and *Orbitolina concava*, from the Greensand. In this year Mr. William Gray, M.R.I.A., one of the Honorary Secretaries of the Club—well known as an acute observer—found some four or five species of Foraminifera in the Lias shales of Ballintoy, County Antrim, and supplied the reader with a large quantity of the shale for examination. This material had the property, when steeped in water, of falling down into a soft mud, which, when washed and sifted, yielded large numbers of Foraminifera. This mud rewarded Mr. Wright's laborious and exhaustive search with twenty species of these shell-bearing Rhizopods, the names of which were published in an Appendix to the Annual Report of the Club for 1870-71. The reader went on to say that in February, 1872, he had expressed an opinion that Foraminifera, which abound in the English Chalk, and which assume forms so varied and so exquisite, would be found in our flints, if any soft material could be secured from the cavities that so often occur in them. This powdery material being, in fact, a portion of the old sea bottom of the Cretaceous times, and should yield the shelly coverings of the Microzoa of that period. Mr. Thomas Galloway, an indefatigable and successful collector of the fossils that frequently occur in these flints, undertook to procure some of the required powder, and next day brought for examination a small quantity obtained from the vicinity of Ligoniel. On carefully washing this powder it yielded Foraminifera, Entomostraca, and sponge spicules in abundance, and in wonderful variety of the most beautiful forms. Here was a discovery of the utmost interest, opening up for this locality an entirely new field of research. Of these Microzoa 142 different kinds have already been discovered in our flints; a full list of them will be found in the Appendix accompanying the present number. In conclusion, Mr. Wright stated that, though all the time he could possibly spare for the past two years had been given to working out this subject, yet he believed it would take several years more of patient investigation to complete our knowledge of these tiny but exquisitely symmetrical fossils, and also of the Corals and Polyzoa that often occur associated with them, The lecture was well illustrated with diagrams and specimens; and, at the close, several of the leading members of the Club expressed themselves highly gratified with the important results of Mr. Wright's researches.

On 11th March, a paper was read by Mr. W. F. WAKEMAN, of Enniskillen, entitled "Remarks on Irish Crannogs, and on their contents as usually found," of which the following is an abstract:

The word Crannog is a formation from the Irish word Crann— a tree—and means a wooden edifice. Up to a period of about thirty-five years ago remains of this interesting class were unknown to modern antiquaries. Since that time a large number have been discovered and carefully examined. The Irish Crannog was simply an island, usually circular or oval, altogether or in part artificial, constructed of alternate layers of brushwood, heath, gravel, &c. The margin of the Crannog was strongly staked with oak, pine, or other suitable round or split timber; but in some few cases the body of the island was constructed of stone. The whole was encompassed by rows of palisading, of which the bases only remain. Upon these structures were erected the rude buildings which protected the inhabitants from the severity of the weather, while the insular position and the encircling palisade served as a defence against wild animals or more dangerous human enemies. The boats used by these island-dwellers are frequently found near Crannogs, or embedded in bogs or lake margins surrounding their sites. These boats or canoes were usually of great length, and constructed of a single oak tree. The Irish Crannogs are, doubtless, very ancient defensive structures—as such they are frequently referred to in the Irish Annals, some notices dating as far back as the 9th century; but long before that period they must have been occupied as places of security. This is shown by the character of the numerous examples of flint, stone, and bronze tools, weapons, and personal ornaments found in them, indicating an age as remote as the earliest settlements of Britain. Many of our oldest Crannogs were occupied until comparatively recent times, and were even then important strongholds. The great length of time during which several of the Crannogs continued to be occupied is proved by the enormous quantities of refuse animal remains contained in and around their sites. Upwards of 150 cartloads of bones were dug from the Crannog of Lagore, County Meath. Similar collections occurred at the Crannogs subsequently discovered at Lough Gur, County Limerick; Strokestown, County Roscommon; Ballinderry, near Moate; and in numerous other localities, including about twenty Crannogs personally examined by Mr. Wakeman in Fermanagh and its neighbourhood.

The reader, after giving a comprehensive view of what is understood by the several periods recognised by archæologists as the Stone, the Bronze, and Iron ages, proceeded to give a summary of the various remains found in Crannogs, and the conditions under which they occur, dealing more especially with such as have come under his own observation in Fermanagh and adjoining counties, a district peculiarly rich in these interesting structures, and fortunate in having earnest workers, who make them a special study and give the public the benefit of their research.

Numerous specimens of stone weapons, and implements of horn and bone, jet ornaments, and those curious and even mysterious beads of glass or vitreous paste, illustrative alike of the warlike and domestic habits of long-forgotten races, were exhibited and described, together with a very large collection of rude pottery of a domestic character, of a type apparently peculiar to Irish Crannogs, which occurs in their immediate neighbourhood. Of the remains of the true Bronze period many good examples have been found, though doubtless many interesting specimens have been lost by falling into the hands of ignorant dealers, and through them into the smelting pot.

Perhaps the most curious antiquity found in the Ulster Crannogs is the Ogham Stone, discovered in the long-submerged island in the small lough of Ballydoolough, near Enniskillen. This has been pronounced by Dr. Ferguson to be the most northern example of the class noticed in Ireland. The fact of a monument of this kind being discovered in a Crannog confirms the opinion that these artificial structures are of extreme antiquity.

An animated discussion took place at the close of the lecture. The speakers referred to numerous examples of Crannogs in Antrim and Down, from which stone, bronze, bone, and other objects have been taken in as large quantities, and in as great variety, as from any of those referred to by Mr. Wakeman.

The specimens kindly brought by Mr. Wakeman to illustrate his paper having been examined with evident interest, a vote of thanks was accorded to that gentleman for his kindness in coming from Enniskillen to bring the subject before the Club.

On 15th April, Dr. T. H. KEOWN, R.N., read a paper, entitled " Notes of the Aurora Borealis, taken at Belfast during the years 1870 and 1871, with suggestions as to the source of the Aurora, and also that of the Earth's Magnetism and Magnetic Currents," of which the following is a summary :—

Impressed with the frequent appearance of the aurora in disturbed states of the atmosphere, especially after heavy rains and storms, he noted the weather, on the days of its appearance, also the weather of the two preceding and two succeeding days, and was thus led to form an opinion of its connection with the weather in this island. This subsequently led him to seek for the true source of the aurora, and to see its identity with the earth's magnetism, and thence followed his theory of the connection of magnetic polarity with the currents running south and north. The chief reference was made to the years 1870 (when it was visible on forty-five nights), and 1871 (when it was noted on ninety-six nights). These satisfactorily proved that all unusual demonstrations near us are accompanied with excessively disturbed states of the air at a distance, which generally reach us; and that in proportion to the quantity of the auroral light, so we may predict unsettled weather in the line of the ocean, which not unfrequently extends to the British Isles. This was further proved by detailing the phenomena connected with the storms of October, 1839, October, 1870, and February, 1871; all illustrating the fact that the aurora does not appear until more or less condensation has taken place. He next passed on to the acknowledged connection between the aurora and the magnetism that directs the magnetic needle; quoting the observations of M. Arago, also those of Messrs. Lotin and Bravais. Having satisfied himself that the usual appearance of the aurora was always connected with, and consequent on condensation of watery vapour, this naturally led to the question, whence the source of this element? The phenomena exhibited on the nights of October, 1870, and February, 1871, rendered the usual explanations altogether unsatisfactory; and having subsequently, on the 2nd of November last, during a storm from the north-west, seen the aurora mingled with the clouds, he felt that we must now look outside our atmosphere for its source. He assumes, then, that all space is filled with a rare elastic medium called ether, which forms, as it were, a bond of union between the visible universe; and that this is probably of the nature of hydrogen combined with magnetism, and that this is the true source of all magnetism; that it is also the medium of luminous undulations between us and the sun and stars, and when exposed to friction becomes luminous, as is seen in the transit of meteoric bodies and comets of all kinds, and also when it comes in contact with our atmosphere. After giving his reasons for forming these opinions, he stated it as probable that the magnetism on entering our atmosphere, and before reaching the earth, leaves the hydrogen, and allies itself to the oxygen of our air; and that the extraordinary power oxygen possesses, of supporting animal life, combustion, and chemical action, seems to point to its being associated with it. He next proceeded to show how this magnetic ether is drawn into our atmosphere. This generally takes place in the hot tropical regions, where evaporation is going on to an extent unknown to us here, and where the heated vapour ascends to the limits of our air; and there being immediately condensed, it causes gaps or partial vacuæ, into which rushes, as it were by insuction, the external magnetic ether—the earth's rotation, onward motion, and attraction helping it inwards to us. Being thus enveloped in cloudy vapour, it naturally, in company with it, is pressed towards the polar regions, where condensation takes place, and there it is set free, and reaches the earth. This may be taken as its daily course. Exceptional inbursts occur in the track of great rainfalls or snowstorms; and it is also probable that it assists in the condensation, and promotes the storms. The coronæ formed on rare occasions, when in our latitude the auroral light is seen in excess, he looks on as points where it is actually entering our lower atmosphere, in the line of the earth's orbit. After referring to the highly electrical state of our upper air, and the fact that auroral currents may be seen in the above cloud region, travelling in a direction S.E., he gave it as his belief, that the magnetism on landing in the north polar region, passes in a direction S.E. to the south polar regions, and that which lands in the south polar regions passes also in the same lines to the north polar regions; that, in short, the south pole of a magnet is directed by the north polar current, running south, and that the north pole of the magnet is directed by the south polar current running north. And that this belief is strengthened in seeing what takes place in the making of an artificial magnet, showing that there are not two distinct kinds of magnetism, but only two distinct currents running north and south, which will explain all the phenomena connected with polarity. After giving his idea of what takes place in the conversion of a steel bar into a magnet, he stated that, as far as he had been able to learn, nothing had been hitherto added to the explanation given by Dr. Gilbert in 1600—viz., that the two kinds of magnetism are separated in the act of magnetisation. The artificial magnet Dr. Keown looks on as a centre for the induction of all passing magnetism, and that it becomes overcharged of necessity only at its poles, hence he attributes the attraction at the poles for that which will help it to pass on its overcharge of magnetism. The currents running south and north, on the magnet, are supposed to overlap each other spirally, one current being stronger than the other in winter and less so in summer; and that this may take place is proved in the example of sending a telegram from each end of a wire at the same moment. All these considerations make it certain that the extreme poles of the earth are in intimate connection with each other through these currents, and show why the intensity at the poles is double of what it is at the equator. After stating that the magnetic needle was solely influenced by the passing currents of magnetism, and that these again are subject to variations from local causes, he referred to the north magnetic pole, which has, during the past sixty years, occupied a limited space, shifting a little from time to time; and that as this locality lies at the head of and between the two great oceans, the sources of continual evaporation and condensation, they may have much to do with its position. He concluded with a suggestion as to the possible influence the shifting of the magnetic pole in past times may have had on the climate of western Europe.

The Annual Meeting of the Club was held on Wednesday evening, 29th April, 1874. The chair was occupied by the President, John Anderson, Esq., J.P., F.G.S. Mr. William Gray read the Secretaries' Report, and Mr. Greer Malcomson the Treasurer's, both of which were unanimously adopted and ordered to be printed.

After the election of the office-bearers for the ensuing year, and the discussion of the arrangements for the year's excursions, the several collections submitted in competition for the prizes offered were exhibited. Mr. S. A. Stewart exhibited flowers and fruit of the Broad Bitter-vetch (*Vicia orobus*). The specimens of this very rare plant were collected during the summer of 1873, from the inland cliffs near Larne, known as the "Sallagh Braes." *Vicia orobus* has been found in Galway, and in King's County; but the locality mentioned above is the only certain station in the North of Ireland. It has been stated, on the authority of one of the early British botanists (Sherrard), that it grew at Rostrevor, in County Down; but the record has been discredited, it being thought that there was an error in the identification of Sherrard's specimen. The effect of the finding of the plant in an almost inaccessible portion of the Sallagh cliffs is, however, to render it more probable that the early record was correct, and that the plant may still grow on the Mourne mountains.

NOTICE.

EXCHANGE OF PROCEEDINGS.

THE Committee of the Club have been desirous of establishing a yearly exchange of their published proceedings with those of kindred organisations in other places, and have during the past year forwarded copies of their Tenth Annual Report to other societies. They acknowledge with thanks the receipt of the following publications, and hope that other societies whose objects are similar will favour them with copies of their proceedings as published.

American Association for the Advancement of Science.
Proceedings. Vol. XXI.—1872.

Berwickshire Naturalists' Field Club.
Proceedings.—1872-3.

Brighton and Sussex Natural History Society.
Twentieth Annual Report.—1873.

Bristol Naturalists' Society.
Annual Report, &c., for 1872-73.

Canadian Institute.
Canadian Journal of Science, Literature, and History. Vol. XIII., No. 6.—1873.
Do.   do.   Vol. XIV., No. 1.—1873.

Cardiff Naturalists' Society.
Transactions. Vol. III., Part 2.—1872.
Do. Vol. IV.—1873.

Eastbourne Natural History Society.
Fifth Annual Report.—1873.
Lists of Local Fauna and Flora.—1873.

Edinburgh Geological Society.
Transactions. Vol. II., Part 2.—1873.

Essex Institute, Salem, Mass., U.S.A.
Bulletin of Essex Institute. Vol. I. 1869.
Do. Vol. II.—1870.
Do. Vol. III.—1871.
Do. Vol. IV.—1872.

Geologists' Association, London.
Annual Report for 1873.
Proceedings. Vol. III., Part 1.—1873.
Do. Vol. III., Part 2.—1873.
Do. Vol. III., Part 3.—1873.
Do. Vol. III., Part 4.—1874.
Do. Supplemental Number, Opening Address, Session 1873-74.

Geological Survey of England and Wales.
Geological Report on Londonderry and parts of Tyrone and Fermanagh; Portlock.—1843.
Sub-ærial Denudation; W. Whitaker, B.A., F.G.S.—1867.

Glasgow Society of Field Naturalists.
Annual Report and Transactions.—1872-73.

Liverpool Geological Society.
Annual Report for 1872-73.

Liverpool Naturalists' Field Club.
Proceedings for 1872-73.—1873.

Manchester Field Naturalists' Society.
Annual Report.—1873.

Norfolk and Norwich Naturalists' Society.
Transactions for 1872-73.

Peabody Academy of Sciences, Salem, Mass., U.S.A.
Fourth Annual Report of Trustees.—1872.

Philadelphia, U.S.A., Academy of Natural Sciences of.
Proceedings for 1873.—1873-74.

Philadelphia, U.S.A., Natural History Club of.
Sixth Annual Report.—1873.

Plymouth Institution.
Transactions. Vol. IV., Part 4.—1873.

Quekett Microscopical Club.
Eighth Report.—1873.

Royal Geological Society of Ireland.
Transactions. Vol. III., Part 3. (New series).—1873.

Royal Institution of South Wales.
Thirty-seventh Annual Report.—1872.

St. Louis, U.S.A., Academy of Science of.
Transactions. Vol. III., No. 1.—1873.

Scottish Arboricultural Society.
Proceedings of Twentieth Annual Meeting.—1873.

Smithsonian Institution, Washington, U.S.A.
Report of Board of Regents for 1871.

Warwickshire Natural History and Archæological Society.
Thirty-seventh Annual Report.—1873.

[*From the respective Societies.*]

BELFAST NATURALISTS' FIELD CLUB.

TWELFTH YEAR—1874-75.

LIST OF OFFICERS AND MEMBERS.

President.
REV. WILLIAM M'ILWAINE, D.D.

Vice-President.
WILLIAM GRAY, M.R.I.A.

Treasurer.
GREER MALCOMSON, CASTLE PLACE.

Secretaries.
| WILLIAM GRAY, M.R.I.A., | HUGH ROBINSON, |
| MOUNT CHARLES. | DONEGALL STREET. |

Committee.
JOHN ANDERSON, J.P., F.G.S.	W. H. PATTERSON, M.R.I.A.
HENRY KNIGHT.	S. A. STEWART, F.B.S.E.
F. W. LOCKWOOD.	WILLIAM SWANSTON.
Dr. J. MOORE, M.R.I.A., H.R.H.A.	SAMUEL SYMINGTON.
Rev. E. M'CLURE, A.M., M.R.I.A.	J. WRIGHT, F.G.S., F.R.G.S.I.

Members.

Any changes in the Addresses of Members should be communicated by them to the Secretaries.

John Aickin, Lincoln Avenue.
William Aickin, M.D., Murray's Terrace.
Miss Alder, Fernbank, Holywood.
W. J. C. Allen, J.P., Faunoran, Whiteabbey.
Edward Allworthy, Mountview.
John Anderson, J.P., F.G.S., Hillbrook, Holywood.
John Anderson, Lower Crescent.
Robert Anderson, Balmoral.
Mrs. Andrews, Chlorine Place.

E. N. Banks, Botanic Avenue.
Jas. M. Barkley, Coleen, Strandtown.
William Batt, Ormeau Road.
J. G. Bell, Tullylish, Gilford.
J. M. D. Bermingham, A.R.I.A.I., Mount Charles.
Arthur Black, Reid's Buildings, Mountpottinger.
W. J. Boucher, Landscape Terrace.
W. H. Braddell, St. Ives, Malone Park.
Edward Braddell, St. Ives, Malone Park.
Rev. S. A. Brenan, A.B., Pomeroy, County Tyrone.
Charles H. Brett, Dunedin Terrace.
John Brown, Crumlin Road.
James Bryce, A.M., LL.D., F.G.S., F.R.G.S.I., &c., Bowes Hill, Blantyre, Glasgow. (Hon. Mem.)
Henry Burden, M.D., Prospect, Ballynafeigh.

James Calwell, Cushendun, County Antrim.
Jno. Campbell, Mossley, Carnmoney.
Miss Carruthers, Claremont Street.
John Charley, College Park.
J. C. Clarke, Parkville.
Wm. Clibborn, Windsor Terrace.
Sir Edward Coey, J.P., D.L., Merville, Whiteabbey.

John Collins, Nottinghill, Malone.
Miss Connery, Victoria Place.
David Corrie, Custom House.
W. F. C. S. Corry, Mountpottinger.
John Cramsie, Lisavon, Strandtown.
John Cramsie, jun., Lisavon, Strandtown.
Alex. Crawford, Fitzwilliam Street.
Wm. Crawford, jun., Fitzroy Avenue.
Henry C. Cronhelm, Ulsterville Avenue.
W. M. Cunningham, Windsor.

Edward Dale, Fitzroy Avenue.
John H. Davies, Glenmore, Lisburn.
Robert Day, jun., F.S.A., Patrick Street, Cork.
George Donaldson, Mount Collyer.
William Doubleday, College Square North.
Charles Druitt, Elmwood Avenue.
William Duff, Cambridge Street.

John Eagleson, Brandon Towers, Strandtown.
J. R. Edeson, Mount Charles.
Mrs. Edeson, Mount Charles.

W. J. Gilmore, Cliftonville.
G. T. Glover, Kew Cottages, Mountpottinger.
Jas. Gourlay, Killinchy, County Down.
Rev. John Grainger, A.M., D.D., Broughshane, County Antrim. (Hon. Mem.)
Rev. Jas. Graves, Inisnaig, Stoneyford, County Kilkenny. (Cor. Mem.)
William Gray, M.R.I.A., Mount Charles.
Forster Green, Derrievolgie, Malone.
Henry Green, Derrievolgie, Malone
Henry Greenhill, Balmoral.
Mrs. Greenhill, Balmoral.
Miss Greer, Tarbat Villa, Strandtown.

Jas. C. Greer, Annadale, Ballynafeigh.
Mrs. Greer, Annadale, Ballynafeigh.
Wm. Gregg, Willowbank, Antrim Road.
William Greig, Richmond, Antrim Road.

Hugh Hamilton, University Square.
William Hancock, Manor House, Lurgan.
Mann Harbison, Newtownards.
William Harte, C.E., Buncrana, County Donegal. (Cor. Mem.)
W. T. Harvey, Kinnaird Street.
Jas. Haslett, Franklin Street.
W. B. Haynes, Lincoln Villa, Knock.
W. D. Henderson, University Street.
Jas. Hewitt, Ballymacreely, Killinchy, County Down.
Stephen Hicklin, Ligoniel.
Prof. J. F. Hodges, M.D., Derrievolgie, Malone.
John Hogg, Richmond Terrace.
J. Sinclair Holden, M.D., F.G.S., Sudbury, Suffolk. (Cor. Mem.)
F. C. Holmes, Belmont.
Alex. Hunter, Northern Bauk.
Thomas Hunter, Holywood.

H. H. Jamieson, Casaeldono, Castlereagh.
F. M. Jennings, Brown Street, Cork. (Cor. Mem.)
Miss Johnston, Dalriada, Whiteabbey.
Miss Johnston, Glenavy, County Antrim.
James Johnston, Alma Terrace.
Samuel Johnston, Antrim Road.
W. J. Johnston, Dunesk, Strandmillis.
J. F. Johnstone, Royal Botanic Gardens.
R. S. Joyce, Mountpottinger.

W. Thompson Kelly, Regent Street.
Mrs. Keogh, Crumlin Road.
Dr. T. H. Keown, R.N., Dundela, Strandtown.
Wm. Kernahan, Sydenham Avenue.
Rev. J. A. Kerr, A.B., Whiteabbey.

William King, Mountpleasant.
Henry Knight, Gloucester Villa, Antrim Road.
W. J. Knowles, Cullybackey, County Antrim.

Miss Lamb, Divis View.
W. W. Lamb, Divis View.
George Langtry, Mount Charles.
G. D. Leathem, Thornlea, Malone.
F. R. Lepper, Sydenham, Strandtown.
Miss Lester, Lonsdale Street.
T. M. Lindsay, Wilmont Terrace.
Mrs. Lindsay, Wilmont Terrace.
F. W. Lockwood, Corn Market.
John Love, Oldpark Terrace.
Wm. Lowry, Kinkora, Strandtown.

Henry Major, Lisburn.
Greer Malcomson, Shamrock Lodge.
James Malcomson, Mountpottinger.
Mrs. Malcomson, Mountpottinger.
John Marsh, York Street.
Joseph C. Marsh, Donegall Street.
Rev. Jas. Martin, Eglintoun, Antrim Road.
Mrs. Martin, Eglintoun, Antrim Road.
John Martin, M.D., Clarence Place.
P. C. Mayne, Sydenham Avenue.
John Millar, J.P., Lisburn.
Miss Millar, Lisburn.
William Millar, Durham Street.
John K. Mitchell, Carrickfergus.
James Moore, M.D., M.R.I.A., H.R.H.A., Chichester Street.
John Moore, M.D., Carlisle Terrace.
W. R. Molyneux, Florence Place.
Miss Monteith, Claremont Street.
William Morris, Fitzroy Avenue.
Hugh Morrison, Ligoniel.
David Morrow, Clarence Place.
Rev. W. E. Mulgan, A.B., Dunaghy Rectory, Clough, Co. Antrim.
J. J. Murphy, F.G.S., Oldforge, Dunmurry.
J. W. Murphy, Strandmillis.
J. R. Musgrave, J.P., Drumglass, Malone.
Robt. M'Adam, College Square East.
John M'Caw, Carlisle Street.

James M'Clenahan, Ardoyne.
Rev. Geo. Macloskie, A.M., LL.D., Limestone Road.
Miss M'Clure, Belmont.
Sir Thomas M'Clure, Bart., V.L., Belmont.
Rev. Edmund M'Clure, A.M., M.R.I.A., Richmond Terrace.
Rev. William M'Ilwaine, D.D., Ulsterville.
Mrs. M'Ilwaine, Ulsterville.
Daniel M'Kee, Adela Place.
John Mackenzie, C.E., Balmoral.
Thos. MacKnight, Balmoral Terrace.
William M'Millan, Ballinasloe.

Nicholas Oakman, Prospect Terrace.
George O'Brien, Holywood.
W. D. O'Brien, Holywood.
Capt. S. P. Oliver, 22nd Brigade R.A., F.R.S., F.R.G.S., &c., Buncrana, County Donegal.
Rev. Jas. O'Laverty, Holywood.
Alexander O'Rorke, Duncairn.

David C. Patterson, Holywood.
W. H. Patterson, M.R.I.A., Dundela, Strandtown.
W. H. Phillips, Lemonfield, Holywood.
Jas. J. Phillips, Virginia Street.
John Pim, Clifton Park Avenue.
Joshua Pim, Crumlin Terrace.
Thomas W. Pim, Evelyn Lodge, Strandtown.
John Preston, jun., Dunmore, Antrim Road.
Alfred Purdon, Wellington Place.
John Pyper, Oldpark Terrace.

John Reid, Donegall Square West.
Miss Robinson, Antrim Road.
Rev. George Robinson, A.M., Tartaraghan, County Armagh.
Hugh Robinson, Donegall Street.
J. R. Robinson, Woodstock Road.
Ninian J. Robinson, Donegall Street.
W. A. Robinson, Crofton, Holywood.
Edward Rogan, Cromac Street.
Rd. Ross, M.D., Wellington Place.

Rev. Geo. B. Sayers, Raloo, Carrickfergus.
Mrs. Scott, Sydenham Avenue.
Rev. Charles Scott, Elgin Terrace.
J. M. Johnston Scott, M.D., Victoria Street.
R. C. Sedgwick, Holywood.
Thomas Shaw, Pakenham Place.
John Shelly, Whiteabbey.
William Shepherd, Holywood.
Miss Simpson, University Square.
Rowland Smeethe, Queen's College.
George K. Smith, Whiteabbey.
Robert Smith, Mountpottinger.
Thomas Smyth, Kensington Street.
Rev. George C. Smythe, A.M., Coole Glebe, Carnmoney.
Adam Speers, B.Sc., Holywood.
J. H. Staples, Lissan, County Tyrone.
Robert Stewart, M.D., Falls Road.
S. A. Stewart, F.B.S.E., North Street.
Miss Swanston, University Street.
Wm. Swanston, University Street.
Samuel Symington, Brookfield House.

Ralph Tate, A.L.S.F., G.S., &c., High Street, Redcar, Yorkshire. (Hon. Mem.)
A. O'D. Taylor, Upper Crescent.
Wyville Thomson, LL.D., F.R.S., F.G.S., &c., University, Edinburgh. (Hon. Mem.)
James Thomson, A.M., LL.D., C.E., Sardinia Terrace, Hillhead, Glasgow. (Hon. Mem.)
George Thomson, Grosvenor Street.
Henry Thompson, Windsor.
John Thompson, B.E., Harbour Office.
Miss Thorn, Holywood.
John Todd, Regent Street.
W. A. Todd, Regent Street.
R. K. Tomlin, University Square.

William Valentine, J.P., Glenavna, Whiteabbey.
J. W. Valentine, Fortwilliam Park.

W. F. Wakeman, Portora, Enniskillen, County Fermanagh. (Cor. Mem.)
T. R. Walkington, Laurel Lodge, Strandtown.
Isaac W. Ward, University Street.
John S. Ward, Lisburn.
W. R. Ward, Stanpit, Christchurch, Hants.
W. T. Waters, Belmont Park.
W. Watson, Londonderry. (Cor. Mem.)
Alex. C. Welsh, Dromore, County Down. (Cor. Mem.)
T. K. Wheeler, M.D., Clarendon Place.
T. K. Wheeler, jun., Clarendon Place.
David Wilson, Ballymoney, County Antrim.

James Wilson, jun., Albion Place.
James Wilson, Ballybundon, Killinchy, County Down.
John Workman, Windsor.
Rev. Robert Workman, M.A., Glastry, Kirkcubbin, County Down.
Thomas Workman, Windsor.
H. J. Wright, Donegall Street.
Joseph Wright, F.G.S., F.R.G.S.I., Cliftonville.
Samuel O. Wylie, College Square North.
William Wylie, College Square North.

Robert Young, C.E., Rathvarna, Antrim Road.
Robert M. Young, Rathvarna, Antrim Road.
Samuel Young, Malone.

RULES

OF THE

Belfast Naturalists' Field Club.

I.

That the Society be called "THE BELFAST NATURALISTS' FIELD CLUB."

II.

That the object of the Society be the practical Study of Natural Science and Archæology.

III.

That the Club shall consist of Honorary, Corresponding, and Ordinary Members. The Ordinary Members to pay annually a Subscription of Five Shillings; and that Corresponding Members be expected to communicate a paper within every two years.

IV.

That Candidates shall be proposed and seconded at any meeting of the Club by Members present, and then be elected by a majority of votes.

V.

That the Officers of the Club be annually elected, and consist of a President, Vice-President, Treasurer, two Secretaries, and ten Members, who form the Committee. Five to form a Quorum. No Member of Committee to be eligible for re-election who has not attended at least one-fourth of the Committee Meetings during his year of office.

VI.

That the Members of the Club shall hold at least Six Field Meetings during the year, in the most interesting localities, for investigating the Natural History and Archæology of the district. That the place of meeting be fixed by the Committee, and that five days' notice of each Excursion be communicated to Members by the Secretaries.

VII.

That Meetings be held Fortnightly or Monthly, at the discretion of the Committee, for the purpose of reading of papers; such papers, as far as possible, to treat of the Natural History and Archæology of the district. These Meetings to be held during the months from November to April inclusive.

VIII.

That the Committee shall, if they find it advisable, offer for competition Prizes for the best collections of scientific objects of the district; and the Committee may order the purchase of maps, or other scientific apparatus, and may carry on geological and archæological searches or excavations, if deemed advisable; provided that the entire amount expended under this rule does not exceed the sum of £10 in any one year.

IX.

That the Annual Meeting be held during the month of April, when the Report of the Committee for the past year, and the Treasurer's Financial Statement, shall be presented, the Committee and Officers elected, Bye-laws made and altered, and any proposed alteration in the general laws, of which a fortnight's notice shall have been given, in writing, to the Secretary or Secretaries, considered and decided upon. The Secretaries to give the Members due notice of such intended alteration.

X.

That, on the written requisition of twenty-five Members, delivered to the Secretaries, an extraordinary General Meeting may be called, to consider and decide upon the subjects mentioned in such written requisition.

XI.

That the Committee be empowered to exchange publications and reports, and to extend the privilege of attending the meetings and excursions of the Belfast Naturalists' Field Club, to members of kindred societies, on similar privileges being accorded to its Members by such other societies.

*The following Rules for the conducting of
the Excursions have been arranged by the Committee.*

I.—The Excursions to be open to all Members; each one to have the privilege of introducing two friends.

II.—A Chairman to be elected as at ordinary meetings.

III.—One of the Secretaries to act as conductor, or in the absence of both, a Member to be elected for that purpose.

IV.—No change to be made in the programme, or extra expenses incurred, except by the consent of the majority of the Members present.

V.—No fees, gratuities, or other expenses, to be paid except through the conductor.

VI.—Every Member or Visitor to have the accommodation assigned by the conductor. Where accommodation is limited, consideration will be given to priority of application.

VII.—Accommodation cannot be promised unless tickets are obtained before the time mentioned in the special circular.

VIII.—Those who attend an excursion without previous notice will be liable to extra charge, if extra cost be incurred thereby.

IX.—No intoxicating liquors to be provided at the expense of the Club.

Belfast Naturalists' Field Club.

TWELFTH YEAR.

THE Committee offer the following Prizes to be competed for during the Session ending March 31, 1875 :—

I. For the best Herbarium of Flowering Plants,
   representing not less than 250 Species............£1 0 0
II. For the best Herbarium of Flowering Plants,
   representing not less than 150 Species........... 0 10 0
III. Best Collection of Mosses......................... 0 10 0
IV.   Do.   Seaweeds 0 10 0
V.   Do.   Ferns............................ 0 10 0
VI.   Do.   Cretaceous Fossils........... 0 10 0
VII. Do.   Liassic   do. 0 10 0
VIII. Do.   Palæozoic   do. 0 10 0
IX.   Do.   Marine Shells 0 10 0
X.   Do.   Land and Fresh-water Shells 0 10 0
XI.   Do.   Lepidoptera.................... 0 10 0
XII. Best Set of 25 Microscopic Slides................ 0 10 0

XIII. Best Collection of Archæological Objects £0 10 0
XIV. Do. Crustacea........................ 0 10 0
XV. Do. Echinodermata 0 10 0
XVI. Do. Geological Specimens, illustrative of the Mineral Resources of the Province of Ulster.. 1 0 0
XVII. Best Collection of all or any of the above Objects collected *at the Excursions* of the Year 0 10 0
XVIII. Six best Field Sketches appertaining to Geology, Archæology, or Natural History............ 0 10 0

In every case where three or more persons compete for a Prize, a second one of half its value, will be awarded if the conditions are otherwise complied with.

CONDITIONS.

No Competitor to obtain more than Two Prizes in any one year.

No Competitor to be awarded the same Prize twice within three years.

All Collections to be made personally during the Session, within the Province of Ulster. Each Species to be correctly named, and locality stated. The Flowering Plants to be collected when in flower, and classified according to the Natural System. The Sketches, Drawings, and Microscopic Slides to be the Competitor's own work.

No Prizes will be awarded except to such Collections as shall, in the opinion of the Judges, possess positive merit.

The Prizes to be in books or suitable scientific objects, at the desire of the successful competitor.

SPECIAL PRIZES.

XIX. The President offers a Prize of £1 1s. for the best Original Measured Drawing and Details of some Ruined Building in Ireland, of not later date than the fifteenth century. The Building selected to be different from those for which Prizes have been previously given. The Prize Drawings to become the property of the Club.

XX. Mr. J. W. Murphy offers a Prize of 10s. for the best Collection of Recent Sponges, the conditions being the same as those for Prizes I. to XVII.

XXI. Dr. James Moore, H.R.H.A., offers a Prize of £1 1s. for the best Two Studies from Nature, illustrative of Archæology. The Prize Sketches to become the property of the Club, and to be not less than 9 inches by 5½ inches. The subjects of the Sketches to be different from any at present in the Club's Album.

XXII. Mr. William Swanston offers a Prize of 10s. 6d. for the best Two Studies from Nature illustrative of Geology. Conditions same as for Prize XXI.

pp 68-80

NOW READY,

320 pp. Fcap. 8vo. Cloth Gilt, Bevelled Boards, with 48 pp. Illustrations and Map. Price 3/6.

GUIDE TO BELFAST

AND ADJACENT COUNTIES.

BY THE

BELFAST NATURALISTS' FIELD CLUB.

THE BOOK TREATS OF THE FOLLOWING SUBJECTS:

PHYSICAL GEOGRAPHY.
GEOLOGY AND MINERAL RESOURCES.
BOTANY.
ZOOLOGY.
TOPOGRAPHY.
HISTORICAL & DESCRIPTIVE NOTICES OF TOWNS.

ANTIQUITIES—ECCLESIASTICAL AND CIVIL.
AGRICULTURE.
TRADE AND COMMERCE.
EXCURSIONS TO PLACES OF INTEREST.

May be had of all Booksellers, or from the Secretaries of the Club.

Presented
11 FEB 1886

ANNUAL REPORT

AND

PROCEEDINGS

OF THE

Belfast Naturalists' Field Club,

1874-1875.

SERIES II.

Volume I. Part II.

PRINTED FOR MEMBERS ONLY.

ANNUAL REPORT

AND

PROCEEDINGS

OF THE

Belfast Naturalists' Field Club,

FOR THE

YEAR ENDING 31ST MARCH, 1875.

(TWELFTH YEAR)

NEW SERIES.

VOLUME I. PART II.

BELFAST:
PRINTED FOR THE CLUB,
AT THE "BELFAST NEWS-LETTER" STEAM-PRINTING HOUSE,
55, 57, & 59, DONEGALL STREET.

1875.

WINTER SESSION.

NOTE.—The Authors of the various papers, of which abstracts are here appended, are alone responsible for the views expressed in them.

THE opening meeting of the Session was held on 18th November. After some preliminary remarks, the President, Rev. WILLIAM MACILWAINE, D.D., proceeded to deliver the following address :

LADIES AND GENTLEMEN,

Anniversaries, such as that which at this moment affords me the privilege of addressing you, are essentially occurrences of a suggestive character. The moralist, as one year gives place to another, reads in the falling leaves of autumn and the clouded sunsets of winter lessons of value and interest in *his* department which he is not slow to learn for himself, and to impart to others. The anniversary of the community or of the household is equally suggestive ; nor should that of such an Institution as our own be allowed to pass without note, and that for similar reasons to those which lead others to utilise its advent. My own idea respecting the opening meeting of any Scientific Institution, on such occasions as this, is that it should present to those assembled a sort of review and summary in that special department of Science or Literature which comes more immediately within its range. Adopting this view of the year

1874, and of the part which our Club has been permitted to take in the advancement of Natural Science, before adverting particularly to our own operations I may be pardoned if I refer to an event which, in common, I may say, with nearly all our fellow-townsmen, we naturally have been led to view with particular interest.

I allude, of course, to the visit of the British Association to Belfast. While not insensible of the honour conferred on our provincial town by the appearance among us of that eminent scientific body for the second time—and after a lapse of some twenty-five years—I cannot refrain from making some observations on one accompanying circumstance of that visit that has bestowed on it an amount of notoriety hardly accorded to any other meeting of the Association since its very formation. I refer to the inaugural address of its learned President. I am not about to follow the example set by Professor Tyndall by recklessly introducing into the following remarks questions of a purely theological or even of a metaphysical nature. I can conceive but one feeling among my auditory were I to act so unadvisedly, and that feeling would be, I am persuaded, one of entire disapproval. That a religious teacher of any denomination should take advantage of his position, while discussing scientific subjects, by introducing theological topics, which he must have known to be distasteful to not a few of his auditory, would be, in my judgment, little short of a breach of faith, as well as a violation of the rules of good taste. And I equally feel that I shall have the sympathy of all who now hear me when I express the opinion that for a scientific professor, or a scientist (as some prefer to designate themselves now-a-days), on a similar occasion to introduce topics of this description would be equally reprehensible ; with this additional consideration, that the latter is going further in diverging fiom the path of good taste and good feeling than the former, inasmuch as he is volunteering to enter upon debatable ground, entirely alien from his proper subject and his legitimate calling.

Truth obliges me to state my conviction, uttered, let me assure you; with regret, that such a line of procedure is chargeable upon the learned President of the British Association in regard to his now memorable address. In giving expression to this conviction, I plead guiltless of the *odium theologicum*, as well as of any other unworthy motive, consciously entertained. I claim for the remarks which I am about to make, that they are dictated pre-eminently, if not altogether, by regard for the interests of pure science, for the promotion of which the British Association was originally established. If the platform of that Institution and its presidential chair are to be esteemed as lawfully convertible into high places whence attacks may be made with impunity, and without contravention, on the religious convictions of almost all its members, if not of the entire community, then my decided opinion is that, so far as the countenance and support of that community are concerned, the days of the British Association are numbered, and deservedly so. That the sentiments which I have ventured to express regarding the document in question are warranted I now proceed to show as briefly as possible.

I have already expressed my opinion as to the impropriety of debating a religious question in a scientific arena. Professor Tyndall, so far from shrinking from the responsibility of so doing, has most deliberately, and, I must add, in my judgment, most needlessly, so acted. The existence and strong influence of the *religious element* in our nature is insisted on at page 30 of his address. Ascribing the existence of this integral portion of our mental constitution, as of the understanding and all others, "to the play between organism and environment through cosmic ranges of time," the learned professor proceeds to place "the immovable basis of the religious sentiment in the emotional nature of man." And when he further states that "to yield this sentiment reasonable satisfaction is the problem of problems of the present hour," it might well be imagined that the utmost caution ought to have been employed by one occupying the elevated and, at the same time, most delicate position in which he was at that moment placed, as, in a sense, one of the high priesthood of science. Unquestionably a chemist handling a highly explosive substance ought to be careful lest he might produce an explosion. Standing as he then was at the entrance of the temple, and in view, as it were, of the altar whereat so many around him who believed in the religion of Revelation stood, was it wise, was it generous, was it safe, even according to his own showing, to discredit that religion by not only ignoring it, but by virtually offering as its substitute the vague and unsubstantial dreams of Democritus, Epicurus, and Lucretius? That this charge is not a groundless one will appear, I venture to hope, before my present address is concluded.

In point of fact, Professor Tyndall appears to have deliberately adopted the line now questioned, in the very face of the religious difficulty. This he admits when he tells his auditory (p. 33), "I have touched on debatable questions and led you over dangerous ground." That this ground was deliberately chosen is further made plain when he thus states :—"I thought you ought to know the environment which, with or without your consent, is rapidly surrounding you, and in relation to which, some adjustment on your part may be necessary." Might not any one possessed of half the intelligence of the speaker have foreseen the inevitable consequences of the very basis of the religious faith professed by his auditory being assaulted as he assaulted it? Assuredly he might, and that such anticipations were not vain, the event has fully proved. I know perfectly well that Professor Tyndall has, since the delivery of his address, taken pains to disavow his belief of gross Materialism, as well as to repudiate the charge of Atheism. But such disavowal and repudiation do not amount to disproof of these charges. The person accused before a legal tribunal does not substantiate his innocency of the charge made against him by the mere plea of "not guilty." The outspoken words of the address are there, together with the indisputable fact, which presents the truest possible comment on these words, that they have been understood as advocating both Materialistic and Atheistic opinions wherever they have gone, and by the great majority of their readers. That the address itself was, moreover, in some sense abnormal and unsuited to the place and occasion, is evident from the effects produced by its delivery. At once it became the perfect tocsin of a religious warfare. Certain organs and advocates of a party which I need not name, immediately hailed it as spoken in advocacy of their opinions. It was the object of attack from those who hold opposing views on religious subjects. Pulpit, platform, lecture-room opened fire on it. The pamphlets written in reply already, and the reviews in periodicals, would almost constitute a library of polemical theology. It has been noticed with the highest disapproval by public bodies and in public assemblies, while crowded auditories have cheered these sentiments. The Roman Catholic hierarchy in this country have issued a lengthened pastoral to their flocks in condemnation of its tenets; and although differing from portions of this document, I feel bound, in honesty, to add that the objections therein taken to it, on scientific grounds, appear to me to be valid and weighty. A perfect civil, or rather indeed as it might be styled an uncivil warfare, raged on the subject in the daily and weekly papers.

As a specimen of the comments passed on Professor Tyndall's views, I may be permitted to read the following from one of the leading journals in the new world—viz, the *New York Times*:—

"Professor Tyndall attacks these questions with characteristic boldness, but beyond making a somewhat vehement defence of the right of physical science to deal with the ultimate problem of being, he can hardly be said to have robbed them of a single difficulty. What is to be considered the most startling part of the address is the following personal avowal which it contains:— 'Abandoning all disguise, the confession that I feel bound to make before you is, that I prolong the vision backward across the boundary of the experimental evidence, and discern in that matter, which we in our ignorance, and notwithstanding our professed reverence for its Creator, have hitherto covered with opprobium, the promise and potency of every form and quality of life.'"

On which avowal the editor remarks—" This is certainly a close approach to the Lucretian maxim that 'Nature is seen to do all things spontaneously of herself, without the intermeddling of the gods.'"

This, then, is the position which, however reluctantly, still with confidence of its propriety, I feel warranted in taking as regards Professor Tyndall's address, viewed in its general bearing and aspect. We have seen how it was at once understood and received, not only by our fellow-townsmen, but by the public at large. In London and New York alike—by the public journals, from the *Times* to *Punch*, it was understood as advocating materialistic opinions of the most pronounced description. Unmistakably and avowedly, the Christian revelation having been first recognised as a fact, professing as that revelation does to throw light on the origin of life, and on the future, after life is ended, the guesses and dreams of Democritus, Epicurus, and Lucretius are preferred to this proffered guidance. Professor Tyndall now assures the world that not only the members of the British Association who heard his address, but that the public in general are mistaken as to his meaning, that he is neither a Materialist nor an Atheist. Be it so, but my averment is, that in such a case as this, and in the delivery of such an address, the deliverer of it should have taken such precaution in the employment of his terms that no such dubiousness of meaning should have arisen. The blame arising from the general misconception of his meaning which has ensued, evidently rests, not with the many who misunderstood what was intended, but with him who employed such evidently ambiguous language.

If, however, the learned professor prefers to adopt the line of defence which some of his friends have employed on his behalf— namely, that his has been a bold, outspoken, chivalrous avowal of opinion for which he is more to be praised than blamed—I cannot but remark that there is a wide distinction, at times, between chivalry and real courage, and that the former is often exercised at the expense and risk of others, while the latter never exposes to peril and risk any but self. If, in his chivalrous defence of what he believes truth, Professor Tyndall has thrown down the gauntlet, he cannot feel surprised or impute blame that others have taken it up. The interests of Christianity are, perhaps, as dear, or even dearer, to them than those of science to him. The pigmy may have quite as acute sensibilities as even the giant, perhaps, indeed, more acute, for all his more powerful opponent knows. I conclude these remarks on this branch of my subject by observing, that the entire blame of that most undesirable religious controversy which has disturbed society since the delivery of his address, can be fairly imputed to none but to Professor Tyndall himself.

I now pass from what may be called the historical view of the subject, and proceed to offer a few observations on the substance of the address itself—and here let me say at once that, as I understand it, I cannot view it in any other light than as being, in the first instance, derogatory to Christianity, and in the next as, when carefully considered, a most unphilosophical tractate.

To this statement, however, I desire emphatically to add, that I do not appear on the present occasion as the advocate of Christianity. Any such advocacy here would be as ill-timed as unnecessary. While our institution is wholly unsectarian, and numbers among its members persons of all shades of religious opinion, none of those are, I trust, prepared to surrender their title to the common appellation of Christian. Were the case otherwise, however esteemed the honour conferred on me by being chosen to occupy the position in our Club which your kindness has conferred on me, I should have declined its acceptance. I think I may further add that none among our number can notice without regret any disparagement offered to our common faith in a document possessed of such high pretensions as that at present under review. Had Professor Tyndall argued out his positions on purely scientific grounds, and without any reference whatever to Christianity, no room had been afforded for the charge which I now feel authorised in making. Such, you will recollect, was the line of argument adopted in the recent valuable address to your fellow townsmen, by J. J. Murphy, Esq. That address, characterized as it is by cogent reasoning and thorough acquaintance with the subjects handled, conducts its line of reasoning, as it was perfectly lawful to do, without any direct reference to the Christian revelation. Not so Professor Tyndall—Speaking of the hindrances which science encountered in the lapse of time, between the era of Greek and Roman philosophy and that of modern civilization and progress, he employs the following language :—

"Rome, and the other cities of the empire, had fallen into moral putrefaction. Christianity had appeared, offering the gospel to the poor, and, by moderation if not asceticism of life, practically protesting against the profligacy of the age. The sufferings of the early Christians and the extraordinary exaltation of mind which enabled them to triumph over the diabolical tortures to which they were subjected, must have left traces not easily effaced. They scorned the earth, in view of that 'building of God, that house not made with hands, eternal in the heavens.' The Scriptures which ministered to their spiritual needs were also the measure of their science. When, for example, the celebrated question of antipodes came to be discussed, the Bible was with many the ultimate court of appeal. Augustine, who flourished A.D. 4co, would not deny the rotundity of the earth; but he would deny the possible existence of inhabitants at the other side, 'because no such race is recorded in Scripture among the descendants of Adam.' Archbishop Boniface was shocked at the assumption of a 'world of human beings out of the reach of the means of salvation.' Thus reined in, science was not likely to make much progress. Later on, the political and theological strife between the Church and civil governments, so powerfully depicted by Draper, must have done much to stifle investigation."

Now, in briefly commenting on this passage, wherein, as I feel bound to repeat my conviction, the subject of Christianity is rather needlessly introduced, I desire to speak guardedly and without any designed offence, but the interests of truth compel me, at the same time, to speak plainly.

The fact of the appearance of Christianity in the world is here admitted. Its peculiarity as "offering the Gospel to the poor" is noted. Praise, strangely enough, indeed, is bestowed on its early propagators for enduring martyrdom in testimony to its truth. With what consistency or merit, in his view, it is for Professor Tyndall to explain; and yet this is followed by a covert but most real assault on Christianity itself, as an obstacle to the spread of scientific truth, for if the passage in question means anything, in its connexion, it can have no other meaning.

The truth of the charge thus, by implication, made against Christianity I entirely repudiate. There is, indeed, a mistiness in the language employed, as well as an utter confusion of dates and persons, which present a great difficulty to any specific reply. Of whom, for example, is the author speaking when he tells us that "the Scriptures which ministered to their spiritual needs were also the measure of their science?" Does he make the statement of those early Christians, whom he so eloquently describes in the very language of Scripture, in the passage preceding? The "noble army of martyrs" had, I rather think, other employment than the discussion of scientific subjects. I am aware that some *laches* in the matter of natural history, such as belief in the existence of the fabulous Phœnix, are to be found in the very early uninspired Christian writings, but these are easily accounted for, and may be readily condoned. But Professor Tyndall's charge appears to be made against Christianity as a whole, and I deny that it has ever appeared, whether as identified with the revelation which it contains or viewed as a community, in the character of an opponent to really philosophical truth and progress, or as "reining in science."

Professor Tyndall goes on to add to his charge against Christianity in this respect by instancing the theological strife between the Church and civil governments. In what manner, however, this strife has acted in opposition to scientific progress he fails to demonstrate. His charges, then, in their integrity, I repeat, fall to the ground.

It is, I may remark, wholly unnecessary, speaking where I now speak, to give the opposite side in this really momentous question. Need I state my conviction—yours, I trust, also—that real Christianity has ever proved, not the handmaid merely, but the elder sister and friend of true science? Need I point to the line of light, traced on the world's history since the appearance among men of the Founder of Christianity, by so many of His true followers? Has not the history of our race since that period proved that Christianity and civilization, so far as the elevation of that race is concerned, may be viewed as almost synonymous terms? So far from unduly reining in science, Christianity has ever proved its safest and surest guide. I shall not tread on often trodden ground by recalling to your recollection such names as those of Bacon and Newton, in the sister land; Boyle and Berkley in our own, who never considered it necessary, in order to insure their claim to the title of philosopher, to abjure the name of Christian. Still less do I think it necessary or expedient to come down to our own day and the history of our time, in order to mention, in the same connexion, the name of Faraday, the really philosophical and withal humble believer in Christianity; or to quote the emphatic words of the English philosopher, Mr. Prichard, the astronomer, spoken even more recently than the meeting of the British Association, wherein his noble testimony is given to the truth of revelation.

I gladly dismiss such topics in order to advert to another, mor in keeping with the present occasion. At the risk of appearing highly presumptuous, I venture to repeat that a *most unphilosophical character* appears to pervade the greater portion, if not, indeed, the entire of the document under review.

I shall not pause to draw your attention to the very loose and inaccurate *resumé* given of the ancient Grecian and Roman philosophy, betraying what appears to me nothing short of unacquaintance with the writers referred to—at least in their original languages. I prefer, however, to refer to one or two of the subjects more prominently discussed, and the mode of their discussion. I mean the Molecular Theory as bearing on the Origination of Life. In connexion with this subject Professor Tyndall thus expresses himself :—

"Trace the line of life backwards, and see it approaching more and more to what we may call the purely physical condition. We reach at length those organisms which I have compared to drops of oil suspended in a mixture of alcohol and water. We reach the *protogenes* of Haeckel, in which we have 'a type distinguishable from a fragment of albumen only by its finely granular character.' Can we pause here? We break a magnet, and find two poles in each of its fragments. We continue the process of breaking, but however small the parts, each carries with it, though enfeebled, the polarity of the whole. And when we break no longer, we prolong the intellectual vision to the polar molecules. Are we not urged to do *something* similar in the case of life? Is there not a temptation to close to some extent with Lucretius, when he affirms that 'nature is seen to do all things spontaneously of herself without the meddling of the gods?' or, with Bruno, when he declares that matter is not 'that mere empty *capacity* which philosophers have pictured her to be, but the universal mother who brings forth all things as the fruit of her own womb?' The questions here raised are inevitable. They are approaching us with accelerated speed, and it is not a matter of indifference whether they are introduced with reverence or irreverence. Abandoning all disguise, the confession that I feel bound to make before you is that I prolong the vision backward across the boundary of the experimental evidence, and discern in that matter, which we in our ignorance, and notwithstanding our professed reverence for its Creator, have hitherto covered with opprobrium, the promise and potency of every form and quality of life."

Now we are here introduced to a clearly physical investigation, and the mode wherein Professor Tyndall proposes to pursue it is given in the very opening sentence of his address :—

"An impulse inherent in primeval man turned his thoughts and questionings betimes towards the sources of natural phenomena. The same impulse, inherited and intensified, is the spur of scientific action to-day. Determined by it, by a process of abstraction from experience we form physical theories, which lie beyond the pale of experience, but which satisfy the desire of the mind to see every natural occurrence resting on a cause."

These latter words exactly describe the process pursued by

Professor Tyndall and his school in working out their Molecular theory. From an experience, and that one by their own showing more imaginary and transcendental than experimental, they reach, or imagine that they reach, conclusions (better styled, indeed, conceptions) which are "wholly ultra-experiential." I would venture to put it to the judgment of any person of sound mind and unprejudiced opinion whether or not this be a safe basis for any physical system ? What have physical inquiries philosophically to do with ultra-experiential theories ?

You will at once perceive the difference between a science of absolute certainty, such as that of geometry or mathematics, and one whose conclusions rest on such a debatable foundation as this. There is absolute certainty in the one case ; there is none in the other. Similarly, in regard to purely physical science, there is the process of induction, founded on well-ascertained and accumulated facts. Is there any theory, even remotely, resembling this in the professor's process? In no other instance has a molecule such as these philosophers imagine been rendered palpable to sense, however aided by the appliances and instruments of science, nor is it even conceivable that it should so become a matter of cognition. And yet we are asked to receive the existence of such into our catalogue of facts, and to build thereon a theory which is to account for the primary origin, the nature and the properties of all living things, ourselves included. Is this philosophical?

To point out the results of such theorizing, I have but to refer you to the closing paragraphs of Professor Tyndall's address—

" And if, still unsatisfed, the human mind, with the yearning of a pilgrim for his distant home, will turn to the Mystery from which it has emerged, seeking so to fashion it as to give unity to thought and faith, so long as this is done, not only without intolerance or bigotry of any kind, but with the enlightened recognition that ultimate fixity of conception is here unattainable, and that each succeeding age must be held free to fashion the mystery in accordance with its own needs—then, in opposition to all the restrictions of

Materialism, I would affirm this to be a field for the noblest exercise of what, in contrast with the *knowing* faculties, may be called the *creative* faculties of man. Here, however, I must quit a theme too great for me to handle, but which will be handled by the loftiest minds ages after you and I, like streaks of morning cloud, shall have melted into the infinite azure of the past."

If the "still unsatisfied human mind" of any present, "as the yearning of a pilgrim for his distant home"—a feeling, not only admitted, but dwelt on by that philosopher as a necessary part of our being—can find rest in the prospect there held out I am greatly mistaken. Laying aside, for the moment, the light shed upon the future by the Christianity which none present are, I trust, as yet prepared to ignore, I am still persuaded that even the light of reason, and the deductions of sound philosophy, will give us a more consoling and substantial hope for the future than the prospect that "you and I shall be like streaks of morning cloud, melting into the infinite azure of the past."

Having thus essayed to perform, however imperfectly, what I again venture to designate a duty, both in respect of the interests of true science and the position which your indulgence has assigned to me, I very willingly come to the fulfilment of another more agreeable one, namely, to afford to those present some information respecting the position and prospects of our Club. I may also, perhaps, be permitted, as the occasion is a special one, to enter into some details as to its origin and previous history.

"The Belfast Naturalists' Field Club" started into existence in the year 1863, and is now therefore but eleven years old. Its origin is interesting, and may be briefly stated. An anonymous correspondent, in one of the public journals of Belfast, called attention to the want of such a club, as a means of uniting and encouraging in their common object and studies the friends of natural history, many of whom were known to be residents in the town and neighbourhood. This letter was responded to by two who are now office-bearers in our society—then young men—and this led to an acquaintance with the writer of the letter above referred to, and finally to a meeting of a few equally interested in this branch of scientific pursuit, who constituted the members of the future club. Its first published report bears date 1864, just ten years ago, and presents a list of members numbering 100. It is pleasing to compare this first report, occupying some twelve pages, with that issued for last year, which comprises 100 pages, and contains a list of between 200 and 300 members. It is also gratifying to note, on turning over the pages of the reports published annually during this interval, that, while death and other incidents, such as change of residence, have deprived the Club of not a few active and valued members, still many of its original ones remain. Among the latter are two of our earlier hon. secretaries—Messrs. W. H. Patterson and Charles H. Brett; as also Messrs. W. Gray and Hugh Robinson— the latter recorded as a member of the original committee, and the former one of the hon. secretaries of the Club in its third year.

The objects of the society are stated in its first report, namely, "The practical study of Natural Science and Archæology," and these remain unchanged at the present date. The constitution and rules, with slight modifications, continue as they were at its start, and, as they are found in each of its reports, a gratifying proof of the good judgment which guided its original members in this particular. It is in no spirit of self-laudation, but in one of legitimate pleasure and pride at the steady success which has marked its progress from the first, that I notice this onward course, as seen in the several reports of our Club. This I am led to ascribe to that natural feeling of brotherhood and reciprocity, which marks all the real students of natural science, as well as to the uniform spirit of kindness and good fellowship which has prevailed among our members during the same period. It is extremely interesting and gratifying to take even a slight retrospective glance at the list of papers which have been read at our stated meetings, and to note the localities which have been visited in our summer and autumn excursions.

The botanical productions and geological formations, the mineral resources and archæological remains, of the entire surrounding district, have been thus so successfully laid under contribution, that the perusal even of the abstracts of papers above referred to, and given in the successive reports of the society, will be found to convey an amount of information as gratifying and useful, as it is creditable to the members of the Club who have contributed them.

While making this reference I feel bound to specify the list of the Irish Liassic Foraminifera, which is found in an appendix to the report of 1871, by Mr Joseph Wright, one of our most indefatigable and distinguished fellow-members. Those who had the pleasure of hearing the paper read by Mr. Wright, at the recent meeting of the British Association, wherein species of Foraminifera, from the Chalk formation of Antrim, were identified and figured, will share with me the satisfaction which so many others enjoyed at the attention and well-merited praise bestowed on its author by the entire geological section present.

Reference is also due here to the list given in the same appendix, of the fossils of the Estuarine Clays of the counties of Down and Antrim by another valued member of our body, Mr. S. A. Stewart, on whom, as most present are aware, the distinction of Fellow has been bestowed by the Botanical Society of Edinburgh. I may also add, with much pleasure, that Mr. Stewart has recently added another species to our rare mosses in his discovery of "Tayloria serrata," on Benbradagh Mountain, near Dungiven, County Derry. This interesting addition to Irish muscology has been fully identified by Dr. Moore, of the Royal Botanical Gardens, Glasnevin—the only other habitats of the plant known in Great Britain being some one or two of the steep and bleak mountains in Scotland.

With these gratifying proofs of success in scientific pursuits by members of our Club before us, to which, indeed, others might be added, I may well offer to its present meeting my sincere congratulations. My reference to the occurrences of the past year would be incomplete without some further allusion to the visit of the British Association, and to the part which our Club was privileged to take in the endeavour to render that visit a successful one. That such it was is, I believe, universally admitted, with perhaps the painful drawback to which I have felt it necessary to advert at the opening of this address. I cannot but notice, with unmingled satisfaction, the production of the Guide Book, undertaken by members of our body, chiefly in anticipation of the visit to our town by so many distinguished strangers on that occasion. That volume, as possibly all now present are aware, was compiled, illustrated, printed, and published, within the space of three months. That it fully answered the end contemplated was attested by the members of the Association into whose hands it came, as well as by others; and my own hope and expectation are that in some future edition it may reflect even greater credit on its compilers. In this brief notice of its production and success it would be unpardonable were I to omit special reference to the share of the labour bestowed on its composition by our Hon. Secretaries, Messrs. Gray and Robinson. To the artistic skill of the former is due the execution of the characteristic lithographic illustrations of the volume; and to the unwearied labour of the latter is mainly due its successful passage through the press.

While referring thus to our last year's proceedings, I may be permitted also to notice the exhibition of Irish antiquities which, during the meeting of the British Association, was undertaken by our Club, in conjunction with the Royal Historical and Archæological Association of Ireland. It is not too much to say that the collection thus brought together, as indeed was universally acknowledged, contributed in no small degree to the instruction and gratification of the members of the Association and others who visited it during the week of its exhibition. The Minor Hall, where the exhibition took place, was crowded by visitors on the two nights when *conversaziones* were held in the Ulster Hall. Many distinguished strangers were present on those occasions, and expressed themselves in very flattering terms, indeed, as to the extent and variety of the articles exhibited. Sir W. Wilde, who was president of the Anthropological Section of the Association, Sir John Lubbock, and other eminent antiquarians and archæologists, were among the visitors referred to, and took part in the conversations and discussions which arose in connection with many of the more rare objects. In making this reference my fellow-members of the Club will, I feel confident, join with me also when I allude, with feelings of respect and esteem, to the presence, on the same occasion, of the eminent archæologists, the Rev. J. Graves, Hon. Secretary of the Royal Historical and Archæological Association of Ireland, and J. Garstin, Esq , Treasurer of the Royal Irish Academy, both of whom kindly contributed to the exhibition objects of great variety, and manifested much interest in the proceedings.

It would be an omission, also, were I not to mention the admirable sketches of Irish scenery lent for the occasion by our fellow-member, Dr. James Moore, the productions of his own gifted pencil, and which proved so appropriate an addition to the antiquarian collection. The same remarks apply to the sketches of a similar kind contributed by one of our Hon. Secretaries, Mr. W. Gray, and by Mr. W. H. Patterson, as also to the universally-admired measured drawings of Greyabbey, by Mr. J. J. Phillips, which, I am happy to add, have since been published in a volume, likely to be long duly prized by all the lovers of Irish art.

I think, then, that on every account the year now closing may well be considered as marking an era of progress in the affairs of our Club, and of the studies with which it is identified, long to be remembered, and for which all may indulge feelings of content and satisfaction.

A few words remain to be said respecting our future, with which this address, already, I fear, too protracted, must conclude.

Among the many claims for encouragement and consideration which commend institutions like ours to general acceptance, one is this—that it offers to non-scientific persons, popularly so called, a means of cultivating science in those fields which, although perhaps not the most accounted of, are still the more easily accessible and rich in really valuable results. The great feature of our Club, for instance, viewed in its proper light is, that it includes in its ranks and invites to its fellowship persons of all classes (and, I may add, of both sexes too), who are statedly engaged in other pursuits —in professional or business occupations—in the walks of trade, commerce, or manufacture. Now, apart from the fact, referred to in a previous portion of this address, that there is here a platform erected, or rather indeed a wholesome field opened, where persons of all varieties of view on abstract subjects—holding, it may be, different religious creeds, and adherents of various schools of political principles—may meet, and without any compromise of principles whatever, partake of the fellowship and enjoyment which science, in its finest sense, offers. There is another consideration which strongly commends such institutions as our Club to some at least. Man, according to his physical organisation, is an omnivorous animal. In the matter of diet Nature herself dictates that he need not, nor ought he, to make choice between being a vegetarian and a purely carnivorous animal, but, in due moderation, partake of all the varieties of food which the Bountiful Creator has so freely provided for his sustenance. As I have just said, this truth is forced on us, as well by our instincts—for man is certainly a cooking animal, and loves to partake of food well and suitably prepared—as also by our very dental apparatus, not to refer to more latent portions of our organisation. We are furnished with a set of teeth which are neither all incisors, nor canine, nor yet molars, but a combination of all three. We are thus plainly omnivorous, and Nature says so. I have sometimes thought that this circumstance might be turned to a moral account. In point of fact, the mind requires variety of *pabalum* just as much as the body. It is an utter mistake for any of us to addict ourselves to any one kind of mental operation to the exclusion of others. This would be like living on flesh meat and eschewing vegetables, or *vice versa*. If carried to an excess, it would be worse. It would resemble a man who never ate anything but one solitary kind of food.

You will, perhaps, yourselves anticipate my inference. A man who never opens any book but his ledger or day-book—or if he be a so-called professional man, his digests of law or his medical tractates—(I shall say nothing of certain divines, whose only studies are theological)—such a man runs extreme risk of increasing such a mental or moral disease, as the liver on but one sort of food. Naturalists' Field Clubs afford, in my judgment, one of the best and most easily applied remedies for such cases. Let a man, for example, during the summer season, leave for a day his desk and office, or his study, or his shop, or " Change," and take an excursion with our Club. Let him have eyes to see, and a heart to enjoy the wonders and the beauties which the God of nature scatters around field and flood, hill and dale. Let the woman leave for the same season her household cares, and join our excursion, for woman needs variety here as well as men. Then let all the members meet, during wintry months like the present, and listen to the lessons which our more patient and experienced members have learned for themselves, and so willingly impart to others, from their summer-gatherings in Natural History, and I am bold to say the result will be to aid in making all better members of society—better able to take and maintain their place in " the battle of life," and, above all, far more likely to look beyond this lower life, and forward to the prospect which true religion—the religion of revelation as well as of nature—offers in that life which, is to come.

Such considerations as these will, I trust, commend our Club and its pursuits not only to its members, but to many around us, and thus, if appreciated, enable us to look forward in anticipation of a prosperous future, as we this evening enjoy a thankful retrospect of its bygone history, and especially of the year 1874.

On 16th December Mr. W. J. KNOWLES read a paper "On Prehistoric Remains at Portstewart."

The remains in question were found among sandhills in the neighbourhood of Portstewart, and consisted of about 600 manufactured flint implements (arrow-heads, scrapers, &c.), several manufactured bone articles, pottery, pierced stones (netweights, &c.), "Tilhuggersteens," hammer-stones, portions of rough and polished stone celts, querns, grain-rubbers, beads, &c., with bones of man, dog, the ox, horse, sheep, deer, pig, &c., and edible shells of various species. The author had found these while exploring the sandhills during the past four or five years. They were found chiefly in pits among the sandhills, accompanied with great quantities of flint flakes, cores, &c. Some of the articles were found lying exposed on the bottom of the pits, and others were procured by excavation from blackened layers appearing on the sides of the pits. Those blackened layers represent the ancient surface, and the thickness of the sand that has accumulated over them amounts to from 10 to 30 feet. At Portrush and Castlerock, places a few miles distant from Portstewart, pits of a similar nature are found, from which the author procured flakes, cores, bones, &c. The author's attention was first directed to the place by Mr. Campbell Leetch, of Cullybackey, who while strolling among the sandhills sat down to rest, and on casting his eyes about him, discovered an arrow-head among some flint flakes.

On 13th January Mr. MANN HARBISON read a paper "On the Origin of Eskers."*

Beneath the vegetable soil of many of our fields there is a mass of clay, mixed with stones of various sizes, more or less rounded, but not at all occurring in regular layers. The superficial accumulation has been usually termed in Scotland "Till," a word in common use in Ulster also, but is now generally called by geolo-

---

* By a special resolution of the Club this paper is published *in extenso*.

gists "Boulder Clay," or "Drift." This singular deposit has only been accounted for at a comparatively recent period. The earlier geologists called it Diluvium, because they supposed it to have been formed by the Deluge. But when it was ascertained that this deposit is not met with in that region from which the account of the flood has been derived, the idea of its diluvial origin was abandoned. The boulder clay is now believed to have been formed by a capping of glacial ice, which at some remote period covered the greater part of the land in northern and southern latitudes. A similar ice cap covers the northern part of Greenland at present, as well as those almost unknown lands in the Southern Ocean.

Various causes have been assigned for the vast difference in climate necessary to produce such phenomena. Some hold that it may have been brought about by a different degree of inclination of the earth's axis to the plane of its orbit, combined with a greater amount of eccentricity in the orbit itself. Others consider that it may have been caused by a different distribution of land and water, accompanied by a different direction of cold and warm oceanic currents. Whatever may be the cause or causes, there is unmistakable evidence that the climate of any particular district of the earth's surface is not at all permanent. The representatives of plants and animals now inhabiting tropical regions once lived in England, and remains of the reindeer, an animal confined at present to the extreme north, have been found as far south as the Pyrenees. On the other hand, the remains of large forest trees recently discovered in Greenland, show that that inhospitable region has not always been doomed to perpetual ice.

There is evidence that *several* glacial periods have taken place in remote ages, separated by long intervals, in which a milder climate prevailed. It is, however, with the last of these episodes that I am to deal at present. The date of this event has not been determined with any approach to accuracy; but, compared to the time that has taken place since the formation of our coal-fields, or even since the deposition of the white limestone of our coasts, it is but as yesterday. Hence the rock matter formed in this way lies above the earlier deposited and more solid strata. As already mentioned, it may easily be known by its want of stratification. It may be unnecessary for me to inform such an audience as this, that sediments, whether of mud, sand, or gravel, deposited in water, always occur in regular layers, one above another. Further, water always *sorts* the material which it holds in suspension. A river conveying mud, sand, and pebbles seaward, parts with the heavier pebbles first, the sand next, and conveys the mud for a considerable distance into the sea. On the other hand, a glacier, where it melts off, precipitates the stony and earthy matter that had fallen on its surface from the cliffs along its margin, in irregular heaps, called *moraines*, which are utterly devoid of stratification or arrangement. For the same reason, when a glacier in a country like Greenland reaches the coast, and is projected over a cliff, until a portion breaks by its own weight and floats off as an iceberg, the earthy matters contained in such ice-mountains are deposited in the sea bottom when the iceberg melts. It is believed that such accumulations would in most cases be devoid of stratification. The resemblance between the drift deposits and the moraines of glaciers first led Agassiz, who had an opportunity of studying their structure in his native country, Switzerland, to propound the theory that these accumulations were formed by ice, and not by water, as had been formerly supposed.

But there are other proofs of the former presence of an ice cap in these and other northern countries. Many of the boulders are scratched and polished, similar markings being found abundantly in the rocks over which the glacier passed. These markings were well seen by the section of the British Association which visited the Castle Espie quarries in August last. This quarry is covered by a deposit of boulder clay 40 to 50 feet thick. Many of the boulders are ice scratched, and the upper layer of limestone is polished and striated. In the valleys of Switzerland, occupied by glaciers, similar phenomena occur. The boulders found in the moraines are scratched, and the rocks over which former extensions of the glaciers passed are scratched and polished. Further, it is believed that the rounded form of many of our hills, and the curved outline of our valleys, are all due to the same cause—the grinding power of ice.

The rocks from which the boulder clay has been formed are mainly found in the neighbourhood of the deposits. Many of the boulders, however, may be traced to rocks which occur at a considerable distance to the north or north-west of the places in which they are found. Boulders of Scotch granite are met with in England ; masses of Antrim Chalk are found in Cork ; Lias fossils have been gathered in various parts of County Down, which must have been transported from the Lias beds of Antrim.

The work done by glaciers in past ages has been of the greatest importance to the agriculturist of the present day. Many districts which, but for their beneficent action, would have been occupied by bare rocks or sterile sands, are covered with a rich deposit of soil derived from a variety of rocks, and consequently containing all the mineral elements necessary for the food of plants.

But my object to-night is not so much to speak of the Glacial period, as of the events that have taken place since that epoch. It is believed, that at the commencement of this period, Ireland was connected with Great Britain, and Great Britain with the Continent ; and that the land was at a considerably higher level than now. Towards the close of the period, it would seem, that the land sank much lower than it is at present, the sea covering all the lower ground, and reducing these countries to a series of groups of islands, represented at present by the various mountain ranges.* For example, there was probably sea all the way from the foot of the Belfast mountains to the north coast at Portrush, the Antrim hills forming a peninsula at one time, a group of islands at another.† Lough Neagh probably formed the deepest portion of this sea, but after the elevation of the land there was a chain of lakes extending

---

* It was probably during this period that the caves from which the neighbouring hill is named were tunnelled out by the waves of the sea.

† As none of the Antrim hills rise to the height of 2,000 feet, the whole country must have been at one time under water.

all the way to the north coast, most of which have been since silted up by the washings of the land, their sites being now occupied by peat bogs. Shallow lakes may be expected to occur in any district from which the sea has retreated, especially if the land had previous to subsidence been subjected to the scooping out power of glacial ice. Such lakes would be at first salt, but this would soon be carried off by the discharging river. There is unmistakable evidence that this district was covered by the sea for a long period after the deposition of the boulder clay. This deposit has been almost entirely swept away from all the lower lands, its place being occupied by water-rolled pebbles and accumulations of mud, sand, and gravel. Farmers are often puzzled by this circumstance. They wonder why it is that the heavy clay lands are confined to the hills, while the sandy and gravelly soils occur at lower levels. The explanation is, that the sea swept away the boulder clay, except an occasional patch of a tenacious character, which resisted its denuding power. Such patches would appear as islands, while the lower ground would be covered with the sorted and water-rolled materials which the sea had spread along its bottom. Similar occurrences have taken place in Down. There is good ground for believing that since the Glacial period Belfast Lough and Strangford Lough were connected along the valley through which the County Down railway runs. This valley is well seen from the top of the Cave hill. Here, as well as in Antrim, the tenacious unstratified clays are mainly confined to the higher ground, the subsoil of the lower lands consisting of stratified deposits of mud, sand, and gravel.

There are certain low hills or ridges, called "Eskers," found abundantly at low levels in all parts of the country, the origin of which has not been satisfactorily explained. Good specimens may be seen along the line of the Northern Counties railway, also between Dundonald and Comber. They are also very numerous in County Tyrone, particularly between Omagh and Dungannon. They are composed of sand and gravel, usually in regular layers. Now it is plain that such accumulations of stratified materials must have been deposited in water, and that it must have required a long period to form them. But the question remains still to be answered, how were these materials formed into ridges or hills? Water distributes the materials which it holds in suspension evenly along the surface over which it spreads, but it has no power to heap up this matter into hills. After much consideration I have come to the conclusion that the following series of events must have taken place since the Glacial period in the districts to which I have referred. You will please excuse me if, for the sake of clearness, I recapitulate something of what has been already said.

(1.) *Towards the close of the Glacial period the land sank, and the lower grounds were for a long period covered by the sea. This sea swept away much of the Glacial drift, and formed, by water-rolling large quantities of sand and pebbles, which were distributed evenly along the sea bottom.*

Much confusion of thought has been occasioned by the officers of the Geological Survey, and writers on geology generally, using the term "drift" to indicate both stratified and unstratified deposits. Now the *unstratified* accumulations of boulders and clay, to which, I think, the term "Glacial Drift" should be restricted, are mainly, as I have stated, confined to the higher grounds, the low lands being generally covered with water-rolled stratified sands, gravels, or clay beds. Where glacial drift occurs at low levels, as at Castle Espie quarries, or the sandstone quarries near Dundonald, it is of an unusually tenacious nature, and consequently was able to resist denudation. So distinct is the line of demarcation between the ice-formed and the water-formed deposits, that I have often been able to trace on the slope of a hill the exact line to which the water had risen after the submergence of the land.

The islands in this Post-Glacial sea are, I think, represented by the hills at present covered with undisturbed drift, as well as those higher ridges from which the drift has since been removed by atmospheric denudation.

I may here observe, that the land was covered with *sea water*, not *fresh water*, inasmuch as marine shells have been found in the gravel in many places. I am aware that in one of the Memoirs of the Geological Survey (49, 50, 61, p. 13), Strangford Lough is set down as having been formerly a fresh water lake, but no evidence is adduced in support of this assertion. If it ever was such it must have been at a remote period, as in the raised beach in the neighbourhood I have frequently found marine shells. All people engaged in scientific pursuits should beware of indulging in guesses which are not supported by evidence.

Islands similar to those that I suppose to have existed in the Post-Glacial sea are at present to be met with in Strangford Lough. These islands are very numerous, and according to the Memoir of the Geological Survey they are formed of mounds of "boulder clay." Whether any of them are formed of stratified material, such as I have described, I have not been able to ascertain. Here we have an excellent illustration of the effects produced by marine denudation in inland seas. If the islands of Strangford Lough were exposed to the fury of the Atlantic waves, they would soon be swept away; but they will probably be able for a long period to resist the action of the calm waters with which they are surronnded. Similar seas occupied all the low lands of our country and other countries during the Post-Glacial period. These seas were studded with islands, which, when the water retreated, appeared as rounded hills.

(2.) *After having been submerged for a long period, the land slowly rose, leaving lakes and swamps, which were ultimately covered with peat in many places.*

The peat of this period was earlier than our present peat bogs, which form so marked a feature in the landscape in many districts. The town of Newtownards is situated on a bed of stratified gravel, deposited by a former extension of Strangford Lough. A few years ago, when making an excavation for a gasometer, a bed of peat was discovered beneath the gravel, which at this place was four feet thick. In the peat were found the trunk and roots of a large tree, and beneath it was a deposit of fine sand. This succession of beds will illustrate the order of events indicated above. The

Post-Glacial sea formed the deposit of sand beneath the peat. Then it retreated, leaving a swamp in which the peat grew. Afterwards the land sank, the sea returned, swept away most of the peat, and buried the remainder under a bed of gravel. Similar beds of peat have been found beneath the sea-beach in many places on the east coast of Down and near Portrush. The secretary of this Club and I were present at the disinterment of the skeleton of an Irish elk, which was found in a deposit of shell-marl, about half way between Newtownards and Donaghadee. The shell-marl was covered with a layer of peat, which was again overlaid by a deposit of gravel beneath the vegetable soil. The shells (mainly Limnæa) had accumulated in a pool of water, in which the elk had probably been drowned. In time the pool became silted up, and formed a suitable soil for the growth of peat. The peat had been in its turn covered by the sea, which buried whatever portion it did not succeed in removing, beneath a bed of shingle.

(3.) *After the lapse of a probably lengthened period, during which the peat was deposited, the land again sank, but not to so low a level as during the Post-Glacial period.*

The peat which had grown during the previous elevation was now mainly swept away, leaving occasional patches in hollow places, as in the cases to which I have just referred. The inland seas that now covered all the ground at a low level were of a tranquil character. *The more compact portions of the stratified sands and gravels, deposited during the previous submersion, were now able to resist the denuding action of the calm waters with which they were surrounded, the looser portions being at the same time swept away.* There would thus be a second series of islands in these seas, the higher group consisting of the glacial mounds that had resisted denudation during the previous submersion; the lower group—*the ridges of sand and gravel which had not been swept away during the second submersion.*

(4.) *The land rose once more, and ultimately attained its present level. The mounds and ridges that appeared as islands during submersion were now hills, some of them composed of unstratified glacial drift—the rubbish deposited by ancient glaciers and icebergs; others formed of water-rolled stratified gravels and sands, and left behind by subsequent circum-denudation.*

These are the "Eskers," which have hitherto failed to give an intelligible account of themselves to our professional geologists, but which seem to me more easily accounted for than many geological problems which have been successfully solved. Since the last elevation of the land, doubtless, vast masses of rock matter have been removed by *atmospheric* denuding agencies. These have greatly modified the shape of the land, but still have not destroyed the evidence of the sequence of events which I have enumerated.

The frequent oscillations of the level of the land which seem to have been necessary to produce the phenomena of the Eskers, have been common events in all periods of the earth's history. The occurrence of numerous beds of coal at different levels, with intervening layers of clay, shale, or sandstone, can only be accounted for by supposing an intermittent series of disturbances similar to those I have described. Nor have these phenomena ceased. The sea is at present making inroads on our coasts, on account of the slow subsidence of the land. No doubt the process is a slow one, but it may have been always so. The life of any of us, contrasted with the duration of one of the great geological periods, is, to use an illustration borrowed from Holy Writ, like the moment occupied by the shuttle of the weaver in crossing his web, compared with the time required to weave that web.

Mr. WILLIAM GRAY, M.R.I.A., then read a paper, entitled "Notes on the rudely-worked Flints of Antrim and Down—their character, distribution, and similarity to specimens from England, Scotland, and the Continent." Having referred to the various authors who have written on the subject, including Mr. John Evans, F.G.S., the late Mr. G. V. Du Noyer, F.G.S., Mr. J. H. Staples, Mr. Robert Day, jun., F.S.A., and Mr. W. J. Knowles, Mr. Gray explained that he had been collecting flint flakes for more than ten years, and that he visited, and collected flakes in, every locality referred to in his paper, and now only states the result of his personal observation. Mr. Gray further explained that he applied the term "flint flake" only to certain forms of flint, the characters of which prove them to be the result of human workmanship, and as such differ from mere flint chips. Every true flint flake will have—1st, a flat, more or less, conchoidal face, with a bulb known as the bulb of percussion at one end, the other end generally tapering to a point; 2nd, a flat end over the bulb of percussion, being a portion of the flat face that received the blow; and 3rd, on the back of the flake there must be one or more ridges, and two or more facets or inclining surfaces. The combination of these essential features proves design: being the result of a series of operations that could not well be repeated so very uniformly without intention; yet the processes are so simple they may be often closely imitated by natural causes, and occasionally one or more of the resulting features may be found on mere chips of flint, and may lead a casual observer to doubt the artificial character of all flint flakes; but to persons who have given attention to the subject the special characters of every true flint flake are as evidently the result of human workmanship as a watch, a penknife, or a pair of spectacles.

In our flint flakes we have the evidence of various degrees of manipulative skill. Some are extremely symmetrical and well-formed, but the great majority of the flakes are apparently clumsy failures, evidently the result of attempts to produce the typical form of flake already described. Flint flakes include a very great variety of forms, all aiming at one type, but varying according to the nature of the material or the skill of the manipulator. Some are large, clumsy lumps: some are so small and delicate, thin and transparent, that they may be mounted as slides for the microscopic examination of the organic remains in the flint. The latter character is, however, an exception, for the flakes are chiefly opaque, the exterior being converted into a kind of porcelain, which is generally white, particularly in the specimens from open gravels; and as this crust is absorbent, the flakes become stained more or less when in contact with ferruginous clays or carbonaceous deposits. This external coating often penetrates to a depth of an eighth of an inch or more. There are instances where different portions of the same gravels yield flakes of different characters. For example, at Ballygally, on the east coast of Antrim, the flakes near the sea are quite white and worn, while the flakes in the same gravel further from the shore are sharp and of a warm brown colour. It has been carefully ascertained that in the County Antrim, or Down, true flint flakes are not found in the crushed flints that occur so abundantly in the hollow, irregular surface of the Chalk below the Trap rocks, nor are they found in any natural or accidental accumulation of flint debris. They do not occur in the undisturbed Tertiary or earlier Post-Tertiary deposits, although we have numerous examples of these deposits in Antrim and Down frequently containing abundant fragments of chalk and flint, but in every such case the flint fragments are quite shapeless and could not be mistaken for true flakes. The latter are only found in the surface gravels and generally within a few feet of the surface. They were found in great abundance around Ormeau Bridge, Belfast, on sites now covered by streets. On the County Down side of the Lagan they occur in the brickfields at Ballynafeigh; also at Annadale, overlooking the Lagan; and sparingly in the fields on both sides of the river as far as Moira. They occur abundantly in the gravels at both sides of Belfast Harbour, at Carrickfergus, Kilroot, and Whitehead, on the Antrim side, and at Holywood, Bangor, and Ballyholme, on the County Down side. They have also been found in the gravel dredged from Belfast Harbour, off Greencastle, &c., and they may be frequently picked up on the walks gravelled with this material. They are distributed over Islandmagee, and are in enormous quantities in the gravels at Glynn and Larne, particularly at the Curran at Larne, where thousands may be gathered from the surface of the raised beach gravels. They are equally abundant at Ballygally, and are numerous at Glenarm and Carnlough. They occur on the bleak hillsides sloping to Tor Head, and along the cliff heads at Ballintoy, and in the sand dunes from the Giant's Causeway to Downhill. All these places are situated on or near the outcrop of the Chalk, where flints naturally occur in greatest abundance. But worked flints are not confined to the outcrop of the Chalk ; they are also distributed over the Trappean plateau that covers the Chalk of Antrim and Derry, and at some spots they are very numerous, particularly at Toomebridge, where they are found in Lough Neagh, as described by Mr. Evans in the Archæologia, Vol. xli. But the worked flints are not limited to Toomebridge; they are found in the Bann for several miles of its course ; around Portglenone they are very numerous, and are frequently found on the shore of Lough Neagh, particularly near Lurgan. In addition to the gravels of Holywood and Ballyholme, worked flints are found in County Down, in places far removed from the outcrop of the Chalk. In the islands of Strangford Lough, and in the Ards, as far south as Ballyquintin Point, worked flints are found where no kind of flint occurs naturally; and even at Leestone and Cranfield, flakes are found in tolerable abundance, although these localities are removed from the flint-bearing rocks by the entire County Down, including the Mourne range of mountains. A few have been found on the sand dunes at Newcastle and Cranfield Point, County Down ; but here flakes are by no means so plentiful as on the north coast of Antrim.

Now, wherever flakes occur in abundance they are accompanied by other forms of stone implements, &c., more evidently the result of human workmanship, and among them may be frequently found the cores from which the flakes were struck. The uniformly constant character of the cores goes a long way in proving the artificial origin of the flakes struck off. The best examples of cores are found at Belfast, Holywood, Carrickfergus, Kilroot, Larne, Islandmagee, Ballygally, and Ballintoy. They are usually about four inches long, but sometimes not longer than an inch, and partake somewhat the form of a truncated cone, the base being formed by the original flat fractured surface of the flint, and the sides of the cone are formed by a series of facets showing where the flakes were struck off.

In addition to the cores which so clearly show the design of the manipulator, the Antrim and Down flint flakes are found more or less chipped to form. Many are irregularly chipped to no definite pattern; others are very carefully chipped to special patterns. One of these patterns is the flat, tanged flake, made by chipping the end bulb so as to form a tang or handle. This must have been a recognised pattern, because it is found in several places, such as Toomebridge, Ballintoy, Ballygally, Islandmagee, Larne, Belfast, &c., and, like the cores, the tanged flakes are invariably of the same lithological character as the common flint flakes with which they are generally found.

The "scraper"—which has such a wide geographical distribution—is another form found very commonly among the wrought flints of Antrim and Down. A large number of examples occur almost identical with the forms so common in England, France, and Belgium. Some of the elongated forms from near Belfast can scarcely be distinguished from those taken from the ossiferous caves in the south of France. The "scraper," like the tanged flake and core, is found in Antrim and Down, wherever the flint flakes are common. Indeed, the "scrapers" show by the bulb of percussion and other features that they were made out of the ordinary flakes. The best examples of scrapers have been found at Ballintoy, Bannmouth, Ballygally, "The Plains," Belfast; Toombridge, &c. Examples of worked or chipped flakes are found graduating from the simplest form up to the very best type of finely-chipped arrowheads, all showing that the characteristic flint flake was the result and object of special manipulative skill.

Roughly chipped, unpolished flint celts, having all the characteristics of extreme age, are also found in every locality where flakes are abundant. They are usually small—from three to six inches long—highly porcelainous, and rounded by age. The best examples are from Holywood, Ballintoy, Carnlough, Islandmagee, Larne, and "The Plains," Belfast.

The ordinary polished stone celts are also very frequently found in connection with flint flakes, particularly at Belfast, Ballintoy, Islandmagee, and Toomebridge. At the latter place they abound

Thus we have distributed in abundance over Antrim and Down,

particularly the former, worked flint flakes, scrapers, celts, &c., which, in general form, size, and lithological character, are identical with the older types from the gravel of England and the Continent, while we find them here associated with some of those elaborately-chipped arrow heads, exhibiting a perfection of skilful workmanship that cannot be excelled; and as yet we have no facts to justify us in separating our rude worked flints into two classes, "The Palæolithic" and "The Neolithic," as has been done by English and Continental archæologists.

On 10th February a paper was read by Mr. HENRY KNIGHT on "Some of the smaller features and lower forms of Vegetable Life, chiefly in connection with Mosses and other Cryptogams."

The paper was illustrated by a number of water-colour drawings of mosses and ferns, drawn from the microscope; and the microscopic slides, mounted by Mr. Knight, from which the drawings were taken, were laid upon the table. After apologising for the elementary character of his remarks, the lecturer proceeded to allude to the almost universal love of flowers, which led many to give some attention to botany, usually confining themselves to what are called the flowering plants and the ferns. Besides these, there are other forms of plants widely distributed, and to be found at all seasons of the year, that would well repay a little attention being bestowed upon them. The most prominent of these are mosses, which are to be met with everywhere—on walls and buildings in the crowded portions of our large towns, under our feet in the less frequented thoroughfares, by the roadside, in the woods and glens, on the mountains, and rocks of every kind. A large collection of these singular and beautiful objects will occupy comparatively little space, enabling its owner frequently to inspect and compare his specimens. The microscope necessary for the examination of mosses is now within the reach of every botanist, and sufficient facility in mounting botanical slides can be acquired by a little perseverance. It will be seen that these diminutive plants have much in common with those more prominent ones previously known. The beautiful urn or capsule is developed by a process very similar to that which produces the fruits and seed-vessels of trees and other plants. From the growth and appearance of mosses, a casual observer would suppose there was not much difference among them; while a careful examination shows that there is considerable variety, not only of species, but of genera, which last are grouped into orders, and finally arranged in sections. Berkeley divides the British mosses into four sections, chiefly dependent upon the nature and position of the *sporangium* or capsule, commonly called the fruit. These sections are divided into thirty-four orders, and one hundred and twenty genera, in which there are about six hundred species. The most abundant are *Hypnums*, *Tortulas*, and *Bryums*; quite a variety of these is to be found in the shortest walk. Concealed among the leaves, and unknown to all but those who have made these plants their study, are the flowers, consisting of *antheridia* and *archegonia* in separate clusters, the former constituting the male and the latter the female or fertile flower. The *archegonia* become matured into capsules, rupturing as they grow the membranaceous envelope of the germen-like *archegonium*, and carrying a part of it on the summit of the stalk, it becomes the veil or horn; this after a time is thrown off. When the capsule is ripe its lid is got rid of, the beautiful teeth of the *peristome* become erect, and the spores or moss seeds dispersed around. Some of the capsules of the smallest mosses contain a great number of spores, and as each spore produces several plants, the great abundance of mosses can easily be understood. The *peristome*, which forms a very beautiful and characteristic appendage of many mosses, consists of a number of curious tooth-like processes, which are always in number multiples of 4, as 4, 8, 16, or 32. These teeth are sometimes in one row, and sometimes in two rows. They consist of cells transversely jointed and beautifully coloured, and may easily be seen by the naked eye in many mosses. In the genus *Tortula* the teeth are twisted, and project some distance above the capsule—hence the name of screw moss. These teeth are very beautiful under the microscope, and, indeed, the whole moss has usually a very elegant and fairy-like appearance. If, in addition, the polarising apparatus is used, the foliage presents various shades of vivid colours, chiefly green, red, and blue ; the nerve and border of the leaf being usually of the latter colour, resulting from the large portion of silica contained in all mosses. The colour of the teeth of the *peristome* under the polariscope becomes much intensified. Besides their spores, some mosses have other organs of reproduction, called *gemmæ*, of which Mr. Knight had a specimen mounted for the microscope, as well as specimens of the *antheridia* and *archegonia*, before spoken of. Drawings of the peculiar fructification of the Killarney fern and the Filmy fern were shown, also of the *sporangia* of the former, of the *Osmunda regalis*, and *Blechnum boreale*. The cellular structure of plants and the appearance and contents of the vegetable cell were explained, and reference made to some of the smaller *algæ*, as diatoms, red snow, &c. The method of preparing and mounting mosses for the microscope was fully detailed. After a few remarks commending the study of botany as a pleasant recreation for the young, Mr. Knight concluded by expressing his obligations to Mr. S. A. Stewart for the great assistance he had given in the preparation of the paper; to Mr. J. Creeth, for the loan of specimens ; and to Mr. F. W. Lockwood and Miss Mary Bell, of Newtownards, for the excellent drawings which they had so kindly done for him.

On 10th March a paper was read by Mr. WILLIAM SWANSTON on "Graptolites, with special reference to those found in County Down."

The reader commenced by giving a brief review of the conflicting opinions of the early palæontologists, showing the puzzling character of these curious fossil organisms. He then directed the attention of the meeting to the various localities in the County Down where they occur, and alluded to some vain attempts that had been made to find coal in the Silurian rocks of that county,

I

where no person with the least knowledge of geology would ever have thought of trying; as the presence of these fossils indicates that these beds belong to a lower horizon than that in which coal occurs. He stated that the existence of graptolites in the district had long been known to many members of the Club, but that the systematic examination of them had not been undertaken by anyone until the Geological Survey commenced operations in this locality. In its "Memoirs," published in 1871, a number of species are given, mostly from the neighbourhood of Donaghadee, which is by far the richest locality yet known in the North of Ireland. The results of the reader's own labours were then given, which are very encouraging, embracing, as they do, the finding of twelve species of graptolitidæ, and three crustaceans. The discovery of the latter is a most important one, this being the first record of the finding of any crustacean remains in this large Silurian area. After a comprehensive description of the physiological character of the graptolites, illustrated by a comparison with that of their nearest living representatives—sertularian hydroids—the reader went on to give an exhaustive synopsis of the various genera into which this fossil group of graptolites is divided. This part of the paper was made very interesting by a series of large diagrams, illustrating all the species found in our district, and the most marked genera of the typical Silurian rocks in Wales. The various conditions under which the fossils occur were clearly given. Mr. Swanston then read a very interesting and suggestive letter which he had received from Charles Lapworth, Esq., F.G.S., Galashiels, an authority on this special department of palæontology, to whom he had submitted his specimens for examination. That gentleman sums up the result of his examination as follows :—" The beds of black shale, containing this peculiar grouping of forms, must be of middle Silurian age, perhaps Lower Llandovery. They form, in all probability, merely the westerly continuation of one of the black shale bands so common in the Silurians of the South of Scotland. They answer exactly to some of the central beds of the Birkhill shales, or the highest subdivisions of the Moffat group, and also represent almost exactly the Coniston mudstones of Professor Nicholson, which are placed by the Geological Survey of England at the base of the upper Silurians of the Lake District." Mr. Lapworth also directed attention to beds occurring in Scotland that may have been overlooked on this side of the Channel, showing that a vast amount of work has yet to be done before our Silurian rocks are as well understood as they ought to be. At the close of the paper some interesting conversation took place, and the series of specimens on the table were closely examined. Mr. Swanston was highly congratulated on his success for so far in this new field of labour, and hopes were expressed that he would continue his researches.

Mr. S. A. STEWART then read a paper on "The Mosses of the District." Mr. Stewart said that the list recently published by the Field Club was the first attempt at a moss flora of the district.— The number of species ascertained as occurring in the counties of Antrim and Down, with a portion of Derry adjoining, was 238, many of these being reckoned as rare forms. In the list of northern mosses, which was just issued, nine species were for the first time enumerated as Irish plants. Two of these plants had been found by Dr. Moore, of Glasnevin, Dublin, but by oversight omitted from his recent list of Irish mosses. The remaining seven were found by Mr. Stewart—four of these on the Belfast hills, two in County Down, and one in County Derry.

On 7th April Mr. J. J. PHILLIPS read a paper on "The Architectural Remains of the Cistercians in the County Down."

In this condensed paper, which is purely of an archæological nature, it is presumed that the general history and puritanical aims of this great Cistercian order of monks are known to the reader. It is sufficient, therefore, to state that it was founded at Citeaux, in Burgundy, A.D. 1098, and was a reformation of the then relaxed Benedictine order. Although we owe much to these monks for the preservation and multiplication of ancient literature, as an outcome of their silent austerity, they are chiefly known to us from the excellence and simplicity of their architectural arrangements, and also their vast farming and gardening operations. In Ireland, previous to their advent, agricultural operations had been considered as the mark of degradation and suitable only for slaves, but the Cistercians quickly placed such pursuits on the most respectable footing. It is an error to suppose that the Cistercian order was introduced into Ireland by the Normans, or to imagine that because we find such a frequent admixture of "Early Pointed" among its "Romanesque" that, therefore, the Anglo-Norman architects and builders were the authors. The discernment of the Anglo-Romanesque or "Norman" detail, from the characteristic Hiberno-Romanesque, requires training and judgment, the want of which has caused discrepancies to creep into the works of some writers, but we have the unimpeachable authority of St. Bernard that a generation before Strongbow or Henry II. set foot on Irish soil, Malachy, Bishop of Down, had introduced the Cistercians, and they had become naturalised, and, in fact, nationalised in Ireland, and even in the County Down, in Newry, under the native bishop and the native king of Ireland, long before John De Courcy was bitten by his abbey-building mania. The native clergy or Culdee in the North of Ireland were sternly conservative, and in the County Antrim the Cistercians never got foothold, except to rear some small chapel or cell, as that at Jordanstown (appropriate to Grey Abbey).

We give the list of their abbeys in the County Down in the order of their foundation, viz. :—

Newry, or de Viridi ligno, founded in 1144 by St. Malachy, and richly endowed by Maurice M'Loughlan, king of all Ireland, in the year 1157.

Inch, founded in 1180, completed in 1188 by Sir John de Courcy.

Grey Abbey, founded in 1193 by Africa, wife of Sir John de Courcy.

Comber, founded in 1199 by an Anglo-Norman family, the Whites. Also in

Down (or Downpatrick) was founded one of the two Cistercian nunneries of Ireland, but all information as to its site, date of foundation, name of founder, or its ultimate fate, is lost to us.

Of the Cistercian abbeys of Newry and Comber we have little to say, as they have been completely swept away; and there are no architectural remains, unless the font belonging to Newry Abbey, mentioned by the Rev. Dr. Reeves, is still in existence. We therefore have only to treat of Inch Abbey and Grey Abbey, both of which are characteristic specimens of early English architecture at the period when it had worked out its transition in the mother country from the Anglo-Romanesque. Fortunately for our researches, we have sufficient of these two abbeys left to illustrate the subject, which is rendered the more particularly interesting from the fact that we have the means (though scanty), without travelling further than Downpatrick Abbey, of identifying the puritanical individuality (architecturally speaking) of this monastic order, as compared with the more lavish splendour of detail which characterised the buildings of the relaxed Benedictine order, of which the Cistercian was the reformed offshoot.

Before undertaking the investigation of the Cistercian abbeys of Down, I will direct your attention to the model of a monastery belonging to this order, prepared and published by Mr. E. Sharpe, M.A., of Lancaster, who has made Cistercian architecture his peculiar study, and who has, happily for us, enthusiastically focussed his vast researches and profound knowledge on this branch of archæological enquiry. In his model plan you will see how the conventual buildings all group around the cloister quadrangle. Now glance from that plan to this of Grey Abbey, or the less complete plan of Inch, and you will perceive a striking coincidence. If we search every one of the sixteen Irish Cistercian abbeys whose remains we yet have (some of the plans of which you have on the wall), we will find in no case any extensive departure from the general grouping of this model plan,—except such as more recent circumstances, such as the troublous times or relaxing of the severity of their rules, occasioned.

There were general and particular rules which controlled their architecture in the *earlier* centuries of the existence of this order; these rules are embodied in their character of charity *(charta caritatis)*, particularly as regards their conventual churches; the most important of these were, that they should be rigidly plain without lofty bell towers. They were forbidden the use of elaborate carvings or representations of the human form, also all merely ornamental or sensuous features, such as stained glass, pictures, gold ornaments, coloured decorations, &c. These rules obliged their architects to depend for their effect on " excellence of proportion and chasteness of detail ;" to this, combined with the fact that the movement was contemporary with the rise and development of the earlier and most pure of the Gothic styles, may be attributed the excellence of the architecture of all the Cistercian monasteries yet remaining; but it is necessary to state that these rules were relaxed late in the thirteenth century, that the Cistercians more or less followed the Benedictines in employing a greater degree of splendour in their later erections and insertions. That these relaxed rules effected the abbeys of Down, we have some proof, such as in the stained glass in Inch Abbey, found during the recent excavations, and the encaustic tiles of Grey Abbey. We have some strange-looking carvings of human heads in the corbel table in the chancel of Grey Abbey. Having briefly noticed these general rules embodied in their *charta caritatis*, we will proceed to trace out the coincidence in plan of our local abbeys to the Cistercian ideal, and we are enabled to treat them conjointly in consequence of this harmony. First of all then as to site. As enjoined by their code, the sites in both cases were and are in secluded spots—in valleys close to water and supplied by never-failing springs. To the practice of building in solitary places may be attributed the fact, that while the abbey churches of other orders in Ireland are in frequent instances used for divine worship, we have in no case that I know of a Cistercian abbey church so restored to its original purpose.

The *ground plans* of Inch Abbey, but more particularly Grey Abbey, as it is more complete, are eminently Cistercian, and give us the key to the non-existent buildings or foundations yet under the sod. The *church* in each case, in strict accordance with their rule, was and is in its ground plan in the form of a Latin cross.

In my first visit to Inch Abbey I was greatly puzzled by the absence of the western arm or the nave of the church, which apparently had never been in existence. On applying to the proprietor (R. P. Maxwell, Esq., D.L., J.P.) for permission to make some excavations, he promptly placed at my disposal workmen, and they have satisfactorily shown the church at Inch Abbey to have been 170 feet long. It was hitherto considered to have been aisleless, but the excavations have revealed the foundations and some of the walls of these aisles, which were comparatively narrow, about 13 feet wide, and somewhat like those in Dunbrody Abbey. As far as excavations have gone, I am inclined to consider that the clerestory, or triforium, as the case may have been, was borne by massive main arches, springing from piers, and on examination of the corners of the cross wall at the height from which the arches would have started, we find the capitals completely torn away, but up to that height is fair and uninjured. The western end of the nave most probably had a doorway, and from the formation of the ground I suspect had a narrow porch or narthex; the extreme north-west angle of the church now visibly shows itself by a block of masonry, very much ragged away, but still bearing a fair corner. The nave of Grey Abbey has one peculiarity not usual in Cistercian churches: it is aisleless.

The eastern end of Inch and Grey Abbey churches is square; in Inch, pierced by three very long lancet windows, with one smaller similar window over the centre. In Grey Abbey it has a double tier of triplet windows, with smaller similar windows over.

The eastern arm of the churches (variously termed the choir by some, the presbytery and sanctuary by others, but in churchwardens' vocabulary "the chancel"), was lighted north and south by large windows; at Inch by double lancet windows at each side; at Grey

Abbey by single windows north and south, originally, I believe, of similar character and form as the east windows, but at a later date they had decorated stone tracery inserted in the outer jambs, and most probably stained glass windows. In Grey Abbey immediately over these windows will be seen, each north and south, a corbel table, the blocks on the south being of a Norman character, those on the north are carved into human and other heads and grotesques—this is a most unusual peculiarity in a Cistercian monastery, as all carving of the human form was strictly prohibited by their charter. I would conclude that these were inserted at a later date, but that they show a rudeness which does not correspond with the date of the inserted stonework of the window below the corbel table.

The chancel extended eastward from the crossing at Inch Abbey, 42 feet long by 27 feet, at Grey Abbey but 30 feet by 24 feet 2 in. All trace of the high altar in both abbeys has disappeared, but we have in Grey Abbey the fragmentary remains of single sedilia and piscina on the south. In Inch Abbey there were three seats for the officiating priests. All the stonework is torn away, but the line of the cusping is shown in the mortar, and the traces of the corbel blocks from which the cusped arches sprang. The stonework of the piscina and aumbry has also been torn out by the sacrilegious housewives of Down. On the gospel side of the choir we have in both abbeys the remains of arches, in the position usually found over the wall tomb of the founder of the abbey. In both abbeys there were very vigorous explorations made in the neighbourhood of these recesses in the search for treasure; in Grey Abbey the stone lockers for sacred vessels, books, or linen of the altar, were laid bare, and the wall broken through to the adjoining chapel. In Inch Abbey the nave arch, transept arches, and chancel arch have all disappeared; we have only the responds of the moulding, till lately, peeping out of the *debris*, which Mr. Maxwell has had cleared away, revealing the magnificently moulded bases and pier responds, somewhat similar to those in Byland Abbey, Wenlock Abbey, and Rievaulx. We have also some portions of the flagging left to us from the utilitarian spoilations of the late Mr. Jack Martin.

Harris, in describing this abbey in 1774, and Dr. Petrie in later years, writes of the very elegant construction of one of the arches then standing, and we may conclude from their description that some portion of the bell-tower wall was then standing. At Grey Abbey we have some of the walls of this low central tower still remaining over the north transept arch and the nave arch. These fragmentary remains of the walls of the central tower show the stone stringcourses, or weather mouldings, which serve to mark the slope and height of the original nave and transepts. The intersection of the four arms of the crux was covered with groined barrel vaulting, as may be seen from the remains of the springing of four groined stone ribs over the north transept arch.

In both abbeys we find the usual side chapels, opening off the east side of the north and south transepts, that is, two chapels each north and south of the choir. In Inch Abbey the scanty remains of quadripartite groined vaulting of these chapels indicate the architectural magnificence of this abbey. We have the corner corbels with caps from which the ribs sprang. Since my first visit a still more beautiful corbel cluster has been brought to light. We have also found the base of the pillar between the north chapels, with responds of the mouldings. At Grey Abbey, the chapels had a simple barrel vaulting, and the arch moulding was very bold, as the scattered fragments show.

In Grey Abbey we find, in the south transept south wall, the remains of a stone newel winding stair; the existence of this stair is interesting evidence of the Cistercian origin of the building. A pile of *debris* at present covers its site at Inch, which, when removed, will most probably reveal some traces of this Cistercian conventual feature. We have uncovered at Inch a stairway close to the site usual for the night stair, but it is undoubtedly a more modern construction. This abbey was used as a residence and a castle long after the suppression of the monasteries.

Adjoining the south transept of the church in each abbey we find a narrow chamber as usual ; this would be *the sacristy*. In both abbeys we have the doorway of communication between this vaulted chamber and the church. *The chapter-house*, as usual, occurs next in order. At Grey Abbey its remains are more complete and characteristic of the usual plan than at Inch, which seems to have been completely gutted; it has been divested of every scrap of architectural detail, its walls rasped and quarried. The local ancient informs us that at the east wall of this chapter-house was dug out the largest human skull he ever saw. We succeeded in hunting up a fragment of one of the flat cuneiform stones belonging to this chapter-house; for the last twenty years it had served the utilitarian purpose of door-step to a barn or stable; on it is incised the stem of a carved cross and the chalice, indicating the tombstone of an abbot or other eminent ecclesiastic. *The passage or parlour*, which usually lies adjacent to the chapter-house, shows very distinctly in Grey Abbey, but as yet the division wall has not been made visible at Inch. The walls of the *fratry or monks' day-room* are visible in both abbeys—in Inch it has been extensively quarried, and as yet we cannot say how far southward it extended. In Grey Abbey it was evidently vaulted, and we have the moulded bases of a few of the central row of columns. The *kitchen* at Inch and Grey Abbey is visible, but at Grey Abbey unmistakably so, as the open of its fireplace is quite discernible. In Inch Abbey its features are all destroyed. The *refectory* in Grey Abbey is quite in consonance with the Cistercian plan; it lies north and south, and has its ruined pulpit, from which, during meals, a reader " entertained the monks with intellectual, while they entertained themselves with material pabulum;" but in Inch Abbey it has been quarried away. The *buttery* has disappeared in both abbeys, but in Grey Abbey we have the evidence of its former existence in the line of weathering shewn at the west side of the refectory. The *domus conversorum*, as defined by Mr. Sharp, usually lay along the west side of cloister garth, and was allocated to the use of the conversi of the monastery; in neither abbey have we any vestige of its existence. The *cloister garth* in Grey Abbey is oblong; this is somewhat unusual, as the quadrangle is usually found to be a perfect square. Availing myself of the proprietor's permission to make search for some trace of the western wall of the garth, I had excavations made, and disclosed the foundations of a curtain wall with several offsets, and indications of a guard-house or gate-room.

Having concluded this descriptive portion of the paper, we must here remark that both Inch and Grey Abbey were for many years used as quarries to their respective neighbourhoods.

It is matter for congratulation that these venerable ruins are now held in reverent appreciation by their respective owners, and that, as far as can be done by them, they are to be preserved from further dilapidation, and are now cherished for the benefit of field naturalist, archæologist, art student, and architect

---

THE Annual Meeting of the Club was held on Wednesday evening, 28th April, 1875. Mr. Henry Knight occupied the chair. The Secretaries' Report was read by Mr. William Gray, M.R.I.A., and Mr. Greer Malcomson, Treasurer, submitted the financial statement for the past year, both of which were adopted and ordered to be printed for circulation among the members. The election of officebearers for the ensuing year was then proceeded with, after which

Mr. JOSEPH WRIGHT, F.G.S., then said—In rising to propose a vote of thanks to our late senior honorary secretary, Mr. Gray, I think it is well that we should take a glance back and note the part taken by Mr. Gray in the working of the Club since its formation, when it was comparatively weak, until the present time, when it opens its thirteenth year a strong and flourishing society, with an established and creditable reputation among naturalists, not only in this country but even beyond the boundaries of the United Kingdom. The Club was established in March, 1863, prizes being at once offered for the best natural history collections ; and we find that at the close of the first session, the principal prize for Neozoic fossils was carried away by Mr. Gray. He was thus the first member to whom a prize was awarded in a geological subject. Mr. Gray has since that time successfully competed for the prizes offered in several subjects. The series of specimens and sketches he has sent in have in all cases been of a high order of merit. If collected together and carefully studied, anyone might form a very good idea of the geology and archæology of the district. The succeeding session Mr. Gray contributed a valuable paper on the *Megaceros Hibernicus*, and from that time until the present no session has passed over without our being favoured with one or more papers or lectures from him, these being on subjects of local interest, and not only of great value as scientific communications, but also attracting a large amount of public attention on account of the popular manner in which the subjects were handled. Two years after the formation of the Club the first report was issued, and occupied twelve pages. The secretaryship then became vacant by reason of the resignation of the gentleman who then held office. Mr. Gray was then induced to undertake the duties, and the report for 1865-6 was published and distributed to 78 members, the entire number at that time in the Club. At the close of the following session, the fourth year of the Club, the report occupied 55 pages, and the membership had increased to 133, a revival of life and interest seldom paralleled in scientific societies. Our present senior hon. secretary now consented to give his services, in conjunction with Mr. Gray; and the affairs of the Club, administered so efficiently as we have seen by these gentlemen, continued to prosper, so that the tenth annual report of the proceedings of the Society occupied 113 pages, and the membership had increased to over 200. These statistics require no comment— they speak for themselves. Most of us have attended the several conversaziones of the Club, and enjoy the recollection of these pleasant reunions, when the hard lines of science have been softened, and, surrounded by flowers and pictures, she has assumed her holiday aspect. Well, then, we owe to Mr. Gray's perseverance that so many of these meetings have been held; and also, to a great extent, the successful carrying them out has devolved upon him. He had also the principal share in suggesting the several excursions made by the Club, and to him fell mainly the labour of arranging and conducting them. By means of these excursions the members have attained a considerable knowledge of the district as regards its physical features and natural history—a knowledge they could not have attained in a pleasanter manner than by attending these field meetings, which Mr. Gray's tact made so enjoyable. One other matter I would like briefly to mention—I refer to the action taken by the Club on two special points on the occasion of the recent meeting of the British Association in this town. First, the exhibition of antiquities in the Ulster Minor Hall, and, second, the preparation of the Guide to Belfast and adjacent counties, which constitute the most important scientific work done in Belfast for the reception of the *savans* who attended the meeting of the association. The exhibition would not have been attempted save for Mr. Gray's energy and special knowledge, which enabled this Club to carry out the project successfully. On him we depended mainly, and were not disappointed. Had the efforts of Mr. Gray and those associated with him been seconded by all who had it in their power to assist, the exhibition would, owing to the abundance of material, have been not only creditable, but immense. You have all seen the Guide so recently issued by the Club, a work which as yet is unique. To Mr. Gray is due the honour of originating this work, and also the execution of a very considerable portion of it. This work has brought the name of the Belfast Field Club prominently before the naturalists of the kingdom, and our example will doubtless be followed by societies in other places when similarly circumstanced; indeed I am given to understand that already steps have been taken in this direction in view of the forthcoming meeting of the British Association at Bristol. On reviewing the past history of the Club, and the part taken in it by Mr. Gray, I feel confident that the position we now hold is very largely due to his efforts on its behalf, and that I express the feeling of every member here when I move, as I do now, that our very best thanks be tendered to Mr. William Gray in recognition of his services to the Club.

The motion having been seconded by Mr. GEORGE O'BRIEN, it was put to the meeting and carried by acclamation.

The CHAIRMAN then conveyed the thanks to

Mr. GRAY, who, in replying, said—Mr. Chairman and fellow-members, the resolution has taken me quite by surprise. The more than flattering terms in which my friend, Mr. Wright, has referred to the services I rendered our Club, and the approval with which they were received by this meeting, is most embarrassing, and for the moment renders it impossible for me to return anything like a suitable reply. I must say, however, that it is particularly gratifying to me now, in retiring from my official position, to find that my services have been so highly appreciated by you. I can assure you I do not retire without some little regret, and my feelings are akin to those excited in my mind in my boyish days when I lost a cherished pet. Perhaps I may flatter myself that something like the same feelings may be entertained by you, but yours must be like the feelings of those who have lost a certain quadruped, on whom you lavished kindness, and from whom you received a small amount of hard work, sundry fits of stubborness, and an occasional tendency to kick. You must not, however, forget that if I worked in harness I went in tandem, and while I have done the ornamental prancing, my wheeler had to do the hard part of the work. Mr. Hugh Robinson, my co-secretary, really deserves a large share of the credit your kindness assigns to me, and now that he goes to the front, and that your new wheeler is in action, quiet, and goes well in harness, the pair of steeds will, I am sure, carry the Club's chariot over the road of its future career with safety and with credit, and add still further to the Club's success; and I need only say whatever they do to this end shall have my warmest sympathy and my heartiest support.

The CHAIRMAN then, on behalf of the Club, presented to each of the authors of the "Guide to Belfast and Adjacent Counties," a specially bound copy of that work, as a recognition of the services rendered by him in its preparation. Each copy contained an illuminated inscription, stating the special portion of the work undertaken by the person to whom it was presented. The following are the names of the gentlemen to whom the books were given :—

John Anderson, J.P., F.G.S.; William Gray, M.R.I.A; Rev. Edmund M'Clure, A.M., M.R.I.A.; Rev. William M'Ilwaine, D.D.; Rev. George Robinson, A.M.; Hugh Robinson; S. A. Stewart, F.B.S.E.; William Swanston.

The arrangements for the Summer excursions of the Club were then discussed, after which the meeting separated.

ANNUAL CONVERSAZIONE.

The following is an account of the ANNUAL CONVERSAZIONE, held in the MUSEUM, on THURSDAY EVENING, 6th MAY.

(Extract from Local Papers.)

Last evening the Annual Conversazione of this Club took place in the Museum, and was fashionably attended. As usual, there was a large and varied collection of interesting articles, which were inspected with evident pleasure by the visitors. The several apartments of the building, as well as the lobbies, &c., were neatly decorated with evergreens and banners; this work, which must have entailed a large amount of labour, having been carried out in the most artistic manner by a sub-committee of the Club, assisted by Mr. William Darragh, the efficient curator of the Museum. On the tables were placed a large quantity of choice flowers, forwarded by Messrs. Philip Johnston, J.P., E. H. Thompson, J.P., A. J. Macrory, Frederick Bell, and E. H. Bell, some choice plants kindly lent by Mr. R. B. Matthews, and a variety of wild flowers collected by the members. Messrs. Swanston and Gray exhibited their collections of Palæozoic fossils in competition for the prize offered by the Club. The former gentleman carried off the prize, but Mr. Gray's collection was of such high merit that a special prize of equal value was awarded him. Both collections included Carboniferous and Silurian fossils. Mr. Swanston's collection of Silurian Graptolites from Donaghadee were of great interest, while Mr. Gray's fish teeth, from Armagh, formed a rich collection. Both these exhibitors had a great variety of Trilobites, from Pomeroy, County Tyrone. Mr. Gray also exhibited twenty-five carefully mounted microscopic slides, for which the prize was awarded. Mr. Henry Knight obtained the prize for the best collection of Mosses, the value of which was much enhanced by their being mounted as specimens for the microscope. He also exhibited a series of microscopic slides, mainly botanical, Mr. George Donaldson's prize collection of Lepidoptera, included a much greater variety of butterflies and moths and many more beautiful species than are commonly supposed to occur in this neighbourhood, yet all the specimens shown were collected within a short distance of Belfast during the last twelve months. This gentleman also carried away the prize for native Ferns, of which he exhibited twenty species. Mr. F. W. Lockwood exhibited two studies from nature, illustrative of archæology. They displayed considerable merit, and gained the prize offered by Dr. J. Moore, H.R.H.A. Mr. J. J. Phillips was awarded the president's (Rev. Dr. M'Ilwaine) prize for an interesting series of drawings illustrating his recent researches at Inch Abbey, Downpatrick. A case of rare British moths was shown by the Rev. John Bristow, A.M. Much attention was attracted by an American Black-billed Cuckoo, which was exhibited by Dr. John Rea, by whom it was shot in the parish of Killead, County Antrim, in 1873. We understand it is the first specimen of this bird which has been obtained in the three kingdoms, and the second in Europe. Some neatly-mounted aquaria were shown by Mr. Thomas Darragh. They were very tastefully fitted up, and contained a great variety of local fish, shells, and water plants. Mr. Joseph Wright, F.G.S., exhibited a valuable assortment of microscopic fossils from the

Antrim chalk; and Mr. William Darragh some cases of marine birds, which formed a noteworthy feature. A large collection of British medals, the records of victories on both flood and field, were lent by Mr. John Browne. The walls were covered with a great assortment of pictures. Dr. James Moore, H.R.H.A., M.R.I.A., had a very attractive series of cleverly-executed water-colours of picturesque places in the neighbourhood; and Mr. T. M. Lindsay, of the School of Art, and Mrs. Lindsay, had another admirable collection. Dr. Henry Burden showed some water-colours and oil paintings, which embraced specimens by Stannus, Burgess, Lane, &c.; Dr. Meissner, a large number of valuable chromo-lithographs, chiefly after the old masters; and Mr. William Gray, M.R.I.A., a series of water-colours of antiquities, chiefly in the counties of Antrim and Down. They consisted principally of cromlechs, castles, and sculptured crosses, and an especial interest was attached to them from the fact that it was from them the illustrations were taken for the complete Guidebook to the North of Ireland, so spiritedly published by the Club for the late meeting of the British Association. Works of art of various kinds were also shown by Messrs. W. H. Patterson, Robert Young, C.E.; J. J. Phillips, and S. P. Close. There were in addition some beautiful photographs and carbon enlargements by Mr. Church, Donegall Place.

The various prizes which had been awarded to the successful competitors for the Club's and special prizes were on the tables. There were also eight handsomely bound copies of the Guidebook to which we have referred. These have been presented by the committee to the Rev. Dr. MacIlwaine, Rev. Edmund M'Clure, Rev. George Robinson (Tartaraghan), Messrs. J. Anderson, J.P.; William Gray, S. A. Stewart, Wm. Swanston, and Hugh Robinson, who prepared the volume; and the illuminated presentation page which each book contains gives not only a just recognition of these gentlemen's services, but forms the only record of the authorship. The following members had their microscopes in the large room, and exhibited during the evening a great number of interesting objects:—Dr. Burden, Messrs. Henry Knight, Hugh Hamilton,

Simpson, Bond, Anderson, Swanston, and Gray. Refreshments were supplied in the lower room, by Mr. William John Walker, Bradbury Place.

NOTICE.

EXCHANGE OF PROCEEDINGS.

THE Committee of the Club have been desirous of establishing a yearly exchange of the published proceedings with those of kindred organisations in other places, and have during the past year forwarded copies of the Eleventh Annual Report and Proceedings to other societies. They acknowledge with thanks, the receipt of the following publications, and hope that other societies whose objects are similar will favour them with copies of their proceedings as published.

Bath Natural History Society and Antiquarian Field Club.
Proceedings. Vol. III., No. 1.—1874.

Berwickshire Naturalists' Club.
Proceedings, 1872.

Brighton and Sussex Natural History Society.
Twenty-first Annual Report and Abstract of Proceedings, 1874.

Bristol Naturalists' Society.
Annual Report, 1873-74.
Proceedings. New Series. Vol. I., Part 1.—1874.

Canadian Institute.
Canadian Journal of Science, Literature, and History. Vol. XIV. Nos. 2 and 3.—1874.

Cardiff Naturalists' Society.
Report and Transactions. Vol. V.—1873.

Dunedin (Otago) Naturalists' Field Club.
Annual Report, 1873-74.

Edinburgh Botanical Society.
Transactions and Proceedings. Vol. XII., Part 1.—1874.

Edinburgh Geological Society.
Transactions. Vol. II., Part 3.—1874.

Essex Institute, Salem, Mass., U.S.A.
Bulletin of Essex Institute. Vol. V., Nos. 1 to 12.—1873.

Geologists' Association, London.
Annual Report for 1874.
Proceedings. Vol. III., Parts 5 to 8.—1874-75.

Glasgow Society of Field Naturalists.
Transactions. Part 2. Session 1873-74.

Liverpool Geological Society.
Abstract of Proceedings, 1873-74.

Liverpool Naturalists' Field Club.
Proceedings, 1873-74.

New York, U.S.A., Lyceum of Natural History.
Annals, Vol. X., Parts 8, 9, 10, and 11.—1872-73.
Proceedings. Second Series. Part 1.—1873.

Norfolk and Norwich Naturalists' Society.
Transactions, 1873-74.
Supplement—Norfolk Lepidoptera—1874.

Philadelphia, U.S.A., Academy of Natural Sciences of.
Proceedings for 1873.

Peabody Academy of Sciences, Salem, Mass., U.S.A.
Fifth Annual Report.—1872.

Plymouth Institution.
Annual Report and Transactions. Vol. V., Part 1.—1874.

Royal Geological Society of Ireland.
Journal, Vol. IV., Part 1., 1874.

U.S.A. Geological Survey of the Territories.
Bulletin No. 1, 1874.
Flora of Colorado, 1874.

Warwickshire Natural History and Archæological Society.
Thirty-Eighth Annual Report, 1874.

Wiltshire Archæological and Natural History Society.
Wiltshire Archæological and Natural History Magazine, Parts 37 to 43·
1871-75.

[*From the respective Societies.*]

[1874-75.]

BELFAST NATURALISTS' FIELD CLUB.

THIRTEENTH YEAR—1875-76.

President.
REV. WILLIAM M'ILWAINE, D.D.

Vice-President.
WILLIAM GRAY, M.R.I.A.

Treasurer.
GREER MALCOMSON, CASTLE PLACE.

Secretaries.

HUGH ROBINSON, | WM. SWANSTON,
DONEGALL STREET. | COLLEGE SQUARE EAST.

Committee.

JOHN ANDERSON, J.P., F.G.S. | W. H. PATTERSON, M.R.I.A.
JOHN ANDERSON. | S. A. STEWART,
HENRY KNIGHT. | SAMUEL SYMINGTON.
F. W. LOCKWOOD. | ISAAC W. WARD.
Dr. JAMES MOORE, M.R.I.A., H.R.H.A. | JOSEPH WRIGHT, F.G.S.

Members.

Any changes in the Addresses of Members should be communicated by them to the Secretaries.

John B. Aickin, Lincoln Avenue.
William Aickin, M.D., Murray's Terrace.
Miss Alder, Fernbank, Holywood.
W. J. C. Allen, J.P., Faunoran, Whiteabbey.
Wm. B. Allen, Albion Street
Edward Allworthy, Mountview.
John Anderson, J.P., F.G.S., Hillbrook, Holywood.
John Anderson, Gulladuff House, Moville.
Robert Anderson, Balmoral.
Mrs. Andrews, Chlorine Place.

E. N. Banks, Botanic Avenue.
Jas. M. Barkley, Cooleen, Strandtown.
William Batt, Ormeau Road.
J. M'D. Bermingham, A.R.I.A.I., Mount Charles.
W. J. Boucher, Landscape Terrace.
W. H. Braddell, College Square East.
Edward Braddell, College Square East.
Rev. S. A. Brenan, A.B., Pomeroy, County Tyrone.
Charles H. Brett, Dunedin Terrace.
Rev. John Bristow, Chichester Park.
John Browne, Crumlin Road.
W. J. Browne, A.B., Newtownards.
James Bryce, A.M., LL.D., F.G.S., F.R.G.S.I., &c., Morningside Place, Edinburgh. (Hon. Mem.)
Henry Burden, M.D., College Square North.

James Calwell, Cushendun, County Antrim.
Jno. Campbell, Mossley, Carnmoney.
Miss Carruthers, Claremont Street.
John Charley, College Park.
J. C. Clarke, Parkville.
Wm. Clibborn, Windsor Terrace.
Sir Edward Coey, J.P., D.L., Merville, Whiteabbey.

John Collins, Nottinghill, Malone.
Miss Connery, Victoria Place.
David Corrie, Custom House.
W. F. C. S. Corry, Mountpottinger.
John Cramsie, Lisavon, Strandtown.
John Cramsie, jun., Lisavon, Strandtown.
Alex. Crawford, Fitzwilliam Street.
Wm. Crawford, jun., Fitzroy Avenue.
Prof. R. O. Cunningham, M.D., Richmond Terrace.
W. M. Cunningham, Windsor.

Edward Dale, Fitzroy Avenue.
John H. Davies, Glenmore, Lisburn.
Robert Day, jun., F.S.A., Patrick Street, Cork.
George Donaldson, Mount Collyer.

Miss Gibb, Cushleva, Jordanstown.
R. M. Gilmore, Shrigley. Killyleagh
W. J. Gilmore, Cliftonville.
D. Corse Glen, Annfield Place, Glasgow.
G. T. Glover, Kew Cottages, Mountpottinger.
Jas. Gourlay, Killinchy, County Down.
Rev. John Grainger, A.M., D.D., Broughshane, County Antrim. (Hon. Mem.)
Rev. Jas. Graves, Inisnaig, Stoneyford, County Kilkenny. (Cor. Mem.)
William Gray, M.R.I.A., Mount Charles.
Miss Gray, Mount Charles.
Miss Frances Gray, Mount Charles.
Forster Green, Derrievolgie, Malone.
Miss Greer, Tarbart Villa, Strandtown.
Jas. C. Greer, Annadale, Ballynafeigh.
Mrs. Greer, Annadale, Ballynafeigh.
William Greig, Richmond, Antrim, Road.

Hugh Hamilton, University Square.

J. C. Hamilton, University Square.
Mann Harbison, Newtownards.
William Harte, C.E., Buncrana, County Donegal. (Cor. Mem.)
Jas. Haslett, Franklin Street.
W. D. Henderson, University Square.
Jas. Hewitt, Ballymacreely, Killinchy, County Down.
Prof. J. F. Hodges, M.D., Derrievolgie, Malone.
John Hogg, Richmond Terrace.
J. Sinclair Holden, M.D., F.G.S., Sudbury, Suffolk. (Cor. Mem.)
F. C. Holmes, Belmont.
Alex. Hunter, Northern Bank.
Thomas Hunter, Holywood.

H. H. Jamieson, Casaeldono, Castlereagh.
F. M. Jennings, Brown Street, Cork. (Cor. Mem.)
Miss Johnston, Dalriada, Whiteabbey.
Miss Johnston, Glenavy, County Antrim.
James Johnston, Alma Terrace.
Samuel Johnston, Antrim Road.
W. J. Johnston, Dunesk, Stranmillis.
J. F. Johnson, Royal Botanic Gardens.

W. Thompson Kelly, Regent Street.
J. J. Kelso, M.D., M.R.I.A., Lisburn.
Mrs. Keogh, Crumlin Road.
Dr. T. H. Keown, R.N., Dundela, Strandtown.
Wm. Kernahan, Sydenham Avenue.
Rev. J. A. Kerr, A.B., Whiteabbey.
William King, Mountpleasant.
Henry Knight, Gloucester Villa, Antrim Road.
W. J. Knowles, Cullybackey, County Antrim.

Miss Lamb, Divis View.
W. W. Lamb, Divis View.
G. D. Leathem, Thornlea, Malone.
Andrew Ledlie, Victoria Street.
F. R. Lepper, Sydenham, Strandtown.

Miss R. Lester, Newtownards.
F. W. Lockwood, Corn Market.
John Love, Oldpark Terrace.
Wm. Lowry, Kinkora, Strandtown.

S. J. Magowan, Cromwell Road.
Henry Major, Lisburn.
Greer Malcomson, Shamrock Lodge.
James Malcomson, Mountpottinger.
Mrs. Malcomson, Mountpottinger.
John Marsh, York Street.
Joseph C. Marsh, Donegall Street.
Rev. Jas. Martin, Eglintoun, Antrim Road.
Mrs. Martin, Eglintoun, Antrim Road.
John Martin, M.D., Clarence Place.
P. C. Mayne, Sydenham Avenue.
John Millar, J.P., Lisburn.
Miss Millar, Lisburn.
William Millar, Durham Street.
James Moore, M.D., M.R.I.A., H.R.H.A., Chichester Street
John Moore, M.D., Carlisle Terrace.
W. R. Molyneux, Florence Place.
Miss Monteith, Claremont Street.
Hugh Morrison, Ligoniel.
David Morrow, Clarence Place.
J. J. Murphy, F.G.S., Oldforge, Dunmurry.
J. R. Musgrave, J.P., Drumglass, Malone.

Robt. M'Adam, College Sq. East.
James M'Clenahan, Ardoyne.
Miss M'Clure. Belmont.
Sir Thomas M'Clure, Bart., V.L., Belmont.
Rev. Edmund M'Clure, A.M., M.R.I.A., Lincoln's Inn Fields, London. (Hon. Mem.)
Rev. William M'Ilwaine, D.D., Ulsterville.
Mrs. M'Ilwaine, Ulsterville.
Daniel M'Kee, Adela Place.
John Mackenzie, C.E., Balmoral.
Thos. MacKnight, Balmoral Terrace.
Alexander M'Laine, Corporation St.
William M'Millan, Ballinasloe.

Nicholas Oakman, Prospect Terrace.
George O'Brien, Holywood.
W. D. O'Brien, Holywood.

Capt. S. P. Olliver, 22nd Brigade R.A., F.R.S., F.R.G.S., &c., Buncrana, County Donegal.
Rev. James O'Laverty, Holywood.
Alexander O'Rorke, Duncairn.

David Patterson, Holywood.
W. H. Patterson, M.R.I.A., Dundela, Strandtown
J. J. Phillips, Granville Terrace.
W. H. Phillips, Lemonfield, Holywood.
John Pim, Clifton Park Avenue.
Joshua Pim, Crumlin Terrace.
Thomas W. Pim, Evelyn Lodge, Strandtown.
John Preston, jun., Dunmore, Antrim Road.
Thomas Plunkett, Enniskillen.
C. D. Purden, M.D., Wellington Place.
Alfred Purdon, Wellington Place.

Joseph Radley, Prospect Hill, Lisburn.
J. Rea, M.D., Great Victoria Street.
Miss Robinson, Lisanore, Antrim Road.
Rev. George Robinson, A.M., Tartaraghan, County Armagh.
Hugh Robinson, Donegall Street.
J. R. Robinson, Woodstock Road.
Ninian J. Robinson, Donegall Street
W. A. Robinson, Crofton, Holywood.
Edward Rogan, Cromac Street.
Rd. Ross, M.D., Wellington Place.
B. F. Rothwell, Marino, Holywood.
James Russell, A.M., LL.B., H.M. C.S., Hong-Kong, China.

Rev. George B. Sayers, Raloo, Carrickfergus.
Mrs. Scott, Sydenham Avenue.
J. M. Johnston Scott, M.D., College Square East.
R. C. Sedgwick, Holywood.
Thomas Shaw, Pakenham Place.
John Shelly, Whiteabbey.
William Shepherd, Holywood.
Miss Simpson, University Square.
Stewart Simpson, Castle Place.

Rowland Smeethe, Queen's College.
George K. Smith, Whiteabbey.
Robert Smith, Mountpottinger.
Thomas Smyth, Kensington Street.
Rev. George C. Smythe, A.M., Coole Glebe, Carnmoney.
Adam Speers, B.Sc., Holywood.
Sir Nathaniel Staples, Bart., Lissan, Dungannon.
Jas. H. Staples, Lissan, Dungannon.
S. A. Stewart, North Street.
Miss Swanston, University Street.
Wm. Swanston, University Street.
Samuel Symington, Brookfield House.

Ralph Tate, A.L.S., F.G.S., &c., High Street, Redcar, Yorkshire. (Hon. Mem.)
A. O'D. Taylor, Upper Crescent.
Miss Thomson, University Square.
E. H. Thompson, J.P., Slieve-na-Failte, Whiteabbey.
Henry Thompson, Windsor.
John Thompson, B.E., Mountpottinger.
James Thomson, A.M., LL.D., D.C.L, C.E., Sardinia T race, Hillhead, Glasgow. (Hon. Mem.)
Wyville Thomson, LL.D., F.R.S., F.G.S., &c., University Edinburgh. (Hon. Mem.)
George Thomson, Grosvenor Street.
John Todd, Regent Street
W. A. Todd, Regent Street.

William Valentine, J.P., Glenavna, Whiteabbey.
J. W. Valentine, Whiteabbey.

W. F. Wakeman, Portora, Enniskillen, County Fermanagh. (Cor. Mem.)
T. R. Walkington, Laurel Lodge, Strandtown.
Isaac W. Ward, University Street.
John S. Ward, Lisburn.
W. R. Ward, Stanpit, Christchurch, Hants.
W. Watson, Londonderry. (Cor. Mem.)

Alex. C. Welsh, Dromore, County Down. (Cor. Mem.)
T. K. Wheeler, M.D., Clarendon Place.
T. K. Wheeler, jun., Clarendon Place
David Wilson, Ballymoney, County Antrim.
James Wilson, jun., Albion Place.
James Wilson, Ballybundon, Killinchy, County Down.
Rev. Hans Woods, Park Avenue, Ormeau Road.
Rev. Robert Workman, M.A., Glastry, Kirkcubbin, County Down.

Thomas Workman, Windsor.
John Workman, Windsor.
Joseph Wright, F.G.S., F.R.G.S.I. Cliftonville.
Samuel O. Wylie, College Square North.
William Wylie, College Square North.

Robert Young, C.E., Rathvarna, Antrim Road.
Robert M. Young, Rathvarna, Antrim Road.

RULES

OF THE

Belfast Naturalists' Field Club.

I.
That the Society be called "THE BELFAST NATURALISTS' FIELD CLUB."

II.
That the object of the Society be the practical Study of Natural Science and Archæology.

III.
That the Club shall consist of Honorary, Corresponding, and Ordinary Members. The Ordinary Members to pay annually a Subscription of Five Shillings; and that Corresponding Members be expected to communicate a paper within every two years.

IV.
That Candidates shall be proposed and seconded at any meeting of the Club by Members present, and then be elected by a majority of votes.

V.
That the Officers of the Club be annually elected, and consist of a President, Vice-President, Treasurer, two Secretaries, and ten Members, who form the Committee. Five to form a Quorum. No Member of Committee to be eligible for re-election who has not attended at least one-fourth of the Committee Meetings during his year of office.

VI.

That the Members of the Club shall hold at least Six Field Meetings during the year, in the most interesting localities, for investigating the Natural History and Archæology of the district: That the place of meeting be fixed by the Committee, and that five days' notice of each Excursion be communicated to Members by the Secretaries.

VII.

That Meetings be held Fortnightly or Monthly, at the discretion of the Committee, for the purpose of reading of papers; such papers, as far as possible, to treat of the Natural History and Archæology of the district. These Meetings to be held during the months from November to April inclusive.

VIII.

That the Committee shall, if they find it advisable, offer for competition Prizes for the best collections of scientific objects of the district; and the Committee may order the purchase of maps, or other scientific apparatus, and may carry on geological and archæological searches or excavations, if deemed advisable; provided that the entire amount expended under this rule does not exceed the sum of £10 in any one year.

IX.

That the Annual Meeting be held during the month of April, when the Report of the Committee for the past year, and the Treasurer's Financial Statement, shall be presented, the Committee and Officers elected, Bye-laws made and altered, and any proposed alteration in the general laws, of which a fortnight's notice shall have been given, in writing, to the Secretary or Secretaries, considered and decided upon. The Secretaries to give the Members due notice of such intended alteration.

X.

That, on the written requisition of twenty-five Members, delivered to the Secretaries, an extraordinary General Meeting may be called, to consider and decide upon the subjects mentioned in such written requisition.

XI.

That the Committee be empowered to exchange publications and reports, and to extend the privilege of attending the meetings and excursions of the Belfast Naturalists' Field Club, to members of kindred societies, on similar privileges being accorded to its Members by such other societies.

The following Rules for the conducting of the Excursions have been arranged by the Committee.

I.—The Excursions to be open to all Members; each one to have the privilege of introducing two friends.

II.—A Chairman to be elected as at ordinary meetings.

III.—One of the Secretaries to act as conductor, or, in the absence of both, a Member to be elected for that purpose.

IV.—No change to be made in the programme, or extra expenses incurred, except by the consent of the majority of the Members present.

V.—No fees, gratuities, or other expenses, to be paid except through the conductor.

VI.—Every Member or Visitor to have the accommodation assigned by the conductor. Where accommodation is limited, consideration will be given to priority of application.

VII.—Accommodation cannot be promised unless tickets are obtained before the time mentioned in the special circular.

VIII.—Those who attend an excursion without previous notice will be liable to extra charge, if extra cost be incurred thereby.

IX.—No intoxicating liquors to be provided at the expense of the Club.

Belfast Naturalists' Field Club.

THIRTEENTH YEAR.

THE Committee offer the following Prizes to be competed for during the Session ending March 31, 1876 :—

I. For the best Herbarium of Flowering Plants,
   representing not less than 250 Species............£1 0 0
II. For the best Herbarium of Flowering Plants,
   representing not less than 150 Species........... 0 10 0
III. Best Collection of Mosses......................... 0 10 0
IV.   Do.   Seaweeds 0 10 0
V.   Do.   Ferns............................ 0 10 0
VI.   Do.   Cretaceous Fossils........... 0 10 0
VII. Do.   Liassic   do. 0 10 0
VIII. Do.   Palæozoic   do. 0 10 0
IX.   Do.   Marine Shells................ 0 10 0
X.   Do.   Land and Fresh-water Shells 0 10 0
XI.   Do.   Lepidoptera........ .... 0 10 0
XII. Best Set of 25 Microscopic Slides................ 0 10 0

XIII. Best Collection of Archæological Objects........ £0 10 0
XIV. Do. Crustacea........................ 0 10 0
XV. Do. Echinodermata................ 0 10 0
XVI. Do. Geological Specimens, illustrative of the Mineral resources of the Province of Ulster. 1 0 0
XVII. Best Collection of all or any of the above Objects collected *at the Excursions* of the Year.... 0 10 0
XVIII. Six best Field Sketches appertaining to Geology, Archæology, or Natural History........... 0 10 0

In every case where three or more persons compete for a Prize, a second one of half its value will be awarded if the conditions are otherwise complied with.

CONDITIONS.

No Competitor to obtain more than Two Prizes in any one year.

No Competitor to be awarded the same Prize twice within three years.

All Collections to be made personally during the Session, within the Province of Ulster. Each Species to be correctly named, and locality stated. The Flowering Plants to be collected when in flower, and classified according to the Natural System. The Sketches, Drawings, and Microscopic Slides to be the Competitor's own work.

No Prizes will be awarded except to such Collections as shall, in the opinion of the Judges, possess positive merit.

The Prizes to be in books or suitable scientific objects, at the desire of the successful competitor.

SPECIAL PRIZES.

XIX. Mr. William Gray, M.R.I.A., offers a Prize of £1 1s. for the best Six Coloured Sketches of separate Antiquarian subjects, for the Club's Sketch Book. The set to be of a uniform size.

XX. Mr. J. W. Murphy offers a Prize of 10s. for the best Collection of Recent Sponges, the conditions being the same as those for Prizes I. to XVII.

XXI. Dr. James Moore, H.R.H.A., offers a Prize of £1 1s. for the best Two Studies from Nature, illustrative of Archæology. The Prize Sketches to become the property of the Club, and to be not less than 9 inches by 5½ inches. The subjects of the Sketches to be different from any at present in the Club's Album.

XXII. Mr. William Swanston offers a Prize of 10s. 6d. for the best Two Studies from Nature illustrative of Geology. Conditions same as for Prize XXI.

NOW READY,

320 pp. Fcap. 8vo. Cloth Gilt, Bevelled Boards, with 48 pp. Illustrations and Map. Price 3/6.

GUIDE TO BELFAST

AND ADJACENT COUNTIES.

BY THE

BELFAST NATURALISTS' FIELD CLUB.

THE BOOK TREATS OF THE FOLLOWING SUBJECTS:

PHYSICAL GEOGRAPHY.
GEOLOGY AND MINERAL RESOURCES.
BOTANY.
ZOOLOGY.
TOPOGRAPHY.
HISTORICAL & DESCRIPTIVE NOTICES OF TOWNS.

ANTIQUITIES—ECCLESIASTICAL AND CIVIL.
AGRICULTURE.
TRADE AND COMMERCE.
EXCURSIONS TO PLACES OF INTEREST.

May be had of all Booksellers, or from the Secretaries of the Club.

11 FEB 1886

ANNUAL REPORT

AND

PROCEEDINGS

OF THE

Belfast Naturalists' Field Club.

1875-1876.

SERIES II.

Volume I. Part III.

PRINTED FOR MEMBERS ONLY.

ANNUAL REPORT

AND

PROCEEDINGS

OF THE

Belfast Naturalists' Field Club,

FOR THE

YEAR ENDING 31ST MARCH, 1876.

NEW SERIES.

VOLUME I. PART III.

BELFAST:
PRINTED FOR THE CLUB,
AT THE "BELFAST NEWS-LETTER" STEAM-PRINTING HOUSE,
55, 57, & 59, DONEGALL STREET.

1876.

REPORT

OF THE

Belfast Naturalists' Field Club,

FOR THE YEAR 1875-76.

N presenting the thirteenth annual report, the Committee have the pleasure of congratulating the members on the completion of another prosperous year in the Club's history. The year, which is now closed, has been as satisfactory as any of its predecessors, so far as regards the number of the members, the attendance at the excursions and winter meetings, and the general interest of the members and the public at large in the scientific work in which the Club is engaged.

The following excursions were made during the Summer Session :—

    On 22nd May, to Antrim and Tardree.
    On 12th June, to Glynn and Glenoe.
    On 3rd July, to Montalto Demesne and The Spa.
    On 20th, 21st, and 22nd July, to Coast Road and Glens of Antrim.
    On 14th August, to Glenavy and Ram's Island.
    On 4th September, to Knockagh and Carrickfergus.

The Committee take this opportunity of returning their sincere thanks to those noblemen and gentlemen who so kindly threw open their grounds to the members of the Club at the various excursions; as in former years, not a single refusal was met with, but full permission granted immediately on being asked for. They also desire to express their obligations to the managers of the various railway companies, for the special facilities they have been granted in the arrangement of the excursions. To J. J. Gardiner, Esq., resident engineer of the Glenariff Iron Ore and Harbour Company, the Club is specially indebted, he having, in the kindest manner, provided gratuitously a special train for the conveyance of the members and their friends, by that company's mineral railway, to the head of Glenariff, on the occasion of the Coast Road excursion.

In addition to the regular excursions of the Club, several of the members had, during the month of September last, the pleasure of engaging in a series of dredging expeditions. One of the original members of the Club, Thomas Workman, Esq., generously gave the use of his yacht, "Denburn," and, accompanied by him, several days' dredging in and about the mouth of Belfast Lough was accomplished. From these excursions valuable results have already been obtained, and it is hoped that these investigations will be further prosecuted, and that at a future time a complete report upon them will be brought before the Club, thus giving a still more exact knowledge of the marine zoology of the district.

During the Winter Session the following papers were read :—

17th Nov.	"Opening Address." By Rev. W. MacIlwaine, D.D.
15th Dec.	"The Vegetable Parasites of the Human Body." By J. M. Johnston Scott, Esq., M.D.
5th Jan.	"The Natural History of Water, and its Effects in Nature." By Adam Speers, Esq., B.Sc.
2nd Feb.	"The Beginnings of Life." By W. J. Browne, Esq., M.A.
8th March.	"The Birds of Lough Neagh." By Rev. George Robinson, M.A.
29th March.	"Practical Hints to Collectors of Lepidoptera." By Rev. John Bristow, B.A.

The Committee have much gratification in recording the fact that at all the meetings, with one exception, the papers read have been brought forward by members who appeared for the first time before the Club in that capacity. They are glad to find additional members bringing forward the results of their investigations in natural science, and trust that others who have been engaged in the elucidation of special subjects will follow the good example thus set them.

The exchange of publications with other societies has been maintained during the past year, and never at any former period has this exchange been so extensively conducted. The Club has during the year received various publications from no fewer than thirty-two different societies, and the Committee have pleasure in stating that not only from Great Britain, but also from America, they have received additional applications for exchanges. The Committee would here express their obligations to the Smithsonian Institution, Washington, for the facilities afforded them by that body in the distribution of the publications of the Club, and the collection of parcels for it in the United States—an advantage which has now been enjoyed for several years. In addition to the exchanges, the Committee thankfully acknowledge the receipt of a donation of valuable publications of the Geological Survey of Canada, by the courtesy of His Excellency Earl Dufferin, Governor-General of Canada; and also a copy of "Reliquæ Aquitanicæ," presented by the executors of the late Henry Christy, Esq., through the kindness of Professor T. Rupert Jones, F.R.S.

Messrs. S. A. Stewart, William Swanston, William Gray, M.R.I.A., and F. W. Lockwood, were requested by the Committee to act as judges of the collections submitted in competition for the Club and other prizes. The following are their reports:—

"We have examined the specimens of Marine Shells sent in by Mr. Thomas Workman, and have to report that this collection fulfils the conditions annexed to prize No. 9, and we accordingly recommend that the prize be awarded. Mr. Workman's Shells have mainly been obtained by dredging, and amongst them are several of the rarer species. At a former period Belfast was famed for the successful prosecution of this branch of natural science, and we congratulate the Club on the prospect of a revival of interest in the subject.

S. A. STEWART.
WILLIAM SWANSTON."

"We have examined the only set of drawings submitted in competition for the Vice-President's prize; these, in our opinion, are not strictly in accordance with the conditions of competition as to uniformity of size, &c. The object of the prize was more especially the illustration of such monuments of antiquity as were liable to removal or destruction, and could not be preserved in the Museums of public or private collectors. We, however, consider the drawings painstaking and meritorious, and we recommend that the prize be awarded to the author, Miss Carruthers.

WILLIAM GRAY.
F. W. LOCKWOOD."

The Committee, acting upon the recommendations of the judges, have awarded the prize for the best collection of Marine Shells to Mr. Thomas Workman, and to Miss Carruthers Mr. William Gray's special prize, for the best six coloured sketches of antiquarian subjects.

During the Summer Session several special prizes, to be competed for at the excursions, were offered by various members of the Club. To these gentlemen the Committee return their best thanks, and express the hope that, during the ensuing Summer, other members will continue this class of prizes, which adds so much to the interest of the excursions, and tends to inculcate those habits of observation which are so essential to all real naturalists.

The Committee, after a careful consideration of the subject, and acting on the suggestions of a number of the members, have thought it advisable to defer the Conversazione till the opening of the Winter Session, which time, they hope, will better suit the convenience of the members generally.

In conclusion, the Committee would impress upon the members the duty of using their best endeavours to increase the membership of the Club. Though, as has already been stated, the number upon the roll is as large as it has ever been, still, it falls very far short of what it should be, when we consider the advantages afforded in return for a merely nominal subscription, and that the area of the Club's operations is the entire province of Ulster. The Committee have done all that has been in their power to do with the amount of funds at their disposal; but, with an increased membership, and consequently augmented income, much more might be done. The "Proceedings" might assume a more extensive form, and the "Appendices"—which have, as yet, appeared at infrequent intervals, as funds admitted of their publication—could be issued with greater regularity, and so give to the scientific world the results of those valuable observations on the flora and fauna of the district, which are now being made by several of the Club's members.

HUGH ROBINSON, } *Hon. Secs.*
WILLIAM SWANSTON,

Dr. Belfast Naturalists' Field Club in Account with Treasurer. Cr.

	£ s. d.		£ s. d.
To Balance from 1874-75	18 6 0	By Loss on Conversazione	3 9 1
,, Subscriptions	50 5 0	,, Printing Annual Report for 1873-74	34 10 6
,, Arrears of Subscriptions	1 0 0	,, ,, ,, 1874-75	11 17 3
,, Gain on Excursions	1 5 0	,, Advertising, Printing, and Stationery	13 13 1
,, Estimated cost of Printing Annual Report for 1873-74, included in last year's a/cs.	15 0 0	,, Delivery of Circulars	1 10 0
		,, Postages	4 18 6
		,, Prizes	1 10 0
		,, Rent of Museum	8 8 0
		,, Curator	2 0 0
		,, Carriage on Parcels	0 2 11
		,, ,, on Fish from Bundoran	0 10 0
		,, Flags	2 0 0
		,, Timber	0 17 4
		,, Balance on hand	0 9 4
	£85 16 0		£85 16 0

Examined and found correct,

HUGH ROBINSON, Hon. Secretary.

GREER MALCOLMSON, Treasurer.

SUMMER SESSION.

The following Excursions were made during the Summer Session:

On Saturday, 22nd May, to

ANTRIM AND TARDREE.

The ground selected on this occasion was the district of country lying between Antrim and Tardree Mountain—a district alike interesting to the archæologist, the geologist, and the botanist. The heavy rain of the previous days somewhat interfered with the attendance, and caused a number of the members to abandon the idea of joining the party; but, notwithstanding this, there was a fair muster at the Northern Counties Terminus, in time to leave by the 9.30 train for Antrim. Those who had sufficient courage to encounter the rain had no reason to regret their decision, as the fine weather which usually attends the Club's excursions did not desert them on this occasion; and the heavy showers which fell during the day were, with two exceptions, seen at a distance only. On their arrival at Antrim, the party found some members and friends from other districts awaiting their coming. Mounting the cars which were in attendance, they drove off to the first stopping place—The Steeple, the residence of G. J. Clarke, Esq., J.P., who kindly gives the public access at all times to his grounds. Here a halt was made to examine the round tower, from which Mr. Clarke's place derives its name. This "monument of time" ever continues to attract the attention of antiquarians, it being one of the most perfect in existence; and forming one of the most conspicuous objects in the neighbourhood to the passengers by the Northern Counties Railway. It is a tapering tower about 95 feet high, with the conical stone roof common to these structures; and has, near the top, four windows, each of which faces one of the cardinal points. The door is at a height of about 8 feet from the mound on which the tower stands, and is square-headed, with the sides narrowing toward the top. The most remarkable feature of the tower is that the stone forming the top of the doorway has a cross carved upon it in relief. This cross is considered by those who advocate the Christian origin of the Irish Round Towers to be one of the strong proofs of the accuracy of their theory; while those who adhere to the pre-Christian origin are of opinion that this stone has been inserted subsequently to the erection of the tower, and, therefore, of no value in the determination of the question. The many conflicting opinions as to the date of the erection of these buildings, or the uses for which they were intended, seem no nearer being solved than when they first engaged the attention of archæologists. One might conjure up the scenes of the builders at work upon them, the quarrying of the stone and the carrying of it to the spot. What tools were used? How were the sturdy builders attired? By what arrangements of scaffolding were the roofing stones laid on? Was there a solemn dedication service performed by some of the saints whose names are now as household words, or was the foundation laid in the blood of pagan sacrifices? The lost chapter of our history telling of these things we fear can never be replaced; and it would ill befit us to allow the remains of a long-forgotten age to fall into decay. Happily there is little prospect of such being the fate of the Antrim Round Tower; and the care so judiciously bestowed on its preservation by the lord of the soil undoubtedly deserves the thanks of all who are interested in the preservation of our national antiquities. Leaving the mysterious pile, with its grey cap o'ertopping the trees, the route to the Fort Bog—the next stopping place—lay by way of Birchill and Ballynoe, passing through bye-lanes fragrant and white with the blossoms of the hawthorn. A short drive brought the party to the fort, which lies about a quarter mile east of the road, and here a stop was made to examine it. It is of considerable magnitude, and, being in good preservation, is one of the most interesting of the many which occur in this neighbourhood. The fort consists of a central earthen mound, surrounded by a double trench. The mound has a diameter of 140 feet, and is hollowed in the centre; on it the ancient residences were probably situated. The distance from the margin of the mound to the outer edge of the enclosing rath (or rampart between the two trenches) is 45 feet, and from that to the circumference of the outer trench 27 feet, thus giving a total diameter of 284 feet. The depth of the central hollow is 6 feet, and that of the inner and outer trenches 14 feet and 8 feet respectively. The garden of an adjoining house touches upon the outer circular trench for about one-sixth of its circumference, otherwise the fort is perfect in every respect. Leaving the fort, the cars are again taken, and the party proceed to Tardree Mountain (Tardree signifying in Irish the Height of the Heather), and, after a drive of three miles, passing another and much smaller fort at Tardree Cottage, the porphyry quarries are reached. The porphyritic district visited on this occasion occupies an area of some ten square miles, the southern limit of which is about three miles northeast of the town of Antrim, Tardree Hill being nearly in the centre. The rock here found is a trachyte-porphyry, differing remarkably in appearance and in lithological character from the surrounding trap. It is usually of a light grey or almost white colour, highly and coarsely crystaline, and, at first sight, resembling a granite. It consists of a felspathic base, with crystals of glassy felspar, smoke quartz, and several other minerals, and is readily disintegrated by weathering on the slopes of the hills, and the result is a fine gravel or sand, which circumstance gives the name "Sandy Braes" to a district east of Tardree. The porphyry is extensively quarried at Tardree Hill, and is largely used for door steps, gate posts, window dressings, and for headstones in country graveyards. As the stone is durable and easily worked, it answers exceedingly well for such purposes, though, owing to its coarse texture, it is less suitable for finer work. The occasional occurrence of small cavities, due to the presence of soft or earthy spots, somewhat interferes also with its value in this respect, but for ordinary building purposes it is well suited. The occurrence of this material in a wide district that is devoid of freestone is a matter of some consequence to the locality. These quarries at one time supplied curbstones for the streets of Belfast, and the Tardree stone was also used to some extent in the construction of the Queen's Bridge, and of the bridge over the Cave Hill Railway on the Antrim Road. The question of the geological age of the porphyry, as compared with that of the trappean rocks surrounding it, is one on which there has been some difference of opinion. The district has lately been examined by the officers of the Geological Survey, and their observations show that the trachyte-porphyry is older than any of the basalts which surround it. As the latter have been determined, by the plant remains found in the iron ore beds at Ballypalliday, and also by other evidence, to be of Miocene age, we may assign the period of the eruption of the porphyry to at least later Eocene times. After examining the quarry on the south side of Tardree, the hill was crossed, and another exposure on the north side investigated; then, taking the cars again, the return journey was commenced, the route being by way of Carnearny Mountain. On arriving at the north-east side of the hill, the party began the ascent on foot, the cars being sent forward to meet them on their descent on the other side. The monumental carn on the top (from which the hill derives its name, Carnearny, *i.e.*, the Carn of Eire) was soon reached, and here a meeting was held and several new members elected. The view from this carn is one of the most picturesque and extensive which can be had in the county. To the south-east are seen the slopes of the Belfast Hills, extending from Divis to Carnmoney, and lying behind them

Slieve Croob and the Mourne Mountains. Over the valley, between Carnmoney Hill and the Knockagh, a glimpse is obtained of Scrabo, with the monumental tower on its summit, and to the left is seen Helen's Tower, near Bangor. On the north-east the conical top of Slemish is seen, almost at hand; and beyond it the Cushendall Mountains, with Trostan, the highest point in Antrim, bounding the view in this direction. To the north-west is the valley of the Bann, with the Sperrin range in Derry and Tyrone lying beyond; and on the south-west is Lough Neagh, presenting an almost complete view of its entire area. In the level plain surrounding the hill the towns of Ballymena, Kells, Connor, and Antrim are distinctly visible. Leaving Carnearny, the drive was resumed, and a halt made at Potter's Walls to visit Croskennan Fort, in the immediate vicinity. This earthwork is a simple mound, or *dun*, and is of small extent compared with the fort already described as occurring at the Fort Bog. A short drive by way of "The Bush" brought the party back to Antrim station. Arriving there, it was found that sufficient time was available, before the departure for home, to visit the Castle—the residence of Viscount Massereene and Ferrard, but which is at present occupied by Sir Richard Wallace. A castle seems to have existed here at an early date, as it is mentioned in a grant to Walter de Lacy in 1226. Sir Hugh Clotworthy, in the reign of James I., seems to have built a castle on the old site, or to have re-edified the ancient Norman structure. In 1662 his son, Sir John Clotworthy (first Viscount Massereene), re-built the castle, leaving it almost as it at present appears. Sir John dying without male issue, the title and estates passed by his daughter and heiress to the Skeffington family—she having married Sir John Skeffington—in which family they still remain. In the rock garden of the Castle grounds there is an interesting achæological object—one of the ancient canoes or boats used by the early inhabitants as a means of access to their crannoges, or lake dwellings. Several such canoes have been found in the district; they are each hollowed out of a single piece of oak, and are from 12 to 16 feet long. Another of them may be seen in the grounds of Shane's Castle. The short time at the disposal of the party only admitted of a hurried walk through a portion of the park, and returning to the station they were soon on their homeward journey. Belfast was reached soon after seven o'clock, everyone well satisfied with the results of the day's excursion, and with the comparatively fine weather with which they were favoured. During the day the entomologists had every opportunity of indulging in their favourite pursuit; for, notwithstanding the slight and very brief showers which fell at intervals during the day, the spring broods of *Lepidoptera* were to be seen in numbers. The small "Copper" *(Lycæna Phlæas)* was met and captured, and the "Orange-tip" and "Common White" were in abundance. The botanists could not boast of the discovery of any special rarities, but to the naturalist nothing is common, and many interesting plants were met with. The graceful flower of the Buck-bean *(Menyanthes trifoliata)*, so seldom seen by dwellers in towns, was gathered, as also the less beautiful but scarcer Jack-by-the-hedge *(Alliaria officinalis)*. Several specimens were also found of a singular variety or "sport" of the wood horse-tail *(Equisetum sylvaticum)*. This curious form bore not only the usual terminal fruit-bearing spike, but, in addition, smaller spikes at the ends of the branches of the upper whorls, and in some cases axillary spikes as well. Several of the party were in quest of the smaller forms of *Cryptogamia*, and were fairly rewarded, two of the less common mosses being found at Ballynoe, viz., *Politrichum gracile*, and *Entosthodon fasiculare*.

On Saturday, 12th June, to

GLYNN AND GLENOE.

Notwithstanding that the sky and the barometer both indicated coming showers, a good number of ladies and gentlemen assembled at the Northern Counties Railway Station, and took their departure for Glynn, near Larne; the majority being intent on botanical pursuits, though geology and entomology had each their votaries. The manager of the railway, with his usual courtesy, placed a saloon carriage at the service of the Club, and thus enhanced the pleasure of the trip. During the railway journey it was announced that one of the members offered two prizes to be competed for on this occasion, the first prize to be awarded to the member who collected the greatest number of native flowering plants, ferns, and fern allies during the day, the second prize for the next greatest number. The conditions were read out, and judges appointed to make the award; and, as will be seen, the contest was keen, and the number of plants collected very large. On arriving at Glynn, the party proceeded at once to visit the ruins of the old church at that place, a considerable portion of which still remain. The walls of unhewn stones, cemented by a mortar now nearly as hard as the stone itself, claim a considerable antiquity for this building, which was examined with much interest, as also the tombstones in the churchyard, some of which are very ancient. The party now proceeded on their way to Glenoe, and for a considerable distance followed the course of the stream, gathering as they went such of the rarer plants as were required for herbaria, and the common forms for the competition. At the outset the search was rewarded by the discovery of a very rare plant—the dog's mercury *(Mercurialis perennis)*, a species which, in Ireland, occurs only in a very few localities. This plant, which grows in some plenty on the south bank of the stream, was in good flower, and was considered quite an acquisition. The Glynn river finds is way to the sea through a rather wide glen that opens out from the hills, and displays broadly rounded undulating banks that tell of the work of an ancient glacier, gliding down from the higher lands above, deepening, widening, and smoothing the original water-course. In these degenerate days, when ice can seldom be found to skate on, it is difficult to conceive, yet geologists inform us of a time long, long ago, which they call the glacial period, when ice was actively engaged as the great agent in modifying the face of the country: rounding off the ruggedness of our hills, and concealing the bare rocks under a covering of drift clay. The stream that now occupies the channel seems insufficient to have produced the Glynn valley, and it appears reasonable to conclude that, as in the case of so many of our valleys and glens, we owe its present form to the action of ice, a most efficient agent, which, long ages before man had existence, was employed not only to embellish our country and render it so picturesque, but also to prepare its surface for that fertility by which it is now blessed. Be that as it may, the Glynn is now one of those fine valleys or glens which so diversify the County of Antrim, and the ramble over its winding banks was most enjoyable. On taking the road again the route was continued to Glenoe, a primitive village in an out-of-the-way position away up in the hills. The glen at this place is very fine, the wooded banks being high and precipitous, displaying good sections of the chalk and basalt, and yielding several of the scarcer native plants. The name Glenoe signifies the glen of the yew, and is a reminiscence of a time when

"The sacred yew, so feared in war,"

was one of our common trees. Ballynure (the place of the yew) has a similar origin. The yew is now practically extinct, in the wild state, in the North of Ireland; some stunted bushes alone remain on the cliffs in the North and North-west. At Glenoe fine specimens were obtained of that form of the polypody named *Polypodium Hibernicum*, also the shining cranesbill *(Geranium lucidum)*, the cow wheat *(Melampyrum pratense)*, and the wild spinach *(Chenopodium Bonus-Henricus)*.

After visiting the waterfall, on the bank above which the church occupies such a picturesque position, and electing several members, the party took their departure, regretting that, owing to want of time, they could not avail themselves of the kind offer of Mr. Turner, to examine his extensive quarries, close to the village. The day had been very fine, save one brief shower, and the pursuit of lepidoptera, though only casually attended to, was not unsuccessful; the Cinnabar moth was captured, as also the common blue (*P. Alexis*). The red admiral (*V. Atalanta*) was seen at Glenoe, this being very early for this rather scarce species. Both plants and insects seem, however, to be in advance this season. As a proof of this, it may be mentioned that ripe strawberries, of nature's own produce, were plucked during the day. The road to Glynn winds along the side of a hill, and affords a fine prospect. Larne Lough, and the town so picturesquely situated, are seen almost below, with the steamer taking her departure for Stranraer. The huge rock of Ailsa was distinctly in view, and in the dim distance the blue hills of Ayrshire. The return to Glynn was hurried by an unwelcome shower, and on arrival at the station the judges commenced the examination of the collections made during the day, and continued the work in the saloon carriage on the return journey, being busily occupied until Greencastle was reached, when they announced that the first prize was awarded to Miss Gray, who collected 88 species, and the second to Miss Connery—81 species. Mr. Gray, who collected specimens of 96 species, had previously retired in favour of the ladies. The competition was most spirited. The lowest number recorded was 71, and when it is considered that the collections were restricted to native plants in flower or in fruit, it will be seen that the result was highly creditable to the powers of discrimination and observation of the various competitors, none of whom were professed botanists.

On Saturday, 3rd July, to

BALLYNAHINCH, MONTALTO, AND THE SPA.

Owing to the fact of this being the only half-holiday excursion in the programme for this season, and the day being all that could be desired, a large number of the members and their friends availed themselves of the arrangements made, and met at the County Down terminus in time to leave by the 1.15 train. On arrival at Ballynahinch, the party walked leisurely through the neat town, in which there is every evidence of prosperity, to the entrance to Montalto. By the courtesy of Marcus Gage, Esq., J.P., the agent of the estate, the party were given full liberty to botanise through the extensive and varied grounds. It having been announced that a member had offered a prize for the two best "sporting" fronds of any species of ferns collected during the day, the party were soon engaged in the exploration of the extensive glades which, spreading on either hand of the principal avenue, afford habitats to some of our choicest ferns. Passing by the front of the mansion-house, the party proceeded to examine the pond, which adjoins the lower side of the extensive lawn. Its surface was covered by a profuse growth of the yellow water-lily, while its margin was fringed by sedges and other aquatic plants, among which was conspicuous the sweet-flag (*Acorus calamus*), specimens of which were eagerly secured by the botanists of the party for their herbaria. This rare plant was known to exist in County Down so early as 1788, but the precise locality was not on record. It was lost sight of till 1866, when it was re-discovered by members of the Belfast Naturalists' Field Club in the Lagan Canal, between Moira and Lisburn. As this was the only known station for the plant in Ireland, it is interesting to note its occurrence in a second locality, which may possibly be the one from which it was originally recorded. Interesting as many of the plants obtained during the day were from their rarity, others of more common occurrence were equally so from their unusual luxuriance. The spotted palmate orchis (*Orchis maculata*) was obtained fully double its usual height. Miniature forests of the common brake fern (*Pteris aquilina*) overtopped the tallest members of the party, and fronds seven or eight feet in height by four or five in breadth were measured, and even these had not attained their full growth. Leaving Montalto, the party proceeded to the Spa. Here a visit was paid to the Labyrinth, entrance to which was simple enough, but egress was not so readily obtained, and there was some little difficulty in again mustering the party. At length all were gathered together, and the wells were visited. The beneficial effects of the waters of the Spa are well known, but an acquired taste seems necessary to enable one to derive the full advantage of their virtues. It was a matter of observation that with a few exceptions a small quantity of the waters satisfied the curiosity of the members of the party. That they possess valuable medicinal properties there can be no doubt, the fact having been attested by eminent competent authorities, and by those who resort to the district to imbibe them, and enjoy the salubrious climate and delightful scenery of the locality. Tea at the Spa Hotel prepared the party for the return journey, and, driving back by the county road, the site of the celebrated battle of Ballynahinch was passed. Again assembled in the comfortable saloon carriage, which had been provided by the Railway Company for the party on both journeys, the judges commenced the examination of the specimens presented in competition for the prize offered. This was awarded to Mr. O'Brien, who had succeeded in finding two exceedingly fine "sports" of fronds of *Lastrea Filix-mas*, on one of which almost all the pinules were bifurcated; the other possessed peculiarities equally marked. Belfast was reached at 8.25, after a most enjoyable and profitable afternoon's excursion.

On 20th, 21st, and 22nd July, to

THE COAST ROAD AND GLENS OF ANTRIM.

What about the weather? This is the anxious inquiry of most excursionists as the time for their trip draws near, even the Belfast Naturalists, who profess to be independent of the weather, have sundry misgivings prior to their annual "three-day" field meeting; particularly, as on this last occasion, when the weather for days before was cloudy, wet, and stormy.

Although the rain fell thick and heavy on the morning of the excursion, and there was every indication of bad weather, the courage of the party did not forsake them. A large party assembled at the Northern Counties Railway, and, with geological hammers, botanical cases, and sundry other naturalists' implements, took their seats in the saloon carriage provided for them, apparently with a full determination to forget the rain and enjoy themselves. Arriving at Larne they never hesitated to take their seats on the open conveyances provided for them, and good fortune smiled on their courage—the clouds rolled up, the sun shone forth, and the weather became all that could be wished for during the trip. A prize was offered by the Vice-President for the best series of geological specimens collected during the excursion, and another for the best bouquet of wild flowers submitted by the ladies, and the competitors seized the very first opportunity to collect specimens. The familiar section at Waterloo was examined by the geologists, while other members of the party admired the coast scenery, particularly the succession of headlands which are seen to such advantage from this point. Ballygally Head offered another attraction. Here the beds of Lias clay, cropping out under the Chalk rocks along the beach, yielded a goodly number of fossils, including Ammonites, Nautili, Pentacrinites, and other characteristic forms. Here, too, the members extracted from the Lias limestone fragments of fossil wood or lignite of the same geological age and origin as the well-known Whitby jet. The basaltic face of Ballygally Head, decorated with fern fronds, and festooned with wild flowers (amongst which were conspicuous the pretty blossoms of the Wood Vetch *(Vicia sylvatica)* a rare plant in other districts, but which is common on the Antrim coast), and the battered ruins of Carncastle beneath it, looked extremely picturesque. Shaw's Castle, a little further on, and the adjoining coast-guard station, are next passed; and at·a gravel bank, two miles nearer Glenarm, a considerable time was spent examining the post-tertiary beds exposed in a deep section close to the road. It was here at Ballyruther, on the farm of Mr. Joseph Dale, that the remains of the Mammoth were found a few years ago. One of the teeth of this creature is now in the collection of the Rev. Dr. Grainger, of Broughshane, as an evidence that the Siberian elephant (*Elephas primigenius*) once lived in Ireland, perhaps contemporary with the great Irish Elk (*Megaceros Hibernicus*). Several horns are reported to have been found with the Mammoth teeth, but the horns have not been identified. The gravels, &c., which crop out below the face of the cliff at this place yield a large number of shells, all of them being of a boreal or northern type, indicating that the climate at the time the shells lived was very much colder than it is now, and corresponded with the conditions under which the Mammoth is supposed to have lived. Leaving Ballyruther, and driving on to the Deer Park, within two miles of Glenarm, the party again separated—some to explore the landslips, some to botanise among the masses of fallen rocks that cover the under-cliffs, and others to enjoy the magnificent coast scenery from the best points of view; and thus the day was spent until the arrival at the Carnlough Hotel for luncheon. This collation was quickly disposed of, and the party having examined Mr. Reside's observatory, moved off for Garron Point. After a quiet walk through the castle grounds, the mural cliffs and other geological features of the place were examined, and the remainder of the day was spent in the drive from thence to Cushendall. The drive was exceedingly pleasant, the weather being all that could be desired for the thorough enjoyment of the magnificent scenery along this portion of the coast.

The capacity of the Glens of Antrim Hotel at Cushendall was severely tested, when some twenty-five tired naturalists, laden with rocks and plants, claimed the shelter of this quiet hostelry, in addition to about the same number already provided for there, but a little skilful management and the exercise of good humour, soon made all right for the night.

After an early breakfast on Wednesday morning, the party went by their conveyances to the new pier of the Glenariffe Iron Ore and Harbour Company at the south side of Red Bay. By the way specimens of the *Gymnadenia conopsea*, with its pretty purple spike of flowers and delicate perfume, were collected from the sandstone cliffs by the side of the road. Here also was obtained another rather rare plant — the hemp agrimony (*Eupatorium cannabinum*). Arriving at the pier, a special train, which had been very kindly provided for the party by J. J. Gardiner, Esq., C.E., the resident engineer of the company, was awaiting their arrival; and under his personal superintendence they were conveyed by the mineral railway up Glenariffe, tracing the mountain side overlooking the valley. The train was made up of mining trucks, but they were so fitted up with seats under Mr. Gardiner's directions, that all were most comfortable, and the steady motion of the waggon proved the superior construction of line, over which thousands of tons of iron ore are intended to be conveyed to the pier at Red Bay.

This railway ride was one of the most interesting features of the excursion. The magnificent valley looked exceedingly beautiful, and the railway train seemed to run along the face of the mountain, up a quick ascent, sweeping round projecting cliffs, past falling waters and over deep ravines, and then plunging into the deep plantations at the head of the glen, pulled up on the open hill-face to allow the party to pursue their investigations through the rocks, glens, waterfalls, and wild scenes of this remarkable place, which for extent, variety, and picturesque grandeur, are equalled by few of the more familiar and more frequented resorts of summer tourists. In and around Glenariffe several rare insects were captured, and among the ferns collected was the beautiful beech fern (*Polypodium Phegopteris*), which was secured after a very close search over the almost precipitous sides of the glen. Several rare flowering plants were also obtained here, among which were the golden rod (*Solidago Virgaurea*), the bog pimpernel (*Anagallis tenella*), and the frog orchis (*Habenaria Viridis*). A few hours were thus spent through the plantations, and then the whole party resumed their places on the cars, on the north side of the valley, and returned to Cushendall by way of Glenballyemon.

Frequent stoppages were made to explore the various points

of interest along the road, and to add to the number of specimens already collected. Very fine specimens of the common spleenwort (*Asplenium Trichomanes*), and the bladder fern (*Cystopteris fragilis*), occur in profusion about the rocks and caves along the river banks, where the kingfisher was started from its haunts by the exploring members of the party. Dinner was ready on arriving at the hotel about five o'clock, and the remainder of the evening was spent about the beach, till about nine o'clock, when the various collections were submitted in competition for the prize offered for the best series of geological specimens. In anticipation of this the competitors were for some time previous engaged in cleaning, washing, and preparing the specimens. For this purpose they had tubs of water, where they slopped and messed to the no small amusement of the domestics.

After a very close scrutiny of the specimens presented to them, the judges awarded the prize to Mr. R. M. Gilmore, who had collected 60 different forms of minerals and fossils.

Next morning (Thursday) the party left for Glendun valley, soon after breakfast, and rambling about the hedges collected a variety of ferns, including the sweet mountain fern (*Lastrea Oreopteris*). They then visited the caves at Cushendun, where they collected plants of the sea spleenwort (*Asplenium marinum*). In addition to the plants which have already been mentioned, the following, as well as many other rarities, were found during the excursion, viz., the dwarf elder (*Sambucus Ebulus*) and (*Lycopodium selaginoides.*) Returning to the hotel for luncheon the ladies' bouquets of wild flowers were placed upon the table, and the prize for the best awarded to Miss Davidson. This closed the business of the excursion, and the party left Cushendall with regret, and highly pleased with the courtesy of the hotel manager and his staff of assistants. The drive to Larne was very pleasant, and had a few breaks, such as to visit the Whiting Mill at Glenarm, &c. Larne was reached in time for the last train, which arrived at Belfast at 9.15.

On Saturday, 14th August to

GLENAVY AND RAM'S ISLAND.

A goodly number of the members assembled at the Ulster Railway Terminus to leave by the nine o'clock train. Soon after leaving Lisburn, Brookhill was pointed out as a place of some historic interest. It was here that the Irish forces under Sir Phelim O'Neill and Sir Con Magenis rendezvoused prior to their attack on Lisburn in May, 1641. After several ineffectual attempts to capture the town they succeeded in firing it, and in their retreat from it set fire to Brookhill House, which contained a valuable library of Lord Conway's. Arriving at Glenavy the party proceeded by the banks of the river which runs through the picturesque Glenconway to the shore of Lough Neagh. The heavy rain of the previous night had largely increased the volume of water in the stream, and so added much to the beauty of the "Leap" waterfall. On reaching Sandy Bay boats were awaiting the party to convey them to Ram's Island, which, as there was a favourable wind, was soon reached. After visiting "the cottage" and the round tower, the party spread themselves over the island, some to botanise among the shrubberies on the higher portions, and others to examine its geological features. The latter were rewarded by the finding of some exceedingly interesting fossil plant remains. These occurred in waterworn nodular massses of ironstone, which, when broken, exhibited impressions of leaves of exogenous plants in a remarkably fine state of preservation. Similar nodules have been found in this neighbourhood by Mr. M'Henry, of the Geological Survey. They were also found several years ago by Dr. James Bryce, F.G.S., formerly of Belfast, and by the late Mr. G. C. Hyndman. These fossils are probably of the same geological age as the iron ore of Ballypallidy and the County Antrim lignites, both of which are considered to be of Miocene age, and probably contemporaneous with the leaf beds of the Isle of Mull and the lignites of Bovey Tracy in Devonshire. Numerous specimens of the silicified wood, for which the Lough is so celebrated, were also found. The popular notion that the water of the lough possesses the property of converting submerged timber into stone has long since been shown to be erroneous, but the idea is still adhered to by many of the fishermen and others residing along the shores. From the fact of the silicified wood being found in detached and somewhat waterworn masses there can be little doubt of its having been derived from some pre-existing formation, and redeposited here. The origin of the wood and also of the nodules before referred to, are interesting subjects which require further elucidation. During the day the botanists of the party secured, amongst other rarities, specimens of the musk mallow *(Malva moschata)* on Ram's Island, and of the penny-cress *(Thlaspi arvense)* near to the mouth of the Glenavy river, the latter in fruit. In addition to these many of the commoner plants which affect lacustrine habitats were also obtained. Returning to the station by a different route a visit was paid to Whiteside's fort, a short distance from the road. It is a fair specimen of the remains of one of the ancient fortified residences which are common in various parts of the country. Belfast was again reached at a little after seven o'clock, a pleasant excursion having been thoroughly enjoyed by all present.

On Saturday, 4th September, to

THE KNOCKAGH.

The place selected for the sixth and last excursion season was the Knockagh, near Carrickfergus. A large party left by the 1-45 train for Carrickfergus Junction, and in less than half-an-hour were slowly ascending to the base of the cliffs. The broken nature of the ground made progress slow; but, as the party were not pushed for time, a close search was made for the ferns and other plants which affect such habitats. After passing along the base and visiting some of the caves on the way, the party scaled the cliffs at an accessible point near their northern extremity, and reached the table-land above. The rocks of the Knockagh closely resemble those of the Cave Hill, and consist of steep basaltic cliffs that tell of the action of the sea, which at a remote period washed their bases. The restless waves have rolled against the coast with a power almost resistless, and, as these escarpments testify, have made considerable inroads on the solid rock itself. The caves here excavated in the hard rock also indicate the action of the sea, and, with the similar ones which occur at the Cave Hill and at Woodburn, point to a time when the sea stood at a level relatively higher than it does at present. The Chalk and other sedimentary rocks which should appear below the basalt are almost entirely covered up and obscured by an enormous talus or undercliff, the result of many extensive slips and long-continued weathering. The botany of the Antrim coast is extremely interesting to those who delight in the study of our native plants. The sea cliffs yield a large number of species which are not found far inland, and the precipitous basaltic rocks of the Knockagh, which were once sea cliffs, are tenanted by several of them. *Solidago Virgaurea*, the only British representative of the large family of the Golden Rods, was found plentifully; also the Red Broomrape *(Orobanche rubra)*, and the Sea Beet *(Beta maritima)*. No county in the kingdom can boast as many species of Hawkweeds as Antrim, and two tolerably rare forms were found, viz.:—*Hieracium anglicum* and *H. murorum*. In addition to the above the cryptogamic flora of this hill is known to include several good species, but, as the time was rather limited to admit of the minute search requisite, nothing special was procured on this occasion. The edible mushroom, which cannot, however, be styled a rare species, was met with in some plenty and of remarkable size. One specimen found, measuring eight and a-half inches in diameter, and about the same height, was by far the largest that any of the party had ever seen. A pleasant walk on the close sward along the top of the cliffs afforded a magnificent view of the Lough and the surrounding country, and the return journey brought a most enjoyable and profitable afternoon's excursion to a close. It was a matter of congratulation among the members that the Club had been most successful this season with its excursions, both in the interest of the places visited, and the good weather with which they had been favoured, conducive alike to the better attendance, as well as to the enjoyment at these popular outings.

WINTER SESSION.

NOTE.—The authors of the various papers, of which abstracts are here appended, are alone responsible for the views expressed in them.

THE first meeting of the Session was held on 17th November, when the President, Rev. WILLIAM MACILWAINE, delivered an opening address.

After some introductory remarks with reference to the nature of their organisation, and the advantages offered by a " Club" such as theirs for the study of Natural History and connected subjects, he proceeded to give an outline of the proceedings of similar societies, and of the progress of scientific pursuits in general, throughout the past twelve months, commencing with a reference to the visit to Belfast, last year, by the British Association. In so doing, Dr. MacIlwaine drew attention to the inaugural address of the President of that society, during the present year, at the meeting held in Bristol, commenting on that of Sir John Hawkshaw as strongly contrasted with the now celebrated one of Professor Tyndall at Belfast. The former was eminently practical, and far from anything that could give offence, or even wound the prejudices of anyone who professed Christianity; while the latter was the tocsin of a religious and scientific warfare, which spread from Belfast as a centre to all parts of the civilised world. Sir J. Hawkshaw appeared to have these facts in view, in the opening sentence of his address, and all through it, when he referred to certain speculations bearing " on the mind, and perhaps even beyond the reach of mind." That the address of Dr. Tyndall was nothing less or more than a bold assertion of not only materialistic, but even of atheistic, principles was proved by the number and nature of replies which it had drawn forth, some of which were noticed at length, among others that of the Rev. J. Scott Porter, the protest of the Roman Catholic Bishops of Ireland, and a treatise by the Abbé Moigno, all of whom agreed in viewing that document as an attack on the fundamentals of Christianity. Dr. MacIlwaine called attention, with satisfaction, to the different attitude assumed of late by those who might be called the high priests of science, with the notable exception of Dr. Tyndall himself, who had renewed his attack, and endeavoured to re-open the whole atheistic and materialistic controversy in his article in the *Fortnightly Review* for this month. This article Dr. MacIlwaine designated as deeply offensive and insulting to the believers in the Divine records of Christianity, and proceeded to quote some of the language therein applied to them. Referring to the fact that because theologians, past and present had ventured to express any views whatever on the subjects of anthropology and cosmogony, Dr. Tyndall had compared them to "squatters" on land to which they had no title whatever, and asserted that expulsion therefrom was all that they deserved. To this Dr. MacIlwaine retorted by inquiring what title their opponents could show in the shape of any account of creation which could be compared with the Mosaic cosmogony, and asked was such to be found in the Shasters and Rig Veda of Hindostan, or the poetic dreams of Lucretius, the Atheist, whom Dr. Tyndall so lauded, or in the Book of Mormon? He went on to assert the claims of theology to be accounted a science, as distinct from religion, which was a matter between every creature and the Creator, and claimed for those who believed the Scripture record a right to modify their views by the light of reason and discovered fact, just as the philosophers of the present day did with regard to the science of half-a-century ago. Dr. MacIlwaine illustrated this portion of his subject by a full account of the so-called *Bathybius*, which Professor Huxley and Dr. Carpenter had so confidently asserted to be a protoplasmic substance—in fact, lower than the lowest previously known of all living beings, and named accordingly. It was now proved beyond the possibility of contradiction that this was an error, and Dr. Huxley himself had the honesty to avow his mistake. Dr. MacIlwaine reminded the meeting that when this very theory had been broached, in the apartment which they then occupied, in the year 1868, by Dr. Wyville Thompson, in giving an account of the results of the expedition in the *Porcupine*, it was met by one of their number—Mr. Samuel Stewart—by the remark that, instead of being the beginning, this sarcode matter might prove to be only the end of living organisms, being the product of decomposed mollusca and other denizens of the deep. This was now proved to be far nearer the truth than the theories of Drs. Huxley and Carpenter; and Dr. MacIlwaine argued from this fact in favour of philosophers being careful of making positive statements and despising the opinions of others. He went on to remark that the same might apply to the celebrated *Eozoon Canadense*, which Dr. Carpenter and others had so dogmatically pronounced to be the fossil remains of an organism, but which others doubted to be such. Dr. MacIlwaine strongly inclined to the negative in this question, and with their fellow-members, Messrs. Stewart and Wright, coincided in the views of Professor King, of Galway, and others who agreed with him, in opposing those of Dr. Carpenter. Dr. MacIlwaine next referred to the paper by Mr. Stewart, in "Science Gossip," wherein he combated with such success the views of Dr. Carpenter as to the formation of Greensand from the shells of Foraminifera. All these instances should teach scientific men caution in propounding new theories and opposing old. He also referred, at some length, to the recent proceedings of other scientific bodies, remarking with satisfaction their practical character in contrast to the novel theories of so-called scientists. The proceedings at the Social Science Congress at Brighton were referred to as an illustration, and the speech of Mr. Gladstone on "Science and Art," at Greenwich, was also quoted in favour of due regard being shown to the Christian revelation. Dr. MacIlwaine next reviewed, at some length, a remarkable treatise which had recently appeared, entitled "The Unseen Universe," and which was said to be the joint production of two of the most eminent physicists of the day—Professors Tait and Clarke Maxwell. The conclusions at which these distinguished philosophers had arrived, so far from impugning Revelation, distinctly avowed the agreement of the Christian Scriptures with the latest and most recondite theories of the ablest scientific men of the day. The address concluded with an appeal to both the students of science and the theologians of the period to cultivate friendly relations, instead of provoking conflict, where both should be viewed as contingents of one great army whose common object was the promotion and defence of truth. The affairs of the Club, Dr. MacIlwaine stated to be in a highly prosperous state. Their members numbered above 200. One thousand copies of the "Guide Book" prepared for the visit of the British Association had been sold, and the remaining copies were still on sale. He remarked, with allowable pride, on the contributions to science by several members of the Club, to Messrs. Stewart and Wright's papers on the Mosses of the Province of Ulster, and on Foraminifera and other microzoa, and to the researches of Mr. Swanston in the fossils of the lower Silurian deposits. The address, which took an hour in delivery, was listened to throughout with marked attention and interest by all present.

On 15th December (William Gray, Esq., M.R.I.A, Vice-president, in the Chair), Dr. J. M. JOHNSTON SCOTT read a paper on "The Vegetable Parasites of the Human Body."

The sketch given by Dr. Scott of the vegetable organisms which live upon the human subject, showed clearly the importance of the study of these structures, on sanitary grounds, as well as from a scientific point of view. He minutely described their natural history, social and geographical distribution, as well as the peculiar effects produced by their presence in the skin. The *Saprophytes*, or division of parasites which live on the dead and decomposing human body, were passed over with a mere allusion to the labours devoted to their study by several eminent continental workers in this department of natural history. The classes of plants called by botanists *Cellulares* and *Thallophytes* contain all those which are found on the living human body. They have neither stem, leaves, nor stomata. The mycelium, which is analogous to the root fibres of more highly-organised plants, branches out in all directions underneath the cuticle or outer layer of the skin, on which the plants are found, and this arrangement is found to have a different aspect in the different species of these fungi. The spores or germinating cells of the six species of *Dermatophytes* which occur on the human subject were described in minute detail, and an interesting account of the development, life, and effects of each of the forms brought the paper to a close. An animated discussion followed, and the election of a number of new members terminated the business of the meeting.

On 5th January the Chair was occupied by the President (Rev. Dr. MacIlwaine), and a paper was read by MR. ADAM SPEERS, B.Sc., on the "Natural History of Water, and its Effects in Nature."

Among other facts, the reader stated that there is no compound substance so widely diffused and so all-pervading as water. A very large percentage of the bodies of animals and plants consist of it. It is also an essential part of the atmosphere. It has been calculated that the ocean makes up the 1-1786th part of the weight of the entire globe. The rocky masses which constitute the crust are steeped in water, and it flows over the surface in streams of all sizes, from the merest runnels to the mightiest rivers. Thales fancied two thousand years ago that it was the principle of everything; that plants and animals were merely condensed water, and that they were all resolved into it after death. His knowledge of physics and chemistry was, of course, very slender; but, although wrong in his belief, he was impressed evidently with the truth that this substance is an essential part of every living thing. Water exists in three distinct states—gaseous, liquid, and solid. Pure aqueous vapour is quite invisible, and is lighter than either oxygen or nitrogen; hence a falling and a low barometer indicates rain. The latent heat of aqueous vapour is very great, nearly 1,000 degrees Fahrenheit. This, which simply maintains it in the state of gas, without raising its temperature, is given back again as sensible heat when condensation ensues; and thus the heat of a tropical sun, bottled up, as it were, in vapour raised there from the surface of the sea, warms the air of higher latitudes where it is condensed. In this manner aqueous vapour becomes a great modifier of climate. After describing the properties of liquid water, the reader observed that owing to its high specific heat, the sea is a vast storehouse for the heat radiated by the sun within the tropics; and pointed out how countries surrounded by the ocean in temperate latitudes, contrast as to the equability of their climates, with other places on the same parallel, in the heart of a continent. The curious behaviour of fresh water near the freezing temperature, and in the act of freezing, as well as the peculiar deportment of salt water in like circumstances, was mentioned as a clear proof of creative design, no matter how some learned physicists might deride the idea. Dr. Carpenter has shown by a beautiful experiment, which the lecturer described, that the circulation of the waters of the ocean, from the equator to the poles and back again, depends mainly upon the fact that salt water, unlike that which is fresh, contracts all the way down to its freezing point. Having adverted to the climatic effects of oceanic circulation, the reader described the properties of ice, the effects of frost and glaciers, snow, &c. He then pointed out the chemical constitution of water, and its action as a solvent on many of the solid materials in the crust. Its effect when charged with carbonic acid upon felspar and calcic carbonate was specially referred to. Limestone districts contain caverns and underground rivers, as well as beautiful grottos, adorned within in the most fantastic manner, by stalactites and stalagmites. The water was shown to have actually made the grottos and caverns, and the under-ground water courses, by dissolving away limestone; and the stalactites and stalagmites, by the evaporation of the water dropping from the roofs upon the floors. The petrifying and fossilising power of water having been described, it was stated as the reader's opinion that the silicification of soft substances like the bodies of echinoderms, mollusca, and sponges, had been effected by a kind of endosmose, the body of the animal acting as a sort of membrane, and retaining silica, which is a colloidal substance when in the soluble state. How it became changed to the hard and insoluble variety, is a problem still requiring elucidation. The formation of the particles of pisolitic and oolitic rocks, and the cementing together of the mineral constituents of all water-formed accumulations, depend upon the solvent action of water, and its power of precipitating salts from solution, as it trickles among these solid particles. Its mechanical force as a moving liquid constituting it at once a destructive and a renovating agent having been dwelt upon, a concluding reference was made to the oceans, lakes, and rivers of the globe as forming a world in which numberless forms of life abound. Late soundings have shown that organisms exist at nearly all depths. The tiniest creatures in the ocean have produced most extensive and important masses of rock; for example, beds of Chalk, which consist of the limestone remains of microscopic Foraminifera; and also Coral Reefs, some of which are as much as a thousand miles in length. Diatoms, a kind of microscopic vegetables, with flinty coverings, have produced effects quite as marvellous. These lowly organisms— some animal and others vegetable — can propagate themselves with astonishing rapidity, and it is part of their vital processes to separate from solution carbonate of lime or silica, according to their nature. As a parallel to Archimedes, who said " he could move the earth if he had a lever long enough and a proper fulcrum," Bischof has said, " Give us a mailed animalcule, and with it we will in a short time separate all the limestone and flint from the ocean."

On 2nd February, the President, Rev. William MacIlwaine, D.D., in the Chair, a paper on " The Beginnings of Life" was read by Mr. W. J. BROWNE, M.A.

The paper treated of some of the lower forms of living matter, of their relations to inorganic matter and to one another, and of the question in debate between the two schools of biologists as to the origin of life. The reader showed that the definitions hitherto given of life are defective, and leave it as much a mystery as ever. Life being an abstract term can be satisfactorily explained only by considering the material substances in which it inheres. Now, the differences which distinguish living from non-living bodies may be summed up in the characteristic functions of nutrition and reproduction, and in certain relations to the surrounding world. Living bodies grow by assimilating the particles of their food to their own material, they have the power of producing other living bodies, and they have some property inherent in them of resisting the physical and chemical agencies which act on them in common with inorganic matter. Two theories put forward to explain the nature of life were briefly referred to—the physical, by which life is regarded as a form of energy or motion, and co-ordinate with heat, light, and electricity; and the vital, which regards life as a separate principle, different in kind, and not merely in degree, from the physical forces. Various typical forms of living bodies were next described—the Torula, or yeast plant, the cause of fermentation, as the type of fungi; the Protococcus, which forms the green scum on walls, roofs, and trees, after rain, as the type of green plants; and the Amœba, or proteus animalcule, as the type of animals. The two first are characterised as plant-cells, by possessing a mass of protoplasm enclosed in a cellulose sac; the last as an animal consisting of a mere mass of living, moving, apparently structureless, protoplasm. Of aggregations of such cells as the Amœba the animal body is composed, and almost perfect specimens of the Amœba may be obtained from the colourless corpuscles of the blood, showing our affinity to and identity with the very lowest forms of life. Bacteria were next considered. These are the organisms found in decaying infusions of organic matter, and are of various forms—sometimes short staff-like bodies, sometimes spiral structures; all exhibit movements plainly due to their vitality. The result of their life is putrefaction; but some hold that they are rather the effect than the cause. If an infusion of hay or turnip be boiled and kept in a moderately warm place exposed to the air, it soon becomes turbid with Bacteria. The question arises—Where did these bodies come from? This is the great subject of discussion of the present day—the question of spontaneous generation. After tracing the experiments of Redi, Needham, Buffon, Spallanzani, &c., the reader referred to the test experiment appealed to by both the advocates and opponents of spontaneous generation. Fill a flask with some organic infusion, boil it, and, while the whole flask is filled with steam, either hermetically seal the flask, or plug it with cotton wool. Now, Pasteur and his followers, including Professors Huxley and Tyndall, assert that the solution will remain clear and lifeless, keep it as long as you will. Bastian affirms that in such a flask living organisms will soon appear, being formed by some chemical or other process from the particles of the infusion. Both analogy and the weight of the evidence are opposed to this belief, and the probabilities are strongly in favour of the doctrine held by the other side, that life always proceeds from pre-existing life, "*Omne vivum ex vivo.*" Many diseases, such as scarlet fever, cholera, cattle plague, are supposed to be due to germs of the organisms previously described contained in the atmosphere or in food or drink. Hence the subject has important practical bearings. The study of these minute organisms, and the question as to their origin, force on the mind, whatever view may be taken, a conviction of the existence and intelligence of a great First Cause, the source of all life, and fountain of all power.

On 8th March the Chair was occupied by the President (Rev. William MacIlwaine, D.D.), and a lecture was delivered by the Rev. GEORGE ROBINSON, M.A., "On the Birds of Lough Neagh."

The lecturer stated that he had selected to bring under the notice of the Club a short account of the birds of Lough Neagh, chiefly because there had been nothing written specially on the ornithology of that lake, and he thought it was desirable that there should be some record of the birds that frequented it, before that lake should become a thing of the past, as the drainage of the lake had been spoken of and written about, and no doubt, in course of time, would be effected. It had been his lot to live for many years within three miles of the southern shores of the lake, so that he had frequent opportunities of being acquainted with its birds. On referring to the "Guide to Belfast and the adjacent Counties," by your Club, you will see that the number of birds recorded for those counties is 185, and for the lake and its southern shores for a mile inland the number is 103. Of these 68 breed. The lecturer called attention to several of the birds which frequent the lake, one of which was pointed out as especially interesting and almost peculiar to it—the Yellow Wagtail—of which a specimen was exhibited. This bird is found as a summer visitant in both England and Scotland, but the only part of Ireland in which it had been hitherto found breeding is the northern and southern shores and neighbourhood of the lake. Another interesting bird found breeding within a mile of the lake is the Siskin. It has also been found breeding near Belfast, as made known by Mr. Bristow, and also in County Wicklow, confirming the surmise of that excellent naturalist, of whom Belfast has reason to be proud— Mr. Thompson—that it would, some time or other, be found breeding in Ireland. Another bird, which we can claim as breeding in this district, is the Woodcock, which breeds regularly at Churchhill, about a mile inland from the lake. Of gulls, two species breed on the islands in the lake, the Lesser Black-backed Gull and the Black-headed Gull. The common Tern breeds, but the Arctic Tern, so nearly allied to it, has not been observed at the lake. The common Sandpiper breeds abundantly, and the Redshank sparingly on the southern shores. This lake is also the breeding place of another very beautiful bird, the Great Crested Grebe, and it is to be feared that in course of time this bird will become everywhere very scarce, as the skin is used largely by the ladies as material for muffs and tippets. Another grebe, in beautiful summer plumage, was exhibited—the Horned Grebe—shot some years ago on the lake, and the only instance recorded of the bird being found in Ireland in that plumage. In the winter season the lake was the great stronghold of the Duck tribe, eight different kinds—the Wild Duck, Widgeon, Teal, Pochard, Scaup, Tufted Duck, Golden Eye, and Shoveler—have been found frequenting it, all abundant, except one, the Shoveler, and of these, only two species breed, the Wild Duck and Teal. The Wild Duck was the most numerous, occurring in multitudes; Widgeon nearly as numerous; then Tufted Ducks, Golden Eyes, the Pochards next, and the Scaup Duck the fewest of all. Of all the ducks nothing can surpass the Pochard for table purposes; the worst of all the ducks, being nearly as bad eating as a gull, is the Golden Eye. The Wild Swan visits the lake every winter; there was a flock of 100 on it this season. The species, I believe, is Bewick's swan. I have never seen any other kind. The lecturer stated that he had made a list of the birds frequenting and visiting the lake, and occurring on the South, within a mile of the shore. He would now hand that list to the Hon. Secretaries of the Club, to be retained as evidence of the birds that are at present to be found in that district. But when, in the course of time, rich meadows and pleasant homesteads and villages should take the place of the present expanse of water most of the birds would disappear, and then it might be desirable that there should be forthcoming some record of the birds which lived upon and visited the lake. An interesting discussion and the election of several new members brought the meeting to a close.

On 29th March, the President, Rev. William MacIlwaine, D.D., in the Chair, a paper was read by REV. JOHN BRISTOW A.M., entitled "Practical Hints to Collectors of Lepidoptera."*

When I was a school-boy almost every school-boy of my acquaintance was making a collection, either of birds' eggs or of butterflies and moths, yet I learn from the Secretary of the Club, that while among its members there are distinguished botanists, geologists, and archæologists, there are but very few who have paid any attention to entomology. At first sight this appears strange; amongst my boyish friends neither botany or geology were as attractive as entomology, and certainly, so far as beauty of form and colour go, I may challenge any collection of dried plants or drier fossils, to compare with a collection of well preserved insects. That a branch of natural history, which to the beginner is so very attractive and interesting, should have failed to secure a very much larger band of votaries amongst us, while other branches —which in the beginning are less attractive, however absorbing they may afterwards become—have many adherents, seems to me to be due, to a great extent, to ignorance. Ignorance of what may be done in this department, even in a comparatively barren locality, and ignorance of how to do it.

I think, therefore, the best way in which I can give a stimulus to the study of entomology in connection with this society, is to show practically what work may be done, and how to do it.

It has often been said to me by persons, when looking over my collection, and these persons well informed on many other matters, "Surely these insects are not to be met with in this country. I never saw these large and beautiful moths flying about." And when asked how many different kinds of butterflies and moths were to be met with in this country, the answer given was often, "about half a dozen butterflies, and a few dingy moths that come to the lamps on a summer's evening, beside the troublesome little clothes' moths." All small moths are by them classed in that mischievous brotherhood, clothes' moths.

* In accordance with a special resolution of the Club this paper is printed *in extenso*.

The collector who seeks only the day-flying Lepidoptera, in the imago state, soon comes to the end of his captures and finds his occupation gone. He likewise, however enthusiastic, can only follow his pursuit at certain seasons of the year, and in certain states of the weather, and speedily retires from a field of investigation so limited in extent and intermittent in its opportunity of pursuit. The collector who goes a step farther, and endeavours to add the night-fliers, has a wider scope, and for a season or two may have enough to occupy his leisure time during the summer months. But what of the long dreary months of winter! when but one or two species of moths are found, and they at rare intervals on mild evenings, and so he also soon tires, having exhausted his mine of interest.

The collection I exhibit this evening will, however, convince most of you that there is in this department of Field Naturalist science sufficient to engage the attention, not only for one or two years, but for many years; and to show that the lepidopterist may have occupation every month in the year, in winter as well as in summer, nay, I would say must occupy himself every month if he is to make a complete, or nearly complete, collection of the insects of his locality. Of this collection every specimen has been captured in Ireland, and with few exceptions every one captured by myself. A few specimens I received from Rev. Joseph Greene, author of "Insect-hunter's Companion," a few from Mrs. Battersby, of Rathowen, Co. Meath, and a few from Mr. Birchall, who has done more for Irish Lepidoptera than any other. All these were most liberal in sending me valuable specimens unsolicited; but the sum total of the specimens not taken by myself would not amount to 12. Most of the specimens are from 15 to 20 years old, yet they retain their colour and freshness as if taken yesterday. I would add, this is far from a complete collection of the Lepidoptera of Ireland, or even of this immediate neighbourhood; fully one-half more kinds have been captured and recorded as Irish, and species which are unrepresented in my collection, have been captured by Mr. Brunton, Glenarm Castle, and by Mr. John

Preston, jun., Dunmore, Belfast. I believe that were the collecting of Lepidoptera taken up intelligently and enthusiastically by some of the younger members of the Belfast Naturalists' Field Club, one hundred species might be added to those which are found in my collection. The County Antrim, with many rich localities, has been quite unexplored by me; the whole basin of Lough Neagh, rich in flora and in birds, must from analogy be rich in insect life, and that remains, so far as I am concerned, a "terra incognita." I exhibit of butterflies, 30 species; of sphinges, 14; of other moths 284, making a total of 314 species, and 1100 specimens, and these are only the Macro-lepidoptera; the Pyrales, Plumes, Tineidæ, Tortricidæ, and Veneers, far more in number, and in the exquisite beauty of their minute perfections by far excelling their larger brethren, still remain to be investigated with ever increasing delight and admiration.

Ignorance of the manner of collecting and preserving insects has also, I believe, prevented many from becoming collectors. A gorgeous Fritillary (*A. Paphia*) as it glances past in the golden splendour of its new-born beauty, or a noble Admiral (*V. Atalanta*) as it quivers its velvet wings in the bright sunlight on a rich dahlia, is a sight on which the most insensible could not gaze without admiration; but the same insect, with a large pin stuck through it, with crushed and rubbed wings, the brightness of its colours almost gone through bad catching, and the symmetry of its form destroyed by bad setting, is a very different spectacle. And no wonder that the contrast between the beauty of the living and the deformity of the dead is sufficient to turn many in disgust from a pursuit which takes away life from some of God's most beautiful creatures, and at the same time destroys the beauty it wishes to preserve.

Of the butterflies in my collection (*V. Antiopa*) Camberwell Beauty, was captured by a nursery-maid on the Shore Road, near Greencastle, and given to her young master, a boy who was making a collection. He, in usual school-boy fashion, stuck it unset into his box, and, having tired of the whole thing, it was handed over to me. I believe this is the second recorded capture of this rare and beautiful butterfly in Ireland, the other specimen having been taken in the south. *V. Io* (Peacock Butterfly) though very common in the neighbourhood of Dublin and further south, is almost unknown in the northern parts of Ireland. My friend, the late Mr. G. C. Hyndman, told me many years ago that he had not heard of a specimen being taken in the neighbourhood of Belfast for twenty years. The finest specimen in my collection flew into my drawing-room at Knockbreda Rectory, as if to make the acquaintance of one who would appreciate its beauty and perpetuate its fame. This specimen was evidently fresh from the pupa, and therefore must have been bred in the neighbourhood. Of the other butterflies *C. Edusa* and *Hyale, G. Rhamni, L. Sinapis, H. Tithonus, C. Davus, M. Athalia,* and *Artemis,* and *T. Rubi,* have all been captured in more southern counties; but Rev. George Robinson informed me that he saw the latter (*T. Rubi*) in abundance on the rhododendrons at Tynan Abbey, Co. Armagh.

Of the butterflies, a collector should, I think, be certain of securing his first year in the region over which the Club extends its rambles, of the PIERIDÆ—*Brassicæ, Rapæ, Napi, Cardamines.*

,, VANESSIDÆ—*Atalanta, Urticæ,* perhaps *Cardui.*

,, HIPARCHIÆ—*Janira, Semele, Hyperanthus, Ægeria, Megæra.*

,, POLYOMMATI—*Alexis, Alsus,* perhaps *Argiolus, Phlæas.*

,, ARGYNNIDÆ—*Paphia* and *Aglaia,* with the abundant Lesser Heath (*C. Pamphilus*).

Of these, Brassicæ, Rapæ, and Urticæ will be easiest taken in the larva or pupa state; Alsus is to be found in any quantity on the sea coast, in the neighbourhood of Black and White Heads; Paphia, in the glades of woods. Of the SPHINGES, a collector should obtain his first year *S. Populi,* either in the larva or pupa state, or in the imago on the stems of trees or on palings. *M. Stellatarum* will surely be seen somewhere, flying briskly over inland rocks, or sea-side cliffs, stopping for a few moments to extract honey from the blossoms of bladder campion or sea pink, or, perhaps, hovering over a bed of petunias or verbenas in our gardens. It may, however, often be seen and not caught. *M. bombyliformis*, is also certain to be met with in its haunts, by those who look for it at the proper season, flying backwards and forwards with great rapidity in some narrow woody glade, or along the bed of some stream that passes through a glen. It requires a trained eye readily to distinguish it from a bee, and a trained hand to catch it as it darts past. It may at once be known from a humble bee, however, on the wing, by the projecting antennæ which it carries as a horn in front. *S. bembiciformis* I have found abundantly in the larva state in old willow trees, everywhere. The best way to obtain good specimens is to examine the stems of the trees, and find where the larvæ are at work; leave them in peace until they have changed into pupæ, when the piece of wood in which they are may be sawed out with the pupæ undisturbed within. *Z. Filipendulæ*—the only one of the genus I have found in the North of Ireland, is abundant both in the hilly and sea-side districts. Of the other *Sphingidæ*, *C. Elpenor* has been taken not rarely in the larva state around Belfast. I have captured seven specimens in the imago state the same evening, hovering over a plant of rhododendron, in the County Wicklow. *C. Procellus* I have from County Meath and further South, where it is not uncommon, taken generally at honeysuckle. I have no doubt it is to be found, if looked for, where there are large beds of the plant on which the larva feeds, the yellow bed-straw. *S. Convolvuli* has been taken by Mr. Preston at Dunmore, Antrim Road, at verbenas, in the evening. One specimen taken by me at Glenarm, at rest; and two at phlox the same evening in County Wicklow. I can give no directions for the capture of the other Sphinges I exhibit, *A. Atropos*, *S. Ligustri*, and *Ocellatus*, and the still more rare *Livornica*. The last two were taken at light at night. The collector must patiently wait and watch, before, either from larvæ or from captures of the imago, he is able to add these splendid specimens to his collection. They are, however, to be obtained in Ireland, as you may see.

Of the *Bombyces* a considerable number may be captured the

first year, and among them as a certainty *S. Carpini*, *L. Quercus*, and *Rubi*, which, with the Tiger moth and the Ermines *caja*, *Plantaginis*, *fuliginosa*, *Jacobææ*, will make an attractive drawer. Time would not permit me to go through all the families thus. I would, therefore, briefly summarise. An energetic collector should in this immediate neighbourhood be able to place in his cabinet the first year, 17 Butterflies, 5 Sphinges, 80 stout-bodied Moths, Bombyces, and Noctuæ, and 35 or 40 Geometræ.

I must now say a few words with respect to the mode of capture, and this I will consider under three heads—capture of imago, pupa, and larva.

I.—As to the capture of the day-flying imago, I always use a ring net, two or three tight-fitting tin boxes, with false bottoms of perforated cork, and a small collecting box, corked both above and below, made like a backgammon board. The net is made of strong brass wire, with a joint in the centre, so that when folded it is in the form of a sickle, and hooks on my shoulder under my coat, where it may be carried without inconvenience and without observation. When it is opened two rings, formed by the ends of the wire, come into line, and fit on the end of an ordinary walking-stick. This net can be unfolded in a moment, even when the collector is at full speed, and can be used, either in the hand without a stick or fixed on a stick, without a moment's delay. Its simplicity and cheapness also commend it. The close-fitting tin boxes I use as killing boxes—two or three of these will be found sufficient. They may be made with a perforated bottom of tin, as described in Mr. Greene's Insect-hunter's Companion. I use a bottom of perforated cork. Under this bottom is placed poison, and when an insect is captured and shut into the box a very short time is sufficient to render it insensible. It should as soon as possible be removed to the cork collecting box, and then transfixed with a fine entomological pin, to prevent the down on the wings from being rubbed off by knocking about loose in the box. There should be poison also in a corner of the collecting box, to prevent the return of the insect to life after it has been impaled. If on opening the killing box it is found that an insect is not required it may be left on the grass, and in a short time will again return to life.

There are three different poisons I have tried; each has its advantages and disadvantages. *Chloroform* is the most immediate in its effects, and this is a decided advantage; but it is so volatile that there is much waste in using it, and the insects are apt to come to life after being apparently dead. The insects that are really killed by its agency are likewise rigid and difficult to set properly without being relaxed. Bruised *laurel leaves* have the advantage of preserving the insect in a flaccid condition, even for days, and may, in fact, be employed to relax rigid insects; but this agent is not so rapid in its soporific effects, and there are certain kinds of moths the colour of which is ruined by it. *Cyanide of potassium* is the agent I most generally use, and on the whole find it best. I do not mix it with lime or whiting, but use it in the dry pure state—wrapping up one of the pieces in blotting paper (as it is liquescent). I place it under the cork bottom of my killing boxes, and another piece in the corner of my collecting box, and in most cases I find it to answer every purpose. There are some few insects, however, which seem to have the power of almost entirely resisting its effects, one of which is the Burnet Hawk (*Z. Filipendulæ*), and where insects are in a very active state it is scarcely rapid enough in its effects to save them from much loss of beauty; I therefore carry, besides the cyanide, a small bottle of chloroform—a drop or two of it is quite sufficient to quiet the most restless insect almost immediately, and the cyanide then completes the work. Many have complained to me of the return of the insects to life again, after having been for a long time exposed to the influence of the cyanide. I think it will be found in these cases that the cyanide was mixed, and not used in its pure state. If the insect is taken out soon no doubt it will revive; but I have not found this to be the case where it has been left a reasonable time under the influence.

And now a word about the capture itself of the day-flying

Lepidoptera. I know no excitement more delightful than a hard chase after a desired insect. I will describe one. It is a bright day in the last week of April or the beginning of May, and with net and boxes you start for the nearest heathery mountain or moor. On your way to the hunting-ground you have seen, perhaps, a few specimens of the Small White (*P. Rapæ*) and of the Nettle (*V. Urticæ*), and may have been fortunate enough to have met with an early born beauty of the Orange Tip (*E. Cardamines*). Every flying thing has been an attraction; all are novelties so early in the year. Now you have reached the unenclosed heath, and the elasticity alike of the earth and the air gives fresh buoyancy to your tread and spirits. As your eye roams over the brown expanse before you there appears in the distance an object which fixes your attention—it is a butterfly or moth, flying rapidly and approaching. What can it be? A Nettle Tortoise-shell? No. It is too large; its wings are too round; there is too much flapping movement; the colour is too pale. Is it a hybernated Painted Lady (*V. Cardui*)? It is like it in colour, but the flight is not so smooth, and now it has swerved out of the path in which you had placed yourself to intercept it, and as it passes you see distinctly the round eye-like markings and deep orange under wings which proclaim a male Emperor. At once you give chase, and as the course leads across the mountain slope you just hold your own, with all your striving it *will* keep about two yards beyond reach of your net; but, foolish moth, it turns down the hill; the falling ground enables you to increase your speed, and as you near the prize on which your eyes are fixed your grasp tightens on the net. It is now in reach; you make a swoop; an inch, nay, only half an inch too short—the net is empty—the moth flies on. But now it has turned up the hill, you struggle a few yards with failing knees in the direction it has taken, and fall all of a heap upon the heather, without breath, without muscles, as limp as the empty net which lies beside or beneath you.

Many such chases have I had; but many successful ones too. On one occasion, with my eye fixed on the insect, I was conscious there was a sheet of water suddenly gleaming below, and leaped, to find myself up to my neck in a bog hole, and I almost fancied I heard the Emperor say "ha-ha-ha" as it flew serenely on its royal path. For the capture of day-fliers I have no specific directions; but a quick eye, a swift foot, and a sure hand, acquired by practice, and the caution—never to chase an insect if there is a hope of your catching it without a chase, nor to rush rashly forward, when it is about to settle, so as to frighten it away.

As to the night fliers, there are many different modes of capture, and some species will be taken by one method which will never be taken by another. In the early evening, from about eight o'clock, Geometridæ may be taken on the wing by means of the net. I have found a hedge-row to be the best locality, especially if near a wood or plantation. As you walk along the row, about two yards from the hedge the moths will be distinctly seen, between you and the dark background of the hedge, or if they rise higher, against the sky. Many Noctuæ may also thus be taken, their time of flight is however later, not sooner than half-past eight o'clock in the summer months. Flowers are the feeding grounds of most moths, and should be carefully watched. Early in the evening, in the twilight, many may be captured hovering over the flowers or lighted on them; later in the evening, with the aid of a lantern, they may also be found, and many secured at rest feasting on their favourite sweets. If fortunate enough to capture any of the larger Sphinges on the wing, it will be at flowers either in early evening or early morning. I captured two fine specimens of *S. Convolvuli* the same evening at one plant, and another evening seven specimens of *C. Elpenor*, while *C. Procellus* is generally taken at honeysuckle. The flower resorts which I have found most prolific are the following. In gardens—beds of petunias, carnations, verbenas; shrubs—arbutus, rhododendron, raspberry, gooseberry, privet hedges: of all flower baits, however, the Sally bloom in early spring, and the Ivy bloom in autumn, are by far the most productive. With reference to the former, you may take your stand net in hand at the lee side of the tree which is in bloom, and capture the moths as they arrive, winging their flight against the wind, following the rich honey aroma to its source; or, the sprays of blossom may be examined with a lantern and the insects boxed when at rest. Another method, which I have never tried, is to spread a sheet beneath the tree and beat the branches, when the moths will drop on the sheet, where they may be easily seen and taken. The moths seldom fly away after having settled either on Ivy or Sally bloom, but drop when touched. In autumn the numbers of living insects which are to be found at the Ivy bloom far exceeds anything I have seen elsewhere, on a well covered Ivy wall hundreds of moths may be seen. On a warm, calm evening almost every tuft of blossom will have one or two, and these may be leisurely examined and only such specimens as are required be boxed. Care should be taken, however, not to throw the light of the lantern on those that you are not ready to attend to, or these will quickly drop off among the thick green leaves and be lost. The third method of capturing the night fliers is at sugar. Take some of the coarsest and darkest brown sugar from the bottom of a sugar hogshead, pour a little water on it and boil slowly until it becomes of the consistency of treacle, then add when it is cold a tea spoonful of rum or whisky, to increase the diffusiveness of the smell, and with this paint the stems of the trees, I have found long perpendicular bands from a height of four or five feet to the ground, and about two inches broad, better than shorter and broader patches. I always put the sugar on the sheltered side of the tree, that the moths may not be disturbed by the breeze. The painting should be finished early in the evening before the moths begin to fly. Sugaring will be found almost, if not entirely, useless, on an evening when the moon is shining, or when the wind is easterly or north-easterly. When the trees are visited always begin your examination from the bottom, carefully shading the light from those above. If you begin at the top the moths below will silently slip away. In taking the moths at sugar, it is only necessary to hold an open box below them, and touch them gently with the lid when they will drop] into the box. I find in my note book the following entry regarding an evening's capture at sugar—" 17th June. Sugared eight trees—on visiting them found 96 moths, amongst which were *T. derasa, A. putris, A. suffusa, A. exclamationis, corticeæ, G. trilinea, T. pronuba, M. oleraceæ, Brassicæ, thalassina, C. cubicularis, L. comma, P. meticulosa, H. protea, X. rurea, polyodon, N. plecta.* At flowers the same evening *C. umbratica* in considerable numbers, and *C. Elpenor.*" LIGHT is another trap for catching moths. The plan I have found best is a moderator lamp on a small table at the window, with a looking glass behind to reflect the light. Candles are apt to be blown out, and many moths will singe their wings unless the light is protected from them. Two inverted tumblers on the table, with a piece of cotton wool dipped in chloroform, to which each moth as captured is at once transferred, will enable the collector to examine at rest each specimen, and reject any that he may not require before life is extinct. If the moths are coming in thickly, as they sometimes do, it is very difficult to examine each one in the net without letting many escape, and the moths are excited and restless, and without the chloroform will not remain sufficiently quiet to permit of an inspection. I have read an extract from my note book about sugaring, I will now read one about an evening's captures at light. "June 11th—Found at 8½ this evening, a fine specimen of *Colias Edusa* upon the under side of a leaf of digitalis on the road side. A great deal of thunder and lightning with rain throughout the evening, during which the moths came into the room in immense numbers. I am sure there were not less than 50 of the Ermines, *S. menthrasti* and *lubricepeda*, in the room at once. Captured specimens of *C. Chamomillæ, R. tenebrosa, A. triplasia, L. comma, M. protea,* and *oleracea, A. Rumicis,* and *M. Atriplicis.*" Both these extracts are concerning captures in the County Wicklow, where I was curate at the time. I have, however, a note of an evening's sugaring last year, late in the season, in the neighbourhood of Belfast. " 30th Sept., 1875. At sugar at Chichester Park. *A. Saucia* and *suffusa,* very fine, also *M. Oxyacanthæ, O. lota,* and *macilenta, N. xanthographa,* and *P. meticulosa.*

O

II.—Larva rearing. The rearing of specimens from the larva has many advantages ; by this means insects are secured in a state of perfection which is never to be found in those taken on the wing, and many insects of great beauty may be obtained in abundance from the larvæ, which are seldom to be met with in the imago state, e.g., the Tiger Moth *(A. caja)* is one of the most showy and beautiful of our moths, but we seldom find it in its perfect state, and when so found, much of the rich soft down is rubbed off the wings. This is also true of the Buff Tip, *(P. bucephala)*, yet any collector may, with ordinary care, obtain his first year as many specimens of both these handsome moths as he requires. The larva of *A. caja* actually obtrudes itself upon his observation, in early spring and summer, on almost every dock, or when larger crawling across his path. The larva of *bucephala* may be taken in the autumn. Some beech, or oak, or elm, or lime, for they are omnivorous, may be observed to have one of its branches denuded of leaves, there will be found a colony of Buff Tips at work, and almost any number may be obtained. It is also most interesting to watch the transformation of the larvæ, the changing of skins, and varying colours and appearances after each change, the grotesque attitudes of some, as *C. vinula* or *N. zic-zac*. I will give another extract from my journal, to illustrate the interesting scenes which take place at times in the breeding cage. " May 5th. Got two larvæ on heather, pale brown, dorsal line and sub-dorsal pale, lateral line broad white, oblique strokes meeting on back, particularly conspicious on 11th and 12th segments, where they are black. I have just been watching one of these changing its skin, the process seems a painful one, the larva for a long time going through violent exertions, drawing in its sides as if taking a long breath, and then inflating them until a liquid exudes from the five fore segments, as if perspiration from over exertion. When this had continued for about fifteen minutes, the skin burst at the juncture of the first and second segments, and by degrees the larva crawled forth, apparently much larger than it had been before the skin had come off. The old head, however, still remained, but this it got rid of by a violent jerking gesticulation, and then walked away, much paler in colour than it had been before its moult." Most of the *Bombyces* are much more easily obtained in the larva than in the imago state, and almost all exhibited by me in drawer No. 4 have been thus reared, including *Quercus, Rubi, Potatoria, Carpini, Caja, Jacobææ, Fuliginosa, Plantaginis, Menthrastri, Lubricepeda, Antiqua, Coryli, Pudibunda, Vinula, Bucephala, Dictæ, Zic-zac, Camelina.* The methods of finding the larvæ are—(1st) searching, by which I mean examining plants with eye and hand for the larvæ. If any plant is observed eaten by insects, first examine the character of the notches or holes in the leaves; if these are at the edge, you may be sure that they are the work of the larvæ of a moth. If the edge is green and fresh the depredator is not far distant, and a careful search will find him. Examine the under side of the leaves carefully, most of the larvæ hide on the under side. It is a good plan, where possible, to get under the shrub, and look up at the leaves against the light of the sky. A very little practice will enable one to tell by the notches whether the caterpillar is a small one, or a large one, and also whether it has lately been at work on the plant. Larvæ may also be found on turning up dead or withered leaves which are lying on the ground, of dock or primrose, and some are found conspicuously extended on the surface of leaves or flowers, *e.g., H. Pisi* on clover, and *A. Rumicis* on bramble. (2nd) Beating— this is very simple, obtain a walking stick and an umbrella, a veritable Mrs. Gamp is best. Open the umbrella and hold it close under the branches, if at a distance from the ground, or lay it on the ground under the branch if low, and then beat the branch downwards, taking care to strike the main stem, so as by the sudden concussion to shake off anything that may be on any portion of the leaves or twigs. If the branch is above you keep your head down, and both eyes and mouth shut, especially late in the season, or you may have a big stupid wasp, fat spider, or wriggling beetle dropping into the latter, or a swarm of minute flies or beetles entering the former. Carefully examine the contents first without moving the umbrella, many of the larvæ of the Geometridæ will lie as dead for a time at the bottom of the umbrella, and so like broken twigs as to be mistaken for them, so do not at first invert the umbrella. Examine carefully what can be seen, removing the leaves, &c., with the hand, and then after a time the umbrella may be turned up, and the *debris* gently shaken out, when the loopers will be found to have gained their legs, and to be walking up the ribs of the umbrella, or standing in a defiant attitude with stiff body and elevated head. I strongly recommend collectors not to be satisfied with either beating or searching in daylight, but to practise both at night with the aid of a lantern. Some of my rarest specimens have been thus obtained, and many larvæ are night feeders.

III.—Pupa digging. This is the portion of the collector's work which can be carried on through the winter months. It requires much perseverance, and there are with it many disappointments, and often blank or almost blank days, yet much may be done by this method. Mr. Greene, who has pursued it both in Ireland and England, gives a list of 133 different species he has obtained thus. I have invariably found the north and north-east sides of the trees the best, and the trees at which I have obtained the greatest number of pupæ are the following :—willow or sally, oak, elm, poplar—trees standing alone are best. Time will not permit me to do more than touch on this branch of collecting.

In conclusion, I would urge in the cause of science as well as of humanity, the avoidance of all appearance of cruelty. I say appearance, for it is maintained by some that insects do not feel. No doubt their nervous system is much less complicated than ours, and we may reasonably suppose they do not feel pain to an equal extent; but it would be hard to prove that a living insect did not feel uncomfortable when a pin was stuck through it, and analogy would lead us to the conclusion that insects must feel some pain. However little this may be I do not consider it lawful for reasonable beings, much less Christians, to run the risk of giving unnecessary pain to any of God's creatures. To pin an insect alive will make the insect flutter and injure itself, whereas, if first rendered insensible to feeling, it may be secured so that not one scale be lost.

After the reading of the paper the President intimated to the meeting that an application had been made by him, on behalf of the Club, to his Excellency the Governor-General of Canada, requesting his Excellency's influence in obtaining a grant of certain of the publications of the Geological Survey of Canada; he further stated that he had that evening received a communication from his Excellency's secretary informing him that the grant had been made. The honorary secretaries next informed the meeting that the books had been received, and proceeded to place them upon the table for the inspection of the members amidst general applause. It was proposed by the vice-president, William Gray, Esq., M.R.I.A., seconded by Joseph Wright, Esq., F.G.S., and carried unanimously, "That the marked thanks of this Club are due and are hereby given to his Excellency Earl Dufferin, Governor-General of Canada, for his prompt and courteous reply to the application of our president, and we beg leave to assure his Excellency that we shall consider the kindness manifested in his recognition of our pursuits in the field of natural science as a high incentive to further efforts of a similar nature."

On the motion of John Moore, Esq., M.D., seconded by S. A. Stewart, Esq., the following resolution was also passed unanimously, "That the best thanks of the members of the Belfast Naturalists' Field Club are due and are hereby given to the Director-General of the Geological Survey of Canada for his kind and liberal grant of the valuable books applied for by the president of the Club, viz., Canadian Fossils, Decade II., "Graptolites," by James Hall; and Geology of Canada.

The Annual Meeting of the Club took place on Wednesday evening, 29th March, 1876. The Chair was occupied by the vice-president, William Gray, Esq., M.R.I.A.

The business of the evening was commenced by Mr. Joseph Wright, F.G.S., giving an account of dredging operations carried on in Belfast Bay, and waters adjacent. During last autumn a number of members of the Belfast Naturalists' Field Club joined Thomas Workman, Esq., in his yacht *Denburn*, for the purpose of dredging in Belfast Bay and Channel outside. All requisite appliances were provided, and, under the guidance of a gentleman so well versed in marine zoology, as also in the best methods of facilitating dredging operations, the party proceeded under most favourable auspices, and met with a fair amount of success. Other dredgings were conducted in conjunction with Mr. Swanston, in yawls procured at Bangor and Donaghadee, and the results of those various operations were now reported on. Mr. Wright said he had been asked to report on the microzoa obtained on these occasions. The material, however, was only partially examined—the Foraminifera alone having been worked up in detail. With reference to the other departments—Mollusca, Crustacea, Echinodermata, and Zoophyta—two other members had undertaken the examination, and had supplied the requisite information, which will be referred to hereafter. Up to 1858, the date when Professor Williamson published his monograph of the British Foraminifera, only 27 of this group were known to occur in Ireland. Shortly afterwards, however, there was a report issued by the committee who had obtained grants of money from the British Association for the purpose of dredging in our lough and its vicinity. This report resulted in the addition of ten species to our list of Foraminifera, raising the total number of Irish species to 37. As compared with these figures, the result of our recent work is most encouraging—already the fine material brought up from our sea bottom and examined for Foraminifera has yielded 81 different forms, and when we bear in mind that the results of several of the hauls remain to be ascertained we may fairly anticipate that others will yet be added to the list. Mr. Wright mentioned the names of the more interesting of the Foraminifera he had found, some of which were amongst the rarest British forms; others were highly interesting on account of their occurring also at great depths in the Atlantic; eight species were common to our lough and the deep-sea dredgings of the *Porcupine* expedition. Further investigations will doubtless show this community of species to be still more intimate. The local Foraminifera are further interesting as showing that many of our forms have continued unaltered since the Cretaceous epoch, there being seven species which are identical with those found abundantly in the Chalk flints of this locality. Four of the species are common to the Chalk, the bed of the Atlantic, and to our lough. When we see that Foraminifera are found living in the shallow waters of our bays and loughs, as also in the abyssmal depths of the ocean, as dredged by the *Porcupine* and *Challenger* explorers, we need not be surprised to find that creatures capable of living under such widely different conditions should also extend through long periods of time; and such we find to be the case, several of our recent Foraminifera being found fossil in rocks as old as the Lias. Mr. Wright then stated some of the results obtained by Mr. S. A. Stewart, to whom had been entrusted the examination of the mollusca dredged up. Mr. Swanston had charge of the Crustacea, Echinodermata, and Zoophyta, and had briefly reported upon these groups.

The Chairman next called upon Mr. Hugh Robinson, hon. sec., to read the report of the committee for the past year, and also (in the absence of the Treasurer) to present the financial statement for the year, both of which were adopted, and ordered to be printed for circulation amongst the members.

In accordance with a notice of motion given by him, Mr. Hugh Robinson proposed, and Mr. George O'Brien seconded, the following resolution, "That Numbers 3 and 4 of the Club's rules be altered to the following :—

Rule 3.

" That the Club shall consist of Ordinary, Corresponding, and

Honorary Members. The Ordinary Members to pay annually a subscription of Five Shillings, and that candidates for such Membership shall be proposed and seconded at any meeting of the Club, by Members present, and elected by a majority of the votes of the Members present."

Rule 4.

"That the Honorary and Corresponding Members shall consist of persons of eminence in Natural Science, or who shall have done some special service to the Club; and whose usual residence is not less than twenty miles from Belfast. That such Members may be nominated (in writing, addressed to the Committee, through the Secretaries) by any Member of the Club, and on being approved of by the Committee, may be elected at any subsequent meeting of the Club by a majority of the votes of the members present. That Corresponding Members be expected to communicate a paper once within every two years."

Mr. Joseph Wright, F.G.S., having referred to a valuable work, "Reliquæ Aquitanicæ," a copy of which had been presented to the Club, proposed the following resolution, which was seconded by Mr. S. A. Stewart, and carried unanimously, "That the best thanks of the members of the Club are due and are hereby given to Professor T. Rupert Jones, F.R.S., Royal Military College, Sandhurst, for his kindness in procuring for the Club a copy of Reliquæ Aquitanicæ from the executors of the late Henry Christy, Esq."

After the election of the office-bearers for the ensuing year, the consideration of the excursions for the summer session was taken up. The election of a number of new members terminated the business of the evening.

[1875-1876.]

NOTICE.

EXCHANGE OF PROCEEDINGS.

THE Committee of the Club have been desirous of establishing a yearly exchange of the published proceedings with those of kindred organizations in other places, and have, during the past year, forwarded copies of the Twelfth Annual Report and Proceedings to other societies. They acknowledge with thanks the receipt of the following publications, and hope that other societies, whose objects are similar, will favour them with copies of their proceedings as published :—

American Association for the Advancement of Science.
   Proceedings of 22nd Meeting.—1874.
      Do.   23rd   ,,   1875.
Bath Natural History and Antiquarian Field Club.
   Proceedings. Vol. III., Part 2.—1875.
Berwickshire Naturalists' Club.
   Proceedings. Vol. VII., Part 2.
Boston, U.S.A., Society of Natural History.
   Proceedings. Vol. XVII., Parts 1 and 2.—1874-1875.
Bristol Naturalists' Society.
   Proceedings. New Series. Vol. I., Part 2.—1875.
   Annual Report for 1874-75. List of Members, &c. Laws.—1875.

Canadian Institution.
Journal of Science, Literature, and History. Vol. XIV., Parts 5 and 6.
—1875.

Cardiff Naturalists' Society.
Report and Transactions. Vol. VI.—1874.

Dunedin (Otago) Naturalists' Field Club.
Report for 1874-1875.

Eastbourne Natural History Society.
Seventh Annual Report.—1874.

Edinburgh Botanical Society.
Transactions and Proceedings. Vol. XII., Part 2.—1875.
Report of Royal Botanic Garden for 1875.

Essex Institute, Salem, Mass., U.S.A.
Bulletin. Vol. VI., Parts 1 to 12.

Geologists' Association.
Proceedings. Vol. IV., Parts 2 to 5.—1875.

Glasgow Natural History Society.
Proceedings. Vol. II., Part 1.

Glasgow Society of Field Naturalists.
Transactions. Parts 2 and 3.—1874-1875.

Leeds Philosophical and Literary Society.
Annual Report for 1874-75.

Liverpool Geological Society.
Proceedings for 1874-75.

Liverpool Literary and Philosophical Society.
Proceedings. Part 29.—1875.

Liverpool Naturalists' Field Club.
Proceedings for 1874-75.
Flora of Liverpool.—1872.
Appendix to ditto.—1873.
Second Appendix to ditto.—1875.

Manchester Scientific Students' Association.
Annual Report for 1874.

Norfolk and Norwich Naturalists' Society.
Transactions. Vol. II., Part 1.—1875.

Philadelphia, U.S.A., Academy of Natural Sciences.
Proceedings for 1874.

Plymouth Institution, and Devon and Cornwall Natural History Society.
Annual Report and Transactions. Vol. V., Part 2.—1875.

Quekett Microscopical Club.
Journal. Part 30.—1876.

Royal Geological Society of Ireland.
Journal. New Series. Vol. IV., Part 2.—1875.

Royal Institution of South Wales.
Fortieth Annual Report.—1875.

St. Louis, U.S.A., Academy of Sciences.
Transactions. Vol. III., Part 2.

Smithsonian Institution, Washington, U.S.A.
Annual Report of Board of Regents for 1873.

U.S.A., Geological Survey of the Territories.
Catalogue of Publications.—1874.
Annual Report of the Geological and Geographical Survey of Colorado for 1873.
Report of the Geological Survey of the Territories. Vol. II. The Vertebrata of the Cretaceous Formations of the West.—1875.
Report of the Geological Survey of the Territories. Vol. VI. Contributions to the Fossil Flora of the Western Territories : Cretaceous Flora.--1874.

U.S.A. Secretary of the Department of the Interior.
Abstract of the results of a Study of the genera *Geomys* and *Thomomys*, &c.—1874.

Warwickshire Natural History and Archæological Society.
Thirty-ninth Annual Report.--1875.

Watford Natural History Society and Hertfordshire Field Club.
Laws and List of Members.— 1875.
Transactions. Vol. I., Parts 1 and 2.—1875.

Wiltshire Archæological and Natural History Society.
Wiltshire Archæological and Natural History Magazine. Parts 44 and 45.—1875.

[*From the respec..ive Societies.*]

Distribution and Correlation of Fossil Insects, &c.
The Lower Lias at Eatington and Kineton, Warwickshire.
From the Author, Rev. P. B. Brodie, M.A., F.G.S.

Reliquæ Aquitanicæ. Parts 1 to 17. (Complete work.)
From the Executors of the late Henry Christy, Esq.

Canadian Fossils—Decade II. Graptolites, by James Hall.
Geology of Canada.—1863.
From the Director-General of the Geological Survey of Canada.

Bristol and its Environs.
From William Gray, Esq., M.R.I.A.

Geological Record for 1874.
From the Editor, W. Whittaker, Esq., B.A., F.G.S.

Geology and Natural History of Minnesota—Second Annual Report (for 1873).
Geographical Survey of Ohio—Reports on Counties of Sandusky, Seneca, Wyandot, and Marion.—1871.
Glacial Features of Green Bay of Michigan.—1871.
Notes on the Drift Soil of Minnesota.—1873.
On the Hamilton, in Ohio.—1874.
The Economical Geology of the region of Cheboygan and Old Mackinac, State of Michigan.
From N. H. Winchell, Esq., University of Minnesota, Minneopolis, Minn., U.S.A.

[1875-1876.]

BELFAST NATURALISTS' FIELD CLUB.

FOURTEENTH YEAR—1876-77.

President.
REV. WILLIAM M'ILWAINE, D.D., M.R.I.A.

Vice-President.
WILLIAM GRAY, M.R.I.A.

Treasurer.
GREER MALCOMSON, Castle Place.

Secretaries.

| HUGH ROBINSON, | WILLIAM SWANSTON, |
| Donegall Street. | College Square East. |

Committee.

F. W. Lockwood.	S. A. Stewart.
Joseph C. Marsh.	Samuel Symington.
Dr. J. Moore, M.R.I.A., H.R.H.A.	Isaac W. Ward.
George O'Brien.	Thomas Workman.
W. H. Patterson, M.R.I.A.	Joseph Wright, F.G.S.

Members.

Any changes in the Addresses of Members should be communicated by them to the Secretaries.

William Aicken, M.D., Murray's Terrace.
Miss Alder, Fernbank, Holywood.
W. B. Allen, Albion Street.
W. J. C. Allen, J.P., Faunoran, Whiteabbey.
Edward Allworthy, Mountview.
John Anderson, J.P., F.G.S., Hillbrook, Holywood.
Robert Anderson, Balmoral.
Mrs. Andrews, Chlorine Place.

E. N. Banks, Botanic Avenue.
Jas. M. Barkley, Cooleen, Strandtown.
Robert Barklie, F.C.S..
William Batt, Ormeau Road.
Penrose Beale, Spencer Street.
W. J. Boucher, Landscape Terrace.
W. H. Braddell, College Square East.
Edward Braddell, College Square East.
Rev. S. A. Brenan, A.B., Pomeroy, County Tyrone.
Charles H. Brett, Dunedin Terrace.
Rev. John Bristow, A.B., Cliftonville
John Browne, Crumlin Road.
W. J. Browne, A.B., Newtownards.
Jas. Bryce, A.M., LL.D., F.G.S., F.R.G.S.I., Morningside Place, Edinburgh (Hon. Mem).
H. Burden, M.D., College Square North.
J. R. Burnett, Holywood.
Rev. S. E. Busby, LL.D., University Square.
Thomas H. Butler, Abington Terrace, Lisburn Road.

John Campbell, Mossley, Carnmoney.
Miss Carruthers, Claremont Street.
John Carson, Corn Market.
John Charley, College Park.
J. C. Clarke, Parkville.
John Clelland, Whitehouse.

Wm. Clibborn, Windsor Terrace.
Sir Edward Coey, J.P., D.L., Merville, Whiteabbey.
John Collins, Nottinghill, Malone.
Miss Connery, Mount Charles.
David Corrie, Windsor.
Thomas H. Corry, Fitzroy Terrace.
W. F. C. S. Corry, Mountpottinger.
John Cramsie, Lisavon, Strandtown.
John Cramsie, jun., Lisavon, Strandtown.
Alex. Crawford, Chlorine Villa.
Alex. Crawford, Fitzwilliam Street.
Elisha Crawford, Cliftonville.
Wm. Crawford, jun., Fitzroy Avenue.
Professor R. O. Cunningham, M.D., Claremont Street.
W. M. Cunningham, Windsor.

Thomas Darragh, Museum.
John H. Davies, Glenmore, Lisburn.
Robert Day, F.S.A., Patrick Street, Cork.
George Donaldson, Church Street.

J. H. Ferguson, Cliftonville.

William Gault, Christopher Street.
Miss Gibb, Cushleva, Jordanstown.
R. M. Gilmore, Shrigley, Killyleagh, Co. Down.
W. J. Gilmore, Cliftonville.
David Corse Glen, Annfield Place, Glasgow.
Jas. Gourlay, Killinchy, Co. Down.
G. T. Glover, Kew Cottages, Mountpottinger.
Rev. John Grainger, A.M., D.D., Broughshane, County Antrim. (Cor. Mem.)
Rev. Jas. Graves, Inisnaig, Stoneyford, Co. Kilkenny. (Cor. Mem.)
William Gray, M.R.I.A., Mount Charles.
Miss Gray, Mount Charles.
Miss Frances Gray, Mount Charles.
Edward Gregg, Model School.

Miss Greer, Tarbat Villa, Strändtown.
Joseph Hall, Dunluce Street.
Hugh Hamilton, University Square.
J. C. Hamilton, University Square.
Mann Harbison, Newtownards.
William Harte, C.E., Buncrana, County Donegal. (Cor. Mem.)
James Haslett, Franklin Street.
W.D.Henderson, University Square.
Arthur Herdman, College Sq. North.
James Hewitt, Ballymacreely, Killinchy, County Down.
Prof. J. F. Hodges, M.D., Derrievolgie, Malone.
John Hogg, Richmond Terrace.
J. Sinclair Holden, M.D., F.G.S., Sudbury, Suffolk. (Cor. Mem.)
F. C. Holmes, Belmont.
Alex. Hunter, Northern Bank.
Thomas Hunter, Holywood.

H. H. Jamieson, Casaeldono, Castlereagh.
F. M. Jennings, Brown Street, Cork. (Cor. Mem.)
Miss Johnston, Dalriada, Whiteabbey.
Miss Johnston, Glenavy, County Antrim.
James Johnston, Alma Terrace.
W. J. Johnston, Dunesk, Strandmillis.

W. Thompson Kelly, Regent Street.
J. J. Kelso, M.D., M.R.I.A., Lisburn.
Dr. T. H. Keown, R.N., Dundela, Strandtown.
Rev. J. A. Kerr, Whiteabbey.
Wm. Kernahan, Sydenham Avenue.
Wm. King, Mountpleasant, Strandmillis.
Henry Knight, Antrim Villa, Ashcombe, Weston-super-Mare.
W. J. Knowles, Cullybackey, County Antrim.

Miss Lamb, Divis View.
W. W. Lamb, Divis View.
G. D. Leathem, Thornlea, Malone.
Andrew Ledlie, Victoria Street.

F. R. Lepper, Sydenham.
Miss R. Lester, Newtownards.
F. W. Lockwood, Mountpottinger.
John Love, Oldpark Terrace.
William Lowry, Oakley, Strandtown.
Richard Lynn, Banbridge, County Down.

Henry Magee, Waring Street.
John Magee, Annesley Street.
S. J. Magowan, Northern Bank.
Henry Major, Lisburn.
Greer Malcomson, Shamrock Lodge.
Jas. Malcomson, Mountpottinger.
Mrs. Malcomson, Mountpottinger.
John Marsh, York Street.
Joseph C. Marsh, Donegall Street.
Rev. James Martin, Eglintoun, Antrim Road.
Mrs. Martin, Eglintoun, Antrim Road.
John Martin, M.D., Clarence Place.
P. C. Mayne, Sydenham Avenue.
John Millar, J.P., Lisburn.
Miss Millar, Lisburn.
William Millar, Durham Street.
James Moore, M.D., M.R.I.A., H.R.H.A., Chichester Street.
John Moore, M.D., Eglinton Terrace.
W. R. Molyneux, Florence Place.
Miss Monteith, Claremont Street.
Hugh Morrison, Ligoniel.
David Morrow, Clarence Place.
J. J. Murphy, F.G.S., Oldforge, Dunmurry.
J. R. Musgrave, J.P., Drumglass, Malone.

Robert M'Adam, College Square East.
Jas. M'Clenahan, Ardoyne.
Miss M'Clure, Belmont.
Sir Thomas M'Clure, Bart., V.L., J.P., Belmont
Rev. Ed. M'Clure, A.M., M.R.I.A., Lincoln's Inn Fields, London. (Hon. Mem.)
Rev. William M'Ilwaine, D.D., M.R.I.A., Ulsterville.
Mrs. M'Ilwaine, Ulsterville.

H. C. M'Ilwaine, Ulsterville.
Daniel M'Kee, Adela Place.
John Mackenzie, C.E., Balmoral.
Thomas Macknight, Windsor.
Alexander M'Laine, Corporation Street.
Francis P. M'Lean, Botanic Avenue.
William M'Millen, Ballinasloe.

Nicholas Oakman, Prospect Terrace.
George O'Brien, Botanic Avenue.
Joshua O'Brien, Botanic Avenue.
Rev. James O'Laverty, Holywood.
Captain S. P. Oliver, 22nd Bde., R.A., F.S.A., F.R.G.S., Buncrana, Co. Donegal.
Jas. O'Neill, A.M., Upper Townsend Street.
Alexander O'Rorke, Duncairn.
Rev. Richard C. Oulton, St. Lawrence Terrace.

David C. Patterson, Holywood.
William H. Patterson, M.R.I.A., Dundela, Strandtown.
James Phillips, Granville Terrace.
William H. Phillips, Lemonfield, Holywood.
John Pim, Clifton Park Avenue.
Joshua Pim, Crumlin Terrace.
Thomas W. Pim, Evelyn Lodge, Strandtown.
Thomas Plunkett, Enniskillen.
William Porter, Percy Street.
John Preston, jun., Dunmore, Antrim Road.
C. D. Purdon, M.D., Wellington Place.
Alfred Purdon, Wellington Place.

Joseph Radley, Prospect Hill, Lisburn.
John Rea, M.D., Great Victoria Street.
Miss Robinson, Lisanore, Antrim Road.
Rev. George Robinson, A.M., Tartaraghan, Co. Armagh.
Hugh Robinson, Donegall Street.
J. R. Robinson, Woodstock Road.
Ninian J. Robinson, Donegall Street

W. A. Robinson, Crofton, Holywood.
Edward Rogan, Cromac Street.
B. F. Rothwell, Howard Street.
Richard Ross, M.D., Wellington Place.
John Russell, Adelaide Street.

Rev. G. Brydges Sayers, Ballinderry, Lurgan.
Mrs. Scott, Sydenham Avenue.
J. M. Johnston Scott, M.D., College Square East.
R. C. Sedgwick, Holywood.
Thomas Shaw, Pakenham Place.
John Shelly, Whiteabbey.
Thomas Shepherd, Whitehouse.
William Shepherd, Holywood.
Rowland Smeeth, Queen's College.
Charles Smith, F.G.S., Barrow-in-Furness.
George K. Smith, Whiteabbey.
Robert Smith, Pottinger Terrace.
Thomas Smith, Kensington Street.
Rev. George C. Smythe, A.M., Coole Glebe, Carnmoney.
Adam Speers, B.Sc., Holywood.
Sir Nathaniel Staples, Bart., Lissan. Dungannon.
James H. Staples, Lissan, Dungannon.
Richard Stevenson, Donegall Pass.
S. Alex. Stewart, North Street.
Miss Swanston, University Street.
Wm. Swanston, University Street.
Samuel Symington, Dundonald.

Prof. Ralph Tate, A.L.S., F.G.S.
A. O'D. Taylor, Upper Crescent.
Miss Thompson, University Square.
E. H. Thompson, J.P., Slieve-na-Failte, Whiteabbey.
John Thompson, B.E., Harbour Office.
Henry Thompson, Windsor.
George Thomson, Broadway.
Prof. James Thomson, A.M., LL.D., D.C.L., C.E., Sardinia Terrace, Hillhead, Glasgow. (Hon. Mem.)

Sir Wyville Thomson, LL.D., F.R.S., F.G.S., &c., University, Edinburgh. (Hon. Mem.)
Charles H. Todd, Atlantic Avenue.
John Todd, Regent Street.
W. A. Todd, Regent Street.
W. A. Traill, B.E., M.A.I., Geol. Sur., Ballymena.

William Valentine, J.P., Glenavna, Whiteabbey.
Jas. W. Valentine, Whiteabbey.

W. F. Wakeman, Portora, Enniskillen. (Cor. Mem.)
T. R. Walkington, Laurel Lodge, Strandtown.
Isaac W. Ward, University Street.
John S. Ward, Lisburn.
W. R. Ward, Stanpit, Christchurch, Hants.
Robert Waters, Belmont Park.
Wm. Watson, Londonderry. (Cor. Mem.)
Isaac Waugh, Benwell Terrace.
Alex. C. Welsh, Dromore, Co. Down. (Cor. Mem.)

T. K. Wheeler, M.D., Clarendon Place.
T. K. Wheeler, jun., Clarendon Place.
David Wilson, Ballymoney, Co. Antrim.
Jas. Wilson, jun., Albion Place.
James Wilson, Ballybundon, Killinchy, Co. Down.
Rev. Hans Woods, Park Avenue, Ormeau Road.
John Workman, Windsor.
Rev. Robert Workman, A.M., Glastry, Kirkcubbin, Co. Down.
Thomas Workman, Windsor.
Joseph Wright, F.G.S., F.R.G.S.I., Cliftonville.
Samuel O. Wylie, College Square North.

Robert Young, C.E., Rathvarna, Antrim Road.
Robert M. Young, Rathvarna, Antrim Road.

RULES
OF THE
Belfast Naturalists' Field Club.

I.

That the Society be called "THE BELFAST NATURALISTS' FIELD CLUB."

II.

That the objects of the Society be the practical study of Natural Science and Archæology.

III.

That the Club shall consist of Ordinary, Corresponding, and Honorary Members. The Ordinary Members to pay annually a subscription of Five Shillings, and that candidates for such Membership shall be proposed and seconded at any meeting of the Club, by Members present, and elected by a majority of the votes of the Members present.

IV.

That the Honorary and Corresponding Members shall consist of persons of eminence in Natural Science, or who shall have done some special service to the Club; and whose usual residence is not less than twenty miles from Belfast. That such Members may be nominated by any Member of the Club, and on being approved of by the Committee, may be elected at any subsequent meeting of the Club by a majority of the votes of the members present. That Corresponding Members be expected to communicate a paper once within every two years.

V.

That the Officers of the Club be annually elected, and consist of a President, Vice-President, Treasurer, two Secretaries, and ten Members, who form the Committee. Five to form a quorum. No Member of Committee to be eligible for re-election who has not attended at least one-fourth of the Committee Meetings during his year of office.

VI.

That the Members of the Club shall hold at least Six Field Meetings during the year, in the most interesting localities, for investigating the Natural History and Archæology of the district. That the place of meeting be fixed by the Committee, and that five days' notice of each Excursion be communicated to Members by the Secretaries.

VII.

That Meetings be held Fortnightly or Monthly, at the discretion of the Committee, for the purpose of reading papers; such papers, as far as possible, to treat of the Natural History and Archæology of the district. These Meetings to be held during the months from November to April inclusive.

VIII.

That the Committee shall, if they find it advisable, offer for competition Prizes for the best collections of scientific objects of the district; and the Committee may order the purchase of maps, or other scientific apparatus, and may carry on geological and archæological searches or excavations, if deemed advisable; provided that the entire amount expended under this rule does not exceed the sum of £10 in any one year.

IX.

That the Annual Meeting be held during the month of April, when the Report of the Committee for the past year, and the Treasurer's Financial Statement shall be presented, the Committee and Officers elected, Bye-laws made and altered, and any proposed alteration in the general laws, of which a fortnight's notice shall have been given, in writing, to the Secretary or Secretaries, considered and decided upon. The Secretaries to give the Members due notice of such intended alteration.

X.

That, on the written requisition of twenty-five Members, delivered to the Secretaries, an Extraordinary General Meeting may be called, to consider and decide upon the subjects mentioned in such written requisition.

XI.

That the Committee be empowered to exchange publications and reports, and to extend the privilege of attending the Meetings and Excursions of the Belfast Naturalists' Field Club to Members of kindred societies, on similar privileges being accorded to its Members by such other societies.

The following Rules for the conducting of the Excursions have been arranged by the Committee.

I.—The Excursion to be open to all Members; each one to have the privilege of introducing two friends.

II.- A Chairman to be elected as at ordinary meetings.

III.—One of the Secretaries to act as Conductor, or in the absence of both, a Member to be elected for that purpose.

IV.—No change to be made in the programme, or extra expenses incurred, except by the consent of the majority of the Members present.

V.—No fees, gratuities, or other expenses, to be paid except through the Conductor.

VI.—Every Member or Visitor to have the accommodation assigned by the Conductor. Where accommodation is limited, consideration will be given to priority of application.

VII.—Accommodation cannot be promised unless tickets are obtained before the time mentioned in the special circular.

VIII—Those who attend an excursion without previous notice will be liable to extra charge, if extra cost be incurred thereby.

IX.—No intoxicating liquors to be provided at the expense of the Club.

Belfast Naturalists' Field Club.

FOURTEENTH YEAR.

THE Committee offer the following Prizes to be competed for during the Session ending March 31, 1877 :—

I. For the best Herbarium of Flowering Plants,
   representing not less than 250 Species............ £1 0 0
II. For the best Herbarium of Flowering Plants,
   representing not less than 150 Species............ 0 10 0
III. Best Collection of Mosses 0 10 0
IV.   ,,   Seaweeds......... .... 0 10 0
V.   ,,   Ferns... .... 0 10 0
VI.   ,,   Cretaceous Fossils.............. 0 10 0
VII.   ,,   Liassic   do. 0 10 0
VIII.   ,,   Palæozoic do. 0 10 0
IX.   ,,   Marine Shells..................... 0 10 0
X.   ,,   Land and Fresh-water Shells... 0 10 0
XI.   ,,   Lepidoptera...................... 0 10 0
XII. Best Set of 25 Microscopic Slides 0 10 0
XIII. Best Collection of Archæological Objects 0 10 0

XIV. Best collection of Crustacea..........................£0 10 0
XV.   „   Echinodermata................. 0 10 0
XVI.   „   Geological Specimens, illustrative of the Mineral Resources of the Province of Ulster... 1 0 0
XVII. Best Collection of all or any of the above Objects collected *at the Excursions* of the Year 0 10 0
XVIII. Six best Field Sketches appertaining to Geology, Archæology, or Natural History............. 0 10 0

In every case where three or more persons compete for a Prize, a second one, of half its value, will be awarded if the conditions are otherwise complied with.

CONDITIONS.

No Competitor to obtain more than two Prizes in any one year.

No Competitor to be awarded the same Prize twice within three years.

All Collections to be made personally during the Session, within the Province of Ulster. Each species to be correctly named, and locality stated. The Flowering Plants to be collected when in flower, and classified according to the Natural System. The Sketches, Drawings, and Microscopic Slides to be the competitor's own work.

No Prizes will be awarded except to such Collections as shall, in the opinion of the Judges, possess positive merit.

The Prizes to be in books, or suitable scientific objects, at the desire of the successful competitor.

SPECIAL PRIZES.

XIX. The President offers a Prize of £1 1s. for the best set of Three Sketches, contributed to the Club's Album, by one out of three or more Competitors. The set to be of uniform size, not less than 9 inches by 5½ inches, unmounted, and to be Original Coloured Drawings of Irish Antiquarian subjects, liable to removal or destruction.

XX. A Prize of 10s., given by the late Mr. J. W. Murphy, for the best Collection of Recent Sponges, the conditions being the same as those for Prizes I. to XVII.

XXI. Dr. James Moore, M.R.I.A., offers a Prize of £1 1s. for the best Two Studies from Nature, illustrative of Archæology. The Prize Sketches to become the property of the Club, and not to be less than 9 inches by 5½ inches. The subjects of the Sketches to be different from any at present in the Club's Album.

XXII. Mr. William Swanston offers a Prize of 10s. 6d. for the best Two Studies from Nature, illustrative of Geology. Conditions the same as for Prize XXI.

NOW READY,

320 pp. F.cap. 8vo. Cloth Gilt, Bevelled Boards, with 48 pp. Illustrations and Map. Price 3/6.

GUIDE TO BELFAST

AND ADJACENT COUNTIES.

BY THE

BELFAST NATURALISTS' FIELD CLUB.

THE BOOK TREATS OF THE FOLLOWING SUBJECTS:

PHYSICAL GEOGRAPHY.
GEOLOGY AND MINERAL RESOURCES.
BOTANY.
ZOOLOGY.
TOPOGRAPHY.
HISTORICAL & DESCRIPTIVE NOTICES OF TOWNS.

ANTIQUITIES—ECCLESIASTICAL AND CIVIL.
AGRICULTURE.
TRADE AND COMMERCE.
EXCURSIONS TO PLACES OF INTEREST.

May be had of all Booksellers, or from the Secretaries of the Club.

11 FEB 1886

ANNUAL REPORT

AND

PROCEEDINGS

OF THE

𝕭elfast 𝕹aturalists' 𝕱ield 𝕮lub,

1876-1877.

SERIES II.

𝔙olume 𝔍. 𝔓art 𝔍𝔙.

PRINTED FOR MEMBERS ONLY.

ANNUAL REPORT

AND

PROCEEDINGS

OF THE

Belfast Naturalists' Field Club,

FOR THE

YEAR ENDING 31ST MARCH, 1877.

NEW SERIES.
VOLUME I. PART IV.

BELFAST:
PRINTED FOR THE CLUB.
ROBINSON BROTHERS, 25, DONEGALL STREET.
1878.

REPORT

OF THE

BELFAST NATURALISTS' FIELD CLUB,

FOR THE YEAR 1876-77.

OUR Committee, in presenting their fourteenth Annual Report, have the pleasure of again recording another year of progress. The objects for which the Club was founded have been carried out. Most of the subjects treated of at the winter meetings were of local interest, and your Committee believe that the general public heartily sympathize with you in your endeavours to cultivate a taste for Natural Science, and in elucidating some of the problems presented by the Archæology and Natural History of the district. Your Committee have pleasure in stating that the membership, upon which so much of the prosperity of the Club depends, has been more than maintained; and the attendance at the winter and field meetings has been equal to the average of former years.

The localities chosen for the Summer Excursions gave general satisfaction, affording as they did good opportunities for the studies of the geologist, botanist, and archæologist. The localities were as follow :—

19th May.	Ballycarry and Redhall.
3rd June.	Ballymena to Larne *via* Glenwherry.
8th July.	Armagh and Neighbourhood.
1st to 3rd Aug.	Dungiven.
12th Aug.	Collin Glen and Castle Robin.
6th Sept.	Rademon and Killyleagh.

Detailed accounts of the Excursions are here appended.

A Conversazione was held in October. The change of date from the Spring to that more advanced season of the year was considered an advantage. The meeting was numerously attended and very successful, and marked interest was evinced in the work of the Society. During the evening the unusual large number of twenty-seven new members were added to the Club.

At the Winter Meetings the following papers were read : —

1876.
22nd Nov. Opening Address, by the President (Rev. William MacIlwaine, D.D., M.R.I.A.).

1877.
24th Jan. "On the Origin and Progress of Coinage." By Mr. John Browne.
21st Feb. "Notes on the Geology of the Black Mountain." By Mr. William Gault.
,, "On Antiquarian Remains on Lurigethan, and in the vicinity of Cushendall." By Mr. William Miller.
14th March. "On the Correlation of the Silurian Rocks of the Co. Down." By Mr. William Swanston.
21st March. "On Woodpeckers and Kingfishers : Their Points of Resemblance and Difference." By Mr. Joseph Radley.
,, "On Hunting in the Sand Dunes." By the Vice-President, Mr. William Gray, M.R.I.A.

Independent of the work done at the ordinary excursions during the past year, much was accomplished by the patient researches of ardent naturalists connected with the Club, who, as circumstances permitted, joined in many enjoyable excursions and dredging expeditions. Their labours have resulted in the detection here of a large number of species additional to those already known to occur in the North of Ireland, and perhaps in no one year has there been greater progress in our knowledge of the Botany, Zoology, Geology, and Palæontology of the district.

Your Committee take this opportunity of thanking the noblemen and gentlemen who so kindly permitted your Club to visit their grounds. Also to again express their obligations to the members and friends who gave us the benefit of their local knowledge on such occasions. Your Committee would also express their thankfulness to Lachlan M'Laine, Esq., for his hospitality, and for kindly placing his yacht at the disposal of the Club, on the occasion of its visit to Killyleagh; and likewise to Mr. Lowry, who accompanied a party in his yacht, enabling those interested to carry out some dredging operations in Strangford Lough on the same occasion. The results of these dredgings are very interesting, and are embodied in the report of that excursion.

The Sub-Committee appointed to assist in the re-arrangement of the local department of the Natural History and Philosophical Society's Museum, continue their labours, and most of the collections in the building have been put in order. The Herbarium, which promises to be a very complete one, will probably be finished by the end of the year. The collections illustrative of Geology are complete, so far as the material is available. There are arranged in cases 702 species of fossils, 104 minerals, and 85 rock specimens. The Club's members have added much to the value of these collections. The specimens in the Herbarium are almost entirely due to the labours of Mr. S. A. Stewart and Mr. Hugh Robinson. In the Geological department, the comprehensive series of rock specimens presented by your Vice-President, Mr. William Gray, M.R.I.A., deserve special notice. Also the Microzoa presented by Mr. Joseph Wright, F.G.S., of which there are 150 species from the Cretaceous rocks alone, forming a valuable addition to the Museum collections. It is to be regretted that many departments remain almost entirely unrepresented—among others, we might mention Insects, Crustaceans, Echinoderms, Zoophytes, Sponges, &c.,—to the study of which it is desirable some members should give their spare time. It is also hoped that more attention will be given to the collections of Irish Antiquities, with a view to having a more complete series of them, in every way worthy of the town, and representative of this district, which is so rich in such remains.

The exchange of Proceedings with kindred societies still continues with mutual benefit. Frequent applications are received for the earlier parts, of which it is to be regretted there are none remaining in the Secretaries' hands. The result of the exchanges to your Club has been the acquisition of a large number of works containing a vast amount of scientific knowledge not otherwise easily accessible. It is hoped ere long they will be catalogued and made more available to members than they have hitherto been.

The Committee appointed, the following gentlemen, viz.—Mr. William Gray, M.R.I.A., Mr. Robert Young, C.E., and Dr. James Moore, H.R.H.A., as Judges of the collections, &c., submitted in competition for the Club and other prizes. Their award is as follows:—

"We have examined Mr. Gault's collection of Cretaceous Fossils, and we are very much pleased to find such positive evidence of a successful year's work. The collection includes some new and rare forms, and many of the ordinary species are in very good condition. Mr. Gault has not submitted a complete list, and the form in which the list is presented prevents us from ascertaining the number of species in time for this report, but we are satisfied that for many reasons this collection is one of the best ever presented in competition for the Club's prize, No. 7. We have also examined Mr. F. W. Lockwood's sketches submitted in competition for the prize (No. 21) offered by Dr. James Moore,

H.R.H.A., and we are of opinion that the merit of the sketches proves the wisdom and value of Dr. Moore's kind offer; and we award the prize to this artist. Mr. Lockwood's water-colour studies, illustrative of geology, competing for the prize (No. 22), offered by Mr. William Swanston, are such as fulfil the terms on which the prize was offered, and we have pleasure in awarding the prize accordingly."

A Sub-Committee was appointed to co-operate with Sir John Lubbock, in promoting his "Ancient Monuments Preservation Bill;" and with that view prepared and forwarded to the House of Commons a petition in favour of the measure. About 400 signatures were attached, including the names of noblemen, landed proprietors, clergy, professors, merchants, and leading citizens, who, in acknowledgement of the necessity for such a measure, cordially responded to the request of the Committee, and expressed an earnest desire that Sir John Lubbock's object should be attained. The Sub-Committee also communicated with the various members of Parliament in Ulster, and requested them to support the Bill. The issue was that the second reading was carried successfully, which justifies the hope that, after amendment, it will become law.

HUGH ROBINSON, } *Hon. Secs.*
WILLIAM SWANSTON,

Dr. *Belfast Naturalists' Field Club in Account with Treasurer.* **Cr.**

	£ s. d.		£ s. d.
To Balance from 1875-76 ...	0 9 4	By Loss on Conversazione ...	6 14 4
,, Subscriptions ...	52 10 0	,, Printing Annual Report ...	11 17 3
,, Arrears of Subscriptions ...	1 5 0	,, Advertising, Printing, and Stationery ...	11 15 2
,, Gain on Excursions ...	1 11 1	,, Delivery of Circulars ...	1 10 0
		,, Postages ...	3 18 10
		,, Prizes ...	1 11 0
		,, Museum Expenses ...	9 9 0
		,, Balance on hand ...	8 19 10
	£55 15 5		£55 15 5

Audited and found correct,

HUGH ROBINSON.

GREER MALCOMSON, *Treasurer.*

SUMMER SESSION.

The following Excursions were made during the Summer Session:

On Saturday, 19th May, to

BALLYCARRY AND REDHALL DEMESNE.

HE Club opened its series of excursions for the summer session on Saturday, 19th May, the district selected being Ballycarry and Redhall Demesne. The party left Belfast by the twelve o'clock train for Carrickfergus. On their arrival there, cars were awaiting to convey them to Ballycarry; and, passing through the old North or Spittal Gate of the town, and taking the old road by Castle Dobbs and Bellahill, a pleasant drive soon brought them to Templecorran old church. Here the cars were dismissed, and a visit was paid to the church, originally a fine cruciform structure, but which is now in ruins. It and the surrounding graveyard contain many interesting monuments—amongst others that which marks the burial-place of Edward Brice, the minister of the first Presbyterian congregation in Ireland. In the 34th of Philip and Mary a law was passed "against the bringing in of the Scots, retaining or intermarrying with them;" but such was the state of the country it was necessary to repeal that law, from which repeal may be dated the first successful attempt at the introduction of those people into the North of Ireland by King James. (Dubourdieu's Stat. Hist: of County Antrim). It was at this time that Brice settled near Templecorran, in 1611.

On leaving Templecorran the party walked through the village of Ballycarry to Redhall Demesne, which was thrown open to them by the kindness of the proprietor, John Macauley, Esq., J.P. The Demesne, which is well wooded, occupies the slopes of the hills which rise from the western shores of Larne Lough, and is laid out with admirable taste. From the higher grounds a good view is obtained of Larne Lough and the opposite shore of Islandmagee. Near this place a ford formerly existed, of which traces are still visible at low water. It was probably constructed at this particular spot to serve as a communication between two churches, one of which was situated at Ballykeel, in Islandmagee, and the other at the rere of the present mansion of Redhall. Passing along the main avenue, the guide led the way to the foot of the Old Mill Glen, anciently known as Altfrakyn. This beautiful glen has been cut into the Chalk by a stream which finds its way from the higher ground. The wider portion at the foot of the glen affords suitable habitats for some of our choicest wild flowers; and here is situated the "Pin Well," where a spring of sparkling water gushes from the base of the Chalk cliffs. The name is given from the practice of persons, after drinking the water, dropping pins into it. What the origin of the custom was cannot now be told, perhaps it is a relic of some superstition regarding the presentation of votive offerings to the presiding spirit of the well. Legends and superstitions in connection with wells and with their spirits and "kelpies" are by no means uncommon. From this point the glen narrows considerably, till near the top it consists of a deep perpendicular gorge. The narrowest part has obtained the name of the "Madman's Leap," from a legend to the effect that some unfortunate rebel, pursued by the soldiery in 1798 to the verge of the cliff, leaped across the chasm, and so made his escape. The cliffs at the upper end of the glen are completely covered with ferns, amongst which may be seen magnificent specimens of *Polypodium Hibernicum*. Much has been done by judicious care and taste to preserve the natural beauties of the place, the idea having evidently been, not to supplant nature by art, but rather to aid and assist her in her own direction, and to propagate and protect the rarer plants which have their habitat here.

In addition to its picturesque beauties, Redhall is interesting on account of the historical associations connected with it. Situated close to the territory formerly occupied by the Macdonnells of the "Glynns," who long strove with the English for the possession of the north-east of Ulster, this neighbourhood has been the scene of many sanguinary engagements, notably that on the 4th November, 1597, when " James MacSorley Macdonnell (son of the celebrated Sorley Boy) came near this place (Carrickfergus) daring the garrison; when Sir John Chichester, Governor, marched out to attack the enemy with such troops of the garrison as could be spared. On this movement Macdonnell retreated, and Sir John, in the pursuit, fell into an ambuscade placed in the glen of Altfrakyn (the Old Mill Glen). The party were instantly surrounded, and nearly cut to pieces; and Sir John, being taken prisoner, was beheaded by Macdonnell on a stone near 'The Glynn'" (M'Skimin, Hist. of Carrickfergus). As to the precise locality of the battle authors slightly differ, another stating that the engagement took place *prope vadum ac tumulum—i.e.,* near to a ford and a mound. This would indicate that the scene of the fight was at the lower end of the demesne, and close to the shore of Larne Lough, where, as has already been stated, the remains of the ford still exist, and where also the entire mound may yet be seen.

The geology of the district would repay a careful examination, indeed, the glen contains an almost complete epitome of the geology of the County of Antrim. The stream, where it emerges from the glen, cuts into the Triassic marls; farther up, where a landslip has exposed the left bank to a height of about thirty feet, the section shows a thin band of Lias clay, from which a few characteristic fossils were obtained; resting immediately upon it is a band of Glauconitic sand, of the Greensand formation, containing fragments of Exogyya and other well marked fossils. These two latter formations, though almost horizontal and in their proper sequence, do not appear to be *in situ*, but have been probably been forced down the glen during the Glacial period. The rich soil, with its luxuriant growth of ferns, hides the rocks from view, till we reach a rustic bridge, where a beautiful cascade cuts deeply into the Chalk. At the head of the glen we find that the Chalk is overlaid by a capping of Basalt, which in its turn is covered by a thick stratum of Boulder clay, thus giving almost in a single view a representative section of the country. Before leaving the glen a meeting was held, at which a unanimous vote of thanks to Mr. Macaulay was passed, thanking him for his kindness in giving the party access to his grounds, and for the valuable notes on the neighbourhood he had placed at the disposal of the Club. The party then wended their way towards Ballycarry Station, passing through a fine avenue of oaks, which once extended the entire way from the old church at the rere of the house to the point where the ford crossed to Islandmagee. A visit was also paid to the dun or fort which we have already referred to in connection with the defeat of Sir John Chichester. Reaching the station, the return train to Belfast was taken, the party reaching home at seven o'clock, after having had a most enjoyable excursion, at which they were favoured by the fine weather which almost invariably accompanies the Club's excursions.

On Saturday, 3rd June, to

BALLYMENA AND LARNE *VIA* GLENWHERRY.

The district selected for this excursion was "Glenwherry Valley." A number of members and friends left the Northern Counties Terminus at 9-30, *en route* for Ballymena. They were here met by members of the Ballymena Field Club, who kindly accompanied them to the fort to the south-west of the town. This fort is a very perfect example of the combined round and square form, and stands on a commanding position on the high bank of the Maine-water. The trees with which it is now surrounded in some measure hinder the view, but prior to their growth, it must have been a prominent feature in the district, and one of the most important of the many forts studded over the country. Mounted on vehicles, the party proceeded towards Larne, several halts being made by the way. The route lay along the extensive valley of the Kells-water and Glenwherry River, through which the projected railway from Larne to Ballymena will pass. It is to be regretted that the time at their disposal prevented full justice being done to the route; many interesting spots had to be passed. A brief stay was made at Shane's Hill to examine the iron mines. Here several members made a rough over-country scramble in search of a Cromlech noted on the Ordinance Survey Maps. After much hunting, the spot was found. The Cromlech—if the heap of stones had ever been one—must have been overturned long since, and the brambles, &c., with which it was overgrown prevented an examination in the time available. Again mounted, no stop was made till the party reached the railway station at Larne. A rapid run home brought a pleasant but rather hurried excursion to a close.

On Saturday, 8th July, to

ARMAGH AND NAVAN FORT.

Notwithstanding that rain had threatened for the previous day or two, there was a large muster of the members at the Great Northern Terminus to leave by the nine o'clock train, and at various stations along the line the number was increased by members and friends residing in other districts. Arriving at Armagh, the party were met by a number of the members of a kindred organization—the Armagh Natural History Society—who were in waiting to accompany them and act as guides for the day. In a few minutes all were seated in the vehicles which had been provided for their conveyance, and the route taken to Carrickloughran. Here a halt was made to inspect an interesting trap-dyke, which passes through the Carboniferous limestone. The eruptive mass appears as a perpendicular wall, about seven feet in width, and evidently extends for a considerable distance, and as usual, has indurated the limestone at its contact with it. Several good specimens of the junction of the two rocks were obtained, and carried away to enrich the cabinets of the members. The next object of interest visited was a stone circle at Ballybrawley—a rude structure consisting of a number of large blocks of the limestone of the district, set on end in the earth, and forming a circle of about 70 feet in diameter. Similar structures are found in many places throughout Ireland, but for what purpose they were erected cannot well be told—perhaps as temples for worship, and afterwards used for sepulchral purposes; or it may be that they were specially constructed for the latter. In many of the stone circles evidences of interments still exist, and in other cases such evidences may have been destroyed in subsequent searches for treasures supposed to have been buried there. Near to this circle is another of similar diameter and appearance, but as the extent of the day's programme did not permit a visit to it, the conveyances were again mounted, and the party drove off to visit Navan Fort, distant some two miles west from Armagh.

The ancient Emania, or as it is now called "Navan Fort," is one of the most celebrated places in early Irish history. Long before St. Patrick founded upon the hill of Drumsailech (the hill of sallows) his church, and around it laid out a city, Emania was known. There it was that the Ulster Kings had their chief residence for nearly seven centuries (from 350 B.C. to A.D. 332), ranging from Cimbaeth and Macha Mongruadh to Fergus Fogha, who fell at Achalethderg in the latter year. There, too, it was that the Red-Branch Knights, so celebrated in song and story, had their residence. A place close to Navan Fort, still called Crieve Row, from the Irish "Craebh-ruadh," *i.e.*, the Red Branch, perpetuates in its name the memories of these knights of old. The foundation of the palace of Emania by Cimbaeth and his wife, Macha, is assumed in the Annals of Tigernach as the starting point of authentic Irish history; and we find numerous references to it up to A.D. 332, when it was burnt and destroyed, and never inhabited again. The site of the old palace, now called Navan Fort (from the compound An-Eamhain), now consists of an elliptical entrenchment enclosing an area of about twelve acres, and separated from the central "dun," on which the residences were erected, by a deep ditch or fosse. After a thorough examination of the Fort by the party, a meeting was held on its summit, and a vote of thanks conveyed to the members of the Armagh Natural History Society—viz., Edward Rogers, Esq., Rev. J. Elliott, Dr. Riggs, and Rev. George Robinson, A.M.—for their kindness in making arrangements for the reception of the party, and for their accompanying the excursion. Near to Navan is a small lake called Loughnashade, which O'Donovan considers to be probably the same as that called Lough Kirr, in the following notice in the Annals of the Four Masters, under the year 907:—
"The privileges of the Cathedral of Armagh were violated by

Kernach MacDulgen, by dragging a captive out of the church, who had taken sanctuary there, and drowning him in Lough Kirr to the west of the city. But this violation was retaliated on Kernach by Niall Glundubh, then King of Ulster, and afterwards of Ireland, who drowned him in the same lough." Leaving Navan Fort, a visit was paid to a quarry in the vicinity, where good specimens of the characteristic fossils of the Carboniferous limestone were obtained, among which may be mentioned the following genera :—*Lithostrotian, Lithodendron, Psammodus, Cochliodus, &c.*

Soon the whistle was heard as a signal to resume the journey, and, though rather against the inclinations of the geologists, all were promptly on their way to the Primate's demesne. Shortly after entering the grounds, a halt was made to inspect the ruins of the Franciscan Abbey, the building of which was completed in 1266 by the then Archbishop of Armagh, Maelpatrick O'Scannail. The Abbey was occupied till 1565, when it was destroyed, though the friars still maintained a holding in the neighbourhood. In 1620 the Abbey grounds became incorporated with the lands of the see, Primate Hampton having obtained letters patent granting to the see the site and precinct of the late dissolved Abbey or Monastery of the Friars Minors, with all their tenements and buildings in Armagh. A little way from the Abbey is the Palace, which was thrown open to the Club by the kindness of his Grace the Lord Primate. The present archiepiscopal residence was erected in 1770 by Primate Robinson, and contains many valuable paintings, principally of the later kings and queens of England and other members of the Royal family. There is also a series of portraits of the primates from the Reformation till the present time, excepting Lancaster, Long, and Garvey. In addition to these there is a valuable collection of works by various masters, the property of the present Lord Primate. Before leaving the Palace a vote of thanks was unanimously passed to his Grace for his kindness in giving the party an opportunity of inspecting these interesting works of art.

Resuming their seats upon the conveyances, the party drove off to the Museum of the Natural History Society. The building, in addition to containing a valuable series of natural history collections, has a library containing the most recent scientific works; a reading-room, in which are the current scientific periodicals; a lecture and committee rooms, &c. The society is one of the oldest of its class in Ireland, having been established in 1839, and numbers among its members many celebrated in scientific pursuits. It was intended to visit the observatory, in which so many valuable astronomical observations have been made by the venerable Dr. Romney Robinson and his staff of assistants; but time did not admit of such being done, and the party proceeded to the Cathedral.

The site of the present Cathedral Church of Armagh has been occupied by ecclesiastical buildings since the time of St. Patrick, but at what time the present edifice was erected seems to be a matter of uncertainty. The Church has been so often repaired and improved, it is probable that but little of the original structure remains. Its present appearance is due to the liberality of the late Primate, Lord John George Beresford, who furnished the requisite funds for the complete repair of the Cathedral—a work which was commenced on 21st May, 1834. A short time was spent in the examination of the interior of the building, the magnificent stained glass windows, and the many interesting monuments; among the latter we may specially refer to that by Roubiliac, in memory of Sir Thomas Molyneux, M.D.; that by Rysbach, in memory of Dean Drelincourt; and the bust of Primate Robinson, by Nollekins. The tower was then ascended, and a magnificent view of the sorrounding country rewarded those who had undertaken the labour of reaching the roof. Descending again to the Church, the party had the pleasure of attending an organ recital by Dr. Marks, who kindly attended specially for the

B

purpose. In the hands of so accomplished a musician, the full powers of the fine instrument were brought out, and a rich musical treat afforded to those present. The organ is the gift of Primate Lord J. G. Beresford. The history of its predecessor is rather interesting to the people of Belfast—that instrument was presented to the Dean and Chapter by Primate Robinson, shortly aftei his appointment to the See, and at the commencement of the repairs to the Cathedral in 1834, was taken to pieces, and carefully placed in apartments over the stables in the Primate's demesne. In 1840, previous to the re-opening of the Cathedral, the late Primate presented the organ which is now in use, and in 1841 that which was the gift of Primate Robinson was erected in the Tontine Concert-Room for the use of the Armagh Musical Society. At the dissolution of that body, some time afterwards, the organ was disposed of, and placed in Donegall Square Methodist Church, where it was unfortunately destroyed by fire on the first evening it was used there. On leaving the Cathedral, the president of the Club was requested to convey a vote of thanks, which had been unanimously passed by the Club, to Dr. Marks for his kindness. A visit was then paid to the crypt, to view the remains of the Old Market Cross of Armagh. It is much to be regretted that some portions of it are wanting, having been converted to other uses by those who have had no respect for such monuments of antiquity. A unanimous opinion was expressed as to the advisibility of replacing the missing portions, and re-erecting it in some part of the Cathedral grounds, where it would be exposed to the examination of visitors, and still preserved from further interference. A hurried inspection was then made of the library in Abbey Street, founded in 1771 by Primate Robinson, and which contains many rare and curious books. The number of volumes in it is upwards of 12,000, and it is constantly increasing. Time would only admit of a short visit to the new Roman Catholic Cathedral. This building, which is one of the most magnificent belonging to that denomination in Ireland, was commenced in 1840, and finished a few years ago. The cost of erection, which was about £70,000, was entirely defrayed by voluntary contributions. The railway station was reached in time for the five o'clock train for Belfast, and the return journey completed at seven o'clock, so concluding another of the many interesting and pleasant excursions of the Club. Much good botanical work was done during the day, as the party included several of the most earnest botanists of the north of Ireland, intent upon investigating the indigenous vegetation of the country visited. Such opportunities as were afforded on this occasion were largely availed of, the result being to add three plants to those already recorded as occurring in the district (district X. of the "Cybele Hibernica"). The plants in question are—1, The spindle tree *(Euonymus europæus)*—a species not at all rare in the North, though so stated in the floras ; 2, the downy oat-grass *(Avena pubescens);* 3, the yellow oat-grass *(Trisetum flavescens).* The latter, though not very common in the North, is, nevertheless, not nearly so rare as would appear from the statements of the "Cybele Hibernica" and the "Flora of Ulster." It has been found by members of the Club in several localities in Antrim and Down. The hop trefoil *(Trifolium procumbens)* was found plentifully at the quarries. This plant has not been recorded as occurring in the county. There is, however, little doubt but that it will be met with in all the Northern counties. In addition to the foregoing, the white water-lily was found in Loughnashade, close to Navan Fort. *Carex disticha*, a sedge that is quite rare in the North-East, was found plentifully. The skull-cap *(Scutellaria galericulata)* was also met with, and many plants of lesser note.

We must express our acknowledgments for valuable information obtained for the preparation of the historical and archæological notes of this excursion in " A Record of the City of Armagh," by Edward Rogers, Esq. ; and in " The Ancient Churches of Armagh," by Rev. William Reeves, D.D., LL.D.

On 1st, 2nd, and 3rd August, to

DUNGIVEN, LIMAVADY, AND LIGNAPEISTE.

This being the most extended excursion of the year, it was expected that the attendance would have been more numerous than on the ordinary occasions; but unavoidable circumstances having led to a postponement from the week preceding—the date originally arranged—that expectation was not realized. The weather, too, rather militated against a numerous muster of members, the bright glow of summer, which had prevailed during the preceding weeks, being succeeded by clouds and threatened rain. The party, however, as is the wont of the Club, met punctually at the Northern Counties Railway Terminus, at the appointed hour of noon, and started in accordance with their programme.

The first halt was at the town of Limavady, until lately better known by the prefix of Newtown, which has been most properly dropped by Parliamentary license, and the ancient name, signifying "The Dog's Leap," reassumed. Although the cloudy condition of the atmosphere portended rain, the first part of the programme was carried out during the evening; and after dinner a visit was paid to O'Cahan's Rock, and the site of the residence of the last chieftain of that name, on the banks of the Roe. The beauty of the surrounding scenery amply repaid the walk of some three miles to this interesting spot, and some rare plants were discovered by the botanists of the party. The locality abounds with traditions connected with the names of the hostile clans, MacDonnell and O'Cahan, some of which were detailed to the party during their walk by inhabitants on the spot. Among other places of interest, they were shown the position at the site of O'Cahan's Castle whence that chieftain was accustomed, as a pastime, to view those of the hostile tribe who were suspended on the trees overhanging the Roe, which flows beneath the rock.

The Alexander Arms Hotel was regained at the "gloaming,"

and on the following morning the whole party started on well-appointed outside cars for Dungiven, the second station on their route. During the drive the beautiful locality of Carrickrock was visited, with the tasteful church—a modern erection—in its vicinity. The scenery here remarkably resembles that of O'Cahan's Rock, the River Roe winding between the steep declivities on both sides, the banks of which present a strikingly beautiful view from a slight wooden bridge which spans the river at this place. At this point of the excursion the rain, which threatened at the outset, commenced, and continued without cessation during the entire day. The members of the Club, however, true to their antecedents, continued their course towards Dungiven, diverging *en route* to visit Pellipar, the elegant mansion of James Ogilby, Esq., J.P., D.L. This visit was paid through the courteous invitation of Canon Ross, Rector of Dungiven, who met the party and conducted them through the several apartments, which contain the well-known and splendid collection of paintings for which Pellipar is celebrated. Few private collections in Ireland can compare with this one in its riches of pictorial art, comprising, as it does, some masterpieces from Murillo, Rubens, Snider, and others of the earlier foreign schools, as well as many gems of modern art.

The remainder of this day (Wednesday) was spent in exploring some of the glens in the neighbourhood of Dungiven—Canon Ross, who is intimately acquainted with their beautiful and romantic recesses, acting here also as guide. Although the rain descended in anything but an encouraging form, the party were enabled to accomplish their purpose in penetrating to the beautiful waterfall of Lignapeiste, and met with several rare and interesting ferns and other plants during their walk. Among others may be mentioned *Lastrea oreopteris* (the scented fern), *Polypodium phegopteris, Pinguicula lusitanica, Galeopsis versicolor, Melampyrum pratense, Hieracium sylvaticum, Melica uniflora, Viola odorata, &c.,* were also noticed. Among other plants of interest was the wild raspberry, which in one spot appeared in the greatest profusion, and bearing fruit which for size and flavour might rival the garden form. The geological features of this remarkable district proved interesting also, particularly an outcrop of the primary limestone in contiguity with the trap rock, and assuming a metamorphic character. During their inspection of the waterfall of Lignapeiste, which name implies in the Celtic tongue " the den or cave of the monster," the party were entertained by some of the natives relating to them the traditions of St. Muiredach O'Heney, who confined to that spot, and bound beneath its waters, a savage beast or serpent which infested the glen, by first becoming familiarly acquainted with the monster, and then by way of civility placing three rushes on its head. These glens are still inhabited by an aboriginal Irish-speaking race, among whom such traditions are preserved in abundance; and, as report has it, the poems of Ossian are here recited to this day in their original Gaelic language.

On their return journey to Limavady, the excursionists visited a very remarkable kist-vaen, and afterwards the ruins of the ancient church of Banagher, which, with the adjoining building—both partly cyclopean in their structure—are amongst the most interesting ecclesiastical remains in Ulster. The latter was unquestionably a place of residence, most worthy of the chief pastor of the district; and in the graveyard annexed an ancient burial-place and tomb are shown, said to be that of St. O'Heney. These ecclesiastical remains date, as to their origin, from the fifth century, and are extremely interesting. Notwithstanding the increasing inclemency of the evening, some of the party visited, before leaving Dungiven, its ancient church, which stands about a mile from the town. This structure is of 12th century date, and contains an altar tomb, with superincumbent effigy of one of the chieftains, probably the last of the O'Cahan family. The eastern gable still stands, and through the laudable exertions of Canon Ross, some of the stone mullions of its windows, the walls of the nave, and other parts of the ancient structure have been preserved from falling into utter decay. We should mention that the repairs executed on the decaying structure of the old church of Dungiven, and the renovation of the remarkable tomb of O'Cahan, have been carried out at the sole expense of James Ogilvy, Esq., the owner of Pellipar. It may also be added that the zealous co-operation of Michael King, Esq., in procuring plans and assisting in business details, has materially aided the generous efforts of the gentleman above-mentioned in preserving these interesting remains from falling into hopeless decay. After the inspection of the church, the members of the Club were hospitably entertained at tea by Canon Ross and his excellent lady, and shortly after left for Limavady, which they soon reached, to enjoy a night's repose, rendered extremely acceptable by the proceedings of the day, interesting as they proved, although carried out under a continuous rainfall.

On the following morning (Thursday) some of the party extended their route to the City of Londonderry, to which they were enabled to pay a passing visit, and to rejoin their fellow-excursionists at Limavady Junction on their return homewards. Some others, although the rain threatened, visited a portion of the adjoining parish of Balteagh, in the neighbourhood of Keady Hill, and afterwards enjoyed a passlng view of Dreenagh, the beautiful residence of C. T. M'Causland, Esq., through which they were courteously conducted by that gentleman, having been introduced by the Rev. Knox Homan, Rector of Balteagh, who accompanied them. The botanists of the party, here and in the immediate neighbourhood, added to the list of plants observed, the following: —*Sambucus ebulus* (dwarf elder), *Tanacetum vulgare, Arctostaphylos uva-ursi* (bear berry); and also, along the cliffs of Ben Evenagh, whither their walk was extended before their return homeward, *Dryas octopetala* and *Silene acaulis*. While noticing objects of interest pertaining to the natural history of the excursion, it would be unpardonable to omit one which appeared to the members of the Club who were favoured with a sight of it deserving more than a passing record. Before they left Limavady, a lady residing there kindly exhibited to the excursionists a seagull, of the herring species, which had been in her possession and under her constant oversight for the space of forty-two years. This bird, although thus aged, is still, so to speak, possessed of all its faculties. The bill is overgrown somewhat and bent, crossing at its extremity, and the gait of this extraordinary bird somewhat affected by its longevity, but still it is comparatively active, and, when under inspection, quite able to hold its own with the poultry in the yard, who crowded around to share the food which the lady threw to it, and of which it partook with apparently an excellent appetite.

The party reached Belfast on the evening of this day (Thursday), having thoroughly enjoyed their trip, notwithstanding the unfavourable state of the weather, and without a single accident or disappointment, their programme having been carried out with nearly entire completion.

On Saturday, 12th August, to

COLIN GLEN AND CASTLE ROBIN.

The members and their friends assembled at the Ulster Hall at twelve o'clock, and, mounting the vehicles which were in attendance for the conveyance of the party, a pleasant drive by the Lower Falls Road and Andersonstown brought them to the Woodbourne entrance of Colin Glen, admission to which was kindly granted by the courtesy of Finlay M'Cance, Esq., J.P. The glen possesses considerable interest to the botanist, as it is the *habitat* of several rare plants, and many species of our native ferns occur here in great profusion. During Saturday's excursion several well-marked varieties or "sports" of them were met with, particularly of the common hartstongue *(Scolopendrium vulgare)*. It is, however, to the geologist that this district has most attractions, as there are few localities to be found where a series of rocks so varied as those seen in Colin Glen are displayed in so small a compass. Commencing at the lower part of the glen, the geological student may investigate strata of Triassic age, consisting of the variegated marls known as the Keuper formation. These are of very great thickness, and, as usual elsewhere, entirely devoid of fossils. Passing upwards, the strata next in order are the highly interesting "*Avicula contorta* beds," which are more extensively developed in Antrim than anywhere else in Britain. These beds consist of soft friable shales, with thin courses of impure limestone, and are highly fossiliferous. There are also several very thin sandy bands, which are charged with the remains of fish and reptiles, mainly the teeth and scales. Owing to a great mass of stones having fallen from the bank above, and covered up the section where these "bone beds" were best displayed, no specimens of Rhætic fish or reptilian remains were obtained on this occasion. Next in order above the Rhætic beds, and occurring both below and above the bridges crossing the glen, are found shales and limestones belonging to the Lower Lias proper. The sections are not, however, the most interesting or instructive that may be found in the county. The series are not well displayed, and consist of the very lowest members of the Lower Lias—known as the "*Ammonites planorbis* zone"—a zone that contains but few fossils, and these not in good preservation. The more fossiliferous portions of the Lias are only slightly exposed in Colin Glen. Superimposed on the Lias there occur considerable masses of rocks belonging to the Upper Greensand. This formation is largely developed here, and consists of soft, dark green sands (Glauconitic sands), yellow cherty sandstones, and light green sands and sandstones; the whole series being estimated by Professor Ralph Tate, F.G.S., at 54 feet in thickness, though appearing to be much more, owing to repetitions of the same beds in the stream, in consquence of vast rock slips which have occurred long since. The Greensand period was characterized by a rich fauna, and the rocks of that age in Colin Glen yield an extensive suite of fossils, consisting mainly of bivalve shells, echinoderms, and fish teeth. A considerable thickness of white limestone succeeds the Greensand, and represents the Upper Cretaceous period, being correlated with the very highest portion of the Chalk of the Continent. The whole of this extensive series of rocks is covered by the capping of basalt usual in this district; and the denudation by which they have been here exposed has not only prepared a scene of beauty for the lover of the picturesque, but also a delightful retreat where the geologist may pursue his favourite studies with unusual advantages. A considerable number of fossils were collected by the members of the party, amongst which the following may be mentioned from the Liassic beds :—Vertebræ of *Ichthyosaurus, Cardinia Listeri, C. ovalis, Astarte Gueuxii, Lima gigantea, L. punctata, L. Terquemi, Cardium Rhæticum, Ammonites Johnstoni,* and *Fucoidea sp.* The various Greensand rocks yielded the following species :—*Pecten quinquecostata, P. æquicostata, Exogyra plicata, E. lævigata, Cucullæa Ligeriensis, Spondylus spinosus, Pleurotomaria sp., Terebratula abrupta, Echinoconus conicus, Ventriculites sp., &c.* Some few of the members remained at the upper portion of the glen to continue their geological investigations, but the larger portion of the party descended to the Upper Falls Road, whither the cars had proceeded to await their arrival. Once more seated upon them, the route was taken to Castle Robin, and on the way a magnificent view of the valley of the Lagan was obtained from the slope of the hill along which the road passes. A short stay was made at the castle to inspect the ruin and the ancient fort or rath which adjoins it. The castle, which does not appear to have been of any magnitude, is said to have been erected in Elizabeth's reign by Roger Norton, an officer in Essex's army. The fort is said to have been previously known as Lisne-Robin, from which name that of the castle may have been derived. The homeward journey was then commenced, and on the way a halt was made to inspect an interesting geological section formed by a stream passing down by the side of a quarry a little beyond Colin Glen. In this section the Liassic rocks which appear in the glen (and which may be traced along the coast so far north as Ballintoy and Magilligan) disappear entirely, and the Greensand rests directly upon the Keuper marls. This inspection concluded, the business meeting of the excursion was held, and a number of members elected as members of the Club, after which the party returned to town, reaching it shortly before seven o'clock.

On Saturday, 6th September, to

RADEMON, KILLYLEAGH, AND STRANGFORD LOUGH.

The small number of members who availed themselves of the opportunity of attending this excursion, left by train at 10.45 for Crossgar, and on arrival at that station were conveyed by cars to the entrance of Rademon demesne, to which they were admitted by the kind permission of James Sharman Crawford, Esq., M.P. The programme for the day admitted of only a very short stay here; a walk through the grounds, however, satisfied the party that they could scarcely visit a spot more suitable for the study of the various branches of natural history. The woods contain some very fine trees, sturdy old oaks, and tall symmetrical larches, under the shade of whose foliage sylvan plants abound, and insects of various tribes find suitable habitats. Though late in the season, butterflies were numerous. Amongst those captured was the painted lady *(Cynthia cardui)*. On leaving Rademon, the party proceeded to Killyleagh, stopping on the way to visit Shane's Lough, near the latter place. On the wooded borders of the lake the ferns were found to be extremely luxuriant; the bracken *(Pteris aquilina)* was most remarkable, several of the stems measuring nine feet in length, and bearing an unusual number of fronds. The white water-lily *(Nymphæa alba)*, so scarce in Antrim, beautified the surface of this pretty lakelet, even at this late season. On reaching Killyleagh, the party were kindly invited to luncheon by Lachlan M'Laine, Esq., who also placed his fine yacht at their disposal, for the purpose of visiting some of the islands in Strangford Lough. One section of the Club came prepared to avail themselves of the opportunity of dredging in the lough, and under the guidance of Mr. Robert Lowry, who kindly accompanied them in his yacht, had a short but most successful cruise. The sheltered inlet of Strangford Lough has been famed for its marine zoology, and certainly the abundance of animal life brought up by the dredge on this occasion was most surprising. Starfish were in the utmost profusion—the dredge, a very small one, was only a very few minutes down, but when brought up, it was found to be not only filled, but heaped up with brittle stars of at least three species—viz., *Ophiura albida, Ophicoma rosula,* and *O. granulata,* the latter a comparatively rare species. The number of starfishes obtained by this one haul of the dredge was not less than 2,000. Of mollusca, the most noticeable were Chitons, three species of which were found—*C. fasicularis, C. ruber,* and *C. marginata.* Specimens of various species of crustacea, echinodermata, zoophytes, and sponges were collected, and those engaged were convinced that if sufficient time had been at their disposal, the result of the dredging operations would have been of very high interest. The remainder of the party proceeded to visit Green Island, which, like the other islands in the vicinity, is notable on account of the remarkable deposit of Boulder clay of which the surface is composed. The clay contains fragments of rocks of various ages and origin. Large boulders of greenstone were common, and masses of red grit resembling the coarse Devonian sandstone of Cushendall. Nodules of ironstone and fragments of sandstone, containing plant remains, were also found. Chalk and flint chips were scarce, but boulders of Carboniferous limestone, charged with brachiopod shells, encrinites, and corals, were abundant. The glacial deposits of Strangford Lough differ so much from accumulations of similar age on the mainland, they require very careful study, and suggest many questions as to their origin—where were the rocks located which have been denuded to form the boulder clay? and by what agency were the materials transported to their present site? The transporting and denuding power of ice in some of its forms is shown by the grooved and polished rocks exposed along the shore, and by the erratic boulders scattered over the country. Interesting as the study of these newer deposits may be, that of the older rocks occurring in the County Down is equally so ; the latter were examined in the fine sections exposed in Rademon demesne and other places along the route. The history of the various phenomena connected with these rocks, the changes they have subsequently undergone, the study of the fossils they contain, and the examination of the igneous rocks associated with them, afford questions of the highest interest to the local geologist.

WINTER SESSION.

NOTE.—The Authors of the various papers, of which abstracts are here appended, are alone responsible for the views expressed in them.

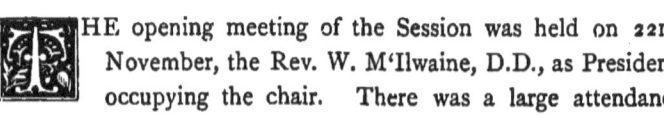

HE opening meeting of the Session was held on 22nd November, the Rev. W. M'Ilwaine, D.D., as President, occupying the chair. There was a large attendance both of ladies and gentlemen, it having been pretty generally known among the members, though not by public advertisement, that the chairman was about to discuss the subject of spiritualism, and to give his opinions thereon, in the address inaugurating the session. The paper read by him commenced with a graphic sketch of the proceedings of the British Association at Glasgow, in the month of August last, in which the address of the president (Dr. Andrews) was highly commended, and reference made to the various subjects discussed in the sections of the Association. Dr. MacIlwaine mentioned with approbation the fact that no topic had been introduced by any of the principal speakers calculated to wound the feelings of any member, with the single exception of that which was read in the Anthropological Section by Professor Barrett, of the Royal College of Science, Dublin, on the subject of spiritualism. Dr. MacIlwaine considered that the introduction of such a subject there was wholly unsuitable, and alluded to the fact that it had been admitted only by the casting vote of the chairman of the Anthropological Section, Mr. Wallace, on whose conduct while acting as president in the section he strongly animadverted. The lecturer proceeded to discuss the subject at length, remarking that he was not answerable for its introduction among topics of a scientific institution; but those who had thus forced it on public notice were so. Dr. MacIlwaine proceeded to examine it in both its physical and psychological aspect. Under the former head, he entered at considerable length into an examination of the nervous system in both man and lower tribes of animals. In the course of his remarks he pointed out the remarkable coincidence between the different grades of animal life, and the divisions of the spinal cord and brain. There are three degrees of life in man—the organic, the animal, properly so called, and the rational. Dr. MacIlwaine traced their connection, from the lowest to the highest, with the spinal cord, the medulla oblongata, and the brain, with its appendages. In so doing, the lecturer was assisted by an admirable diagram, copied from the recent work of Dr. Ferrier on the Functions of the Brain, in which these divisions, and their progress from simple reflex action of the nerves to the highest functions of the brain, were clearly traced. The intimate connection between matter and mind, and the independent existence of each, was fully explained, the seat of the will and the higher mental powers being shown to be located in the frontal lobes of the brain. Dr. MacIlwaine next proceeded to trace the history of the three subjects embraced in Professor Barrett's paper—namely, mesmerism, clairvoyance, and spiritualism—and showed by a historical sketch that the one insensibly, but invariably, led to the other. The cases of Dr. Braid, of Manchester, and Dr. Gregory, of Edinburgh, were quoted in proof that well-meaning, and even scientific, men might be led into absurdities and dangerous errors by bestowing their attention on comparatively worthless subjects. The lecturer proceeded to examine at length the ground taken up by Professor Barrett in his papers, and by Mr. Wallace. He clearly showed that this ground was delusive and unphilosophical, as proved by the exposure made of Slade and others in the police courts, whither the common sense of the English people had relegated the question of spiritualism. He proceeded to examine the examples of clairvoyance adduced in Professor Barrett's paper, and showed their entire similarity to the exploded theories of Spiritualists. The evidence given by Mr. Marshall and Serjeant Cox in the police courts in favour of Slade was next fully gone into, Dr. MacIlwaine observing that it was one thing to collect facts, and quite another to reason correctly on them and to examine evidence. He also exposed the fallacy of comparing the discoveries of Galileo and other pioneers in true science with the alleged facts of spiritualism. In the one case acknowledged phenomena were brought into agreement with known laws; while, in the other, a new and undiscovered law was asserted, in order to account for dubious facts. He considered it certain that the alleged miraculous occurrence of clairvoyance and spiritualism could be accounted for on perfectly natural principles and ingenious juggling, and denounced the charlatanism which lay at the bottom of most of them. While admitting, as he was bound to do, the existence of such a power as mesmerism, Dr. MacIlwaine strongly disapproved of its practice, and read extracts from the *Lancet*, condemning it as highly dangerous even when really exhibited. He showed the absurdity of saying that spirits possessed hands of flesh and blood, and could pull watch chains and write on slates, as Mr. Wallace and Serjeant Cox asserted that they could. The messages alleged to be sent from the spirit-world were puerile and absurd, and could not warrant the belief that they were genuine. Dr. MacIlwaine proceeded to show the dangerous moral tendency when individuals were encouraged to surrender their wills and reason to the control of others. He also referred to the results of such acts in America, and strongly censured their practice on the young especially. Dr. Forbes Winslow had publicly stated that there were 10,000 patients in lunatic asylums in the United States of America who had fallen victims to this delusion. The lecturer proceeded to give a highly satisfactory account of the state of the Club, and to the work done during the past year by some of its members—by Mr. Joseph Wright in his researches connected with the Foraminifera; by Mr. W. Swanston in the Silurian deposits; by Mr. William Gray in the archælogical department, and by others. After referring to some other interesting details, the President concluded his address, and the meeting proceeded to the election of new members, with which the proceedings closed.

On 24th January—Rev. William MacIlwaine, D.D., M.R.I.A., President, in the chair—a paper was read by Mr. JOHN BROWNE, on " The Origin and Progress of Coinage."

After some introductory remarks, the essayist went on to say that he had seen it stated "that much had been well and eloquently written on the interest and study of coins, from the time of Petrarch to the present day, and yet the number who have sought amusement and instruction in that pursuit has been, and still continues small." He then pointed out that, as historic records, coins have proved themselves of the highest importance; and, even from the very infancy of the art of coinage, their valuable testimony commences, and that to the Greeks we owe, if not the invention, at all events the very early general extension of a circulating medium in this form. And, on the coins of the very earliest period, we find the migrations, and the manners, and the mythology, and state of civilization of this great and interesting people. But the Roman series, which rose, as it were, on the ruins of that of Greece, is, perhaps, more generally interesting than any other; at all events, it has been more studied, and, putting the question of art all together on one side, it may fairly, from the number of undoubted portraits, and from the variety of great events recorded on the coins belonging to it, be considered of the highest importance and interest. In addition to the vivid illustrations of history and general civilization, which they convey, the coins of Greece and Rome form, in themselves, a complete history of art from its earliest development to the highest excellence it ever attained in the greatest age of Grecian splendour, some Greek coins of that epoch presenting works unsurpassed by sculptures on a larger scale.

We may trace on the Roman series the gradual decline of art, with the decay of the Empire, until, on the complete prostration of Roman power in the west, art became nearly extinct, to revive, after a dormant period, in a totally new feeling, in the quaint but energetic character known as Gothic, the development of which may be traced in the coinage of modern Europe, from the fifth to the fifteenth centuries. The modern series, consisting of Anglo-Saxon, Anglo-Norman, and English coins, is, perhaps, more perfect and complete than that of any other state, and exhibits every stage of development, from the rude Saxon penny of Ethelbert, to the great coinage of gold nobles in the reign of Edward III., as well as the links of all subsequent progress. The eventful reign of Charles I. might be exhibited very graphically in a small cabinet of his coins. The rude siege pieces, struck without coining apparatus, in different parts of the kingdom, whither the fluctuating fortunes drove that unfortunate prince, serve as monuments of almost each disaster or temporary triumph. Amongst these, not the least remarkable are the great twenty-shilling pieces of silver, struck at Oxford, from the plate given up by the heads of the colleges, to be melted down and coined for the royal cause, in which process perished some of the noblest specimens of the exquisite skill of our early silversmiths, the loss of which will never cease to be regretted by all true lovers of art. The essayist, after showing the interest coins offer to private study, and their advantages in a public light, as being almost as important as a national library, then gave a brief description of the different series of coins in chronological order, from the primitive ring-money, as used in the days of Abraham, and which passed by weight, and not by tale or counting, down to the coinage of the present day. A discussion on the subject of the paper, and the election of new members, terminated the business of the meeting.

On 21st February—Rev. Dr. MacIlwaine, D.D., M.R.I.A., in the chair—two papers were read. The first, by Mr. WILLIAM GAULT, was entitled, " Observations on the Geology of the Black Mountain, with special reference to the Cretaceous Rocks." The Second was by Mr. WILLIAM MILLER, on " Antiquarian Remains on Lurigethan Mountain, and in the vicinity of Cushendall."

Mr. Gault commenced by referring to the great and increasing interest taken by English and continental geologists in the study of the Cretaceous rocks, and the almost total neglect of the same strata in Ireland. As worthy of particular notice, he mentioned the great work on the Upper Cretaceous strata of England and Ireland, by Dr. Charles Barrois, Professor of Geology in the College of Science in Lille. He had no hesitation in estimating the book of this young and ardent French geologist as the best and most comprehensive ever issued on Cretaceous geology. To Mr. William Whitaker, of the Geological Survey of England, he also gave great credit for the way he had detailed the Cretaceous beds in Kent and elsewhere in England. Mr. Whitaker's works might be taken as models of accurate observation, and clear statements of important, though often obscure, facts. The labours of Portlock and Tate, on the Irish Cretaceous beds, were next alluded to; also the maps and memoirs of the Irish Geological Survey, and the merits and deficiencies of each were pointed out.

A brief outline was next given of the order of succession of the Cretaceous strata in those districts in England and France where they are best developed. Their lithological and palæontological characteristics were described, and the very important fact of these beds thinning out to the north and west of Europe was mentioned as explanatory of the comparative thinness of this formation in Ireland. Our Irish strata also illustrate this fact, for they are best developed in the south and east of the County of Antrim, and thin out to the west and north, in the counties of Londonderry and Tyrone their thickness being very insignificant.

The Irish Cretaceous rocks are seen in general cropping out below the basaltic escarpment of the Miocene volcanic plateau of the North-east of Ireland, and they invariably form a smaller escarpment a little in advance of the igneous rocks, as they resist denuding forces, whether sub-ærial or marine, better than the overlying volcanic rocks. On the Antrim side of the Lagan valley, they may be seen stretching along the Belfast hills, like a silver streak below the dark basaltic cliffs, and all around the wave-washed shores of the County Antrim, as far to the northward as the famous Giant's Causeway and Rathlin Island; then turning westwards, by the ruined towers of Dunluce Castle, to Ben Evenagh mountain, overlooking Lough Foyle and the valley of the Roe, along which they stretch southwards past Dungiven, and terminate beyond Tamlaght and Stewartstown, in the County of Tyrone, almost in the very heart of Ulster.

Over this extended area of country, there is great variation in the thickness and composition of the Cretaceous rocks. But it is only in the south-eastern part of this district, particularly in the vicinity of Belfast, where we find anything like completeness in the succession of the beds. Along the elevated escarpment of the Belfast range of hills, from Colin Glen—a few miles south-west of Belfast—to Woodburn, on the north-east, we have good exposures of these rocks in natural cliff sections, in quarries, and in the deep

BELEMNITELLES.	Zone of the BELEMNITELLES.	Zone of the BELEMNITELLES.	Zone of the BELEMNITELLES.
2 Zone of MARSUPITES.			
3 Zone of M. Cor-Anguinum.	Tabular bed of Flint.	Tabular Flint.	Tabular Flint.
Callianassa Bed.		Zone of Marsupites.	
4 Zone of OSTREA COLUMBA.	2	2 M. Cor-Anguinum.	2 Micraster Cor-Anguinum.
Waldheima Hibernica.	3	3	3
4	Ostrea Columba.	4 Ostrea Columba.	
5 Zone of HOLASTER SUB-GLOBOSUS.	5 H. Sub-Globosus.	5 H. Sub-Globosus.	5 H. Sub-Globosus.
6 Zone of PECTEN ASPER.	6 Pecten Asper.	6 Pecten Asper.	6 Pecten Asper.
7 Ammonites Angulatus.			
8 Ammonites Planorbis Zone.	KEUPER MARLS. Motled and Variegated.	KEUPER MARLS. Red and Green Motled and Variegated.	KEUPER MARLS, with Gypsum Veins, and Bands of Sandstone Ripple Marked, &c., and with obscure footprints.
9 White Lias.		Calcareous Sandstones.	
c Avicula Contorta Beds.		Soft Red Sandstones.	
1 Bone Bed.	Bunter Sandstones.		
KEUPER MARLS.			

W. GAULT, DEL.

1. Hard Chalk with flints.—Upper Chalk. }
2. Chalk without flints. } Lower Chalk.
3. Conglomerate and nodular bed of green-speckled chalk (mulatto stone).

4. Light green sandstones. } Upper Greensand
5. Yellowish calcareous sandstones.
6. Dark green argillaceous sands.

SCALE OF THICKNESS-40 FEET TO 1 INCH.

7. Calcareous marls and grit. } Lower Lias.
8. Black shales.
9. Grey limestone.
10. Thin black shales. } Rhaetic Beds.
11. Micaceous shales and sandstones.

⁓⁓⁓ Waved lines denote unconformability.

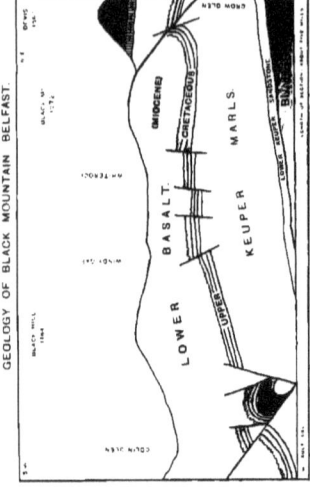

ravines and glens cut through the escarpment by the rapid streams flowing down from the hills to the river Lagan and Belfast Lough.

The reader stated that in the present paper he purposed detailing a few observations made during his study of the Cretaceous strata of the Black Mountain, reserving, for some future occasion, a detailed sketch of the part lying north-east and north of Belfast.

The general geological features of the Black Mountain are shown in the accompanying longitudinal section,* from Colin Glen to Crow Glen. It is drawn from personal survey, and those rocks only are noted about the occurrence of which there is no uncertainty. The scale of length is about one inch to a mile, but the vertical thickness of the formations is not drawn to scale, the Cretaceous and Liassic strata are exaggerated in order to bring them out more distinctly. The section gives the ground plan as far as it possibly could be delineated in a section of this kind, and, of the numerous faults and dislocations of the strata, only the most important are indicated by black lines. A page plate of vertical sections of the most interesting places along the escarpment is given in order to show the minuter details and succession of the various beds. The scale of thickness appended to these sections refers only to the Cretaceous rocks as a whole : some of the minor sub-divisions being very variable in thickness, whilst others are so thin as to require exaggeration in order to give them their position in the section.

Before giving the details of these sections, the author noticed at some length the underlying rocks, which he said consisted of the Bunter sandstone—a thick-bedded soft red rock, with layers of brown and yellowish sands, well shown in Conway Street, Belfast, and at Milltown and other places. These sandstones are overlaid by a thin course of buff, and reddish-brown sandstone,

* The Committee of the Club desire to express their obligations to the author (Mr. Wm. Gault), who has kindly supplied them with the plates in illustration of this paper.

with marly layers, being the representatives of the Lower Keuper —a division of the Trias only feebly represented in the district. The variegated marls and clays which form the great mass of our Keuper formation, succeed these beds, and are well seen in many fine sections in the various stream courses, perhaps the best of which is Springfield Glen.

In the section given the Keuper marls immediately underlie the Cretaceous beds, and the junction of the two formations may be seen at Whiterock, and at the Windy Gap. At Hannahstown Glen, a fault brings in the Lias and Rhætic beds, but at the detached position of the Cretaceous rocks seen at the waterfall in Colin Glen, we find the marls of the Keuper occupying their usual position at the base of the Greensand.

Strata, belonging to the Rhætic beds, and Lower Lias, rest conformably on the Keuper marls. They are chiefly composed of black shales, argillaceous limestones, and calcareous marls. I use the word calcareous to distinguish these marls from those of the Keuper, which contain little lime, and would be more properly termed clays. These Liassic strata are very fossiliferous, and good sections are seen along the river banks in Collin Glen. In the Glen, at Hannahstown, these strata are very much indurated by a large wedge-shaped projection of the basalt, which has curved the strata round into Colin Glen, cut off portions of the Cretaceous rocks, and broken the continuity of the escarpment, so that the beds in Colin Glen are repeated several times as we ascend to the waterfall. The Liassic strata are not continuous round the escarpment, but seem to occupy a trough in the Keuper marls, and occur under the same circumstances in many similar places, as at Carr's Glen, at the Cave Hill.

The lower basalt rests on the Chalk which it has hardened by heat and pressure into the familiar, hard, white limestone, so peculiar to our district. The surface of the Chalk upon which the basalt rests is greatly worn and very uneven, some of the hollows being filled with masses of flint gravel or rather breccia of flints and light grey calcareous clay, derived from the waste of the chalk itself; some of the flints are red, others yellow, or banded with yellow and red, the deepest tint of red being always in the very heart of the flint. This flint breccia is well seen at the quarries at the Black Mountain, near Windy Gap, but it is not found at any other place along the escarpment of the Black Mountain.

Owing to their varied composition, the great number of fossils contained, and the fact of it being the locality where the richest and most complete section of Upper Greensand beds are found, the Cretaceous rocks of the Black Mountain are the most interesting rocks of this formation occurring in Ireland. The section so well exposed for examination in the rocky gorge of Colin Glen we give in detail, as an index to the other localities, and in order to show the nature and composition of the various sub-divisions. A list is appended of the characteristic fossils occurring in the strata exposed at the various sections seen along the escarpment so far as the Crow Glen.

SECTION IN COLIN GLEN.

No. of Beds.　　　　　　　　　　　　　　　　　　　　　　Thickness in Feet.

1.A. Hard white chalk, thin bedded, and with flint, nodules occurring irregularly. Fossils not plentiful - - 6　0

BELEMNITELLA MUCRONATA　　RHYNCHONELLA OCTOPLICATA
LIMA HOPERI　　　　　　　　　　"　　PLICATILIS
PECTEN CRETOSUS　　　　　　MAGAS PUMILIA
ANANCHYTES OVATUS　　　　　PARASMILIA CENTRALIS
CIDARIS SP.　　　　　　　　　CŒLOPTYCHIUM FURCATUM
SPONDYLUS SPINOSUS　　　　　PARAMOUDRA BUCKLANDI
TEREBRATULA CARNEA　　　　　AMORPHOSPONGIA

1.B. Hard white chalk, in thicker beds, and the flints in regular rows about 18 inches apart on an average. The Fossils are not at all plentiful - - - 14　0

BELEMNITELLA	TEREBRATULA CARNEA
NAUTILUS	,, SEMIGLOBOSA
OSTREA VESICULARIS	RHYNCHONELLA PLICATILIS
,, DILATATA	,, LIMBATA
SPONDYLUS LATA	SERPULA
TURRITELLA UNICARINATA	AMORPHOSPONGIA PERRETICULATUM

1.c. Tabular bed or layer of grey flint, averaging about - 0 6

2. Hard white chalk, thick bedded, fossils numerous, and usually coated with a layer of glauconitic chalk Flints very rare and small, - - - - 2 6

AMMONITES LEWESIENSIS	ANANCHYTES GIBBUS
,, RHOTOMAGENSIS	,, PYRAMIDATUS
,, PORTLOCKI	ECHINOCONUS CONICUS
NAUTILUS LÆVIGATUS	,, SUB-ROTUNDUS
,, RADIATUS	MICRASTER, 2 SPECIES
BACULITES ANCEPS	CIDARIS
,, FAUJASI	MARSUPITES ORNATUS ?
BELEMNITELLA PLENUS	SERPULA
,, QUADRATA	AMORPHOSPONGIA GLOBULARIS
,, MUCRONATA	SIPHONIA CERVICORNIS
PLEUROTOMARIA PERSPECTIVA	TEREBRATULA CARNEA
,, MAILLEANA	,, ABRUPTA
TROCHUS CIRRUS	RHYNCHONELLA PLICATILIS
,, REGALIS	,, OCTOPLICTA
OSTREA CRASSA	,, MARTINI
,, VESICULARIS	TEREBRATULINA STRIATA
OTODUS APPENDICULATUS	INOCERAMUS SP.
CORAX ?	VENTRICULITES ALTERNANS
ANANCHYTES OVATUS	,, RADIATUS

3. Hard green speckled chalk, coarsely conglomeritic at the base; large rounded pebbles of quartz and other rocks, the glauconitic grains are very large and thickly scattered throughout, giving the bed its well-known name of mulatto stone. The fossils, except the sponges and brachiopods, are broken and worn, being probably derived from the waste of

an older bed. Sponges are very numerous, but other fossils are rare

RHYNCHONELLA LIMBATA (rare)	ETHERIDGIA MIRABILIS
,, PLICATILIS (rare)	CEPHALITES FUNGIFORMIS
TEREBRATULA CARNEA	AMORPHOSPONGIA GLOBULARIS
,, OBLONGA	,, PERRETICULATUM
PECTEN QUINQUECOSTATUS	VENTRICULITES DECURRENS
TROCHUS SP.	,, RADIATUS
CIDARIS SERRATA	,, ALTERNANS
SERPULA FILIFORMIS	,, CAMPANULATUS
SPONDYLUS SP.	,, MURICATUS
OTODUS APPENDICULATUS	CŒLOPTYCHIUM SP.
LAMNA ACUMNINATA	SIPHONIA ,,
GYRODUS SP.	BELEMNITELLA
PTYCHODUS MAMMILARIS	ANANCHYTES GIBBUS
ECHINOCONUS CONICUS	,, OVATUS
,, TUMIDIOR	,, SULCATA
,, SUB-ROTUNDUS	MICRASTER COR-ANGUINUM

(UNCONFORMITY.)

4.A. Whitish silicious sandstone, hard and compact, with glauconitic grains sparingly disseminated. The fossils are not numerous, and are chiefly fragmentary. The crustacean fragments are very plentiful - - - - - - - 9 0

CALLIANASSA, fragments of nipping claws and other portions of this crustacean	PECTEN QUINQUECOSTATUS
	NATICA SP.
	ECHINODERM fragments

4.B. Light green uncompacted sands, with layers of soft calcareous sandstone, with grains of glauconite and coarse grains of quartz. Fossils abundant - 6 0

OSTREA (EXOGYRA) COLUMBA	OTODUS APPENDICULATUS
,, PLICATA	LAMNA ACUMINATA
,, CANALICULATA	CORAX FALCATUS
,, LACINIATA	PTYCHODUS MAMMILARIS

INOCERAMUS STRIATUS	EPIASTER DISTINCTUS
PECTEN ASPER	BOURGUETICRINUS SP.
,, DUTEMPLEI	BRACHIOLITES PROTENSUS
,, VIRGATUS	SERPULA PLEXUS
,, ÆQUICOSTATUS	,, GORDIALIS
,, QUADRICOSTATUS	,, CONVEXA
,, QUINQUECOSTATUS	DITRUPA DEFORMIS
TEREBRATULINA STRIATA	RHYNCHONELLA DIMIDIATA
CUCULLÆA FIBROSA	TRIGONIA CRENULATA
AMMONITES LEWESIENSIS	

4.c. Light green sands, with nodular masses of hard compact silicious sandstone, full of fossils in fine preservation. The grains of glauconite are very fine, and not very numerous in this sandstone - - - 2 0

CARDIUM GIBBOSUM	WALDHEIMA HIBERNICA
PINNA SUB-TETRAGONA	LIMA SIMPLEX
PECTEN ASPER	,, SEMIORNATA
,, DUTEMPLEI	BULLA SP.
,, VIRGATUS	INOCERAMUS STRIATUS
,, ÆQUICOSTATUS	OSTREA LACINIATA
,, QUINQUECOSTATUS	,, CANALICULATA

5. Buff - coloured calcareous sandstone, with cherty masses, and layers of soft brown argillaceous sandstone, becoming at the base black and shaley. Fossils are plentiful, but not in very good preservation - - - - - - - - 34 0

AMMONITIES VARIANS (rare)	PECTEN ASPER
,, INFLATUS (rare)	,, ORBICULARIS (rare)
NAUTILUS DESLONGCHAMPSIANUS	,, DUTEMPLEI
OSTREA CARINATA	,, MEMBRANACEUS
,, CONICA	HOLASTER SUB-GLOBOSUS
,, PLICATA	DISCOIDEA MINIMA
,, HALIOTOIDEA	CIDARIS SP.
SCALPELLUM TRILINEATUM	RHYNCHONELLA LATISSIMA
SERPULA AMPULLACEA	DITRUPA DEFORMIS
MICROBACIA CORONULA	BRACHIOLITES PROTENSUS
PECTEN ÆQUICOSTATUS	PLANT REMAINS (obscure)
,, QUINQUECOSTATUS	

6. Dark green argillaceous sands and marls, almost entirely made up of grains of glauconite, in an argillo-calcareous paste. Nodules of phosphate of lime occur in small quantity, chiefly in the medial portion of the bed, where the fossils occur in the phosphatic matter. Fossils are numerous, but mostly in a bad state of preservation, and often as casts only - 9 0

AMMONITES VARIANS	BELEMNITES ULTIMUS
,, INFLATUS	LITTORINA ROTUNDATA
OSTREA (EXOGYRA) CONICA	SOLARIUM ORNATUM
,, PLICATA	MYACITES MANDIBULA
,, HALIOTOIDEA	AVICULA SUBLINEATA
,, LACINIATA	TEREBRATULA SQUAMOSA
PECTEN GLAUCONEUS	RHYNCHONELLA NUCIFORMIS
,, ASPER	DITRUPA DEFORMIS
,, DUTEMPLEI	SERPULA ANTIQUA
,, VIRGATUS	,, QUINQUECARINATA
,, QUINQUECOSTATUS	OTODUS APPENDICULATUS
TRIGONIA, several species	LAMNA ACUMINATA
CUCULLÆA CARINATA	PLANT REMAINS (obscure)
PLICATULA BRONNI	

Beds No. 1.a., 1.b., and 1.c. represent, without doubt, the zone of Belemnitelles. Beds Nos. 2 and 3 are usually grouped as part of the latter, but it is evident from a proper comparison and examination of the fossils found in them that they belong to an older portion of the Chalk series ; in fact, their true position is in the Lower Chalk division of English writers. No doubt, their thickness is comparatively trifling, but it is as great relatively to the English Lower Chalk as the upper bed is to the corresponding division in England. It will thus be seen that these beds are of importance, as they are the only representatives of the Lower Chalk we possess, and their persistence is very marked over a wide area, extending as far as Ballintoy, in the north of County Antrim.

These Chalk beds repose on the worn surface of the Upper Greensand, to which the beds numbered 4.a., 4.b., 4.c., 5, and 6 belong. These last-mentioned beds are the representatives of the Upper Greensand beds of Blackdown, and other parts of England, being our oldest Cretaceous strata, and belong to the Cenomanien division of French geologists. Beds Nos. 4.a., 4.b., and 4.c. thin out to the north-east end, and are limited in this direction by a fault south-west of Crow Glen. In the section at this latter place they are not seen, rocks belonging to bed No. 3 resting on the eroded surface of No. 5 ; nor are they seen again in any of the sections to the north-east, as far as Woodburn and Islandmagee; their place being taken by a bed of bluish-coloured calcareous grit, with large grains of quartz and glauconite, the fossils of which prove its affinity to the beds below the lower chalk of England, called the chalk marls of the Turonien division of the French geologists. That this is the true position of the Woodburn beds, the reader stated that he had no doubt, whatever; lithological and palaeontological evidence prove it to be so, and the discovery by him of *Terebratulina gracilis* in the Woodburn bed is a further proof of this statement. This very characteristic fossil has not been found in any other bed in this locality. *Spondylus spinosus* is also a Chalk fossil, and proves that the beds containing it have no claim to be considered as true members of the Upper Greensand division of the Cretaceous formation. The following table gives the classification of our Irish Cretaceous strata by the geologists who have written on the subject, for comparison with the correlation here adopted :—

France	England			R. Tate	C. Barrois	W. Gault	
				Uppermost Chalk			
Senonien	Upper Chalk			White Chalk	Zone of Belemnitelles	Zone of Belemnitelles	Upper Chalk
				Chloritic Chalk	Zone of Marsupites	Zone of Marsupites	
					Zone of Micrasters		
Turonien	Lower Chalk			Absent	Absent	Zone of Micrasters	Lower Chalk
		Chalk Marl		Zone of Exogyra Columba	Zone of Holaster Planos	Zone of Inoceramus Crispi (Unconformity)	Chalk Marl
Cenomanien	Upper Greensand			Zone of Inoceramus Crispi	Zone of Terebratulina Gracilis	Zone of Ostrea Columba	Upper Greensand
				Zone of Ostrea Carinata	Zone of Holaster Sub-Globosus	Zone of Holaster Sub-Globosus	
				Zone of Exogyra Conica	Zone of Pecten Asper	Zone of Pecten Asper	

Our Irish Cretaceous strata have suffered great denudation, and have been subjected to many viscissitudes which the English and Continental strata never had to endure. That they formerly extended further north to the Western Highlands of Scotland we have evidence of in the remnants of Cretaceous beds still found there, and which the reader has himself seen. They were probably continuous along the great Cretaceous basin of the north—with the Chalk of Sweden—and, doubtless, continued round the flanks of the Lammermuir Hills, and joined the Yorkshire basin, which is a prolongation of the South English and Continental Cretaceous formation.

Mr. MILLER then read his paper on "Some Antiquarian Remans on Lurigethan Mountain and in the vicinity of Cushendall." After a brief description of the locality, the reader showed from numerous remains of earthworks and the manner in which they were constructed, that Lurigethan was at one time a great central fortress. He also quoted and explained a number of local names, showing how they corroborated some of the local traditions which associated this—the most picturesque spot in the Antrim Glens—with the heroes of Finn and Ossian. After pointing out a few of the more prominent objects around Cushendall, he concluded by calling attention to the great number of antiquarian remains in the glens, most of which have as yet received very little attention.

An animated discussion followed the reading of the papers. The interest evinced in Mr. Miller's subject led to the formation of a sub-committee to communicate with Sir John Lubbock, M.P., in reference to the Bill which he was then about to bring before Parliament concerning the preservation of national monuments.

On 14th March, the President (Rev. William MacIlwaine, D.D., M.R.I.A., in the chair), a paper was read by Mr. WILLIAM SWANSTON on "The Correlation of the Silurian Rocks of the County Down." The paper *in extenso*, appears as an appendix to this number of the Club's proceedings.

On March 21st (the President, Rev. Dr. MacIlwaine, M.R.I.A., in the chair), two papers were read —The first was by Mr. JOSEPH RADLEY, of Prospect Hill, Lisburn, on " Woodpeckers and Kingfishers, their points of resemblance and difference." The reader, after giving the classifications of Linnæus, more particularly referred to the order *Picidæ*, which embraced a great variety of birds, some of which had little affinity to each other, including woodpeckers, crows, trogans, cuckoos, kingfishers, humming birds, hoopoes, creepers, and others. He stated that the woodpecker was more strictly a climbing bird than a percher, and the kingfisher finds its place more properly among the passerine birds. Few parts of the animal kingdom have, however, exercised the ingenuity of classifiers, more than that under notice. A convenient arrangement of the birds allied to the woodpeckers is that of M. Meyer; he calls them *Picæ*, and makes two divisions—the first, containing those with stiff feathers—viz., the genera *Picus* and *Certhia;* and secondly, those with soft feathers, *Yunx* (the wryneck), *Sitta* (the nuthatch), and *Tichodrama* (the wall-creepers). The true woodpeckers and the wryneck have one feature in common in the long and extensile tongue which is projected when the bird is in search of its food. Of the European varieties of the woodpecker, five are known in England—viz., the great black, the green, the great black and white, and the middle and lesser spotted varieties. Only two of these are recorded in Ireland—the great spotted *(Picus maior)*, and, more doubtfully, the lesser spotted *(Picus minor)*. The question was discussed as to whether the scarcity of old timber in Ireland is, or is not, a cause of the absence of the common green woodpecker *(Picus viridis)*. In Thompson's "Birds of Ireland," this idea is maintained. The reader suggests a connection between the geological strata, and the food and other conditions of life necessary, showing by reference to the geological map, that the woodpeckers in England flourished on secondary, and particularly Oolitic strata, the latter of which is entirely unknown here. These birds are becoming rare in England. The wryneck and woodcreepers still abound, the latter are plentiful in Ireland, but the presence of the former has not yet been recorded.

This part of the paper was illustrated by diagrams, and by specimens of several varieties from the museum collections, and by two very fine examples of the green woodpecker, shot near Witney, in Oxfordshire, by C. Clinch, Esq. The subject of kingfishers was also well illustrated by diagrams, and an extensive series of specimens belonging to the museum, including several of our native species (*Alcedo hispida*), which were obtained near Belfast. Some interesting remarks were made by members of the Club as to localities near Belfast where kingfishers were met with. One member stated that a brood of seven was last year brought out by a pair near Lisburn; others gave information respecting the appearance of the birds this spring on the Lagan, or on familiar spots on both sides of the Lough; but, acting on the advice of the president, members appeared unwilling to publish, for the benefit of the sporting world, information better appreciated by the true admirers of animated nature. The vice-president, Mr. William Gray, made an eloquent appeal to the ladies of Belfast, a fair sprinkling of whom graced the meeting, to desist from, and discourage, the wearing of kingfishers in the so-called bonnets of the period. His remarks were loudly cheered.

Mr. WILLIAM GRAY, M.R.I.A., communicated some of the results of "Hunting in the Sand-dunes." He explained that sand-dunes were heaps of blown or drifted sand that occurred at several places round the coast of Ireland, in common with most other countries. Those heaps are called "dunes," from an old Saxon word for mound or hillock. Sand-dunes are favourite resorts for rabbits, and are frequently thereby converted into rabbit warrens, and in some places the rabbits are so numerous at to be a source of trade. When sand-dunes occur, as they frequently do, at the mouths of rivers, or on prominent points near natural harbours, they become good stations for fishing as well as hunting, and as fish, particularly river fish, can be readily captured by simple means, sand-dunes were very probably selected as camping grounds by the very earliest inhabitants of Ireland as well as of England and Scotland. The evidence of this early occupation is afforded by the quantity and variety of ancient stone implements, pottery, &c., so frequently found in the sheltered hollows of sand-dunes. The principal stations yielding implements in quantity are the following, commencing at the north and going southwards :—

BANNMOUTH.—At both sides of the mouth of the River Bann there are extensive sand-dunes, indeed, the probability is, that the river at one time ran into the sea more to the east than at present, and that at that time both the groups of sand dunes were continuous; now the river turns to the east at its mouth, and cuts the sand-dunes into two groups. In both these divisions the number and character of the flints, &c., are the same.

PORTRUSH.—The sand-dunes at Portrush have yielded a large number of flakes, scrapers, &c., but owing to the great number of visitors to this station, the variety of implements, &c., found here is not so great as at Bannmouth.

BUSHFOOT.—The sand-dunes at Bushfoot, at the mouth of the River Bush, have yielded a fair number of implements.

BALLINTOY.—The sand-dunes at Whitepark Bay, near Ballintoy, have yielded a very large number of implements.

TORR HEAD.—Quantities of flakes have been found in the flats along the shore here. Those places are now under cultivation.

At such stations as Carnlough, Ballygally, Larne, Kilroot, Carrickfergus, Holywood, Ballyholme, and Leistone, where worked flints are very abundant, the beds in which they are found close to the sea are more like raised beaches than sand-dunes; but the sand-dunes at both sides of Dundrum Bay are in every respect similar to the dunes at Bannmouth, and yield similar implements. Mr. Gray also explained that, like the ancient camping grounds of North America, the kitchen middens of Denmark, and the lake dwellings of Switzerland, there are usually a number of sepulchral

D

monuments in the neighbourhood of implement-bearing sand-dunes. He referred particularly to a rude stone monument he found in the sand-dunes at the south side of Bannmouth, and to the stone circle, perched on a sand heap in Whitepark Bay; here flint implements were abundant, and the frequent finds of urns from this locality indicate that several early burials took place in the slopes of the adjoining cliffs.

Some years ago similar remains were found at the mouth of the River Bush, having been exposed by a storm that stripped off the sand. They were examined by Dr. W. Peard, of Bath, who happened to be in the locality, and Dr. Peard confirms Mr. Gray's opinion, that the site was an ancient camping ground, and was particularly selected from its proximity to the sand-dunes, and the well-known salmon pool in the neighbourhood. Mr. Gray concluded by directing attention to what he considered errors by the authors of the Geological Survey Memoirs, with reference to our northern worked Flints.

The explanatory memoir description of sheets 21, 28, and 29, refers to the Flint flakes, and miscalls them " Palæolithic," and further states that the flakes were "discovered" in the neighbourhood of Carrickfergus, Kilroot, &c., in 1867, by one of the officers of the Survey, Mr. Du Noyer; whereas Mr. Du Noyer himself states, in a letter to the Secretary of the Royal Geological Society of Ireland, dated December, 1868, that they were discovered five years before. This "discovery" was made by Mr. Gray and the members of the Belfast Naturalists' Field Club, who at first had some difficulty in convincing Mr. Du Noyer that the flints were artificial. The Club's report for 1866—the year before Mr. Du Noyer came to Carrickfergus—describes the finding of flint-flakes by members during an excursion to the localities referred to by Mr. Du Noyer.

Mr. Gray also exhibited a collection of coins recently found in peat neár Dervock, Co. Antrim. They consisted of base silver coins of Edward VI., Mary, and Queen Elizabeth. Of the latter there were examples of no less than twenty-three mintages from 1561 to 1594. The greater portion of the coins were sixpences. Mr. THOMAS DARRAGH brought under the notice of the meet-

Since the abstract of my paper was written, Professor Hull, Director of the Geological Survey of Ireland, has published his work on "The Physical Geography of Ireland," in which he has again erroneously referred to the worked flints of Larne and Kilroot as "Palæolithic." He also incorrectly describes the raised beach of Larne as "*composed of stratified and water-worn gravel, with numerous blanched marine shells, and with flint-flakes of human workmanship;*" and concludes from "*the presence of the worked flints, associated with the shells in the stratified gravels at Larne and Kilroot, that the coast has been raised since the occupation of the British Islands by the ancient Celtic tribes.*" In my opinion all this is untenable, inasmuch as the gravels are *not* mixed with worked flints, nor are the latter associated with marine shells; the worked flints are only found on the surface, and up to the present there is no evidence whatever to show that the worked flints of Larne, Kilroot, or any other part of Ireland are of the Palæolithic age.—WILLIAM GRAY.

The Fourteenth Annual Meeting of the Club was held in the Museum, College Square, on Wednesday evening, 18th April.

The chair was occupied by the Vice-President (Mr. Wm. Gray, M.R.I.A.).

In opening the business of the evening, the chairman stated that he presided in consequence of the unavoidable absence of their president, Dr. MacIlwaine, who was detained by illness, which he in common with all the members of the Club very much regretted. He was happy, however, to state that Dr. MacIlwaine was rapidly recovering, and he trusted soon to see him again presiding at their meetings.

Mr. JOSEPH WRIGHT, F.G.S., who was requested to report on the recent dredgings in this vicinity, stated that much material had been collected for future examination, but the only forms as yet worked up in detail were the Foraminifera. Referring to the report on this subject submitted at the last annual meeting, he mentioned that the number of Foraminifera found up to that date was eighty-one species. Since then the Club had visited Strangford Lough, and a large quantity of material from the sea-bottom was there procured. A second visit was made to Killyleagh, and further dredgings taken in the deepest parts of the lough; the results of these operations proving that Strangford Lough is tenanted by a rich Foraminiferal fauna. Other dredgings were also taken near the Maiden Lighthouses, in which very good results were obtained. The dredgings on the Antrim and Down coasts had yielded many rare species, the total number found up to the present date being 110, making 20 species additional to those reported last year. The Foraminifera found on the British coasts number from 170 to 180 species. It will thus be seen that those already obtained from our immediate vicinity amount to about 65 per cent. of the total British forms. Amongst those found in Strangford Lough was the very rare LAGENA TRIGONOMARGINATA. This little rhizopod has also been dredged by Mr. David Robertson, of Glasgow, off the Durham coast, about two years since, this being the only other record of its occurrence in

Britain. Mr. Wright then referred to the fossil Foraminifera, and stated that he had discovered them in the Lower Lias at Barney's Point, Islandmagee, a locality extremely rich in fossils, but in which these little rhizopods had not hitherto been detected. The species found are as follows—those marked (*) being additions to our Irish lists :—*TROCHAMMINA INCERTA (*D'Orb.*) ; *LAGENA STRIATA (*D'Orb.*); *NODOSARIA RAPHANISTRUM (*Linn.*); *N. RAPHANISTRUM, var. approaching SCALARIS (*Batsch.*) ; DENTALINA COMMUNIS (*D'Orb*) ; *MARGINULINA GLABRA (*D'Orb*) ; M. ENSIS (*Reuss*); CRISTELLARIA ACUTAURICULARIS (*F. & M.*) ; *POLYMORPHINA COMPRESSA (*D'Orb.*) ; FRONDICULARIA STRIATULA (*Reuss*) ; LINGULINA TENERA (*Bornemann*); *DISCORBINA SP. In the Club's proceedings for the year 1870-71 a good series of these interesting forms is recorded from Ballintoy, the only other Lias locality in Ireland which has hitherto yielded them. Although Liassic Foraminifera have as yet been recorded only from the above two localities, there is every reason to believe they will be found at many other places throughout the North of Ireland.

Mr. WM. GRAY, M.R.I.A., stated that in addition to the two localities mentioned by Mr. Wright, he (Mr. Gray) had found Lias Foraminifera in other localities, such as Glynn, Ballygally Head, Glenarm Deer-Park, and under Straidkelly.*

Mr. S. A. STEWART, F.B.S. Edin., exhibited a rare and very

---

* These shales have since been examined by Mr. Wright, and were all found to contain microzoa in more or less abundance ; that from Ballygally Head yielding Ostracoda and Foraminifera in great profusion and variety. The following species were found at this station :—NODOSARIA RAPHANUS (*Linn.*); N. RAPHANISTRUM (*Linn.*); N. RAPHANISTRUM (*Linn.*), approaching SCALARIS (*Batsch.*) ; DENTALINA COMMUNIS (*D'Orb.*) ; D. OBLIQUA (*Linn.*); MARGINULINA GLABRA (*D'Orb.*); M. LITUUS (*D'Orb.*); *VAGINULINA HARPA (*Römer*) ; CRISTELLARIA SP. ; FRONDICULARIA STRIATULA (*Reuss.*) ; LINGULINA TENERA (*Bornemann*) ; *CYTHERELLA CIRCUMSCRIPTA (?) (*Blake*) ; *BAIRDIA DISPERSA (*Blake*) ; *B. LACHRYMA (?) (*Blake*); *B. NOV. SPEC. ; *POLYCOPE CERASIA (?) (*Blake*); *CYTHERE NOV. SPEC., near C. BLAKEI (*Jones*).

minute moss, Anodus Donianus, discovered by him last summer on Greensand rocks in Colin Glen, and new to the Irish flora. He also handed round examples of Tortula papillosa from a beech tree near Glencairn. This rare moss was mentioned with doubt in the list of the mosses of the North-East of Ireland, published by the Field Club, no specimens being forthcoming at the time. Its detection near Belfast renders it certain that Mr. J. H. Davies was right in referring his Lisburn plant to this species. Mr. Stewart showed other rare mosses, and stated that since the publication of the list referred to five species had been added to the record.

Rev. GEORGE ROBINSON exhibited some fine specimens of lepidoptera. Amongst these was the clouded yellow (C. edusa), a species usually quite rare in the North of Ireland, but which occurred in considerable numbers during the past summer. Another was the green hairstreak (T. rubi), a butterfly which may be considered as a great acquisition to the cabinet of a local collector.

The Club, anxious to encourage amongst its members a taste for natural history and antiquarian studies, annually award prizes for collections and sketches illustrative of those subjects. On this occasion a prize was awarded to Mr. William Gault for the best collection of Cretaceous fossils made during the past year. The collection, which was displayed on the table, consisted of a large number of forms, and well illustrated the palæontology of the Cretaceous epoch, many being good examples of already recorded species, and two at least are new to to the geology of our district. Mr. F. Lockwood obtained the special prize offered by Dr. James Moore, M.R.I.A., &c., for the best two drawings illustrative of archæology; the subjects were Kirkiston Castle, County Down, and the doorway of Newtownards Old Church. Mr. Lockwood was also awarded the special prize offered by Mr. Wm. Swanston for the best two studies from nature illustrative of geology. The difficulty of treating geological subjects from an artistic point of view was successfully surmounted in the two admirable drawings which were exhibited.

The report of the committee and the treasurer's statement of accounts were then read, which showed that the Club was in a flourishing and progressive condition, the number of members being on the increase, and the interest in the Club's work unabated. The Treasurer's statement showed a small balance to credit, which, considering the trifling amount of the annual subscription and the work accomplished, is highly satisfactory.

The following addition to No. 3 of the Club's Rules was proposed by Mr. Hugh Robinson, seconded by Mr. Wm. Swanston :— " Ordinary Members may compound for future subscriptions by payment of Three Guineas."

The election of officers for the ensuing year was then proceeded with, and also the admission of new members, after which a conversation ensued regarding the work of the Society, and suggestions were made in reference to the places to be visited during the coming summer session. The specimens exhibited were inspected with much interest by the members, and the meeting was brought to a close.

NOTICE.

EXCHANGE OF PROCEEDINGS.

HE Committee of the Club have been desirous of establishing a yearly exchange of the published proceedings with those of kindred organizations in other places, and have, during the past year, forwarded copies of the Thirteenth Annual Report and Proceedings to other societies. They acknowledge with thanks the receipt of the following publications, and hope that other societies, whose objects are similar, will favour them with copies of their proceedings as published :—

Bath Natural History and Antiquarian Field Club.
Proceedings. Vol. III., Part 3.—1876.

Berwickshire Naturalists' Field Club.
Proceedings for 1875.

Boston (U.S.A.) Society of Natural History.
Proceedings. Vol. XVII., Parts 3 and 4.—1875.
Do. Vol. XVIII., ,, 1 and 2.—1875-76.

Bristol Naturalists' Society.
Proceedings. Vol. III.—1868.
Do. Vol. IV.—1869.
Do. New Series, Vol. I., Part 3.—1876.
Annual Report for 1875-76.

Canadian Institute.
Journal of Science, Literature, and History. Vol. XV., Parts 1 to 4. 1876-77.

Cardiff Naturalists' Society.
Report and Transactions. Vol. VII.—1875.

Dunedin (Otago) Naturalists' Field Club.
Report for 1875-76.

Eastbourne Natural History Society.
Papers.—1875-76.

Edinburgh Botanical Society.
Transactions and Proceedings. Vol. XII., No. 3.
Report of Royal Botanic Gardens for 1875.

Essex Institute, Salem, Mass., U.S.A.
Bulletin. Vol. III., Nos. 1 to 12.—1876.
Art Department, Catalogue of Paintings, Bronzes, &c.—1875.

Geologists' Association.
Annual Report for 1875.
Do. Do. 1876.
Proceedings. Vol. IV., No. 6 to 9.—1876.

Glasgow Geological Society.
Transactions. Vol. V., Part 1.

Glasgow Natural History Society.
Proceedings. Vol. II., No. 2.—1876.

Glasgow Society of Field Naturalists.
Transactions. Part 4.—1875-76.
Flora and Fauna of West of Scotland.—1876.

Leeds Naturalists' Club and Scientific Association.
Constitution.
Sixth Annual Report.—1876.

Leeds Philosophical and Literary Society.
Annual Report for 1875-76.

Lewes and East Sussex Natural History Society.
Twelfth Annual Report.—1876.

Liverpool Philosophical and Literary Society.
Proceedings. No. 30.—1876.

Liverpool Naturalists' Field Club.
Proceedings for 1875-76.

Manchester Field Naturalists' and Archæologists' Society.
Report and Proceedings for 1875.
Do.   do.   1876.

Norfolk and Norwich Naturalists' Society.
Transactions. Vol. II., Part 2.—1876.

Peabody Academy of Sciences, Salem, Mass., U.S.A.
Sixth Annual Report of Trustees.—1874.
Memoirs. Vol. I., No. 4.
American Naturalist. Vol. VIII., Nos. 2 to 12.
Do.   do.   Vol. IX., Nos. 1 to 4, 6 to 12.

Philadelphia (U.S.A.) Academy of Natural Sciences.
Proceedings for 1875.

Plymouth Institution, and Devon and Cornwall Natural History Society.
Annual Report and Transactions. Vol. V., Part 3.—1876.

Quekett Microscopical Club.
Journal. Nos. 31 to 33.—1876-77.

Royal Institution of South Wales.
Forty-First Annual Report.—1876.

U.S.A. Geological Survey of the Territories.
An Account of the Publications Relating to the Travels of Lewis and Clarke.—1876.
Some Account, Critical, Descriptive, and Historical, of Zapus Hudsonius.—1875.

Warwickshire Naturalists' and Archæologists' Field Club.
Proceedings for 1875.
Do.   for 1876.

Warwickshire Natural History and Archælogical Society.
Fortieth Annual Report.—1876.

Watford Natural History Society, and Hertfordshire Field Club.
Transactions. Vol. I., Parts 4 and 5.—1876.
List of Members, &c.

Wiltshire Archæological and Natural History Society.
Wiltshire Archæological and Natural History Magazine. Parts 46 to 48.—1876.

[*From the respective Societies.*]

Check List of Ferns of North America.
From the Author, John Robinson, Esq., Salem, Mass., U.S.A.

The Ancient Churches of Armagh.—1860.
From the Author, Rev. Wm. Reeves, D.D., M.R.I.A.

BELFAST NATURALISTS' FIELD CLUB.

FIFTEENTH YEAR—1877-78.

LIST OF OFFICERS AND MEMBERS.

President.
REV. WILLIAM MacILWAINE, D.D., M.R.I.A.

Vice-President.
WILLIAM GRAY, M.R.I.A.

Treasurer.
GREER MALCOMSON, CASTLE PLACE.

Secretaries.

HUGH ROBINSON,	WM. SWANSTON, F.G.S.,
82, DONEGALL STREET.	50, KING STREET.

Committee.

JOHN BROWNE.	S. A. STEWART, F.B.S.E.
F. W. LOCKWOOD.	SAMUEL SYMINGTON.
Dr. J. MOORE, M.R.I.A., H.R.H.A.	ISAAC W. WARD.
GEORGE O'BRIEN.	THOMAS WORKMAN.
W. H. PATTERSON, M.R.I.A.	JOSEPH WRIGHT, F.G.S.

List of Members.

Any changes in the Addresses of Members should be communicated by them to the Secretaries.

William Aickin, M.D., Murray's Terrace.
Miss Alder, Kinnegar, Holywood.
W. J. C. Allen, J.P., Faunoran, Whiteabbey.
Edward Allworthy, Salem, Crumlin Road.
John Anderson, J.P., F.G.S., Hillbrook, Holywood.
Robert Anderson, Donegall Place.
W. C. F. Anderson, Springbank, Dunmurry.
Mrs. Andrews, Chlorine Place.
Thos. D. Atkinson, Donegall Place.

Rev. B. Banks, Claremont Street.
E. Neville Banks, Milton Terrace.
James M. Barkley, Cooleen, Strandtown
Robert Barklie, F.C.S., Carlisle St.
William Batt, Ormeau Road.
Miss L. Bell, Lucyville, Whitehouse.
E. H. Bell, Knockdarra, Strandtown.
George E. Bell, High Street.
Thomas D. Bottomley, Calender Street.
Joseph Boucher, Landscape Terrace
W. J. Boucher, The Mount, Mount Pottinger.
Davis Bowman, Calender Street
Charles H. Brett, Dunedin Terrace.
Rev. John Bristow, A.M, Cliftonville.
D. H. Brown, Fortwilliam Park.
John Browne, Crumlin Road.
W. J. Browne, A.M., I.N.S., Longford.
Henry Burden, M.D., College Sq. North.
J. R Burnett, Holywood.
Charles Bulla, Brougham Street.

John Campbell, Mossley, Carnmoney.
R. G. Campbell, Mossley, Carnmoney.

R. J. B. Canning, Knock Cottage, Knock.
W. J. Canning, Belgrave Cottage, Knock.
Miss Carruthers, Claremont Street.
John Carson, Holywood.
John Charley, College Park.
Miss Maud Charley, College Park.
A. Norman Charley, College Park.
J. C. Clarke, Dunedin, Antrim Road.
John Clelland, Model School, Newtonstewart.
William Clibborn, Windsor Terrace
Sir Edward Coey, J.P., D.L., Merville, Whiteabbey.
Edwin Collier, Alexandra Terrace.
Miss Connery, Mount Charles.
David Corbett, Coolavin, Malone.
Thomas H. Corry, Benvue, Windsor.
W. F. C. S. Corry, Ormeau Road.
Major John Sharman Crawford, M.A., T.C.D. ; J.P., D.L, Crawfordsburn.
Alex. Crawford, Chlorine Villa.
Alex. Crawford, Fitzwilliam Street.
Elisha Crawford, Cliftonville.
W. Crawford, Jun., Windsor Av.
Jas. Creeth, Brookhill Avenue.
Prof. R. O. Cunningham, M.D., F.L.S., Claremont Street.
W. M. Cunningham, Windsor.
Right Hon. Lord Dufferin and Clandeboye, K.P., Governor-Gen. of Canada (Hon. Mem.)
W. S. Davidson, Linen Hill, Armagh.
Thos. Darragh, Museum.
John H. Davies, Glenmore, Lisburn.
Robert Day, F.S.A., Patrick St., Cork.
L. D. Devlin, Ulster Villas, Lower Windsor.
John M. Dickson, Cromwell House, The Plains.
George Donaldson, Church Street.

Charles Elcock, Fitzroy Avenue.
J. George Fennell, Ardmore, Windsor Park.
J. H. Ferguson, Cliftonville.
W. A. Firth, Whiterock.
J. Firth, Whiterock.

William Gault, Christopher Street.
R. M. Gilmore, Shrigley, Killyleagh, Co. Down.
W. J. Gilmore, Richmond.
D. Corse Glen, Annfield Place, Glasgow.
G. J. Glen, Durham Street.
Jas. Gourley, Killinchy, Co. Down.
Henry Gowan, Greenwood, Belmont.
Mrs. Gowan, Greenwood, Belmont.
G. T. Glover, Kew Cottages, Mount Pottinger.
Rev. John Grainger, A.M., D.D., Broughshane, Ballymena (Cor. Mem.)
Rev. Jas. Graves, Inisnaig, Stoneyford, Co. Kilkenny (Cor. Mem.)
William Gray, M.R.I.A., Mount Charles.
Miss Gray, Mount Charles.
Miss Frances Gray, Mount Charles.
Edward Gregg, Prospect Street.
Miss Greer, Tarbat Villa, Strandtown.
Alexander Guild, Bedford Street.

Joseph Hall, Dunluce Street.
Hugh Hamilton, University Square
Jas. C. Hamilton, University Sq.
Thomas Hampton, Mount Charles.
Mann Harbison, Model School, Newtownards.
Wm. Harte, C.E., Buncrana, Co. Donegal (Cor. Mem.)
James Haslett, North Street.
W. D. Henderson, University Sq.
John Louis Henry, Donegall Pass.
Arthur Herdman, College Square North.
F. A. Heron, Greenmount, Craigavad.
Mrs. Heron, Greenmount, Craigavad.
James Hewitt, Ballymacreely, Killinchy, Co. Down.
Prof. J. F. Hodges, M.D., F.C.S., Derrievolgie, Malone.

John Hogg, Corporation Street.
J. Sinclair Holden, M.D., F.G.S., Sudbury, Suffolk (Cor. Mem.)
F. C. Holmes, Belmont, Strandtown.
J. J. Howard, Clifton Park Avenue.
Miss Hunter, Orchard Street.
Alex. Hunter, Northern Bank.
Thomas Hunter, Holywood.

James Imrie, Magdala Street.
Rev. Richard Irvine, A.M., Hampton, Windsor.
R. H. Irwin, Holywood.

F. M. Jennings, Browne St., Cork (Cor. Mem.)
Miss Johnston, Dalriada, Whiteabbey.
Miss Johnston, Glenavy, Lurgan.
Jas. Johnston, Derrivolgie, Malone.
W. J. Johnston, Dunesk, Stranmillis.

W. Thompson Kelly, Grasmere Terrace, Antrim Road.
J. J. Kelso, M.D., M.R.I.A., Lisburn.
Rev. J. A. Kerr, A.B., Whiteabbey.
William Kernahan, Antrim Terrace.
George Kidd, Suffolk, Dunmurry.
Henry Knight, Antrim Villa, Ashcome, Weston-super-Mare.
W. J. Knowles, Cullybackey.

Miss Lamb, Divis View, Lisburn Road.
W. W. Lamb, Divis View, Lisburn Road.
Geo. D. Leathem, Hollymount, Malone Park.
F. R. Lepper, Clonoriel, Strandtown.
Miss R. Lester, Newtownards.
F. W. Lockwood, Brookhill Avenue
John Love, Oldpark Terrace.
William Lowry, Oakley, Strandtown.
Richard Linn, Banbridge.

Henry Magee, Eglinton Avenue.
S. J. Magowan, Albion Place.
J. J. Major, Belvoir Hall, Newtownards Road.

Greer Malcomson, Shamrock Lodge.
Jas. Malcomson, Mount Pottinger.
Mrs. Malcomson, Mount Pottinger.
John Marsh, Richmond, Antrim Road.
Joseph C. Marsh, Donegall Street.
Rev. James Martin, Eglintoun, Antrim Road.
Mrs. Martin, Eglintoun, Antrim Road.
P. C. Mayne, Sydenham Avenue.
Miss Meadley, Eton Terrace.
John Millar, J.P., Lisburn.
Miss Millar, Lisburn.
William Millar, Shankhill Road.
James Moore, M.D., M.R.I.A., H.R.H.A., Chichester Street.
John Moore, M.D., Carlisle Terrace.
W. H. Moreland, Bloomfield House.
W. R. Molyneux, Florence Place.
John Morton, Donegall Place.
Miss Monteith, University Road.
Hugh Morrison, Ligoniel.
David Morrow, Dunluce Street.
J. R. T. Mulholland, Tyne Cottage, Whiteabbey.
J. J. Murphy, Old Forge, Dunmurry.
J. R. Musgrave, J.P., Drumglass, Malone.

Robert M'Adam, College Square East.
James M'Clenahan, Ardoyne.
Rev. Edmund M'Clure, A.M., M.R.I.A., Lincoln's Inn Fields, London (Hon. Mem.)
Sir Thomas M'Clure, J.P., V.L., Belmont.
Miss M'Clure, Belmont.
W. J. M'Clure, Divis Street.
John M'Connell, North Street.
John M'Ferran, Fortwilliam Park.
Joseph H. M'Ferran, Elmwood Terrace.
Rev. William MacIlwaine, D.D., M.R.I.A., Ulsterville.
Mrs. MacIlwaine, Ulsterville.
Herbert C. MacIlwaine, Ulsterville.
John B. S. MacIlwaine, Stephen's Green, Dublin.
Mrs. M'Ilwrath, Dunluce Street.
Daniel M'Kee, Adela Place.
John MacKenzie, C.E., Balmoral.

Thos. MacKnight, Windsor.
Alex. M'Laine, Corporation Street.
Francis P. M'Lean, Botanic Avenue.
William M'Millan, I.N.S., Ballinasloe.

Richard Niven, Chrome Hill, Lisburn.

Nicholas Oakman, Prospect Terrace.
George O'Brien, Botanic Avenue.
Joshua O'Brien, Botanic Avenue.
W. D. O'Brien, Botanic Avenue.
Rev. Jas. O'Laverty, Holywood.
James O'Neill, M.A., Upper Townsend Street.
Alexander O'Rorke, Manor House, Antrim Road.
Rev. R. C. Oulton, St. Lawrence Terrace.

David C. Patterson, Holywood.
R. Lloyd Patterson, Martello Terrace, Holywood.
W. H. Patterson, Dundela, Strandtown.
J. J. Phillips, Granville Terrace.
W. H. Phillips, Lemonfield, Holywood.
E. W. Pim, Elmwood Terrace.
John Pim, Chichester Park, Antrim Road.
Joshua Pim, Crumlin Terrace.
Joshua Pim, Lisnagarvey, Lisburn.
T. W. Pim, Evelyn Lodge, Strandtown.
Thomas Plunkett, Enniskillen.
R. L. Praeger, Holywood.
W. E. Praeger, Jun., Woodburn, Holywood.
John Preston, Jun., Dunmore, Antrim Road.
C. D. Purdon, M.D., Wellington Place.
Alfred Purdon, Wellington Place.

Joseph Radley, Prospect Hill, Lisburn.
John Rea, M.D., Great Victoria Street.
Jas. Theodore Richardson, Glenone, Lisburn.
Miss Robinson, Lisanore, Antrim Road.

Rev. Geo. Robinson, A.M., Tartaraghan, Co. Armagh.
Hugh Robinson, Donegall Street.
J. R. Robinson, St. Helen's Terrace, Mount Pottinger.
N. J. Robinson, Foxvale House, Cregagh Road.
W. A. Robinson, Tudor Park, Holywood.
W. G. Robinson, Dunluce Street.
Richard Ross, M.D., Wellington Place.
John Russell, Adelaide Place.
William Russell, University Street.

Rev. G. Bridges Sayers, Ballinderry, Lurgan.
Mrs. Scott, Fountainville Terrace.
J. M. Johnston Scott, M.D., Chichester Street.
Rev. Jonathan Seaver, A.B., Atlantic Avenue.
Thomas Seaver, B.E., Botanic Avenue.
A. F. Shaw, Belmont Park.
Thomas Shaw, Pakenham Place.
Thomas Shepherd, Whitehouse.
F. W. Smith, Rugby Road.
Charles Smith, F.G.S., Barrow-in-Furness.
George K. Smith, Meadow Bank, Whitehouse.
Robert Smith, Mount Pottinger.
Rev. Geo. C. Smythe, A.M., Coole Glebe, Carnmoney.
Major-Gen. Smythe, R.A., M.R.I.A. Abbeyville, Whiteabbey.
Adam Speers, B.Sc., Holywood.
Sir Nath. Staples, Bart., J.P., Lissan, Dungannon (Life Mem.)
Jas. H. Staples, Lissan, Dungannon.
John M'N. Stevenson, Model School, Carrickfergus.
Richard Stevenson, Donegall Pass.
S. A. Stewart, F.B.S.E., North Street.
J. M. Harris Stone, F.L.S., Wilmont Terrace.
Miss Swanston, University Street.
William Swanston, F.G.S., University Street.
Saml. Symington, Ballyoran House, Dundonald.

Prof. Ralph Tate, A.L.S., F.G.S., University of Adelaide, South Australia (Hon. Mem.)
A. O'D. Taylor, Upper Crescent.
Edward M'C. Thompson, Walton, Fortwilliam Park.
E. H. Thompson, Slieve-na-Failthe, Whiteabbey.
Henry Thompson, Windsor.
Prof. Sir Charles Wyville Thompson, LL D., F.R.S., &c., University Edinburgh (Hon. Mem.)
Prof. Jas. Thomson, A.M., LL.D., F.R.S., &c., Sardinia Terrace, Hillhead, Glasgow (Hon. Mem.)
Robert Thompson, Jun., Walton, Fortwilliam Park.
George Thomson, Broadway, Falls Road.
John Todd, Regent Street.
Wm A. Todd, Regent Street.
Wm. A. Traill, M.A.I., B.E., H.M. Geol. Survey, Glenarm.
A. Chevenix Trench, Upper Crescent.
Miss Thorpe, University Street.

Wm. Valentine, J.P., Glenavna, Whiteabbey.
J. W. Valentine, Greenisland.
W. F. Wakeman, Portora, Enniskillen (Cor. Mem.)
T. R. Walkington, Laurel Lodge, Strandtown.
Isaac W. Ward, University Street.
John Ward, Lennoxvale, Malone Road.
John S. Ward, Lisburn.
W. R Ward, Stanpit, Christchurch, Hants.
Robert Waters, Belmont Park.
E. H. Watson, Ardmore, Windsor.
W. Watson, Londonderry (Cor. Mem.)
Isaac Waugh, Everton Terrace.
T. K. Wheeler, M.D., Clarendon Place.
Wm. Whitford, A.M., Magdala Street.
David Wilson, Ballymoney, Co. Antrim.
Jas. Wilson, Ballybundon, Killinchy, Co. Down.

Rev. Hans Woods, A.M., Cooke Street, Ormeau Road.
John Workman, Windsor.
Rev. Robt. Workman, A.M., Glastry, Kirkcubbin, Co. Down.
Thomas Workman, Windsor
Joseph Wright, F.G.S., F.R.G.S.I., Albertville, Crumlin Road.

Saml. O. Wylie, College Square North.
William Wylie, Belgrave Terrace.
Robert Young, C.E., Rathvarna, Antrim Road.
Robert Young, Jun., Rathvarna, Antrim Road.

RULES
OF THE
Belfast Naturalists' Field Club.

I.

That the Society be called "THE BELFAST NATURALISTS' FIELD CLUB."

II.

That the objects of the Society be the Practical Study of Natural Science and Archæology.

III.

That the Club shall consist of Ordinary, Corresponding, and Honorary Members. The Ordinary Members to pay annually a subscription of Five Shillings ; and that candidates for such Membership shall be proposed and seconded at any Meeting of the Club by Members present, and elected by a majority of the votes of the Members present. Ordinary Members may compound for future subscriptions by one payment of Three Guineas.

IV.

That the Honorary and Corresponding Members shall consist of persons of eminence in Natural Science, or who shall have done some special service to the Club, and whose usual residence is not less than twenty miles from Belfast. That such Members may be nominated by any Member of the Club, and, on being approved of by the Committee, may be elected at any subsequent

Meeting of the Club by a majority of the votes of the Members present. That Corresponding Members be expected to communicate a Paper once within every two years.

V.

That the Officers of the Club be annually elected, and consist of a President, Vice-President, Treasurer, Two Secretaries, and Ten Members, who form the Committee. Five to form a quorum. No Member of Committee to be eligible for re-election who has not attended at least one-fourth of the Committee Meetings during his year of office.

VI.

That the Members of the Club shall hold at least Six Field Meetings during the year, in the most interesting localities, for investigating the Natural History and Archæology of the district. That the place of meeting be fixed by the Committee, and that five days' notice of each Excursion be communicated to Members by the Secretaries.

VII.

That Meetings be held Fortnightly or Monthly, at the discretion of the Committee, for the purpose of reading papers, such papers, as far as possible, to treat of the Natural History and Archæology of the district. These Meetings to be held during the months from November to April inclusive.

VIII.

That the Committee shall, if they find it advisable, offer for competition Prizes for the best collections of scientific objects of the district ; and the Committee may order the purchase of maps, or other scientific apparatus, and may carry on geological and archæological searches or excavations, if deemed advisable, provided that the entire amount expended under this rule does not exceed the sum of £10 in any one year.

IX.

That the Annual Meeting be held during the month of April, when the Report of the Committee for the past year, and the Treasurer's Financial Statement shall be presented, the Committee and Officers elected, Bye-laws made and altered, and any proposed alteration in the general laws, of which a

fortnight's notice shall have been given, in writing, to the Secretary or Secretaries, considered and decided upon. The Secretaries to give the Members due notice of such intended alteration.

X.

That, on the written requisition of twenty-five Members, delivered to the Secretaries, an Extraordinary General Meeting may be called, to consider and decide upon the subjects mentioned in such written requisition.

XI.

That the Committee be empowered to exchange publications and reports, and to extend the privilege of attending the Meetings and Excursions of the Belfast Naturalists' Field Club to members of kindred societies, on similar privileges being accorded to its Members by such other societies.

The following Rules for the Conducting of the Excursions have been arranged by the Committee.

I. The Excursion to be open to all Members ; each one to have the privilege of introducing two friends.

II. A Chairman to be elected as at ordinary meetings.

III. One of the Secretaries to act as conductor, or, in the absence of both, a member to be elected for that purpose.

IV. No change to be made in the programme, or extra expenses incurred, except by the consent of the majority of the members present.

V. No fees, gratuities, or other expenses to be paid except through the conductor.

VI. Every member or visitor to have the accommodation assigned by the conductor. Where accommodation is limited, consideration will be given to priority of application.

VII. Accommodation cannot be promised unless tickets are obtained before the time mentioned in the special circular.

VIII. Those who attend an excursion, without previous notice, will be liable to extra charge, if extra cost be incurred thereby.

IX. No intoxicating liquors to be provided at the expense of the Club.

Belfast Naturalists' Field Club.

FIFTEENTH YEAR.

The Committee offer the following Prizes to be competed for during the Session ending March 30, 1878 :—

1. For the best Herbarium of Flowering Plants, representing not less than 250 Species............ ......£1 0 0
2. For the best Herbarium of Flowering Plants, representing not less than 150 Species................... 0 10 0
3. Best Collection of Mosses................. .. .. 0 10 0
4. ,, ,, Seaweeds............... .. .. 0 10 0
5. ,, ,, Ferns........... .... 0 10 0
6. ,, ,, Tertiary and Post Tertiary Fossils................ .... 0 10 0
7. ,, ,, Cretaceous do. 0 10 0
8. ,, ,, Liassic   do. 0 10 0
9. ,, ,, Palæozoic do. 0 10 0
10. ,, ,, Fossil Plants...................... .. 0 10 0
11. ,, ,, Marine Shells...................... 0 10 0
12. ,, ,, Land and Freshwater Shells...... 0 10 0
13. ,, ,, Lepidoptera 0 10 0
14. Best set of 25 Microscopic Slides........................ 0 10 0

15. Best Collection of Archæological Objects............ £0 10 0
16.   ,,   ,,   Crustacea........ ... .,....... 0 10 0
17.   ,,   ,,   Echinodermata. 0 10 0
18.   ,,   ,,   Geological Specimens, illustrative of the Mineral Resources of the Province of Ulster... ... 1 0 0
19. Best Collection of all or any of the above Objects collected *at the Excursions* of the year............ 0 10 0
20. Six best Field Sketches appertaining to Geology, Archæology, or Natural History................... 0 10 0

In every case where three or more persons compete for a Prize, a second one of half its value will be awarded, if the conditions are otherwise complied with.

CONDITIONS.

No Competitor to obtain more than Two Prizes in any one year.

No Competitor to be awarded the same Prize twice within three years.

All Collections to be made personally during the Session, within the Province of Ulster. Each species to be correctly named, and locality stated. The Flowering Plants to be collected when in flower, and classified according to the Natural System. The Sketches, Drawings, and Microscopic Slides to be the Competitors' own work.

No Prizes will be awarded except to such Collections as shall, in the opinion of the Judges, possess positive merit.

The Prizes to be in books, or suitable scientific objects, at the desire of the successful competitor.

SPECIAL PRIZES.

21. The President offers a Prize of £1 1s. for the best set of Three Sketches, contributed to the Club's Album, by one out of three or more Competitors. The set to be of uniform size, not less than 9 inches by 5½ inches, unmounted, and to be Original Coloured Drawings of Irish Antiquarian subjects, liable to removal or destruction.

22. The Vice-President offers a Prize of 10s. 6d. for the best Sketch contributed to the Club's Album, by one out of two or more Competitors, not taking the President's Prize. Conditions otherwise same as for Prize No. 21.

23. Mr. William Swanston offers a Prize of 10s. 6d. for the best Two Studies from Nature, illustrative of Geology.

24. A Prize of 10s., given by the late Mr. J. W. Murphy, for the best Collection of Recent Sponges, the conditions being the same as those for Prizes 1 to 20.

25. Mr. W. A. Traill, M.A.I., H.M. Geological Survey, offers a Prize of £1 10s. for the best Collection of Rock Specimens—Igneous and Metamorphic—from the North of Ireland, tabulated with names and localities. The number need not exceed 36. Size recommended, 3 inches by 2 inches, by 1 inch.

Presented

11.FEB 86.

320 pp. Fcap. 8vo. Cloth Gilt, Bevelled Boards, with 48 pp. Illustrations and Map. Price 3/6.

GUIDE TO BELFAST

AND ADJACENT COUNTIES.

BY THE

BELFAST NATURALISTS' FIELD CLUB.

THE BOOK TREATS OF THE FOLLOWING SUBJECTS:

PHYSICAL GEOGRAPHY.
GEOLOGY AND MINERAL RESOURCES.
BOTANY.
ZOOLOGY.
TOPOGRAPHY.
HISTORICAL & DESCRIPTIVE NOTICES OF TOWNS.

ANTIQUITIES—ECCLESIASTICAL AND CIVIL.
AGRICULTURE.
TRADE AND COMMERCE.
EXCURSIONS TO PLACES OF INTEREST.

May be had of all Booksellers, or from the Secretaries of the Club.

11 FEB 1886

ANNUAL REPORTS

AND

PROCEEDINGS

OF THE

Belfast Naturalists' Field Club,

1877-78——1878-79.

SERIES II.

Volume I. Parts V. and VI.

PRINTED FOR MEMBERS ONLY.

ANNUAL REPORT

AND

PROCEEDINGS

OF THE

Belfast Naturalists' Field Club,

FOR THE

YEAR ENDING 31ST MARCH, 1878.

NEW SERIES.
VOLUME I. PART V.

BELFAST:
PRINTED FOR THE CLUB.
ROBINSON BROTHERS, 25, DONEGALL STREET
1879.

REPORT

OF THE

BELFAST NATURALISTS' FIELD CLUB,

FOR THE YEAR 1877-78.

IN meeting the members at the close of the fifteenth year of the Club's existence, the Committee have pleasure in being able to report that the society continues to enjoy a fair degree of prosperity. The work of the various branches of study contemplated by the Club has been steadily pursued by an increasing number of members, who devote their attention to special subjects, and the interest in the Club's work manifested by the members in general, and the public is in no way diminished. During the year there has been a considerable increase in the membership, this is mainly due to the efforts of a few who have, as occasion offered, placed the claims and the advantages of the Club before those who were unacquainted with them. The Committee are still of opinion that much more might be done in this direction, and as the efficiency of the Club depends to a very considerable degree upon the extent of its membership, they trust that further efforts will be made to increase it.

The localities selected for last Season's Excursions seemed to give general satisfaction. They were as follow :—

	19th May.	Duncrue and Woodburn.
	9th June.	Slate Quarries and Greyabbey.
	30th June.	Tartaraghan and Lough Neagh.
17th, 18th, &	19th July.	Greenore and Carlingford.
	18th Aug.	Downpatrick, Ardglass, &c.
	8th Sept.	Dundonald and Neighbourhood.

Detailed accounts of the Excursions are appended hereto.

Although the season was by no means a favourable one for excursions, the programme was, with one exception, carried out, and the attendance in some cases was much above the average. The exception referred to was the excursion arranged to Greenore and Carlingford. It is to be regretted that the unsuitable weather which prevailed at the time, and the high charges incident to the occasion, deterred all but a few from sending in their names, and on the morning of the excursion it was considered advisable to abandon it for the year.

At several of the field meetings short papers were read on subjects for the study of which the localities were more or less suitable. This is a feature which the Committee would be glad to see more generally adopted at future excursions.

As in the previous year, the Conversazione was held at the beginning of the Winter Session, and not at its close as formerly. The experience of the past two seasons fully justifies the change, and warrants the Committee in recommending to their successors in office the continuance of this arrangement. The general response of the members and friends to the invitations, and the interest evinced in the various objects exhibited and displayed around the room, were highly gratifying to those who were charged with the arrangements.

The Winter Session was opened by an address from the President (Rev. Canon MacIlwaine, D.D., M.R.I.A.), and during the session a number of interesting papers were read, of which the following is a list :—

1877.
20th Nov. Opening Address of the President (Rev. Canon MacIlwaine, D.D., M.R.I.A.)
11th Dec. "Water as an Agent of Denudation." By Mr. J. R. Robinson.
1878.
23rd Jan. "Something about Old Finger-rings." By Mr. Robert Day, F.S.A.
19th Feb. "Antiquarian Remains on Knock Dhu, the probable site of the Battle of Ollarbah." By Mr. William Millar.
19th Mar. "Notes on Birds." By Mr. Thomas Darragh.
,, "Our Northern Rocks, and where to find them." By Mr. William Gray, M R.I.A.

The Committee take this opportunity of thanking those who have, during the past year, added to the interest of the excursions by their kindness in throwing open their private grounds for the inspection of the members of the Club—a boon which was highly appreciated. Special thanks are due to the Belfast Mining Company, for the facilities afforded to a large party for examining the extensive salt mines at Duncrue; to Hugh Montgomery, Esq., D.L., for the privilege of visiting the interesting ruins of Greyabbey, and the slate quarries in the neighbourhood; and to the Belfast Slate Company for permission to view their extensive works. The Committee desire to express their appreciation of the kind hospitality extended to the members of the Club by William Valentine, Esq., J.P., of Glenavna; the Rev. George Robinson, A.M., of Tartaraghan; John Mawhinney, Esq., of Newtownards; and Samuel Symington, Esq., of Ballyoran House, on the occasion of the Club's visit to their respective localities. The Club still continues to receive contributions to its small stock of books. These consist principally of Transactions and Reports of kindred societies, and contain a vast amount of information ·not available by other means. Several valuable additions have also been received from the United States Government, &c., and it is gratifying to learn that the copies of the Club's Reports and Proceedings sent out are highly valued by those who receive them.

Two of the prizes offered by the Club have this year been competed for. The following is the report of the Judges :—" The first, a collection of Liassic Fossils, was sent by Mr. William Gault, in competition for Prize 8. This collection fairly represents the fauna of this formation, from the various exposures in the immediate vicinity of Belfast, some of the specimens being very good examples of characteristic forms. It is, however, noticeable that the zones occuring at Ballintoy are not represented, and in consequence the number of species is less than those which gained prizes on previous occasions ; but taking the collection as a whole, we consider it worthy of the prize, and have pleasure in recommending that it should be awarded." " The second collection is a series of mounted Microscopic Objects, prepared by Mr. W. A. Firth, for Prize 14. This collection includes specimens illustrating minute structures of several groups of the animal and vegetable kingdom—the Diatomaceæ, represented by some beautiful and rare forms, each slide showing a group of these minute organisms arranged with consummate skill. We cannot too highly speak of the manner in which these objects have been prepared. They might be taken as models of careful and skilful manipulation, and would compare favourably with any microscopic work which we have hitherto seen by the most eminent mounters in Britain. We have great pleasure in recommending that the prize be awarded." The prize offered by Mr. Swanston for the two best Studies from Nature illustrative of Geology was awarded to Mr. F. W. Lockwood, for two coloured sketches of remarkable trap dykes in the north of County Antrim. Mr. Lockwood also sent in a series of four water-colour drawings of Irish Antiquities, in competition for the prize offered by the President, but owing to there being less than three competitors, this prize could not be awarded.

HUGH ROBINSON. } *Hon. Secs.*
WILLIAM SWANSTON.

Dr. Belfast Naturalists' Field Club in Account with Treasurer. **Cr.**

	£	s.	d.		£	s.	d.
To Balance from 1876-77 ...	8	19	10	By Loss on Conversazione ...	6	8	10
,, Subscriptions ...	56	15	0	,, Advertising, Printing & Stationery	11	4	9
,, Arrears of Subscriptions ...	1	10	0	,, Delivery of Circulars ...	1	10	0
,, Life Member's Subscription ...	3	3	0	,, Postages	2	16	4
				,, Prizes	1	0	0
				,, Loss on Excursions ...	0	4	2
				,, Museum Expenses ...	8	8	0
				,, Subscription to Palæontographical Society (2 years) ...	2	2	0
				,, Balance on Hands ...	36	13	9
	£70	7	10		£70	7	10

Audited and found correct,

HUGH ROBINSON, *Hon. Secretary.*

GREER MALCOMSON, *Treasurer.*

SUMMER SESSION.

The following Excursions were made during the Summer Session:

On Saturday, 19th May, to

DUNCRUE AND WOODBURN.

THE Club successfully opened its Summer Session by a very pleasant excursion to Woodburn Glen and Duncrue Salt Mines. The party, including a number of ladies, left by the 9-30 train for Trooper's Lane station, and walked thence to Woodburn Glen. The day was exceedingly fine, and the country looked remarkably well. Reaching the Glen the geologists were soon busy with hammer and pick at the fossiliferous bands of Greensand, &c., that crop out at the sides of the Glen. The exposed sections of Cretaceous rocks and basalt were described by Mr. Gray, the Vice-President, who acted as conductor; and then the party went rambling about the Glen, following their various pursuits. At a pre-arranged hour all met at the Duncrue Salt Mines, and were received by the Company's very courteous Secretary, J. A. Cochrane, Esq., under whose careful superintendence, assisted by his efficient staff, the whole party, numbering upwards of forty, descended the shafts, which are about 620 feet deep. The Vice-President, complying with the request of the members, gave a short description of the mine, in which hes tated that the place in which they were assembled was about 300 feet below the level of the deepest part of Belfast harbour. After briefly stating the geological position of the salt-bearing strata, and giving a history of the discovery and the progress of mining, the business meeting of the Club was held, and a number of new members elected. Mr. Cochrane aftewards conducted the party through the workings, which are very spacious, averaging 30 feet high, and about 21 yards between the supporting pillars, these latter are very striking features in the high cavern, and measure 36 feet by 24 feet at the base. On the present occasion the mine was well lighted with blue lights, Roman candles, &c., and had a strange, weird effect, intensified by the loud explosions of gunpowder and dynamite, which were given occasionally. All having again assembled safely at the surface, they were hospitably entertained at the office, and afterwards visited the ancient castle of Carrickfergus.

Leaving Carrickfergus by train, the party again stopped at Jordanstown station, where they were met by Wm. Valentine, Esq., J.P., who conducted them through his fernery, conservatory, and ornamental grounds—a treat thoroughly appreciated by the Naturalists, who only regretted that they could not spare more time to enjoy the visit. Thankfully acknowledging Mr. Valentine's kindness, the Club took train at Whiteabbey for Belfast, and there separated, after a most enjoyable and interesting day.

On Saturday, 9th of June, to

GREYABBEY, &c.

Notwithstanding the threatening appearance of the weather on starting, those Members who ventured were well repaid by the advent of a bright summer's day. A few minutes were devoted to the Dun, or fort, of Dundonald, and a few more to the quarries of deep red sandstone recently opened about a mile further on. These are attributed to the Bunter sandstone, of which the great mass of Scrabo Hill is composed. After passing Newtownards a visit was paid to Mountstewart Demesne, through the kindness of J. Brownlow, Esq., J.P. As on a former visit, the little fern, Ophioglossum vulgatum, or Adder's tongue, was speedily detected amongst the grass. The small, but very perfect Cromlech, near the outskirts of the Demesne, was also visited. This originally formed the centre of a large tumulus, now removed, in which were several other structures nearly similar, containing sepulchral urns.

On reaching Greyabbey the company, after a general ramble among the picturesque ruins, assembled to hear a detailed description of them from Mr. J. J. Phillips, whose unsurpassed acquaintance with the mediæval antiquities of the County of Down, well fitted him for the post of cicerone which he had so kindly undertaken. The general substance of his communication was similar to the paper recently read by him before the Club, and which appears in the Proceedings for the Session 1874-5. To this the reader is referred for full particulars of the Church, Refectory, and other buildings, which have perhaps undergone fewer changes from the time of their erection, towards the close of the twelfth century, except from neglect and decay, than most other of the Cistercian abbeys of the British Islands. The gratitude of all antiquarians is due to Colonel Montgomery for having so generously placed funds at the disposal of Mr. Phillips for the excavations and other researches, which produced such interesting results, and to that gentleman himself for the knowledge and zeal with which the works have been carried on.

After leaving the Abbey the Slate Quarries lately opened in the vicinity were visited. These have now been assigned their true position in the group of Silurian rocks, stretching from the

Copelands to the County Cavan, and evidently form part of the Llandovery group, the passage formation between the Upper and Lower Silurians, their exact equivalent being the Gala beds in Scotland, with which they correspond fossil for fossil. The force of dynamite was here experimentally shown by several explosions, Many specimens of the slate, in the form of slabs, hearths, tombstones, &c., were also examined. Whilst returning to the cars the brilliant blossoms of the Yellow Broom, *Sarothamnus scoparius*, were particularly noted. The ride home was as enjoyable as the earlier portions of the day had been.

On Saturday, 30th June, to

TARTARAGHAN AND LOUGH NEAGH.

The district selected for the third excursion was Loughgall, Tartaraghan, and Lough Neagh. On arrival at Armagh the party were met by the Rev. George Robinson, who very kindly undertook to conduct them to the best localities, both botanical and geological. Conveyances were in waiting, and a start was at once made for Loughgall, a highly-interesting botanical locality. The fragrant Gymnadenia *(Gymnadenia conopsœa)* was collected on the way, though scarcely in flower yet, and some limestone quarries were examined, from which a few of the common fossils of the Carboniferous period were obtained. In one quarry a large trap dyke was exposed. The igneous rock, penetrating the limestone, had considerably indurated the latter, and a good opportunity was thus afforded of studying the metamorphism thus effected. By the kind permission of R. B. Templar, Esq., J.P., the fine old demesne of Loughgall was visited, and proved highly interesting by reason not only of its charming sylvan scenery, but also because it affords habitats for some rare plants. The drive was continued *via* Tartaraghan to Maghery, on the shore of Lough Neagh. At the former place the Rev. Mr. Robinson pointed out the Adder's tongue fern in some plenty, and the Royal fern near the latter. The Osmunda, however, is becoming quite scarce in this locality, and evidently is hard pressed to hold its ground.

At Maghery the Rev. Mr. Robinson entertained the party with a sumptuous dinner, which, being served up on the grassy shore of the noblest lake in Britain, after many hours spent in the field, was partaken of with unusual zest. At the conclusion of the repast the usual business meeting of the Club was convened—the Vice-President, William Gray, Esq., M.R.I.A., in the chair. One new member was elected, and on the motion of Mr. J. Harris Stone, F.L.S.; seconded by Mr. S. A. Stewart, F.B.S., the hearty thanks of the members were accorded to Mr. Robinson for his kindness in conducting them to so many points of interest, as well as for his generous hospitality. At Maghery boats were in attendance and the majority of the party paid a visit to Scawdy Island, a short distance off. This little island is interesting as being the principal locality in Britain for a very rare native grass, best known as *Calamagrostis stricta*. This plant occurs nowhere in Ireland save in two or three spots about Lough Neagh, and as it differs in some of its characters from the *Calamagrostis stricta* of Oakmere, in Cheshire, Dr. Boswell has re-named it as *C. Hookerii*. Good specimens were obtained of this plant, as well as others less rare. Nests of several species of birds were observed on the island, including the common fern, sandpiper, and black-headed bunting.

Returning from Scawdy Island the journey was resumed to Annaghmore, for the train due at 7-34. This route was by the way of Churchhill demesne, where the immense profusion of rhododendrons and their marvellous luxuriance surprised and delighted the party. The Rev. Mr. Robinson also pointed out, in the woods close to the lake, a number of extraordinary ant-hills. These hillocks, composed of leaves and small twigs of fir trees, measure three to four feet, or even more, in diameter, and were found to be tenanted by prodigious numbers of a very large and lively ant, *Formica Herculanea*, the great wood ant, Churchhill is also interesting as being the habitat of one of the rarer British butterflies, the green hairstreak (*Thecla rubi*), which Mr. Robinson has repeatedly observed here. The season was, however, too far advanced to admit of any specimens of it being procured on this occasion. Many rare plants were obtained during the day in addition to those already mentioned. The following are the most noteworthy:—The wood betony *(Stachys betonica)*, the gladden *(Iris fœtidissima)*, greater spearwort *(Ranunculus lingua)*, meadow rue *(Thalictrum flavum)*, and a rare form of the water crowfoot *(Ranunculus trichophyllus)*. The beautiful quaking grass *(Briza media)* was in profusion in pastures about Loughgall, and sedges were numerous, including *Carex curta, C. paniculata*, and a peculiar form of *C. stricta*, which is very distinct and still awaits a varietal name.

On Saturday, 18th August, to

DOWNPATRICK AND ARDGLASS.

Notwithstanding the unsatisfactory weather a goodly number started, and on leaving Downpatrick drove first to Legainaddy, to examine the very fine stone circle at that place. This is one of the few complete circles in the North of Ireland. The outer ring is 105 feet in diameter, and the inner one 57 feet, composed in all of about seventy stones, many standing seven feet high and weighing fully twelve tons each.

The weather prevented the intended visit being paid to Castle Skreen, Bright's Castle, St. John's Church, and other interesting objects on the route, leaving, however, the more time to be devoted to Ardglass. This spot appears to have early been of importance, many battles having been fought in the locality, and traces of its occupation still remain in the earthwork known as " The Moat," just outside the town.

To John de Courcy and his Anglo-Norman followers we are indebted for the numerous castles in this district.

The family of Jordans settled in Ardglass, 1177, and King John, in company with Mariadac, King of Limerick, is recorded to have visited " Castrum Jordani de Sankeville." In 1217 Jordan de Sankeville was confirmed in his possessions " de Ardglass" by Henry III, and in Elizabeth's time the Jordans were said to be still the principal gentry about Ardglass. Jordan's Castle in the centre of the town, is the best preserved of the castles, and is named after Simon Jordan, who held it for three years against the rebels, till June, 1601, when he was relieved by Deputy Mountjoy. Margaret's Castle is the fragment of a square tower of which little is known. King's Castle, once the chief stronghold, is now a modern building, of which nothing is ancient except the name. " Newark," or " Ardglass Castle, " is an extensive group of buildings chiefly modern, but some portions may date from before 1426, as an inquisition of Henry VI. in that year mentions " One Messuage called Newark, in Ardglass." It is thought to have been erected by a company of London Merchants who settled here early in the fifteenth century.

The customs of the port were granted by Henry VIII. to Gerald, Earl of Kildare, but were afterwards re-sold to Charles I. in 1637. Ardglass fell behind in competition with Belfast, Carrick, Newry, &c., and in 1810, when the Fitzgeralds sold the estate it was a mere fishing village. The new purchaser, the late Mr. Ogilvie, set zealously to work to raise the status of the place.

Sir John Rennie was employed, and much money spent on harbour works, but the injuries caused by storms, the competition and jealousy of its wealthier rivals, and the apathy of successive

Governments, have long retarded its advancement. The present Government, however, have granted £20,000, which, added to the £5,000 raised in the district, will, it is expected, in two years place the harbour in complete repair. Some idea of the service these works are likely to prove to the community, may be derived from the fact, that in the ten weeks of the present Summer £160,000 worth of fish have been brought into Ardglass by between two and three hundred boats, about one-fifth of which were Irish, one-fifth Manx, a few Cornish, and the remainder Scotch. Much of the fish goes to Scotland, *via* Downpatrick and Belfast, but the greater portion is taken direct to Holyhead, in which trade two steamers are engaged, making runs daily during the season. In spite of the weather, the party were able to return to Belfast with a store of recollections, of amusement, and instruction, derived from their day's trip to Ardglass.

On Saturday, 8th September, to

DUNDONALD AND NEIGHBOURHOOD.

The Club brought its Fourteenth Summer Session to a close by a most successful excursion to Dundonald and neighbourhood.

By twelve o'clock, the time appointed for starting, about forty members and friends had assembled at the Ulster Hall, and were soon seated in the vehicles, and on their way to Dundonald. No halt was made until the extensive sandstone quarries at Ballyoran were reached. Much surprise was manifested at the fine bed of stone which is being worked here, and at its uniform character and rich brown colour, closely resembling the well-known Dumfries stone, at present so much in favour. After examining the quarry, and witnessing the mode of raising and squaring the stone for the market, the party retired to a sheltered spot, where a paper was read by one of the members on the geology of the neighbourhood, with special reference to the sandstones. The reader gave it as his opinion that the entire sandstones of the Scrabo district were of Carboniferous age, rocks of which age were unmistakably represented at Cultra and Castle Espie. Several members spoke on the subject of the paper, and expressed opinions differing from those of the reader as to the geological age of the rocks, but all agreeing with him as to the economic value of the Ballyoran stone, and the desirability of substituting it for the expensive Scotch and other sandstones introduced into Belfast, the character of which is often very unsatisfactory with respect to their endurance.

John M'Whinney, Esq., proprietor of the quarries, then invited the party to a substantial luncheon which he had kindly provided, and to which full justice was done. A vote of thanks having been passed to him for his hospitality, and hopes expressed that the undertaking so energetically carried on would continue to prosper, the party again mounted the conveyances and proceeded to Summerfield, the residence of R. A. Gordon, Esq., J.P. These grounds are beautifully situated, and contain some fine trees, particularly beeches and sycamores. Before leaving the grounds a short visit was paid to a remarkable chalybeate spring which was once in great favour, and famous for its remedial properties. This well was referred to by Richard Dobbs, Esq., as early as 1683, who states that it was then much resorted to.*

After leaving Summerfield the party divided, a section proceeding to visit West Dunledy Glen, interesting to geologists as exhibiting the contact of the sandstone with the underlying Silurian rocks. The main party left the Newtownards Road near Dundonald village, and proceeded by a narrow old road in the direction of the Kempe stones, passing on the way, the moat, and a fine example of a "standing stone" in a field near the railway station.

* The Macdonnels of Antrim—Hill. (Appendix).

A short drive brought them near Ballyoran, where a halt was made to visit an ancient rath or fort. It is in very good preservation, the circular trench around it being nearly perfect, and the farmer on whose land it is has made no attempt to level or labour it.

The party next proceeded to Ballyoran House, the residence of Samuel Symington, Esq. The house is delightfully situated, and has been erected with a view more to internal comfort and convenience than mere outward show, and has a site remarkable for its mildness—a fact indicated by the luxuriance of the trees around it, one of which, an Auricaria, near the terrace on which the house is built, is perhaps one of the finest in the north of Ireland. The vehicles were put up here, and the party went on foot to visit the Kempe stones, which are close by, and where they were soon joined by the contingent who had been visiting Dunledy Glen. This remarkable monument—one of the largest cromlechs in the North, and so well worthy of a visit—is probably unknown to nine-tenths of the inhabitants of our modern Athens. The massive block forming the table, and weighing upwards of twenty tons, is perhaps unique in the manner in which it it supported. In the adjoining hedges a number of large stones were observed, which probably formed part of an extensive circle characteristic of erections of this class. It is to be hoped that this interesting relic of a bygone age will long survive the hand of the *improver (?)* who has helped in too many cases to remove such valuable remains. The party then adjourned to Ballyoran House, where all were soon seated around a sumptuous table, and for a time natural science and archæology gave way before the more stimulating cup of tea. After tea, the formal business meeting of the Club was held, a number of new members elected, and a vote of thanks passed to Mr. Symington for his hospitable kindness. Some time was then spent in examining the extensive flower garden and grounds, which are laid out with exceeding neatness and taste. A fine specimen of *Eschalonia macracantha* completely embowers an extensive summer house, and attains dimensions which are seldom seen here, except in localities so mild and salubrious as the one under notice.

Assembling again on the terrace in front of the house, a short communication was brought before the members on cromlechs and similar megalithic remains. A lively discussion ensued, but time did not admit of its continuance; and the conveyances being again ready, the start was made for home. Leaving Ballyoran by the main entrance, the Newtownards Road was soon reached, and a few minutes brought the party to Dundonald. Here a halt was made to inspect an antique chest in the Presbyterian church. The chest is of wrought iron, and is of a peculiar construction, having the lock occupying the entire of the inner side of the lid. Bolts are shot out on each of the four sides, and catch on a projecting flange on the edges of the chest, so preventing the lid being raised till the key is turned round, a process which requires a lever passed through the bow of the key. The chest is very similar in appearance to those in the Tower of London, and which are said to have been recovered from the wreck of the Armada. That this chest is also Spanish there can be little doubt, as the arms of Spain appear inside the lid.

Darkness was now setting in, and the homeward journey was resumed. The party arrived in town about half-past eight, after one of the most enjoyable excursions which the Club has as yet had, whether with regard to the weather, the interest of the district visited, or the hospitable treatment they received.

ANNUAL CONVERSAZIONE,

26TH OCTOBER, 1877.

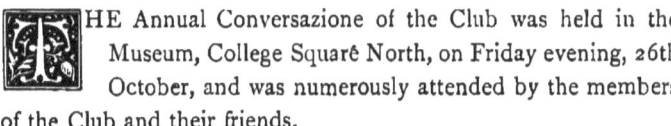HE Annual Conversazione of the Club was held in the Museum, College Square North, on Friday evening, 26th October, and was numerously attended by the members of the Club and their friends.

The Museum was tastefully decorated by the committee for the occasion with flags, evergreens, &c., their principal efforts, however, being lavished on the large hall or lecture room upstairs, the centre of which was occupied by an artificial palm tree constructed most artistically from fern fronds, &c., by Mr. William Darragh, of the Museum, to whose assistance, in the decorations generally, the committee are largely indebted.

Amongst the various objects exhibited was the collection of Cretaceous fossils made by Mr. William Gault, and for which the Club's prize was awarded, containing over 300 specimens, illustrating a very large number of species and genera. This collection is one of the best that has been made from the Irish Cretaceous rocks, and includes many very rare forms, some of which are new to our Irish strata. Mr. Gault also exhibited a number of beautiful specimens of chalcedony, semi-opal, amethyst, &c., all obtained from the old volcanic vent at Rathfern, near Carnmoney.

A series of dredgings, the result of several most successful expeditions to the deep water near the Maiden Lighthouses, and at the entrance to Belfast Lough, was shown by Mr. William Swanston, F.G.S. It included about 60 specimens of Terebratula caput-serpentus, all brought up by a single haul of the dredge in 70 fathoms of water. The collection also contained a number of the rarer Mollusca, Crustacea, Echinodermata, &c. In these dredgings many fine sponges were obtained, which have been sent for identification to Dr. Carter, F.R.S., the best authority on these obscure creatures. It is interesting to learn that one of these has been pronounced new to science, and another is excessively rare, not having been hitherto recorded from our shores. The Foraminifera obtained at the same time, were shown by Mr. Joseph Wright, F.G.S. Many of the forms shown were of the most exquisite beauty.

Occupying a prominent position in the principal room was a table devoted to the exhibition of a few of the objects presented, through the Club, to the natural history department of the Museum, during the past year. Conspicious amongst these was a cast of a gigantic Ammonite in flint—new to Ireland—from the Antrim Chalk, presented by Mr. Walter Jamieson, of Glenarm. Also a fine series of Graptolites including many which were not previously known as Irish, one of them—a type specimen *(Dimorphograptus Swanstoni)* obtained by the late William Bullock, Esq., and presented by his son. On the same table was a remarkable group of fossil fishes preserved on a slab of limestone from one of the rich fossiliferous localities in the south of England, and presented by Captain Wichelo, R.N., through David Cunningham, Esq.

Mr. Robert Day, jun., F.S.A., of Cork, sent a fine collection, filling three cases, containing nearly one hundred beads and ornaments (mostly from the County Antrim) of rock crystal, amber, stone, glass, &c., (with enamel settings of various colours), many of which are of extreme interest and beauty. He also sent an interesting series of arrow points, flakes, scrapers, spindle whorls, &c., from nearly all parts of the world. They are made of quartz, flint, chert, and obsidian—the beauty of those made of the latter material being much commented on. Mr. Day also sent the hauberk of chain mail lately found in the Phœnix Park, Dublin, with the silver badge of the O'Neills attached to it. This is the finest specimen of chain armour that has yet been discovered in the country : each link is rivetted separately, and the hauberk is of that kind known as "a grain d'orge," from the links resembling barleycorns. The badge is of great interest, and by it we are enabled to assign with certainty the hauberk to one of the great O'Neill sept. It is of silver, on a backing of bronze, shield-shaped, and bears within the shield, the red hand of the O'Neills resting upon the three steps of a calvary supported by two lions rampant. Mr. W. A. Traill, M.A.I., H.M. Geological Survey of Ireland, exhibited a rich pendant, set in topazes from the granite of the Mourne Mountains.

During the evening Professor Everett, F.R.S., kindly conducted a number of scientific experiments which were the source of much instruction and amusement.

As usual on these occasions a number of microscopes were exhibited. The Vice-President (Mr. W. Gray, M.R.I.A.) illustrated geological subjects, and Dr. H. Burden, Mr. John Charley, Mr. I. W. Ward, Mr. W. A. Firth, and other gentlemen showed a series of well mounted slides pertaining to various departments of natural history. Mr. William Darragh kindly lent for the evening a large case of sea birds of the Lough, two specimens of owls shot at the People's Park during the past season, and two groups of foreign birds under glass shades. An imposing feature at one end of the room was a large case belonging to Mr. Greer Malcomson, containing many of the rarer British Raptores.

A number of valuable paintings and drawings were courteously lent to add to the interest of the evening. Foremost among these was a fine set of six water-colour paintings lent by Professor A. L. Meisner, comprising works by Prout, David Cox, Nash, Jackson, and Paul Marny. Mr. Rd. Niven contributed a masterly pen-and-ink drawing by T. A. Jones, R.H.A., representing the "Farewell" of an Irish emigrant. Two water-colour sketches by the late G. V. Du Noyer were exhibited by Mr. W. H. Patterson, M.R.I.A. Mr. Thomas M. Lindsay and Mr. John Teasdale covered two large screens with a series of striking views of local scenery, and other drawings and sketches of interest. One of the most valuable contributions in the room was lent by Mr. Charles Elcock. It consisted of a bound portfolio of exquisite sketches of the fishes of the Ganges, done many years ago by an artist whose name has been forgotten. Mr. Robert Young, C.E., exhibited two cases of ancient illuminated manuscripts and engravings. The quaintness of some of the latter attracted considerable attention.

The album of the Club has received during the year several additions. Amongst these is a set of drawings of Irish antiquities (some of which are no longer in the country) executed by Miss Carruthers, to whom was awarded a prize offered by the Vice-President, Mr. Wm. Gray. Also, two water-colour drawings by Mr. F. W. Lockwood; one of these represented Kirkistown Castle, County Down, a typical and nearly perfect specimen of the series of Anglo-Norman castles built round Strangford Lough in the fourteenth century, but now nearly all destroyed through neglect and other causes. The second is an elaborate drawing of the curious doorway of Newtownards old church, the quaint and rapidly decaying carvings of which have thus been rescued from oblivion. The album also contains some interesting drawings of geological subjects which recently obtained the prize offered by Mr. William Swanston.

Mr. Joseph Radley (Lisburn) exhibited a valuable copy of De Imitatione Christi, bound with the Passion Book, in black-letter, Milan, 1488. This interesting volume was formerly in possession of the family and descendants of William Penn, founder of Pennsylvania, and bears an excellent autograph of that eminent man, dated 1690½, 2mo., 2. Mr. Radley also contributed a monograph on the famous Rosetta stone now in the British Museum, the discovery of which gave the key to the reading of the Egyptian hieroglyphics. An autograph letter from Wellington, containing some severe strictures on the outrages committed by the British troops on their retreat from Burgos was also exhibited. It is dated November 20, 1812. This valuable document is carefully protected by a neat framing of glass, fitting into leather case, and was kindly sent in by David Cunningham, Esq. The President (Rev. Dr. MacIlwaine, M.R.I.A.) showed a volume of facsimiles of ancient Irish manuscripts; also a richly-carved bog oak walking-stick, and revolving stereoscope.

Mr. W. H. Phillips contributed several varieties of the common native fern, *Blechnum spicant*, collected by him in the immediate neighbourhood, the varietal peculiarities of which are well marked.

A series of Nature-printed ferns, illustrating many rare and curious forms, and printed by a new process from the plants themselves, was shown by the same gentleman; also three live specimens of the common English toad—a reptile non-resident in Ireland. Mr. Greer Malcomson sent in a number of growing ferns, which were much admired, and greatly enhanced the beauty of the rooms.

WINTER SESSION.

NOTE.—The Authors of the various papers, of which abstracts are here appended, are alone responsible for the views and statements expressed in them.

HE first meeting of the fifteenth winter session of the Club took place on the 20th November, when the usual opening address was delivered by the Rev. CANON MACILWAINE.

Dr. MacIlwaine commenced his address by a review of the proceedings of the British Association at its late meeting in Plymouth, and remarked that the number of members present fell short of those attending the Belfast meeting in 1874 by upwards of 700, while the receipts fell short of those at the same meeting by above £700. Dr. MacIlwaine stated his impression that one cause of such a falling off was the evident departure of the British Association from its original programme, in allowing so many subjects which could not properly be called scientific to be discussed at its meetings, such as the absurdities of spiritualism, which had disgraced the Glasgow meeting, and also such a subject as temperance, which was hardly to be counted scientific. He also suggested that steps might become necessary for bringing back the Association to its original bounds in this respect. The address of the president was referred to, and reviewed at length, Dr. MacIlwaine remarking that the subject chosen by Dr. Allan Thompson, namely, "Development of the Forms of Animal Life," leading to a thorough endorsement of evolution, as advocated by Darwin, seemed hardly an appropriate one for such an occasion. The address was, in a great measure, a lecture on embryology, in the treatment of which terms were introduced which could hardly be intelligible to any mixed audience, the whole being more suited to an anatomical lecture-room than to the assembly then present. In his remarks upon the address, Dr. MacIlwaine took occasion to draw a comparison between it and that delivered by Dr. Andrews, at Glasgow, which was a complete contrast to its successor, being a comprehensive review of the progress of science generally, and delivered in terms which were level with the comprehensions of all who heard it.

A review of the subjects discussed and of the several addresses delivered by the presidents of the various sections was then entered upon, chiefly those connected with the subjects in which the Club was most interested—geology and anthropology, as brought forward at Plymouth, were fully examined, and the interesting results of "cave hunting," which had been almost erected into a science of late years. It was at this point that several sciences might, in a sense, be said to meet, such as geology and biology and, in a sense, archæology and history. Dr. MacIlwaine gave an interesting sketch of the subjects discussed by Dr. Gwynn Jeffreys and Mr. Pengelly in the biological section, remarking that the former distinctly avowed an entirely opposite conclusion to that of Dr. Allan Thompson, on the subject of evolution, and also showed how much moderation ought to be used by those who attempted theorising on insufficient grounds. An instance of this occurred in the case of the assertion made by several of late, that the process of a chalk formation was going on in the mud of the Atlantic, as evidenced by the late deep-sea dredgings, which Mr. Jeffreys showed to be utterly untenable. Dr. MacIlwaine compared such hypotheses to those referring to Bathybius and the Eozoon Canadense, as also Dr. Carpenter's assertions about the formation of the Greensand deposits, some of which, as he reminded the members, were first pronounced untenable by members of this Club.

The subjects of anthropology and the "Antiquity of Man" were afterwards introduced, the President speaking with high approval of the good feeling prevailing at the late meeting between the students of science and the professors of religion. In connection with the antiquity of the human race, Dr. MacIlwaine gave an outline of a theory which identified the bones found in the caves and drift with the glacial period, as well as the rudely wrought stone implements, and further advocated the possibility of these being the remains of an extinct race of bimana, which had perished in that geological era. It was remarked that such a theory was not opposed to anything contained in the Mosaic record. It remained, however, as a hypothesis only. In giving details of the proceedings of the Club during the past year, the President stated them to be in a very prosperous and favourable condition. The results of their fellow-members' researches in the various fields of natural history were highly creditable. The geological collection of Mr. Gault from the Cretaceous rocks of Antrim, which included several forms new to Ireland, was one of the best ever made from these deposits. Mr. Swanston still continued his researches in the Silurian rocks of the County Down with marked success. Mr. Joseph Wright also continued his labours among the recent Foraminifera, his list at present numbering as many as 110 species. An interesting conversation took place after the address, the meeting being brought to a close by the election of several new members.

On 11th December, the President, Rev. Canon MacIlwaine, D.D., M.R.I.A., in the chair, Mr. J. R. ROBINSON read a paper on "Water as an Agent of Denudation."

After some remarks, he proceeded as follows :—By " Denudation" we understand the wearing away of rocks, so as to expose others beneath them. The object of this paper is to show how water performs its work as a denuding agent. The idea has been entertained that clouds consist of vesicles of water, and not of spheres. However that may be, two facts must be borne in mind—viz., that small particles of water can float in the air without being vesicular; and that water is capable of forming crystals at great elevations. Snow is not simply a collection of ice particles, when perfectly formed, as it will be in a calm atmosphere, its atoms arrange themselves in beautiful figures. These blossoms form the white caps of our mountains, but here their fragile forms are soon destroyed. The mountain caps are limited by a snow line, below which the snows do not extend in summer. That mountains have not attained an amazing altitude shows that the annual augment or its equivalent must in some way or other be removed from the mountain peaks. True, we have masses descending as avalanches, but this is not the only motion of these masses. As each layer of snow is superimposed upon its predecessors, the superincumbent mass is sufficient not only to consolidate the lower stratum and gradually cause it to assume the properties of ice, but also to squeeze out the lower stratum. There is also a sliding motion of the entire mass, which when received by a valley undergoes still further solidification, and moves still further down the great slope, scratching and grooving the rocks over which it passes, as well as suffering on its own lower surface; till from melting, the consumption below equals the supply above, when the mass terminates. The portion below the snow-line is called the "glacier," while that above gets the name of "névé," or "feeder of the glacier." From the action of the frost on the cliffs above, blocks of stone fall on the surface of the glacier, which are enabled by the glacier's slow motion to form lines of stones, called "moraines." These stones are deposited from the melting of the ice at the end of the glacier, forming terminal moraines. It was formerly thought that ice was capable of yielding to strain, from the action of the glacier in accommodating itself to the valleys through which it passes, but experiment fails to detect this property of ice. It would appear rather that it is the property of ice in uniting its parts after fracture which enables the glacier to do this. The grooves and scratches in the lower parts of the glacier valleys, as well as the evidence of these in districts now entirely void of glaciers, give us some idea of the part taken by these masses in the denudation of past ages. Referring similar results to similar causes, we must conclude that where these effects exist the cause did. It is this cause which in past times rounded our Irish, Scotch, and Welsh hills. We are able to distinguish the stones transported by glaciers from those carried by rivers from the angularity of the former and the roundness of the latter. It is these marks which form an important part of the alphabet of the geologist.

The effect of elevations in condensing vapours carried by winds appears to me to be imperfectly explained. It is usually stated that the wind, say, meeting with a mountain range, has its vapour condensed, from which one is to gather that this is brought about by the direct cooling effects of the mountain, as in the case of dew. I think it would be better explained by the wind, having to ascend to greater elevation, is subjected to less pressure, when by its elasticity it expands, does work, loses heat, and has its vapour precipitated. The portion of rain water which is not re-evaporated or absorbed by plants appears again as rivers. These give an example of what water may do in a liquid state.

Mr. Robinson then explained the chemical action of river water, and the important work effected by this means, especially on limestone rocks. He also referred in detail to the mechanical action of rivers and of the ocean in promoting the work of denudation, the aqueous agency being seen to be opposed to the igneous.

On 23rd January, a paper was read by Mr. ROBERT DAY, F.S.A., M.R.I.A., entitled, "Something about Old Finger Rings."

The reader commenced by saying—While glancing at the antiquity of such memorials, and at their value as links in the chain of not merely national, but family, histories, we will come down the stream of time to those days of the nineteenth century in which the ring is still of so much importance that, when the humblest peasant weds his chosen wife, if too poor to purchase a golden circlet, he marries her with a simple ring of plaited rushes. In the circle of a ring we have the old and favourite emblem of eternity —without beginning or ending—something that clasps the finger closely round, true emblem of the union which should subsist where friends have joined their hands and pledged their troth, something that sticks close to you through evil report and good report, and that is capable of being made, not merely from the associations surrounding its reception, but from its delicate workmanship and artistic merit, a thing of beauty and of joy. After referring to several passages in the Old Testament in which signets are mentioned, Mr. Day stated that those passages did not refer to finger rings as now understood, but were more properly seals of stone, of cylindrical form, upon which various devices were engraved. Whenever signets are mentioned in the Old Testament it is always as borne upon the hand, not upon the finger. Thus Tamer demanded her lover's "seal and twisted cord"—chotham and pethill —incorrectly rendered "ring and bracelet." This seal and twisted cord was a seal cylinder, through which a thick, coloured, twisted cord was passed, and secured to the hand or wrist.

Ancient rings have been preserved in the Egyptian tombs, and may be seen in any of our great public museums; they are met with in gold, bronze, porcelain, and painted ivory, and with settings of engraved gems and scarabei. The Egyptians made this scarabeus, or beetle, the emblem of valour and manly power; hence they forced all the soldiers to wear a ring upon which a beetle was engraved. The Estruscans, Greeks, and Phœnicians, who borrowed many of the customs and superstitions of the Egyptians, adopted the scarabeus as an ornament. Whilst the Egyptians mounted the beetle in the plainest and most simple fashion, the Etruscans, who have ever been the first gold workers in the world, made the settings of their scarabei of the boldest and most artistic forms. The earliest Greek rings were of base metal, not gold, and had the signet devices cut on their faces. Many of the rings found in Greek graves were made not for the living but for the dead. These were of a hollow and light description, set with pastes imitating jacinth, opal, and carbuncle. Rings were exhibited of this kind set with a paste to imitate the opal, also a gold finger ring from a grave in Cyprus, evidently that of a child, for there the infants of wealthy families wore tiny gold rings.

The custom of wearing finger rings was believed to have been introduced at ancient Rome by the Sabines, who were described in the early legends as wearing golden rings with precious stones of great beauty. During the Empire, rings made of silver were only worn by the emancipated slaves, and those of gold were always wrought with the hammer and finished with the same tool, the ductility of the gold permitting such a mode of treatment. Hollow rings of this kind had often death within their compass, and afforded convenient receptacles for poison. Of this practice there are many instances recorded in ancient history, as the death of Hannibal and of Demosthenes. Pliny relates how the custodian of the Capitol, when apprehended for the gold which Crœsus had carried away from beneath Jove's throne, " broke the gem of his ring in his mouth and at once expired." The key rings of the ancient Romans are sometimes met with in Roman sites; they are made of bronze, and were worn on the finger. Formerly it was the custom with the bridal ring to deliver the keys of the house. In the Saxon formula of matrimony the father of the bride is made to say, " I give thee my daughter to be thy honour and thy wife, to keep thy keys," &c. In Pliny's time it was most customary to wear but one ring, and that on the little finger, although previously the ring had always been worn on the fourth finger of the left hand, from a notion that a vein passed down it direct to the heart, and to our time this same finger is known as the ring finger. As the Roman people lapsed into sensuality and foppishness the intrinsic value of the ornament outweighed and vanished all regard for art, so that "some people made a boast of the weight of their rings," and the hand was encumbered with rings worn on every joint of the fingers. In 1863 four rings were found at Tarsus weighing upwards of two ounces each. In the days of the Roman Republic iron rings were worn by the citizens. These rings, we are told by Pliny, were worn as badges of martial courage, and that under the Republic the senators only had the privilige of wearing rings of gold. As a relic of the ancient usage, the bride's betrothal ring continued to be made of iron in Pliny's time. And in later times, during the Prussian war of independence in 1813, the custom was strangely revived, for the women contributed their wedding rings to the Patriotic Fund, and received in exchange for them rings of iron, with this legend, "*Ich gabe gold für eisen*," which rings are now preserved as precious heirlooms in the German empire.

The practical purposes for which rings, or rather the figures engraved on them, were used at all times were the same as those for which we use our seals. Besides this, however, persons when they left their houses used to seal up such parts as contained stores or valuables in order to secure them from thieves. Plain gold wedding rings which are at present used as visible pledges of matrimony seem to have descended to us from very early times. The Egyptian gold, before the introduction of coinage, usually circulated in the form of a ring, and the Egyptian at marriage placed one of these pieces of gold on his wife's finger, thereby showing that he entrusted her with his property. The early Christians, says Clemens, saw no harm in following this custom, and in our own marriage cermony the man places the gold ring on his wife's finger, when he says, "With all my worldly goods I thee endow." During the seventeenth and the early part of the eighteenth centuries, it was the custom to engrave the inner surface of the wedding ring with the date of the marriage and the initials of the bride, or of both the bride and the bridegroom. The marriage ring could thus be identified, and handed down from father to son as a family memorial. This custom, though gone out of fashion, might well be revived, as it would enable the ring to tell its own wedding story. Gem rings were considered to possess certain virtues, which were contained in the various stones with which they were set. Thus, for instance, the bloodstone had much power superstitiously attached to it—among other things, that of checking bleeding at the nose. The same influence was attributed to the lovely sapphire, which, says Reginald Scott in his ' Discovery of Witchcraft," "hath virtue against venome, staieth bleeding at the nose, being often put thereto." The turquoise was said to have the property of looking pale or bright, as the wearer was ill or well in health.

> As a compassionate turquoise, which doth tell
> By looking pale, the wearer is not well.

Religious rings are not uncommon in this so-called Island of Saints, and have come down to us from mediæval times. They are met with in brass, silver, and gold ; and may be easily recognized by the cog-like projections upon their circumference. These knobs usually number ten, hence the name decade rings, by which they are known to collectors. These ten projections stand for as many *aves*, while the round or oval central head, which is generally engraved with the letters I.H.S. and the ancient and mystic symbol of the three nails, represents the *Pater Noster*.

At the conclusion of the paper some of the Members present took part in an interesting conversation regarding the subject ; and, after the election of several new Members, and an examination of Mr. Day's very valuable collection, the meeting separated.

On 19th February, the President, Rev. Canon MacIlwaine, in the chair—a paper was read Mr. WILLIAM MILLER, entitled "Antiquarian remains on Knock-Dhu, the probable site of the Battle of Ollarbah," of which no abstract has been furnished to the Secretaries.

On 19th March, the President, Rev. Canon MacIlwaine, in the chair—two papers were read. The first, entitled, "Notes on Birds," by Mr. THOMAS DARRAGH; and the second, "Our Northern Rocks, and where to find them," by Mr. WILLIAM GRAY, M.R.I.A. Abstracts of these papers have not been supplied by the authors.

The fifteenth annual meeting of the Club was held in the Museum on 18th April, 1878—the President, Rev. Canon MacIlwaine, D.D., M.R.I.A., in the chair. The Senior Hon. Secretary, Mr. Hugh Robinson, read the Report of the Committee; after which, the Treasurer (Mr. Greer Malcomson) presented the financial statement, from which it appeared that the income of the Society for the year was in excess of that of former years, owing to increase of the membership, and would about balance the expenditure after providing for the cost of printing the Proceedings, which, though later than usual in being printed, will, nevertheless, be the most extensive and valuable part yet issued by the Club.

Mr. William Gray, in accordance with notice of motion given by him, proposed certain alterations in Nos. 2 and 6 of the Club's rules. The suggested alterations were accepted by the meeting and the rules made to read as follows :—

Rule 2. "That the Objects of the Society shall be the Practical Study of Natural Science, and Archæology in Ireland."

Rule 6. "That the Members of the Club shall hold at least

Six Field Meetings during the year, in the most interesting localities, for investigating the Natural History and Archæology of Ulster. That the place of meeting be fixed by the Committee, and that five days' notice of each excursion be communicated to Members by the Secretaries.

The election of office-bearers for the ensuing year was next proceeded with, and the following gentlemen elected:—President—Rev. Canon MacIlwaine, D.D., M.R.I.A.; Vice-President—Wm. Gray, M.R.I.A.; Treasurer—Greer Malcomson; Honorary Secretaries—Hugh Robinson, and William Swanston, F.G.S.; Committee—John Browne, F. W. Lockwood, James Moore, M.D., M.R.I.A., H.R.H.A.; George O'Brien, W. H. Patterson, M.R.I.A.; S. A. Stewart, F.B.S.E.; Samuel Symington, Isaac W. Ward, Thos. Workman, Joseph Wright, F.G.S.

The Members present then engaged in a discussion as to the best means of advancing the interests of the Club, and also regarding the localities to be visited during the ensuing summer session, after which Mr. William Gault exhibited a fine series of Cretaceous Brachiopoda from the vicinity of Belfast; among which were some very rare species, and in addition a number of good specimens from the neighbourhood of Cambridge were shown. Mr. Gault also showed several fossil Patellidæ found near Belfast, and which were new to the Irish strata. Mr. S. A. Stewart exhibited specimens of *Orthotrichum Sprucei* found by Mr. J. H. Davies near Drumbridge. This moss, which is abundant on trees in that locality, is an addition to the Irish flora, and is one of the rare British mosses. At the Drumbridge it occurs with *Orthotrichum rivulare*, new to the flora of the North of Ireland, and also *Tortula latifolia*, another very rare moss. An examination of the collections on the tables brought the meeting to a close.

ANNUAL REPORT

AND

PROCEEDINGS

OF THE

Belfast Naturalists' Field Club,

FOR THE

YEAR ENDING 31ST MARCH, 1879.

NEW SERIES.
VOLUME I. PART VI.

BELFAST:
PRINTED FOR THE CLUB.
ROBINSON BROTHERS, 25, DONEGALL STREET
1879.

REPORT

OF THE

BELFAST NATURALISTS' FIELD CLUB,

FOR THE YEAR 1878-79.

N meeting with the members at the close of the sixteenth year of the Club's existence, your Committee are gratified at being able to report that the Society continues to enjoy a fair amount of prosperity. The membership is about as numerous as it has been at any time, and a considerable degree of interest in the Club's operations is manifested, not only by its members, but also by the public at large.

During the Summer Session the usual field meetings were arranged for, and localities selected which possessed considerable interest. The majority of these Excursions were well attended, and proved both instructive and interesting to the members. It is, however, to be regretted that in some instances, owing to unfavourable weather and other causes, the attendance was insufficient, and that on one occasion it became necessary to abandon an excursion after it had been announced. Any failure in this respect is unfortunate, as field work constitutes one of the main objects for which the Club was founded, and is one of the principal means of exciting and maintaining an interest in archæological and natural history studies.

The following is a list of the Excursions arranged for the Session, and detailed accounts of each are appended :—

25th May.	Dundrum and Newcastle.
18th and 19th June.	Carlingford.
29th June.	Crow Glen.
24th July.	Glenarm.
17th Aug.	Crumlin River.
7th Sept.	Roughfort and Carnmoney.

The alteration in the time of holding the Conversazione, which the Committee considered it advisable to make some time ago, has been continued, and the result has proved eminently satisfactory, the attendance at the Conversazione of the past year having been much larger than at the latter of those held at the close of the Winter Session.

During the winter months meetings were held as usual in the Belfast Museum, at which a number of interesting papers were read, having special reference to Irish Natural History and Archæology, and which it is hoped proved instructive and tended to further the purpose of our organisation.

The following is a list of the papers, abstracts of which appear in the Proceedings :—

1878.
26th Nov.   Opening Address by the Vice-President (Mr. William Gray, M.R.I.A.).

17th Dec.   "On the supposed Pliocene Fossiliferous Clays near the shore of Lough Neagh." By Mr. William Swanston, F.G.S.

,,   "On Rude Stone Monuments in Antrim, with notes on the Ancient Graves recently discovered near Glenarm." By Mr. William Miller.

1879.
14th Jan.   "A Trip from Galway to Dingle." By Mr. S. A. Stewart.
,,   "On the mode of occurrence and probable origin of the Hullite and other Siliceous Minerals found in the Volcanic neck of Carnmoney, and elsewhere in Antrim." By Mr. William Gault.
18th Feb.   "Ferns and Fern-collecting." By Mr. W. H. Phillips.
18th March.   "Notes on the occurrence of Bauxite in Antrim." By Mr. William Gray, M.R.I.A.
,,   "Notes on the Round Tower and Cathedral of Kildare." By Mr. F. W. Lockwood.

The Committee, as on former years, offered a series of prizes for competition, and have appointed a sub-committee to adjudicate thereon, who report as follows :—" The only collection submitted is one in competition for the special prize offered by Mr. William A. Traill, M.A.I., H.M. Geological Survey of Ireland, for Igneous and Metamorphic Rocks, with reference to which we cannot express any opinion until we have the advantage of Mr. Traill's assistance."

During the winter the number of Proceedings for 1876-7 has been issued to the members, and copies sent to the various scientific magazines. This number, though long delayed, was rendered valuable by its accompanying appendix, contributed by Mr. Joseph Wright, F.G.S., and Messrs. Swanston and Lapworth. As the papers by these authors contain the only complete account yet published of the subjects treated therein, they are not only valuable to members of the Club, but have been appreciated by naturalists at home and abroad as tending to a more perfect acquaintance with the living Rhizopoda of Great Britain, and also to a more exact knowledge of the Silurian geology of our country. Mr. Gault's paper in the body of the proceedings will be perused with interest by students of Cretaceous geology. The issue of appendices giving complete local lists is to be continued as valuable material is presented, and as funds are available for the printing of such; of necessity, however, these publications must be intermittent. Our Proceedings continue to be much sought after by other societies having objects similar to our own; and during the year new applications for exchanges have reached the Secretaries from several British and Continental societies, and the Club has received a considerable number of the publications of other bodies.

The Committee regret to record the fact that during the year now closed the Club has lost a number of members by death—perhaps a larger number than in any previous year. They would point out the necessity which exists for the replacement, by new members, of those who are removed by death and other causes. The membership must necessarily be of a fluctuating character, and on the addition of new members whose tastes are in harmony with the objects for which the Club was established, much of its prosperity and success must depend. Our society has its aims comprehensive and well defined—the study of the various branches of natural history as displayed in our own locality, and the elucidation of the archæology of the district. These objects we seek to promote by practical methods, by field work during the summer season, when outdoor meetings of the Club are held in the most suitable localities for investigation; and by evening meetings during the winter season, when papers are read and the Club is made acquainted with the conclusions arrived at by those members who are working at special departments. It is to be regretted that whilst Field Clubs are spreading extensively in England and Scotland, yet so little has been done in this direction in Ireland, whose antiquities have surpassing interest, and whose fauna, flora, and geology are such as to attract the special attention of some of the most distinguished *savans* of other countries. There are, however, indications of a desire for the establishment of Field Clubs in other districts of Ireland, and doubtless it is only required that some parties should undertake the labour of organisation in order to multiply such societies. The Committee are confident that there are many persons in Belfast who only require the aims of our Club and the advantages of its membership to be pointed out to them to induce them to enrol themselves in its ranks, and so not only enable them to associate with those whose tastes are similar, but add to the efficiency of an organisation which is the oldest Field Club in the country, and which is doing good work in popularising the study of the archæology and natural sciences of the North of Ireland.

HUGH ROBINSON. } *Hon. Secs.*
WILLIAM SWANSTON.

Dr. **Belfast Naturalists' Field Club in Account with Treasurer.** **Cr.**

	£ s. d.		£ s. d.
To Balance from 1877-78 ...	36 13 9	By Loss on Conversazione ...	6 18 10
,, Subscriptions	52 0 0	,, Printing Annual Report ...	49 13 8
,, Arrears of Subscriptions ..	3 5 0	,, Advertising, Printing & Stationery ...	9 7 4
,, Gain on Excursions ...	0 5 8	,, Delivery of Circulars	1 10 0
		,, Postages	3 11 9
		,, Museum Expenses	8 8 0
		,, Balance on Hands... ..	12 14 10
	£92 4 5		£92 4 5

Audited and found correct,

HUGH ROBINSON, *Hon. Secretary.*

GREER MALCOMSON, *Treasurer.*

SUMMER SESSION.

The following Excursions were made during the Summer Session:

On Saturday, 25th May, to

DUNDRUM AND NEWCASTLE.

HE Club opened its Sixteenth Summer Session by an excursion to Dundrum and Newcastle. A party of twenty-four members and friends met, and, after a pleasant run by rail, were soon busy examining the extensive ruins of Dundrum Castle. The buildings appear to be the work of different periods, the circular keep on the summit being, perhaps, the most ancient portion. This castle, like many others scattered over the country, is said to have been erected by Sir John de Courcy, in the twelfth century. It has had an eventful history, having been frequently stormed, taken and retaken, and been in the hands of many proprietors. As late as 1571, we find that the Earl of Kildare—then Lord Deputy—took it by storm from the Irish, who had a short time before driven the English from it. It is again taken by the Magennises, and retaken by Lord Deputy Gray. It afterwards got into the hands of Phelim M'Ever Magennis, who was subsequently obliged to yield it to Lord Mountjoy, after which it was held for the English. In 1641, Cromwell—apparently as a precautionary measure—ordered it to be demolished; and the old historians, from whom the foregoing notices have been taken, suggestively state that "it has since been suffered to run entirely to ruin." It affords us great pleasure to state that this latter remark no longer holds good. The noble family of Downshire—the present proprietors—have, within the past few years, judiciously spent a large sum upon the ruins, to prevent their further decay.

Several "good plants" were observed about the castle grounds, among others, the hairy rock-cress *(Arabis hirsuta)* was found flourishing on the old walls; this plant is not known to occur elsewhere in Down or Antrim. Leaving Dundrum by the road leading to Newcastle, the party, after an easy walk of a couple of miles, visited the Cromlech, near Slidderyford Bridge. Many theories have been advanced to account for these rude erections. Perhaps the most generally accepted is, that they were raised as monuments over the graves of great warriors who had fallen in battle. It was noted by members present who had visited this cromlech about a dozen years ago, that the hand of the modern improver(?) had been busy on it, and that a series of large stones which then encircled it has since been removed. Now it stands bleak and bare on a closely-cropped grazing field, and it is sincerely hoped that the few square feet of ground that it now occupies will not tempt to the further injury of this interesting relic. Crossing the railway near this point, the party entered the extensive area of sandhills which here skirt the shore for several miles. This wild waste of sand is interesting in many ways. To the botanist it yields its peculiar plants, most of which are passed by as possessing neither beauty nor interest for the majority; but even those who do not make botany a special study, cannot refrain from admiring the wild pansies which occur here in such variety and profusion. The heart's-ease, so dear to poets, displays on this waste its most brilliant colours; but the species so abundant on these links is the sea-pansy *(Viola Curtisii)*, a near ally of the field pansy, the original stock from which sprung the magnificent pansies that adorn our gardens. *Polygala oxyptera*, a rare variety of the milkwort, was also found here, together with the Portland spurge *(Euphorbia Portlandica)* and the hound's-tongue *(Cynoglossum officinale)*. The geologist sees in the sandhills one of the most recent geological formations, and from a study of them is enabled to better understand many of the puzzling phenomena presented in the more ancient deposits. Here also, as elsewhere in Down, Antrim, and Derry, where similar formations occur, rude stone implements have been found, of which a few were picked up on the present occasion. Several members repaired to the beach to search for zoological treasures, and were amply rewarded by many good examples of Echinodermata, Mollusca, &c. Heavy rain having set in, caused naturalists and archæologists alike to beat a hasty retreat to the railway refreshment rooms, where an ample tea was enjoyed. Before leaving the room a meeting was held for the election of new members; and soon after the party were on their way home, having spent a very pleasant day, notwithstanding the heavy rain of the afternoon.

On the 18th and 19th June, to

CARLINGFORD AND NEIGHBOURHOOD.

This formed the long excursion of the season, and few places within reach can be more calculated to interest a Naturalists' and Archœologists' Field Club, This was amply realised by the small party which made the present excursion. The route selected was *via* Newry, and then along the lately opened Greenore and Carlingford Railway, by which, skirting the Newry canal, and the southern shore of the most beautiful of our east coast loughs, and under the frowning mass of Carlingford mountain, the ancient town of that name is reached. Situated on the extreme northern frontier of the English pale, Carlingford has played an important part in Irish history, of which its many ruined castles are still monuments. On leaving the station an old tower in good preservation is first seen, apparently once of much importance, the date of which is uncertain, but it probably belongs to the early part of the fifteenth century.

Carlingford, like many other places, has been claimed as the landing place of St. Patrick. This, however, is merely tradition. Of another, as notorious, if less revered personage, viz., King John, we have numerous documentary notices, in connection with Carlingford. We find from these that he occupied the castle as early as A.D. 1210, apparently soon after its erection. Amongst other entries in the state papers of the time are the following:—July 10, 1210, "at Carlingford, to Henry FitzEarl, for 2 galleys going with a message for the King—10 marks." Another dated August 2, 1210, "to Robert de Ros, for play at Carlingford, with Warin FitzGerald, when the King was his partner—37s 4d." At the same place "to Nicholas the carpenter—20s." "Master Osbert, quarryman, and Alberic, ditcher, 10s." "To Barberill, to buy wax, 4 marks." Many other items of later date are scattered through the records. The castle as it now stands forms an imposing pile of massive masonry, covering the irregular outline of a rocky point, and it passed through many vicissitudes before being finally dismantled about the middle of the seventeenth century. On its grey walls are to be found several plants not of common occurrence. The wall flower (*Cheiranthus cheiri*), and the red valerian (*Centranthus ruber*), both grow here spontaneously, and truly wild. There are besides, the wall barley (*Hordeum murinum*), and the hard meadow grass (*Sclerochloa rigida*), whilst the lovely little *Asplenium Trichomanes* is especially luxuriant and abundant.

A second old tower, also near the railway station, is interesting on account of the curious carvings of grotesque figures, and early Irish interlaced work which embellish the stone facings of the windows. Close by is the curious old building known as the " Tholsel," erected over an archway which spans one of the main streets. This was formerly a prison, but is now disused—though still a quaint feature of the place.

The monastery, on the south side of the town, is well deserving of a visit. It consists of the walls of the church, including the base of the square central tower springing from lofty pointed arches at the intersection of nave, &c. The West end is flanked by two castellated towers, giving it an appearance quite as warlike as ecclesiastical, which is not, however, without precedent in Irish Gothic architecture. Portions of the lay buildings still remain, but of no marked interest. This monastery was founded for the Dominicans early in the fourteenth century, by Richard de Burgh, Earl of Ulster, of which province Louth then formed a part. It was finally ruined, like the castle, about the middle of the seventeenth century.

The quarries, of the Carboniferous limestone, were next visited, the dense blue stone of which is so justly in demand for burning into hydraulic lime. The dykes were a source of great interest, ramifying in all directions, and sometimes having been forced between the beds of limestone.

The remainder of the day was spent in a botanical ramble, with the most interesting results, many rare plants being collected. Amongst others were the musky stork's bill *(Erodium moschatum)*, the corn salad *(Valerianella dentata)*, the dwarf spurge *(Euphorbia exigua)*, the knotted hedge parsley *(Torilis nodosa)*, the sea beet *(Beta maritima)*, and the lesser broom rape *(Orobanche minor)*, which latter plant seems not to have been previously noted in the north or centre of Ireland. In this locality it occurs in a considerable quantity as a parasite on the roots of white clover, and it will be interesting to observe if it is permanently established, or merely a "casual," as some suspect. *Anthriscus vulgaris* was found near Greenore plentifully, and *Geranium pyrænaicum* at the same place. The horned poppy *(Glaucium luteum)* also occurs on the sandy shores. The low ground of Greenore point is formed in part of a raised beach, indicated on the Survey map as a locality for worked flints, and in which many layers are formed entirely of the Carlingford oyster, which has still survived to be a feature in Irish gastronomy. The surface of the limestone in the quarry near Greenore bears marks of ice action, the grooves and striations of which bear ample testimony to the enormous mass of ice which must at one time have helped to plough out the rock basin which now forms the Newry valley and Carlingford Lough. Testimony is also borne to the same facts by the soundings shewn on the charts, the rocks which nearly close the entrance opposite Greenore, with the depth of water (seven fathoms) within, indicating that Carlingford Lough is one of the true rock basins which, according to the theories of Professor Forbes and Mr. Geikie, are to be found opposite most of our glacier valleys.

During the ascent of Carlingford mountain fifteen species of ferns were found, amongst which was an abundance of the beech fern *(Polypodium phegopteris)*. Of the parsley fern *(Cryptogramme crispa)*, two specimens were seen, on nearly inaccessible cliffs, but were not gathered, in conformity with the wise rules laid down by the Club, whose motto "protection, not extinction" might be more often kept in mind by collectors.

Near the summit were found the Cow berry *(Vaccinium vitis-idæa)*, Rose root *(Sedum rhodiola)*, and the mountain meadow rue *(Thalictrum montanum)*, the two latter being additions to the flora of district 5 of the Cybele Hibernica.

This closed the work of a most interesting and successful excursion.

On Saturday, 29th June, to

CROW GLEN.

Although within an easy half-holiday's ramble of Belfast, and possessing many attractive features, Crow Glen is a *terra incognita* to many. To the lovers of nature it has, however, long been known as one of the choicest nooks in the neighbourhood. The party set out from the Museum on cars shortly after two o'clock, and on alighting at the Forth River Bridge proceeded to the grounds of Glencairn House, the residence of J. Cunningham, Esq. Adjoining the house is part of an extensive fort, the embankments of which are covered with well-grown timber, and the centre cultivated. More than a dozen similar erections are known in this neighbourhood within a very limited area, and it is from them that the stream which flows close by receives its name of Forth River. The origin and history of these forts is but little known, and their study offers a good field for the researches of our local archæologists. After a leisurely walk, the party left the road and entered the almost dry bed of the stream, which is here cut through the red Keuper marls of the Triassic series. Many examples of trap dykes may here be seen, and the disturbance and alterations which they cause to the almost horizontal strata of the marls is admirably shown along the stream banks. The Rhætic and Lias beds, which in these districts usually overlie these marls, are here absent, and the next beds in ascending order belong to the Cretaceous formation, and are the yellow sands and marls forming the central division of the Hibernian Greensand of Professor Ralph Tate. The Chalk, or ordinary white limestone, rests upon these, and forms a broken escarpment, capped by the traps of the Antrim plateau. The junction between the Cretaceous rocks and the underlying marls gives rise to many fine springs. The fissured character of the former allows the water to pass through, until

D

intercepted by the impervious strata of the marls, along which it finds its way to openings in the hill-side.

An active section of the party were busy in search of rarities to add to their herbaria, and were by no means unsuccessful, the broken ground along the stream-course being rich in vegetation. Among the rarest were the wood cow-wheat (*Melampyrum sylvaticum*), the bay-leaved willow (*Salix pentandra*), and the Dutch rush (*Equisetum hyemale*). The slopes of the adjoining mountain were also searched, and yielded the small wintergreen (*Pyrola minor*) and the intermediate wintergreen (*Pyrola media*). A little east of the Glen, in the broken ground at the foot of the Chalk, is one of those subterranean buildings known as *souterrains*. The entrance to it is by an opening caused by the falling in of one of the covering stones. Inside the structure is seen to be of unhewn stones regularly built, but without cement. Unfortunately, the chamber is greatly filled with rubbish, and the fallen roofstone shuts off half its length. If cleared, it would measure about twenty feet in length by five or six in width, and as many high. Several square openings can be seen in its eastern end, which may probably lead to other chambers. The western end shows no openings, but is rounded and neatly built, in shape like the sections of a bee-hive. It is probable if the floor were cleared to a greater depth here that openings would be discovered, as part of another chamber is distinctly seen several yards off in this direction. Subterranean buildings of this character are not uncommon throughout Antrim and Down—(see Guide to Belfast and Adjacent Counties, by the Belfast Naturalists' Field Club, p. 211)—and various opinions have been advanced to account for their probable use. That most generally accepted is, that they were formed as dwellings at a very early period, and are by some antiquaries considered among the most ancient specimens of architecture in the country. The party returned by way of Ligoniel, having enjoyed a most profitable ramble.

On Wednesday, 24th July, to

GLENARM.

A fair muster of members and friends assembled at the Northern Counties Terminus in time to start by the 9-30 train, the weather being most unfavourable. The heavy mists which hung round the slopes of the cliffs and along the shore hid from view everything except those in the more immediate neighbourhood, and shut out entirely the glorious prospect afforded by the succession of bold headlands which characterise the coastline beyond Larne. The party were, however, still in hope that the weather would clear up, and, despite appearances to the contrary a few members left the car to examine the Lias deposits exposed near Glenarm. A short time, however, proved that this part of the day's programme would be barren in results, the heavy rain having formed the tenacious clay into an almost impassable waste of mud, making progress almost impossible. A few of the commoner Lias and Rhætic fossils were found on the surface; an unusually fine vertebrate joint of an Icthyosaurus was, perhaps, the only specimen worth recording. The rain coming on heavily drove all to seek for a shelter, several finding the Madman's Window a welcome retreat under the circumstances. Those who went on by the vehicle were scarcely more fortunate; they had managed to reach Glenarm before the downpour came on, and had set out on foot to visit the demesne so kindly thrown open to them by the noble proprietor. The grounds are most extensive and varied, and have the advantage of a fine stream running through them, which in its course forms some choice pieces of scenery. Its banks and the thick wood that fringe them are just the sort of places that the botanist would wish to search for rarities; to-day, however, botanising was out of the question, the rain compelling all to beat a hasty retreat to the Antrim Arms Hotel, where all the party eventually assembled, and were shortly after comfortably seated at a refreshing tea. The start for home was made about six o'clock. A more extended view was obtained on the way than that which was had in the morning, the sea cliffs coming out at times wonderfully distinct from the mists that had all day enshrouded them; even the distant Maiden Lighthouses were occasionally seen through the haze. It was acknowledged that the day, though wet and gloomy, was far from being without enjoyment.

The excursion arranged to Crumlin River in the second week of August was abandoned in consequence of unfavourable weather.

On Saturday, 7th September, to

ROUGHFORT AND CARNMONEY.

A party of above thirty members and friends assembled at the Ulster Hall at noon, and left shortly after *en route* for the Antrim Road. The morning was in every way favourable for out-door work, the clear atmosphere affording a good view of the Lough and surrounding country. A halt was made for a short time at Whitewell quarries. On returning to the vehicles, the Vice-President, Mr. William Gray, pointed out that a person walking from the sea level to the top of the hill would pass over several geological formations. Beginning with the Triassic, the Bunter sandstone occupies the low ground, while the slopes are composed of the Keuper marls. Near the quarries the Lias clays occur, their plastic character forming a bad foundation for the road which for some distance passes over them. These are succeeded by the Greensand and Chalk of the Cretaceous formation, which in their turn are overlaid by basalts and volcanic ashes, supposed to be of the Miocene age,

The party being again seated, the route was by Glengormley and the old road to Templepatrick, through a richly cultivated country. Roughfort was soon reached, after a pleasant drive. This fort, which gives its name to a quiet little village, is but one of a series of earthen erections, about twenty of which are noted on the six-inch map of the district. In a field a short distance to the east of the fort is Carngraney, or more properly Cairn Graine, a fine example of an entirely different type of erection, known to archæologists as Kistvaens, but more familiarly known as giants' graves by the country people. These rude stone erections, like the cromlechs for which the North of Ireland is so celebrated, are supposed to be ancient sepulchral monuments. They are formed of large blocks of stone set on edge a few feet apart, the spaces between which are spanned by other blocks, thus forming a low chamber or series of chambers. The one visited is in good preservation, and is constructed of about 37 large stones, forming a chamber of about 40 feet long, covered by nine of the largest blocks. The various arguments regarding the age and uses of these erections formed an animated theme of conversation, and the origin of the name came in for a fair share of attention. By some authors it is conjectured to mean " the heap of the sun." This, however, is a very far-fetched meaning; more probably it means the grave or cairn of Graine, an Irish proper name formerly of common occurrence.

Again mounting the cars, a visit was paid to Carnmoney quarries, where a close search was made for the newly-discovered mineral *Hullite*, of which a notice was brought before the late meeting of the British Association. After a brief stay here, the party scrambled to the hill above the quarry, on which is another entrenched fort of a circular form in good preservation, the view from which commands a wide expanse of country. The party then proceeded to Coole Glebe, the residence of the Rev. George C. Smythe, A.M., who had kindly invited them to dinner, which, as may be supposed, was very welcome, after the long drive. Before leaving Coole Glebe, the usual business meeting of the Club was held, the Vice-President in the chair. Some new members were elected; and on the motion of the Rev. Geo. Robinson, seconded by Mr. W. H. Patterson, M.R.I.A., and passed by acclamation, a hearty vote of thanks was given to the host and hostess for the kindness extended to the Club on this occasion, the chairman reminding the members that this was not the first time that Mr. Smythe had hospitably entertained the members of the Belfast Naturalists' Field Club. Such of the Members as take a special interest in the department of Botany, were gratified by securing specimens of the scaly hart's tongue (*Cetarach officinarum*), a fern of some rarity, but which was found in plenty in the neighbourhood of Roughfort.

THE

ANNUAL CONVERSAZIONE

AS held on Friday Evening, 1st Nov., in the Museum, and was largely attended by members and their friends. As is well known, the objects of the Club are the study of natural history, geology, and archæology in the North of Ireland. The local collections exhibited on the present occasion were of much interest, and were, for the most part, collected by the members during the past session. It is gratifying to find that the study of these subjects is on the increase in this locality, and this was at once manifest from the collections exhibited. The Club have at all times taken a warm interest in the study of archæology, and in this department Mr. William Gray, M.R.I.A., exhibited a variety of ancient American stone implements, with some antique Irish forms for comparison. The Rev. Dr. Grainger, of Broughshane, exhibited a series of prehistoric remains, found by him on the 19th October in ancient graves disclosed by the fall of material in the quarry near the "Madman's Window," Glenarm. Among other things it contained many rude flints and stones, which had probably been used by the ancient inhabitants for various purposes—domestic and warlike. Associated with these were human remains, including a skull supposed to be that of a young female. The type of skull was that known as the dolicho-cephalic. There were also evidences of many of our domestic animals, deer, &c.; and in addition there were a few shells of limpet and periwinkle. The graves were rudely built of unhewn stones, of which Dr. Grainger had secured a large number. Mr. William Miller also exhibited a series of remains from the same locality, among which was a well-developed human skull in fine preservation. He illustrated the position in which the graves occured, by large diagrams. Mr. John Browne, M.R.I.A., showed a valuable series of coins, both ancient and modern.

The votaries of geological science were strongly represented, and the result of their labours occupied a prominent place in the principal room. Mr. Gault had a good set of Liassic fossils, intended to compete for the Club's prize. It was very characteristic of these rich deposits, and represents a considerable amount of close attention to these beds. Mr. Charles Bulla had an extensive collection of Pleistocene fossils from South Carolina, which attracted considerable attention, on account of the unusually fine fish teeth it contained. A fine display of granites, marbles, limestones, &c., was shown by Mr. William Miller, and was intended to illustrate the resources that Ireland could boast of in this department of economic geology. A large table was devoted to the exhibition of fossil wood, for the most part local. This exhibition was supplemented by a series of cut and polished agates, chalcedonies, crystals, &c., many of which were of great beauty and some of special interest, having been obtained on the Club's excursions. Mr. W. Traill, M.A.I., of her Majesty's Geological Survey, exhibited sheet 71 of the Irish survey map, and explanatory memoir of the same, both of which he also kindly presented to the Club. Mr. Traill also shewed the nest of a small and rare wasp, recently found by him in the locality.

In zoology, Mr. Thomas Workman had a case of British and foreign Arachnidæ or spiders, a class of animals not very popular, but when mounted and arranged as those shown in Mr. Workman's case are found to possess points of great interest. Mr. John Hamilton showed two cases containing various species of silk-producing moths and their cocoons, reared by him from the larval state. Mr. Thomas Darragh had an interesting ornithological rarity. That gentleman was so fortunate during the past season as to secure a specimen of the red-backed shrike *Lanius collurio*) or butcher bird, the first-known instance of its occurrence in Ireland. Dr. Rea contributed two oval cases of novel design containing stuffed birds, the work of a French taxidermist, which made very effective wall ornaments. Mr. Edward M'Fee placed on the table several live musquitoes, captured during the past summer in the neighbourhood of Whiteabbey.

In the upper room of the building a series of successful experiments were conducted by Mr. J. O'Neill by means of a magneto-electric machine. Mr. O'Neill also exhibited the Geissler and vacuum tubes, water hammer, and other scientific novelties. A set of plans and drawings of old Belfast, kindly lent by Dr. Chas. Purdon, and a series of geological maps and sections by Mr. Wm. Swanston, F.G.S., were also exhibited here. Various other interesting objects, which it would be impossible to enumerate in detail, were scattered throughout the rooms. As usual several members presided at their microscopes during the evening, and illustrated the various branches of natural science, each being a centre of attraction. The brilliancy of the rooms was much enhanced by the number of paintings which adorned the walls. With his usual kindness, Dr. James Moore, one of the oldest members of the Club, and a Royal Hibernian Academician, exhibited a selection from his extensive series of studies from nature.

Miss Thorpe lent a most admirable study of flowers, and Mr. W. A. Firth contributed several very clever water-colour drawings, principally of local subjects. The White Rocks, by Stannus, and two oil paintings, by Armfield, were contributed by Mr. William Swanston, and a series of fifty photographs of Rome and Venice were lent by Mr. James Wright.

[1878-1879.]

WINTER SESSION.

NOTE.—The Authors of the various papers, of which abstracts are here appended, are alone responsible for the views and statements expressed in them.

THE first meeting of the Session was held on Tuesday evening, 26th November, when the Vice-President (Mr. William Gray, M.R.I.A.) delivered an opening address, reviewing some geological and archæological questions connected with the North of Ireland. Mr. Gray explained that he was obliged at short notice to open the Session, owing to the illness of the President, and that as the President's annual address usually referred to the previous meeting of the British Association he would follow the President's example to some extent, and review those questions in geology and archæology, brought before the late meeting of the British Association, which had reference to the North of Ireland. There was a group of papers introduced which gave rise to a considerable amount of discussion on the vexed question of metamorphism. Mr. Gray explained that there were three kinds of rock familiar to the geologist—the sedimentary rock known to have been deposited in water, of which our Chalk and Lias are examples; the plutonic rocks, which at one time were poured forth as lava, of which our granite and trap rocks are types;

and the metamorphic rocks, which include a great variety, supposed to have been altered by volcanic, hydro-thermal, or chemical agencies. But the real distinction between these rocks has not been clearly settled by geologists. On this point they are divided into two schools—one holding that our granites, dolerites, and their associated greenstones, and even our schistose rocks, are of plutonic origin; while the other school claims for all these rocks, and even for granite, an aqueous origin. Mr. Gray reviewed the arguments for and against both theories, and explained that we have in the North three varieties of granite—first, the Slieve Croob granite, supposed by some to be a truly metamorphic granite, because it appears to pass from the typical granite, through schistose varieties, into unaltered Silurian Shales; second, the Mourne granite, an undoubted *intrusive* plutonic rock; third, the Carlingford granite, like the Mourne, manifestly plutonic. In addition to these we have the metamorphic rocks of Antrim, Derry, Tyrone, and Donegal, affording examples from which to study the debated question of metamorphic action. In studying the origin of the crystalline rocks we can be materially assisted by a careful examination of the basaltic rocks of the North of Ireland. We have thus two remarkable groups of rocks—the granites and the basalts—and both associated with a variety of the sedimentary rocks, ranging from the Cambrian to the Chalk. Mr. Gray described the basalt and its central zone of iron ore, with the associated bauxite clays, and lignite beds, and the very remarkable plant remains found in the iron ore, bauxite clays, and carbonaceous shales. The late meeting of the British Association gave a grant towards the expense of exploring these beds.

Of the several papers read before the British Association having reference to our district, one of the most suggestive was a paper by Mr. Traill, of the Geological Survey, on the "Rocks of Ulster as a Source of Water Supply." In reference to this paper, it might be stated that in the opinion of Mr. Traill, the water-bearing rocks of the trappean area of Antrim and Derry form a basin which, on being tapped by boring through the basalt, must yield an abundant supply of good water. But the practical value of such a communication depends upon considerations which seem to have been overlooked by Mr. Traill. All things being equal, a gravitation scheme is manifestly superior to a supply from wells of any depth requiring pumping. This being chiefly an engineering scheme, we need not discuss it here. But before any depreciatory comparisons be drawn between our practice in Ireland and the practice in some places in England, it should, in Mr. Gray's opinion, be shown from a knowledge of the geology and physical geography of the North, that gravitation schemes are not available for our towns, either from a deficiency in the height of water commanding the towns or from the defective quality of such waters. And he was disposed to suspect that no such difficulty existed, when he considered the schemes already projected for the supply of such towns as Ballymena, Ballymoney, Cookstown, Coleraine, and Portrush. Let us take any point within the basaltic area and consider the source and quality of the water. If the supply is to come from the basalt, then there is a chance, if not a certainty, that the water will be charged with iron. If we take our supply from the underlying Cretaceous rocks the water must be hardened by the lime; if we go deeper into the Keuper marls, we can scarcely avoid the injurious effects of salt and gypsum; and the waters from these sources being beyond our reach, we cannot test them by chemical analysis until expensive boring operations have been resorted to. The height at which the Chalk is occasionally found around the margin of the trappean area does not necessarily prove the existence of a basin-like depression under the basaltic rocks. Indeed, the more uniform level at which the Chalk occurs along the entire boundary rather indicates that the intermediate beds below the basaltic area are tolerably level, and the outcrop of the Chalk at Templepatrick would indicate the same. But admitting the existence of the basin-like depression below the trappean area, the impervious beds relied upon as forming the basin must be the Lias clays of the Keuper marls of the New Red Sandstone. Either are sufficiently impervious to retain the water; so that, in the possible or probable absence of the Lias, the marls will be sufficiently retentive. Our basin being admitted, it is evident cannot hold water above the level of its margin, and if the basin is tilted the level of its lower edge will be the level of the contained water. Now, we know that while the New Red Sandstone marls maintain a tolerably uniform level on the west, south, and east boundaries, it drops below the sea to the north of the country; and therefore, the level of the contained water in this our basin must stand at or about the sea level. Again, the entire trappean area is traversed by intersecting dykes in every direction, materially intercepting the uniform flow of the underground waters, and complicating in a most serious manner the data upon which we have to rely in estimating the probable supply from any one locality. But, granting the existence of an unbroken basin, full of pure water, to what level will the water rise in a boring, say at Ballymena?—after all, the practical value of any boring depends upon this. Clearly, we cannot rely upon the existence of any artesian system, because we have no impervious bed overlying the permeable water-bearing strata. These and other considerations may very fairly prompt any session of County Antrim ratepayers to question, if not absolutely refuse to entertain, any scheme for the supply of water to towns from deep wells.

Mr. Gray next referred to the valuable work done by the Geological Survey, but stated that the benefit resulting to the public was hindered by the high prices at which the maps and memoirs were issued. Mr. Gray then alluded to the caves of Fermanagh. In that county the limestone hills are traversed by rivers which frequently disappear into the ground and burst out again at the opposite side of the mountain. The effect of these waters is that deep channels or tunnels are cut through the rocks along their courses. Besides the present rivers, it is evident that many more existed in former times ; but their courses are now dried up, and in some cases all that remains of them consists of great caves or irregular chambers approached only by contracted passages, often in the shape of perpendicular shafts or chimneys. When favourably situated, these caves are frequently encrusted with a coating of carbonate of lime, assuming every conceivable form, pendant stalactite hanging from the roof, and bosses of stalagmite covering the floor, and the sides festooned with petrified folds of curious drapery, or garnished with mimic cascades like frozen water. It is to the intelligent zeal and enterprize of a local field naturalist—Mr. Thomas Plunkett, of Enniskillen—we owe our knowledge of those caves. Prompted by the discovery of the very earliest evidences of man in the ossiferous caverns of England, France, and Germany, Mr. Plunkett undertook the exploration of the caves of Fermanagh, and after recording some discoveries the British Association gave a grant of money towards prosecuting the work. The result was reported to the late meeting from which we find that Mr. Plunkett, in addition to the remains and works of man, found a great quantity and variety of animal bones. Objects of interest were found in every one of the fifteen caves explored, indicating in each case that the cave was occupied by man in very early times. But not one of the many extinct animals has yet been found associated with man in Fermanagh, or any other part of Ireland, either in our caves, cranoges, or gravels. Since Mr. Gray first described the occurrence of flint implements in so many northern localities, the officers of the Geological Survey and others have devoted considerable attention to the subject, and published the results of their investigations. Amongst those inquirers, perhaps Mr. Knowles, of Cullybackey, has been the most industrious as a collector, a worker in the field, and a writer. He has brought the subject before the British Association three times, and very fully described the results of his exploration in the sand dunes of Portstewart and Ballintoy. Mr. Knowles' last communication referred to a number of additional facts and observations in confirmation of what had been published in our reports with reference to flint implements, and shows, as Mr. Gray had previously done, that many of our Irish forms are almost identical with the well-known palæolitic implements of England and the Continent ; and he concludes from this that in Ireland we must carry man farther back than the so-called neolithic period, or else give up some of our theories regarding the distinguishing characters of the palæolithic and neolithic implements. There were many questions yet unanswered even in connection with the few topics which Mr. Gray had just referred to, and similar questions will arise in connection with every subject which may be discussed in the wide domain of natural science, the solution of which is the object of the Club, and a promising source of interesting employment for all members who will only work.

On 17th December—Mr. William Gray, M.R.I.A., Vice-President in the chair, two papers were read—the first in order being by Mr. WILLIAM SWANSTON, F.G.S., on "The Supposed Pliocene Fossiliferous Clays near the Shore of Lough Neagh." The reader, after mentioning the circumstances which led him to examine the beds in question, stated that the extent of these beds and their geological age had been the subject of a paper read before the British Association in 1874 by a gentleman connected with the Irish Geological Survey, and again before the Royal Geological Society of Ireland in 1875. The substance of the papers referred to had also been embodied in the explanatory memoir accompanying sheet thirty-five of the Geological Survey map of Ireland. The author of the paper to which reference had been made considered the Lough Neagh clays to be of the Pliocene age, and the discovery by that gentleman of a bed of shells in the Crumlin river caused considerable importance to be attached to the beds, as may be learned from the concluding paragraph of the paper to the Irish Geological Society, which is as follows :—" In the meantime it is right to place it on record, seeing that this place is the only locality in the British isles yielding lacustrine fauna of Pliocene date." Mr. Swanston's examinations having led him to form a different opinion, not only regarding the fossils, which had been referred to the genus Unio, a fresh water shell, but also respecting the age of the containing beds, he proceeded to point out the evidence on which that opinion was founded. The shells having all the appearance of a marine, and not a fresh water mussel, a good series of them were forwarded to Dr. J. G. Jeffreys, F.R.S., for identification, who, with his usual kindness, states— " . . . . After examining them I can come to no other conclusion but that the shells belong to our common mussel, *Mytilus edulis*, which occurs in all our newer tertiary formations. The colour, structure, and composition agree."

A quantity of the material of which the beds is composed was submitted to Mr. Joseph Wright, F.G.S., of Belfast, for microscopic examination. Mr. Wright states that the only microzoa which he was able to detect in it were a few Foraminifera, referable to four species, all of which are found living on our coasts, and are also of frequent occurrence in the Pleistocene boulder clay. An examination of the stratigraphical position of the fossil-bearing beds, proves that they repose upon the true boulder clay, which is full of ice-marked stones. As the Mytilus is a sea shell, and Foraminifera essentially marine organisms, it is clear that the beds are not of lacustrine origin. The fact that they repose upon boulder clay proves that they must be either glacial or interglacial deposits, not Pliocene. The author of the paper referred to seems to have fallen into an error in supposing that the beds in question belong to the white plastic clay series which occur along the southern shore of Lough Neagh, whereas the latter do not seem to extend to within half a mile of the spot where the fossils occur, nor is the lithological character of the two beds at all similar. As the conclusion regarding the fossiliferous beds in the Crumlin river is erroneous, and as the evidence on stratigraphical grounds in favour of the Pliocene age of the Lough Neagh clays is not conclusive, the exact epoch to which the latter beds must be referred is still an open question. Granted that they repose upon basalt, nevertheless they may be of any age between that of the lower miocene basalt and that of the upper boulder clay of the glacial epoch. The reader suggested that they spanned almost the entire interval, and are in part contemporaneous with the lacustrine iron ores, bauxite and lithomarge of the Antrim hills, which beds rest similarly on basalt, and contain plant remains closely resembling, if not indeed identical, with those found in the ironstone nodules of Lough Neagh. Should further researches prove that the plants of the two deposits are the same, and that the plastic clays are really of later Miocene age, it may safely be inferred that one reason why these have retained their clayey character is the simple fact that they were not covered by the outflows of later Miocene basalt, to which is attributed the consolidation of the iron ores and their associated beds.

Mr. Swanston then briefly referred to the well-known silicified woods of Lough Neagh, and brought forward a number of strong arguments tending to supplement the opinion that they are associated with the black lignites, and are derived from the Lough Neagh beds. A number of most interesting specimens were exhibited, including the fossils and scratched boulders from the Crumlin river, pieces of wood partially silicified while the remainder still retains its woody character; with examples of the black lignite and ironstone nodules, enclosing plant remains from the Lough Neagh beds.

The second paper was by Mr. WILLIAM MILLER, on "Rude Stone Monuments in Antrim, with notes on the recently-discovered graves near Glenarm." This was an attempt on the part of the author to establish some connection between the stone-built graves occasionally brought to light and the remains of dwelling places known as "coves" or "souterrains," often found in these countries. These generally consist of a group of narrow underground chambers, twelve to twenty feet long, and five or six feet high, connected by a small passage close to the floor, and roofed generally with very heavy blocks of stone. They would seem to be of quite distinct character from the chambers for sepulchral or monumental purposes, found in connection with raths, cairns, tumuli, &c. They are probably the oldest remains of human workmanship in the country. The probable order of age would be—first, these souterrains; second, the lises or forts, the cromlechs, and the class of monuments represented at Cairngraney; and lastly, a long way inside the historic period, the raths, cairns, and pillar stones, of which there are many in this county. The graves recently found in a limestone quarry at Glenarm, and those found some years ago at Gransha, Islandmagee, were described. Of the latter there may have been, it is supposed, two hundred. All lay facing the East, in rude graves built of stone slabs. Of those at Gransha no skulls have been preserved, and those from Glenarm are very few in number. The one exhibited in the Museum falls within the brachy-cephalic, or broad-headed type, the dimensions being— length, 7⅛ inches, breadth, 5⅝ inches, and circumference, 20⅝ inches. A few flint flakes were the chief objects found in these graves. The teeth, as is usual, were very much worn. There were also some indications of cremation, and some burials without any stone graves at all.

On 14th January

Rev. Canon MacIlwaine, D.D., President in the chair—a paper, entitled " A Trip from Galway to Dingle," was read by Mr. S. A. STEWART, Fellow Botanical Society, Edinburgh.

In this paper the author gave an account of a trip during the latter part of last July from Galway to Dingle. The first halt was at the Burren of Clare, situated on the south side of Galway Bay, which exhibits a singular geological structure. It is an elevated country, whose strata consists of Carboniferous limestone, the hills displaying in most cases series of rock terraces reaching from the base to the summit. These terraces are commonly as flat as our Post Office steps, and their height varies from one foot to six or eight feet. The rocks are split up by innumerable joints, with fissures from one or two inches to two feet wide, filled with a rich soil derived from the decomposition of plants, and of the limestone rock. It is in these fissures that the greater portion of the vegetation of the hills is found, and they afford a rich crop to the botanist, some of the rarest members of the Irish flora being found in them. Mr. Stewart succeeded in finding the maidenhair fern (*A. capillus-veneris*) growing luxuriantly on Blackhead. This is the original locality from whence the maidenhair fern was brought to Dublin for sale 150 years since. Extremely fine plants of the scaly harts tongue fern (*Ceterach officinarum*) were also obtained, and the rare orchid, *Epipactis ovalis*, was found in some plenty, with many other scarce plants. The cliffs of Moher were also visited. They rise perpendicularly to the height of 660 feet, and are tenanted by innumerable sea-birds. The mountain pansy (*Viola lutea*), the true plant of Hudson, was found plentifully on the short pastures. At Tralee, where another halt was made, *Ranunculus Baudottii* was found in brackish marshes near the harbour. Three days were spent on the Dingle promontory, a district which combines so many attractions—geological, botanical, and archæological—as to constitute it, in these respects, the most interesting part of Ireland. Some very rare plants were collected here. The geological structure of this western promontory is very striking. The rocks are mainly sedimentary, in most cases Silurian strata that rise to the summit of the mountains, reaching on Brandon an elevation of over 3,000 feet. Mr. Stewart referred at some length to the antiquities of Dingle, which embrace types of great interest. There are ancient churches and religious buildings dating back some 800 years; grand old castles, pillar stones, bullan stones, ogham inscriptions, and singular archaic structures whose date is unknown. These were illustrated by sketches made on the spot by Mr. W. Swanston, F.G.S., who kindly consented to exhibit them on this occasion.

A paper "On the mode of occurrence and probable origin of the Hullite and other silicious minerals found in the volcanic neck of Carnmoney, and elsewhere in the County Antrim" was next read by Mr. WILLIAM GAULT, who stated that, for a lengthened time, he had been making observations and collecting specimens at this very interesting locality, and that the volcanic neck in which these minerals occur has been exposed to denudation, and may be observed as a rounded protruberance on the escarpment on the southern side of Carnmoney Hill. It has cut through the Triassic and Cretaceous strata, but its relation to the beds of lower basalt is not so clearly seen owing to the heavy covering of drift and decomposed rocks. At its northern end volcanic ash is found in small exposures. The neck measures about 400 yards across, and is formed of hard, coarsely crystalline grey dolerite rock, containing glistening crystals of augite, and vesicular cavities filled with various silicious and ferruginous minerals, very often with a black substance resembling cannel coal. This black mineral was found at Shane's Castle, in 1837, by Dr. Scouler, who supposed it to be pitchstone; at a later date Portlock refers to it as obsidian; the Geological Survey call it by the same term. Mr. E. T. Hardman, F.C.S., of the Geological Survey, however, determined its real nature by chemical and microscopic examination. The result of his researches proved the black mineral to be a remarkably distinct new mineral, belonging to the chlorito-ferruginous group. He named it Hullite, after Professor Hull, F.R.S., a gentleman well deserving the compliment for his zeal in working out the sequence of the volcanic rocks of his native County Antrim.

Before describing in detail the various minerals and their mode of occurrence, Mr. Gault briefly noticed these volcanic necks, as they are very seldom visible. It is only when denudation has removed all the covering from the top, or cut for us a section along some hillside or seashore, that we find oval or circular masses of hard crystalline basaltic rock, very often prismatic in structure, standing out from or elevated above the surrounding strata. These bosses of basalt rock are the plugs of the volcanic orifices, and differ in form and other peculiarities from the longitudinal dykes that are so numerous in this district. They are not the original cones from which the lava and ashes were ejected, for these would be higher than the deposited material, and in this district have been entirely obliterated by the severe denudation they suffered during the Pliocene and glacial epochs. This is proven by the fact of the removal of all the beds of iron ore and sheets of upper basalt, in thickness amounting to about 500 feet, that covered the whole of the County Antrim south of the great downthrow fault of the Six-milewater valley. Only a few patches of these important deposits now remain on some of the higher elevations to attest their former wide extension. The Pliocene clays of Lough Neagh have been largely made up with the material denuded from the South Antrim plateaux. Some of the masses of dolerite and other basaltic rocks in the North Antrim district said to be volcanic necks, are very doubtful examples, but the Carnmoney neck is one of the best. It was first recognised by Mr. Du Noyer, in 1868, to be a great pipe or feeder of the volcanic flows. Other good examples of volcanic necks are seen at Greenisland, near Carrickfergus, and at Ballygalley head, near Larne.

The silicious minerals found in Carnmoney "neck" comprise many varieties of quartz, rock-crystal or Irish diamonds, and amethyst. A variety of opal is found in abundance, some specimens of which, on being pressed against a rapidly-revolving grindstone, become filled in the interior with flashes of golden light, rendering them most interesting and beautiful objects. This light seems quite different from the phosphorescent glow produced on silicious minerals by the application of heat. The reader stated that he had not yet seen any notice of this in the works he had read on this subject. Chalcedony is common in many stalactitic and mammilated forms, and in sheets and veins, varying from the thickness of notepaper to upwards of one foot. It forms a casing around all the other minerals, and passes into silicious tuff and grey flint, resembling the flints of the chalk. Hydrophane and cachalong occur very rarely, also hyalite or Muller's glass. Zeolites are rare, and have been formed quite recently compared with the silicious minerals; they occur filling up the hollows in quartz prisms and cavities between the chalcedony and rock-crystal. Hullite occurs abundantly in the cavities of the dolerite; it is also got in large masses in the heart of the mammilated chalcedony, and sometimes interlaminated with chalcedony, opal, and iron pyrites. This iron pyrites is found disseminated through the dolerite in great plenty; sometimes it is scattered in bronze-coloured blotches over the entire surface of some fissures. Chlorite and terra verte are plentiful, and are often found mixed up with the Hullite, chalcedony, and iron pyrites in a confused manner very difficult to account for. A bright blue film is found on the surface of the dolerite. It is like the fumes from a furnace, but its nature has not been determined. It occurs likewise in the altered Portrush rock, and is thought to be Hauyn, a volcanic mineral found near the Rhine, in Germany. These are only the most prevalent kinds of minerals; others occur which have not yet been identified. Nowhere in our district can such a variety be found in so small a compass, nor in such abundance as in this old volcanic vent. Hullite also occurs as a thin glaze or film on the joints and fissures of basalt at other localities near Belfast, the Giants' Causeway, and Knocklayde, and has caused the igneous rocks to be mistaken for coal by not only the unlearned, but by "men of science." Although it looks like coal, it contains no carbonaceous matter, and the simple test of putting it into a fire would increase the knowledge of many individuals, and keep them from indulging in useless conjectures.

Mr. Gault concluded by stating his views regarding the origin of the Hullite and other silicious minerals referred to. Into the volcanic neck of Carnmoney, long after the volcanic forces had spent their vigour, and were fast dying out, alkaline water at a high temperature found access. This would dissolve the silica in the basalts, and form a sort of gelatinous or colloid state of silica that would percolate through the fissures and cavities in the dolerite rocks, and would probably combine with some of the many varieties of iron to form the Hullite and other ferruginous silicates. These fluid combinations would solidify and crystallise. Violent explosions of gaseous matter would take place from time to time, and blow off portions of the walls of the vent. Some of these solid basalt fragments would fall back again into the fissures, and after some time would be enveloped by the layers of silicious matter. Thus often do we find hard masses of dolerite forming a nucleus, around which the opal and chalcedony is gathered in many concentric layers. This process would be continued until the volcanic forces became extinct in Antrim, and moved northward to Mull, Staffa, and other Hebridean islands; and finally shifting to Iceland and Jan Mayen islands, where they still burn with great intensity. The paper was illustrated by specimens, and by a diagram of Carnmoney Hill.

On 18th February, the President, Rev. Canon MacIlwaine, D.D., M.R.I.A., in the chair, when a paper was read by Mr. W. PHILLIPS, entitled, "Ferns and Fern Collecting." The lecturer commenced by saying that up to a very recent period ferns were unknown as cultivated plants in our houses—that this was owing to a want of knowledge of their habits, but from the accidental growth of a fern in some earth put in a bottle along with the chrysalis of a moth, the idea was first originated, which afterwards developed into miniature cases for our rooms and glass-houses with rockeries, &c., in which ferns could be planted and grown with great success. The ease with which ferns may be gathered, and the low prices at which they may be purchased, enabling the dwellers in towns to provide themselves with a means of enjoyment, whose green fronds would look refreshing almost all the year, thus commending themselves to a large number of admirers.

Ferns have been present on the earth from a very early period, forming a large part of the tropical vegetation, which, afterwards subsiding under the mud and waters of ancient seas, became hardened into coal, their delicate forms revealed to our curious eyes in the shales of the coal formations. M. de Saporta recently announced the discovery of fossil ferns in the Silurian Rocks of Angers, in France. In a slab of schistoze rock, from the middle Silurian strata, containing *Calymene tristana*, he has found the remains of a large fern, tolerably well preserved, the outline, however, rather imperfect, as though the plant had suffered by long exposure in water. The vegetable matter has disappeared, and its place taken by iron pyrites. In the venation, which is well marked, the specimen approaches to some of the ferns from the Devonian, or lower Carboniferous strata.

The number of species now known is about 2,500, occurring in almost all parts of the world, more plentifully in mountainous tropical countries. They are of varied size and aspect, some very minute and of delicate structure, others noble trees, with stems 50 feet and upwards in height, crowned with magnificent plumy heads of fronds, their form or cutting not less varied, and all intermediate states of division between the simple or undivided frond to that in which division and sub-division of the parts is so many times repeated as to produce highly composite characters. As many as 35,000 divisions have been counted in a frond of the lady fern. These elegant characters of outline and division of parts have led to their being associated with all that is graceful and fascinating among vegetable forms; they are, indeed, the very prototypes of gracefulness.

The distinguishing characters of ferns were then enumerated, showing the differences between them and flowering plants, both as to absence of flowers and seeds, and in their places spores and spore-cases, which are borne on the fronds, either on the back or margin, some in round clusters, others in lines or broken up into irregular masses. The difference between seeds and spores was then shown; that after the germination of the spores organs similar to stamens and pistils are developed, and after fertilisation the fronds are produced.

For successful fern-collecting it is necessary to have a knowledge of the normal forms and their habits, otherwise many an excursion will be unsuccessful. One of the greatest charms about ferns is that they are spread so bountifully over the country, that they are available to those of limited time and means, and when found may be captured and cultivated. The hunter must have indomitable perseverance. Every nook, dell, rock, roadside, hedge, and ditch must be examined thoroughly, so that nothing may escape the eye. The hunter should always be prepared with tools—a fern trowel, a naturalist's pick to fasten on a walking-stick, a pocket knife, some string, and a good canvas bag with shoulder straps. These will enable any plant to be lifted and carried home. The reader then gave some humorous episodes of fern-hunting, as also the finding of other objects of interest, and peeps into the privacies of vegetable and animal life.

Some interesting details were given as to the way of growing ferns from spores, and the mode in which any peculiar character in the parent may be transmitted to the seedlings, and also on cross-fertilisation.

The walls of the lecture-room were hung round with a very fine collection of upwards of 150 sheets of impressions of ferns, nature-printed by a new process, showing in series some of the newest forms, many of them so exquisitely divided and so fragile that it seems almost impossible that the impressions could have been printed from the ferns themselves. Some of the lecturer's own findings from this neighbourhood were amongst those printed: they were—*Blechnum spicant trinervum*, from the Mourne Mountains; *Polystichum angulare rotundatum*, from Ligoniel; *Athyrium filixfœmina Phillipsii*, from Holywood. Besides these, a number of very beautiful fronds were exhibited, showing different characters; and in a pot the beautiful new variety, *Blechnum spicant foliosum*, found by the lecturer on the Mourne Mountains.

On 18th March, the Vice-president, Mr. Wm. Gray, M.R.I.A., in the chair—when two communications were brought forward. The first, entitled "Notes on the occurrence of Bauxite in Antrim," was by Mr. WM. GRAY, M.R.I.A. The lecturer, after explaining an extensive series of coloured diagrams illustrating the manner in which this mineral was associated with the basalts, iron ores, and lignites of County Antrim, proceeded to note the history of its discovery, and point out the uses to which it is being applied. This latter part of the subject was illustrated by specimens both Irish and Continental, showing the mineral in its natural state, as well as several of its products in the form of alum, alum-cake, &c.

The second communication was by Mr. F. W. LOCKWOOD, who had for his subject "Notes on the Round Tower and Cathedral of Kildare"—a place which has been of some note according to the earliest traditions. Saint Bridged or Bridget founded a nunnery here in the fifth century, and the place then became known as Kill-dara, or the church of the oak. Kildare was fourteen times pillaged by the Danes within the space of 190 years, and on ten of these occasions was wholly or partly burnt. The legends of St. Bridged are numerous, the most curious is that relating to the sacred fire which was kept up by the nuns even till the time of the Reformation. Cambrensis, in the twelfth century, was informed that nineteen nuns guarded the fire in turn, and on the 20th night it was left to the saint, by whom it was miraculously sustained without fuel. The fire was strictly watched, and no male was permitted to approach it. The round tower is a very fine one, and the highly ornamented doorway a good example of Irish Romanesque work of the eighth or ninth century, which would lead us to infer that the original cathedral, probably about the same date, was also highly decorated. It was divided down the middle by a wooden screen, so as to keep the nuns and other females separate from the remaining worshippers. The early Irish Christians possibly derived many of their ideas in architecture from the Eastern Church, and not from Britain or those parts of Europe which had formed the western branch of the Roman Empire; for the churches before the Anglo-Norman invasion have no aisles, being generally small, and sometimes in groups of seven, as at Glendalough. The present cathedral, built by the Anglo-Normans about 1229, retained some of the native arrangements, having no aisles, and a separate north door for the entrance of the nuns. It is almost unique in the buttresses of the nave, which are very massive, with bold arches nearly on a line with their outside face springing from one to another, entirely separated from the wall, and casting a deep shadow over the heads of the windows. The effect produced is most striking and picturesque. Mr. G. E. Street, R.A., the eminent architect of Christ Church Cathedral, Dublin, is now restoring this building, which was rapidly becoming a complete ruin.

Some discussion followed on the protection of our ancient monuments, a work which the Club has always taken a special interest in. The election of several new members brought the business of the evening to a close.

The Sixteenth Annual Meeting of the Club was held in the Museum, College Square North, on Tuesday evening, 29th April, Mr. William Gray, M.R.I.A., Vice-President, in the chair.

The Chairman called upon Mr. Hugh Robinson, one of the Hon. Secretaries, to read the Annual Report of the Committee, and upon Mr. Greer Malcomson, the Treasurer, to submit his Statement of Accounts for the preceding year.

Mr. Gray moved that rule 5 be altered, the alteration being to the effect that the office of President or that of Vice-President shall not be held by the same person for more than two years in succession. After some discussion the motion was put to the meeting and carried.

The Rev. Canon MacIlwaine having intimated his intention to retire from the office of President, it was resolved, on the motion of Mr. Joseph Wright, F.G.S, seconded by Mr. Frederick

Lockwood, that Mr. William Gray, M.R.I.A., be elected President for the ensuing year.

On the motion of Mr. William Miller, seconded by Mr. George O'Brien, Professor J. F. Hodges, M.D., was elected as Vice-President.

Mr. Greer Malcomson was re-elected as Treasurer, and Messrs. Hugh Robinson and William Swanston, F.G.S., as Secretaries.

After the Election of the committee for the year, Major-General Smythe, M.R.I.A., in complimentary terms, moved that the best thanks of the Club be tendered to the Rev. Canon MacIlwaine, M.R.I.A., for the valuable services which he had rendered the Club during the time in which he had occupied the presidential chair.

The vote of thanks was seconded by Mr. Joseph Wright, F.G.S., and passed by acclamation.

On the motion of Mr. Swanston, Mr. Charles Lapworth, F.G.S., of St. Andrew's, was elected an honorary member of the Club.

The Chairman requested the members present to express their opinions as to the places to be visited during the summer, and also regarding the general business of the Club.

A number of suggestions having been made and discussed, Mr. John Hamilton showed a living specimen of the long-eared bat *(Placotus auritus)* recently captured near Belfast.

Mr. Gault's collection of rock specimens was also exhibited. This extensive series consists of about sixty different varieties of igneous and metamorphic rocks, and was sent in competition for Mr. 'Traill's prize, which, on account of the absence of Mr. Traill, was not adjudicated.

NOTICE.

EXCHANGE OF PROCEEDINGS.

HE Committee of the Club have been desirous of establishing a yearly exchange of the published proceedings with those of kindred organizations in other places, and have, during the past year, forwarded copies of the Fourteenth Annual Report and Proceedings to other societies. They acknowledge with thanks the receipt of the following publications, and hope that other societies, whose objects are similar, will favour them with copies of their proceedings as published :—

Aberdeen Natural History Society.
Transactions for 1878.

American Association for the Advancement of Science.
Proceedings of Buffalo Meeting.—1876.

Ballarat School of Mines.
Annual Reports for 1875 and 1876.

Barrow Naturalists' Field Club.
Transactions. Vol. I.—1877.
Do. Vol. II.—1878.
Do. Vol. III.—1879.

Bath Natural History and Antiquarian Field Club.
Proceedings. Vol. III., Part 4.—1877.
Do. Vol. IV., Part 1.—1878.
Do. Vol. IV., Part 2.—1879.

Berwickshire Naturalists' Club.
Proceedings for 1876.
Do. for 1878.

Boston (U.S.A.) Society of Natural History.
Memoirs. Vol. II., Part 4.—1877.
Proceedings. Vol. XVIII., Parts 3 and 4.—1877.
Do. Vol. XIX., ,, 1 and 2.—1877.

Brighton and Sussex Natural History Society.
22nd Annual Report and Abstract of Proceedings. —1876.
23rd ,, ,, ,, ,, 1877.
24th ,, ,, ,, ,, 1878.

Bristol Naturalists' Society.
Proceedings. New Series, Vol. II., Part 1.—1877.
Do. do. Vol. II., Part 2.—1878.
Do. do. Vol. II., Part 3.—1879.

Canadian Institute.
Canadian Journal. Vol. XV., Parts 5 to 7.—1877.
Do. New Series, Vol. I., Part 1.—1879.

Cardiff Naturalists' Society.
Report and Transactions for 1876.
Do. do. 1877.
Do. do. 1878.

Dublin University Biological Association.
Proceedings. Vol. I., Part 2.—1876.

Dunedin (Otago) Naturalists' Field Club.
Report for 1876-77.

Eastbourne Natural History Society.
Papers.—1876-77.
Do. 1877-78.
11th Annual Report.—1878.

Edinburgh Botanical Society.
Transactions. Vol. III., Part 1.—1877.

Edinburgh Geological Society.
Transactions. Vol. III., Part 2.—1877.

Essex Institute, Salem, Mass., U.S.A.
Bulletin. Vol VIII., Nos. 1 to 12.—1877.
Do. Vol. IX., Nos. 1 to 12.—1878.

Geologists' Association.
Proceedings. Vol. V., Parts 1 to 4.—1877.
Do. Vol. V., Parts 5 to 8.—1878.
Do. Vol. VI., Parts 1 to 3.—1879.
Annual Report for 1877.
Do. do. 1878.

Glasgow Natural History Society.
Proceedings. Vol. III., Part 3.—1878.

Glasgow Society of Field Naturalists.
Transactions, Part 5.—1877.

Leeds Naturalists' Field Club and Scientific Association.
Seventh Annual Report. — 1877.

Leeds Philosophical and Literary Society.
Annual Report for 1876-77.
Do. do. 1877-78.
Do. do. 1878-79.

Lewes and East Sussex Natural History Society.
Thirteenth Annual Report.—1877.

Liverpool Geological Society.
Proceedings for 1875-76.
Do. for 1876-77.

Liverpool Literary and Philosophical Society.
Proceedings. Vol. XXXI.—1877.
Do. Vol. XXXII.—1878.

Liverpool Naturalists' Field Club.
Proceedings for 1876-77.
Do. for 1677-78.
Do. for 1878-79.
Notes by a Field Naturalist in the Western Tropics.

F

Manchester Field Naturalists' and Archæologists' Society.
Report and Proceedings for 1877.
Do.   do.   for 1878.

Manchester Scientific Students' Association.
Report and Proceedings for 1878.

Norfolk and Norwich Naturalists' Society.
Transactions.   Vol. II., Part 3.—1877.
Do.   Vol. II., Part 4.—1878.
Do.   Vol. II., Part 5.—1879.

Philadelphia (U.S.A.) Academy of Natural Sciences.
Proceedings for 1876.
Do.   for 1877.
Do.   for 1878.

Plymouth Institution, and Devon and Cornwall Natural History Society.
Annual Report and Transactions.   Vol. VI., Part 1.—1877.
Do.   do.   Vol. VI., Part 2.—1878.
Do.   do.   Vol. VII., Part 1.—1879.

Quekett Microscopical Club.
Journal.   No. 34.—1877.

Royal Irish Academy.
Transactions.   Vol. XXV. (Science), Parts 10 to 18.—1875.
Do.   Vol. XXV. (Science), Part 20.—1875.
Do.   Vol. XXVI. (Science), Parts 1 to 21.—1876-79.
Do.   Vol. XXVII. (Polite Literature and Antiquities), Parts 1 to 3.—1877-79
Proceedings.   Vol. I., Series 2 (Polite Literature and Antiquities), Parts 12 and 13.—1877-79.
Do.   Vol. II., Series 2 (Science), Parts 5 to 7.—1876-77.
Do.   Vol. III., Series 2 (Science), Parts 1 to 3.—1877-79.

Royal University of Norway, Christiania.
Caranologiske Bidrag til Norges Fauna af G. O. Sars.
De i Sondre Bergenhus Amt hidtil observede Coleoptera og Lepidoptera af J. Sparre Schneider.—1875.
Enumerantum Muscorum quadrundum rariorum sedes in Norvegia, quas obseravit.   N. Wulfsberg.—1875.

Jætegryder og Gamle Strandlinier i Faste Klippi af S. A. Sexe (with Translation).—1874.
Monographi over de ved Norges Kyster Fore Kommende Mysider. Forste Hefte.—1870.
Do. do. Andet Hefte.—1872.
Transfusion und Plethora, eine Phylogische Studie. Von Jacob Worm Muller.—1875.

St. Louis Academy of Sciences.
Transactions Vol. III., Part 4.—1878.

U.S.A. Geological Survey of the Territories.
First, Second, and Third Annual Reports for 1867-68 and 69.—1873
Bibliography of North American Invertebrate Palæontology.—1878.
Birds of the North-west.—1874.
Bulletin of the U.S. Entomological Commission. Parts 1 and 2.
Descriptive Catalogue of Photographs of the North American Indians. —1877.
Descriptive Catalogue of the Photographs of the U.S. Geological Survey of the Territories for the years 1869—1875 inclusive.
List of Elevations, principally in that portion of the United States west of the Mississippi River.—1875
List of Elevations, principally in that portion of the United States west of the Mississippi River.—1877
Meteorological Observations during 1872 in Utah, Idaho, and Montana. —1873.
Meteorological Observations during year 1873-74 in Colorado and Montana Territories.—1874.
Preliminary Report of U.S Geological Survey of Montana, and portions of adjacent territories.—1872.
Report of the U.S. Geological Survey of the Territories. Vol. I., viz., "Contributions to the extinct Vertebrate Fauna of the Western Territories."
Report of the U.S. Geological Survey of the Territories. Vol. V., viz., "Acrididæ of North America."
Report on Rocky Mountain Locust and other Insects.—1877.
Synopsis of Flora of Colorado.

Warwickshire Naturalists' and Archæologists' Field Club.
Proceedings for 1877.
Do. for 1878.

Warwickshire Natural History and Archæological Society.
Forty-first Annual Report.—1877.
Forty-second   do,   —1878.

Watford Natural History Society, and Hertfordshire Field Club.
Transactions. Vol. I., Parts 6 to 10.—1877-78.
Do.   Vol. II., Part 1 to 4.—1878-79.

Wisconsin, Naturhistorischen Vereins von.
Jahres-Beucht für das Jahr 1878-79.

Wiltshire Archæological and Natural History Society.
Wiltshire Archæological and Natural History Magazine. Vol. XVII.,
Parts 49 to 51.—1877-78.
Wiltshire Archæological and Natural History Magazine. Vol. XVIII.,
Parts 52 and 53.—1878-79.

[From the respective Societies.]

Aeneidea, or Critical, Exegetical, and Aesthetical Remarks on the Aeneis. Vol. I. and Vol. II., Books 1 to 4.
From the Trustees of the late James Henry, Esq., Dalkey.

Bulletin of the Minnesota Academy of Natural Sciences for 1876.
Geological and Natural History of Minnesota. Fourth Annual Report, 1876.
Do.   do.   Fifth Annual Report, 1877.
From N. H. Winchell, Esq., Minneopolis, U.S.A.

Geological Survey of Ireland. Map No. 71.
Memoir to accompany ditto.
From the Author, W. A. Traill, Esq., B.E., M.A.I., H.M. Geol. Sur.

Notes on the Scenery and Geology of Ireland.
From the Author, T. Mellard Reade, Esq , C.E., F.G.S.

On the Distribution of the Brachiopoda in the Oolitic Strata of Yorkshire.
From the Authors, W. H. Huddleston, Esq., M.A., F.G.S.; and John Francis Walker, M.A., F.G.S.

On a Remarkable Volcanic Agglomerate near Dundalk.
From the Author, J. Nolan, Esq., M.R.I.A.

On the Recent and Extinct Irish Mammals.
Report on the History of Irish Fossil Mammals.
From the Author, A. Leith Adams, Esq., F.R.S., F.G.S.

[1878-1879.]

BELFAST NATURALISTS' FIELD CLUB.

SEVENTEENTH YEAR—1879-80.

LIST OF OFFICERS AND MEMBERS.

President.
WILLIAM GRAY, M.R.I.A.

Vice-President.
PROFESSOR J. F. HODGES, M.D.

Treasurer.
GREER MALCOMSON.

Secretaries.

HUGH ROBINSON,   WM. SWANSTON, F.G.S.,
82, DONEGALL STREET.   50, KING STREET.

Committee.

JOHN BROWNE, M.R.I.A.	GEORGE O'BRIEN.
W. A. FIRTH.	S. A. STEWART, F.B.S.E.
F. W. LOCKWOOD.	ISAAC W. WARD.
DR. JAS. MOORE, M.R.I.A., H.R.H.A.	THOMAS WORKMAN.
REV. CANON MACILWAINE, D.D., M.R.I.A.	JOSEPH WRIGHT, F.G.S.

Members.

Any changes in the Addresses of Members should be communicated by them to the Secretaries.

Charlton R. Aickin, Murray's Terrace.
Miss Alder, Holywood.
W. J. C. Allen, J.P., Faunoran, Whiteabbey.
Edward Allworthy, Longford Villa.
John Anderson, J.P., F.G.S., Hillbrook, Holywood.
John Anderson, Richmond Terrace.
Robert Anderson, Donegall Place.
W. C. F. Anderson, Springbank, Dunmurry.
Samuel Andrews, Chlorine Place.
Mrs. Andrews, Chlorine Place.
Thomas D. Atkinson, Bangor, Co. Down.

James M. Barkley, Mountpottinger.
Robert Barklie, F.C.S., Carlisle St.
William Batt, Ormeau Road.
E. H. Bell, Sydenham.
Miss Bell, Lucyville, Whitehouse.
George E. Bell, High Street.
James Bennett, Botanic Avenue.
Richard S. Birch, Thornhill, Dunmurry.
Joseph Boucher, Cliftonville Avenue.
W. J Boucher, Mountpottinger.
Davys Bowman, University St.
Charles H. Brett. Dunedin.
Rev. John Bristow, M.A., Cliftonville.
D. H. Brown, Crumlin Terrace.
John Browne, M.R.I.A., Park Place, Ormeau Road.
John Browne, J.P., Ravenhill.
W. J. Browne, M.A., Longford.
W. W. Brydon, Greenisland.
Charles Bulla, Brougham Street.
H. Burden, M.D., College Square North.
J. R. Burnett, Holywood.

John Campbell, Mossley.
R. G. Campbell, Mossley.
William Campbell, Argyle House, Donaghadee.

R. J. B. Canning, Knock.
John Carson, Holywood.
Miss Carruthers, Claremont Street.
J. C. Clarke, Dunedin.
John M. Clelland, Newtownstewart.
William Clibborn, Windsor Terrace.
Foster Coates, Derryvolgie, Windsor.
Sir Edward Coey, J.P., D.L., Merville, Whiteabbey.
Miss Connery, Mountcharles.
David Corbett, Coolavin.
Thomas H. Corry, M.A., F.B.S.E., Benvue, Windsor.
W. F. C. S. Corry, Chatsworth.
Major John Sharman Crawford, M.A., T.C.D.; J.P., D.L., Crawfordsburn.
Alexander Crawford, Chlorine.
Elisha Crawford, Fortwilliam Park.
James Creeth, Brookhill Avenue.
William M. Cunningham, Sydenham.

Right Hon. Lord Dufferin and Clandeboye, K.P., Clandeboye.
Thomas Darragh, Museum.
John H. Davies, Glenmore, Lisburn.
Robert Day, F.S.A., Cork.
L. D. Devlin, Ulster Villas.
Thomas P. Devlin, Ulster Villas.
George Donaldson, Church Street.
Charles Dundee, Carnmoney.
J. J. Dougan, Claremont Street.
Mrs. Dougan, Claremont Street.

Charles Elcock, Fitzroy Avenue.

William Faren, Mountcharles.
J. George Ffennell, Ardmore, Windsor Park.
J. H. Ferguson, Antrim Road.
J. Firth, Whiterock.
W. A. Firth, Whiterock.
S. Joseph Flynn, Franklin Place.
Thomas Fraser, Wellington Park.

William Gault, Westmoreland St.
R. M. Gilmore, Portstewart.
William J. Gilmore, Windsor Crescent.
D. Corse Glen, F.G.S., Annfield Place, Glasgow.
George G. Glen, Durham Street.
G. T. Glover, Holywood.
Major Goldsmid, Hopefield Avenue.
Jas. Gourley, Derryboy, Killyleagh.
Rev. Canon Grainger, A.M., D.D., M.R.I.A. (Cor. Mem.)
Rev. James Graves, Inisnaig, Stoneyford, Co. Kilkenny (Cor. Mem.)
William Gray, M.R.I.A., Mountcharles.
Miss Gray, Mountcharles.
Miss Frances Gray, Mountcharles.
Miss Greer, Tarbat Villa, Sydenham.
Edward Gregg, Virginia Street.
H. H. Greenhill, University Street.

Joseph Hall, Windsor Avenue.
Hugh Hamilton, University Square.
J. C. Hamilton, University Square.
John Hamilton, Mount Street.
Thomas Hampton, Mountcharles.
L. Hanlon, Heath Cottage, Knock.
Mann Harbison, Model School, Newtownards.
William Harte, C.E., Buncrana (Cor. Mem.)
James Haslett, University Street.
H. A. Hawkins, Kin-Edar, Strandtown.
W. D. Henderson, University Sq.
J. L. Henry, Donegall Pass.
Arthur Herdman, College Square North.
John O. Herdman, College Square North.
F. A. Heron, Greenmount, Craigavad.
Mrs. Heron, Greenmount, Craigavad.
Prof. J. F. Hodges, M.D., F.C.S., Derryvolgie, Malone.
F. Hodges, Derryvolgie, Malone.
John S. Holden, M.D., F.G.S., Sudbury, Suffolk (Cor. Mem.)
F. C. Holmes, Belmont.
J. J. Howard, Clifton Park Avenue.
Alexander Hunter, Northern Bank.
Miss Hunter, Orchard Street.
Thomas Hunter, Holywood.

James Imrie, Fitzroy Avenue.
Rev. Richard Irvine, A.M., Hampton, Windsor.
R. H. Irwin, Holywood.

John Jaffé, Cambridge Villa, Sydenham.
Mrs. Jaffé, Cambridge Villa, Sydenham.
F. M. Jennings, Cork (Cor. Mem.)
James Johnston, Derryvolgie.
Miss Johnston, Glenavy.
W. J. Johnston, J.P., Dunesk, Stranmillis.

Stuart C. Kelly, Seaview House, Greenisland.
W. Kernahan, Antrim Terrace.
Rev. J. A. Kerr, LL.D., Whiteabbey.
George Kidd, Suffolk, Dunmurry.
Henry Knight, Antrim Villa, Weston Super-Mare.
W. J. Knowles, Cullybackey.
Robert Kyle, Richmond.

W. W. Lamb, Divis View.
Miss Lamb, Divis View.
Charles Lapworth, F.G.S., St. Andrews, N.B, Hon. Mem.
David Laurie, Richmond Place.
George D. Leathem, Malone Park.
F. R. Lepper, Sydenham.
Miss R. Lester, Newtownards.
Rev. H. W. Lett, Ardmore Glebe, Lurgan.
Joseph F. Lewis, Cooke Street.
Joseph Lewis, Schomburg Terrace.
F. W. Lockwood, Brookhill Avenue.
Wm. Lowry, Oakley, Strandtown.

Henry Magee, Eglantine Avenue.
J. J. Major, Belvoir Hall.
S. J. Magowan, Granville. Villas.
Greer Malcomson, Shamrock Lodge.
James Malcomson, The Mount, Mountpottinger.
Mrs. Malcomson, The Mount, Mountpottinger.
John Marsh, Richmond.
Joseph C. Marsh, Clifton Park Avenue.
Rev. James Martin, Eglantoun, Antrim Road.

Mrs. Martin, Eglantoun, Antrim Road.
John Martin, M.D., Clarence Place.
Robert Masterson, Summer Street.
William Miller, Shankhill Road.
W. R. Molyneux, Florence Place.
Miss Monteith, University Road.
James Moore, M.D., M.R.I.A., H.R.H.A., Chichester Street.
John Moore, M.D., Carlisle Terrace.
David Morrow, Dunluce Street.
John Morton, Donegall Terrace.
Robert Mullan, Willowfield.
J. R. T. Mulholland, Tyne Cottage, Whiteabbey.
J. J. Murphy, F.G.S., Old Forge, Dunmurry.
J. R. Musgrave, J.P., Drumglass.

John M'Callum, Botanic Avenue.
James M'Clenahan, Tennent Street.
Samuel M'Cloy, Magdala Street.
Rev. E. M'Clure, A.M., M.R.I.A, Lincoln's Inn Fields, London, (Cor. Mem.)
Sir Thomas M'Clure, Bart., M.P., Belmont.
W. J. M'Clure, Divis Street.
John M'Connell, North Street.
Edward M'Fee, Whiteabbey.
Joseph H. M'Ferran, Elmwood Terrace.
John M'Hutchinson, Wesley Terrace, Cooke Street.
Rev. Canon MacIlwaine, D.D., M.R.I.A., Ulsterville.
Mrs. MacIlwaine, Ulsterville.
H. C. M'Ilwaine, Ulsterville.
John MacIlwaine, Sydenham.
Mrs. MacIlwaine Sydenham.
J. B. S. MacIlwaine, Stephen's Green, Dublin.
Mrs. M'Ilwrath, Dunluce Street.
Daniel M'Kee, Adela Place.
W. S. M'Kee, Fleetwood Street.
John MacKenzie, C.E.
Alexander M'Laine, Altmore.
F. P. M'Lean, Huntly Villas, Derryvolgie Avenue.
William MacMillan, Sallow Mount, Ballinasloe.
W. K. M'Mordie, M.D., College Square East.

Lucien Nepveu, Fitzwilliam Street.
Chas. A. Nicholl, Rathmore, Greenisland.
Richd. Niven, Chrome Hill, Lisburn.

Nicholas Oakman, Prospect Terrace.
George O'Brien, Botanic Avenue.
Joshua O'Brien, Botanic Avenue.
W. D. O'Brien, Botanic Avenue.
F. H. O'Flaherty, Fitzroy Avenue.
Mrs. O'Flaherty, Fitzroy Avenue.
Dr. O'Flaherty, R.N., Botanic Terrace.
Rev. Jas. O'Laverty, P.P., M.R.I.A., Holywood.
James O'Neill, M.A., College Square East.
Thomas E. Osborne, Marino Cottages.

D. C. Patterson, Holywood.
R. L. Patterson, Martello Terrace, Holywood.
W. H. Patterson, M.R.I.A., Dundela, Strandtown.
James J. Phillips, Granville Terrace.
W. H. Phillips, Lemonfield, Holywood.
E. Wakefield Pim, Elmwood Terrace.
John Pim, Chichester Park.
Joshua Pim, Crumlin Terrace.
Thos. W. Pim, The Lodge, Strandtown.
C. D. Purdon, M.R.I.A., Wellington Place.
Miss Nellie Purdon, Wellington Place.

Joseph Radley, Prospect Hill, Lisburn.
W. J. Ramsay, Mauds Terrace.
William Rankin, York Street.
John Rea, M.D., Great Victoria St.
James Theodore Richardson, Glenone, Lisburn.
Miss Robinson Lisanore.
Rev. George Robinson, A.M., Tartaraghan.
Hugh Robinson, Donegall Street.
James R. Robinson, St. Helen's Terrace.
N. J. Robinson, Oakfield, Cregagh Road.

W. A. Robinson, Crofton, Holywood.
W. G. Robinson, Tartaraghan.
Richard Ross, M.D., Wellington Place.
Mrs. Rowland, University Street.
Charles C. Russell, Newtownards

Mrs. Scott, Fountainville Terrace.
Thomas Shaw, Pakenham Place.
Samuel Smiles, Sydenham.
Charles Smith, F.G.S., Barrow-in-Furness.
F. W. Smith, Rugby Road.
George K. Smith, Meadow Bank, Whitehouse.
Rev. George C. Smythe, M.A., Carnmoney.
Maj.-Gen. Smythe, R.A., M.R.I.A., Abbeyville, Whiteabbey.
Adam Speers, B. Sc., Holywood.
Sir N. A. Staples, Bart., Lissan (Life Mem.)
James H. Staples, Lissan.
H. Stevenson, Glenfield Place.
J. M'N. Stevenson, Carrickfergus.
Richard Stevenson, Donegall Pass.
S. A. Stewart, F.B.S.E., North St.
Miss Swanston, Cliftonville Avenue.
William Swanston, F.G.S., Cliftonville Avenue.
Samuel Symington, Ballyoran House

Prof. Ralph Tate, F.G.S., A.L.S., University of Adelaide, South Australia (Hon. Mem.)
A. O'D. Taylor, Upper Crescent.
H. F. Thomas, Lower Crescent.
Mrs. Thomas, Lower Crescent.
E. H. Thompson, J.P., Slieve-na-Failthe, Whiteabbey.
E. M'C. Thompson, Walton, Fortwilliam Park.
Henry Thompson, Windsor.

George Thomson, Broadway.
Prof. Sir C. Wyville Thomson, LL.D., F.R.S., &c., Edinburgh (Hon. Mem.)
Prof. Jas. Thomson, A.M., LL.D., F.R.S., &c., Glasgow.
Miss Thorpe, University Street.
John Todd, Regent Street.
W. A. Todd, Elgin Terrace.
W. A. Traill, M.A.I., B.E, H.M., Geo. Survey, Ballymena.

John Vinycomb, Melrose Terrace.

T. R. Walkington, Laurel Lodge, Sydenham.
Isaac W. Ward, University Street.
James F. Ward, Lennoxvale, Malone.
John Ward, Lennoxvale, Malone.
John S. Ward, Lisburn.
Thomas R. Ward, Holywood.
E. H. Watson, Ardmore, Windsor.
Isaac Waugh, Everton Terrace.
T. K. Wheeler, M.D., Clarence Place.
William Whitla, M.D., Gt. Victoria Street.
David Wilson, Ballymoney.
James Wilson, Jr., Albion Place.
James Wilson, Ballybundon, Killinchy.
James F. Wilson, Ventry Street.
John Workman, J.P., Windsor.
Rev. Robert Workman, A.M., Glastry.
Thos. Workman, Westburne, Windsor.
Joseph Wright, F.G.S., Albertville.
Mrs. Wright, Albertville.
S. O. Wylie, College Square North.
William Wylie, Belgrave Terrace.

Robert Young, C.E., Rathvarna.

RULES

OF THE

Belfast Naturalists' Field Club.

I.

That the Society be called "THE BELFAST NATURALISTS' FIELD CLUB."

II.

That the objects of the Society be the practical study of Natural Science and Archæology in Ireland.

III.

That the Club shall consist of Ordinary, Corresponding, and Honorary Members. The Ordinary Members to pay annually a subscription of Five Shillings, and that candidates for such Membership shall be proposed and seconded at any Meeting of the Club, by Members present, and elected by a majority of the Votes of the Members present.

IV.

That the Honorary and Corresponding Members shall consist of persons of eminence in Natural Science, or who shall have done some special service to the Club; and whose usual residence is not less than twenty miles from Belfast. That such Members may be nominated by any Member of the Club, and on being approved of by the Committee, may be elected at any subsequent

Meeting of the Club by a majority of the votes of the Members present. That Corresponding Members be expected to communicate a Paper once within every two years.

V.

That the Officers of the Club be annually elected, and consist of a President, Vice-President, Treasurer, Two Secretaries, and Ten Members, who form the Committee. Five to form a quorum. No Member of Committee to be eligible for re-election who has not attended at least one-fourth of the Committee Meetings during his year of office. That the office of President, or that of Vice-President, shall not be held by the same person for more than two years in succession.

VI.

That the Members of the Club shall hold at least Six Field Meeting during the year, in the most interesting localities, for investigating the Natural History and Archæology of Ulster. That the place of meeting be fixed by the Committee, and that five days' notice of each Excursion be communicated to Members by the Secretaries.

VII.

That Meetings be held Fortnightly or Monthly, at the discretion of the Committee, for the purpose of reading papers; such papers, as far as possible, to treat of the Natural History and Archæology of the district. These Meetings to be held during the months from November to April inclusive.

VIII.

That the Committee shall, if they find it advisable, offer for competition Prizes for the best collections of scientific objects of the district; and the Committee may order the purchase of maps, or other scientific apparatus, and may carry on geological and archæological searches or excavations, if deemed advisable, provided that the entire amount expended under this rule does not exceed the sum of £10 in any one year.

IX.

That the Annual Meeting be held during the month of April, when the Report of the Committee for the past year, and the Treasurer's Financial Statement shall be presented, the Committee and Officers elected, Bye-laws made and altered, and any proposed alteration in the general laws, of which a

fortnight's notice shall have been given, in writing, to the Secretary or Secretaries, considered and decided upon. The Secretaries to give the Members due notice of such intended alteration.

X

That, on the written requisition of twenty-five Members, delivered to the Secretaries, an Extraordinary General Meeting may be called, to consider and decide upon the subjects mentioned in such written requisition.

XI.

That the Committee be empowered to exchange publications and reports, and to extend the privilege of attending the Meetings and Excursions of the Belfast Naturalists' Field Club to members of kindred societies, on similar privileges being accorded to its Members by such other societies.

The following Rules for the Conducting of the Excursions have been arranged by the Committee.

I. The Excursion to be open to all Members, each one to have the privilege of introducing two friends.

II. A Chairman to be elected as at ordinary meetings.

III. One of the Secretaries to act as conductor, or, in the absence of both, a member to be elected for that purpose.

IV. No change to be made in the programme, or extra expenses incurred, except by the consent of the majority of the members present.

V. No fees, gratuities, or other expenses to be paid except through the conductor.

VI. Every member or visitor to have the accommodation assigned by the conductor. Where accommodation is limited, consideration will be given to priority of application.

VII. Accommodation cannot be promised unless tickets are obtained before the time mentioned in the special circular.

VIII. Those who attend an excursion, without previous notice, will be liable to extra charge, if extra cost be incurred thereby.

IX. No intoxicating liquors to be provided at the expense of the Club.

Belfast Naturalists' Field Club.

SEVENTEENTH YEAR.

THE Committee offer the following Prizes to be competed for during the Session ending March 31st, 1880:—

1. For the best Herbarium of Flowering Plants, representing not less than 250 Species............ ......£1 0 0
2. For the best Herbarium of Flowering Plants, representing not less than 150 Species.................... 0 10 0
3. Best Collection of Mosses................. .. ..- 0 10 0
4. ,, ,, Seaweeds............... . ... 0 10 0
5. ,, ,, Ferns............ ....…... 0 10 0
6. ,, ,, Tertiary and Post Tertiary Fossils................. .... 0 10 0
7. ,, ,, Cretaceous do. 0 10 0
8. ,, ,, Liassic do. 0 10 0
9. ,, ,, Palæozoic do. 0 10 0
10. ,, ,, Fossil Plants..................... .. 0 10 0
11. ,, ,, Marine Shells...................... 0 10 0
12. ,, ,, Land and Freshwater Shells..... 0 10 0
13. ,, ,, Lepidoptera 0 10 0
14. Best set of 25 Microscopic Slides..................... 0 10 0

15. Best Collection of Archæological Objects............ 0 10 0
16.   „   „   Crustacea 0 10 0
17.   „   „   Echinodermata..... .... 0 10 0
18.   „   „   Geological Specimens, illustrative of the Mineral Resoutces of the Province of Ulster 1 0 0
19. Best Collection of all or any of the above Objects, collected *at the Excursions* of the Year 0 10 0
20. Six Best Field Sketches appertaining to Geology, Archæology, or Natural History 0 10 0

In every case where three or more persons compete for a Prize, a second one, of half its value, will be awarded if the conditions are otherwise complied with.

CONDITIONS.

No Competitor to obtain more than two Prizes in any one year.

No Competitor to be awarded the same Prize twice within three years.

All Collections to be made personally during the Session, within the Province of Ulster. Each Species to be correctly named, and locality stated. The Flowering Plants to be collected when in flower, and classified according to the Natural System. The Sketches, Drawings, and Microscopic Slides to be the Competitors' own work.

No Prizes will be awarded except to such Collections as shall, in the opinion of the Judges, possess positive merit.

The Prizes to be in books, or suitable scientific objects, at the desire of the successful competitor.

SPECIAL PRIZES.

21. The President offers a Prize of £1 1s. for the best set of Three Sketches, contributed to the Club's Album. The set to be of uniform size, not less than 9 inches by 5½ inches, and to be Original Pen and Ink or Coloured Drawings of Irish Antiquarian subjects, liable to removal or destruction. If there be only one Competitor, the Judges may award the Prize, if they consider the Drawings possess superior merit.

22. Mr. William Swanston, F.G.S., offers a Prize of 10s. 6d. for the best Two Studies, illustrative of Geology, contributed to the Club's Album. The subjects must be from Nature, and may be either in the form of Drawings or Measured Sections. Size not to exceed 15 inches by 9 inches.

23. A Prize of 10s. given by the late Mr. J. W. Murphy, for the best Collection of Recent Sponges, the conditions being the same as those for Prizes 1 to 20.

N.B.—The Sketches and Drawings to be Competitors' own work.

11 FEB 1886

320 pp. Fcap. 8vo. Cloth Gilt, Bevelled Boards, with 48 pp. Illustrations and Map. Price 3/6.

GUIDE TO BELFAST

AND ADJACENT COUNTIES.

BY THE

BELFAST NATURALISTS' FIELD CLUB.

THE BOOK TREATS OF THE FOLLOWING SUBJECTS:

PHYSICAL GEOGRAPHY.
GEOLOGY AND MINERAL RESOURCES.
BOTANY.
ZOOLOGY.
TOPOGRAPHY.
HISTORICAL & DESCRIPTIVE NOTICES OF TOWNS.

ANTIQUITIES—ECCLESIASTICAL AND CIVIL.
AGRICULTURE.
TRADE AND COMMERCE.
EXCURSIONS TO PLACES OF INTEREST.

May be had of all Booksellers, or from the Secretaries of the Club.

ANNUAL REPORT

AND

PROCEEDINGS

OF THE

Belfast Naturalists' Field Club,

1879-80.

SERIES II.

Volume I. Part III.

PRINTED FOR MEMBERS ONLY.

ANNUAL REPORT

AND

Proceedings

OF THE

Belfast Naturalists' Field Club

FOR THE

Year Ending 31st March, 1880.

(EIGHTEENTH YEAR.)

SERIES II.
VOLUME I. PART VII.

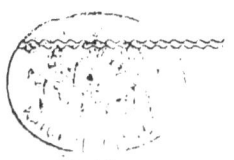

Belfast:
PRINTED FOR THE CLUB.
ROBINSON BROTHERS, 25, DONEGALL STREET.
1881.

AND

REPORT

OF THE

Belfast Naturalists' Field Club,

FOR THE

Year Ending 31st March, 1880.

OUR Committee in meeting you at the close of the seventeenth year of the Club's existence have much pleasure in reporting the continued prosperous state of the Society, both as regards its membership and the interest evinced in the various subjects brought under discussion.

The Excursions selected for the Summer Session were, without exception, carried out. The attendance of members was not, however, so large as could have been wished. This was mainly due to the very unfavourable nature of the season, which was remarkable for cold winds in the opening months, and excessive rains towards its close.

The Committee desire to express the thanks of the Club to those Gentlemen who so kindly allowed the members attending the excursions to visit their grounds, and especially to Mr. Mann

Harbison for his kindness in conducting and entertaining the party on the occasion of their visit to Newtownards and Scrabo. The places visited are as follow :—

Hillhall and Drumbo, on	31st May.
The Gobbins,	21st June.
Antrim Coast Road and Cushendall,	15th, 16th, and 17th July.
Toome Bridge,	9th August.
The Black Mountain,	23rd August.
Newtownards and Scrabo Hill,	13th September.

At the opening of the Winter Session a Conversazione was held in the Museum, which was well attended. It was gratifying to those members on whom devolved the labour of arranging for this meeting to find that their efforts were appreciated by a highly intelligent audience. As an evidence of the continued prosperity of these re-unions, twenty-two members were elected on this occasion. Your Committee take this opportunity of thanking the members and friends who so kindly lent objects of interest, valuable works of art, &c., as well as plants, flowers, and objects suitable for decoration. Through the kindness of the Natural History and Philosophical Society, the Museum was opened to the public the following day, when several members attended, and exhibited their microscopes, &c.

The Winter Session may be considered to have been one of the most active the Club has ever had, and some difficulty was experienced by the Secretaries in affording opportunities to all the members anxious to bring forward communications. Extra meetings were arranged, and nine papers were read, the greater part of which were of a local nature, or bore more particularly on subjects of local interest. The following are their titles ; abstracts of them will appear in the Proceedings :—

1879.
2nd Dec. Opening Address by the President, Mr. Wm. Gray, M.R.I.A. Subject : "Our Club—Its Aims and Objects."
9th Dec. "A few words on British War Medals." By Mr. John Browne, M.R.I.A.

1880.
6th Jan. "Notes on a Tour through Switzerland, with special reference to the Origin of the Swiss Valleys." By Mr. Mann Harbison.
3rd Feb. I. "On the Round Towers; who built them and for what purpose." A Notice of the latest views on this question. By Mr. F. W. Lockwood.
,, II. "On Sponge Remains from the Carboniferous Limestone of Benbulben, Co. Sligo." By Mr. Joseph Wright, F.G.S.
2nd March. "On the Honey Bee and its Treatment." By Mr. Charles Russell.
23rd March. I. "Notes on North of Ireland Cup Markings." By the President, Mr. Wm. Gray, M.R.I.A.
,, II. "On the Palæontology of the Irish Cretaceous Strata." By Mr. William Gault.
,, III. "On the Post Tertiary Foraminifera of the North of Ireland." By Mr. Joseph Wright, F.G.S.

Abstracts of these papers, as well as notices of the various excursions, appeared from time to time in the daily papers, thus keeping the general public acquainted with the work in which your Club has been engaged. The Committee have pleasure in acknowledging the courtesy displayed by the local Press in so readily inserting the communications of the Club.

The Committee, as in former years, have distributed a large number of copies of your Proceedings, and in return continue to receive the publications of kindred societies, both British and Foreign. The Club is also deeply indebted to the United States Government for several parcels of Books, treating on the Geology and Natural History of the States and Territories.

WILLIAM SWANSTON, } *Hon. Secs.*
F. W. LOCKWOOD,

Several Collections were sent in by members in competition for some of the prizes offered by the Club. The Judges appointed to make the awards report as follows :—

"We have examined the twenty-five Microscopic Slides submitted by Mr. Charles Elcock in competition for Prize 14. We are of opinion that the collection is strictly in accordance with the conditions. The mounted objects are chiefly of Foraminifera, illustrated by a great variety of species, and several excellent methods of mounting. All are prepared with artistic skill and superior finish. We recommend that the prize be awarded to Mr. Elcock.

"WILLIAM GRAY,
"S. A. STEWART, } *Sub-Committee.*"
"JOSEPH WRIGHT,

In competition for the prizes offered by the Club for Botanical work, there have been three sets of Plants sent in. The following are the awards :—

II. "The collection made by the Rev. H. W. Lett, M.A., T.C.D., includes 257 species, well mounted and correctly labelled, with dates and localities as prescribed. We have pleasure in awarding to Mr. Lett the prize No. 1 for the best collection of flowering plants.

III. "The Rev. Mr. Lett has also sent a series of specimens of Ferns, representing twelve species, in competition for Prize No. 5 ; but as this collection is meagre in number, and the specimens not prepared with sufficient care, we do not consider that the prize can be awarded.

IV. "Mr. Joseph Radley has sent a large collection of flowering plants ; but having failed to comply with the conditions, which require the specimens to be labelled, with dates and localities, he is thereby disqualified, and no prize is awarded.

"S. A. STEWART, } *Sub-Committee.*"
"G. MALCOLMSON,

A set of original drawings was also sent in, in competition for the prize offered by the President, as to which the following is the award :—

" We have examined the three water-colour drawings sent in by Rev. H. W. Lett in competition for Prize No. 21.

" We consider them careful delineations of most interesting

Archæological remains, and have pleasure in recommending that Mr. Lett be awarded the prize, and in congratulating the Club on so important an addition to its Sketch Album.

"JOHN VINYCOMB, } *Sub-Committee.*"
"SAMUEL M'CLOY, }

DR. Belfast Naturalists' Field Club in Account with Treasurer. CR.

	£ s. d.
To Balance from 1878-79,	£12 14 10
,, Subscriptions—230, at 5/-	57 10 0
,, Arrears of Subscriptions—16, at 5/-	4 0 0
,, Gain on Excursions,	1 1 10
,, Exhibition held 8th November,	0 6 0
	£75 12 8

	£ s. d.
By Loss on Conversazione,	£7 5 4
,, Printing Annual Report,	16 18 6
,, Advertising, Printing, and Stationery,	10 17 8
,, Delivery of Circulars,	1 10 0
,, Postages,	4 8 9
,, Museum Expenses,	8 8 0
,, Prizes, No. XIV.,	0 10 0
,, Do. No. I.,	1 0 0
,, Balance on hands,	24 14 5
	£75 12 8

Audited and found correct,

GREER MALCOMSON, *Treasurer.*
WILLIAM SWANSTON, *Hon. Secretary.*

SUMMER SESSION.

The following Excursions were made during the Summer Session:—

On 31st May, to

HILLHALL AND DRUMBO.

The Summer Session was inaugurated by an excursion, on Saturday, 31st May, to Hillhall, Drumbo, and the Giant's Ring, a most attractive locality for those having archæological proclivities. Though the unsettled weather of the previous day caused some uncertainty, nevertheless a large number of ladies and gentlemen attended, and started at noon from the Ulster Hall, on well appointed vehicles, supplied by Messrs. Thomas Johnston & Sons. The weather proved all that could be desired, and the departure was made with high anticipations of a pleasant day to be delightfully spent in the green lanes and by-ways remote from the beaten tracks of tourists.

Proceeding by the Malone Road, many scenes of local interest were passed, and fine views were obtained of the rich valley of the Lagan, bounded on the west and north by the picturesque range of the Belfast hills.

At the Drum Bridge a halt was made, and an opportunity afforded for collecting botanical specimens by the river bank. The rare moss, *Orthotrichum Sprucei*, was found to be plentiful and in good fruit on several trees close to the bridge. This is the spot at which this well-marked, though minute, moss was discovered by Mr. Davies last year, and is the only locality in Ireland where it is known to occur. The neat and tasteful Church at Drum was thrown open for inspection, and was visited by the party. The churchyard contains several tombstones with inscriptions of early dates.

A drive of two miles southward brought the party to "The Court," where there are still to be seen some remains connected with the ancient seat of the Downshire family. The walls are, however, yielding to the irresistable influence of time, and the frosts of last winter have been fatal to some of the old bastions. The Celandine *(Chelidonium majus)* grows abundantly at these ruins. The Court is one of the places where King William III. is said to have stayed on his passage through this part of Ireland—an incident of which its name, "The Court," still perpetuates the memory.

Tullyard (the high hill), lying more than a mile to the south-east, was the next place visited. This being the highest ground in the neighbourhood, affords a very extensive view, well repaying the toil of the ascent; but the principal object of interest in this place is the old Fort, some traces of which still remain. The structure is to a great extent demolished, and the site partly in crop; however, the greater portion of the central "lis" is still intact, and though the remains are much obscured, yet the stones found in a vitrified or slaggy state are sufficient to attest that this was one of those structures, so rare in this country, which are known as vitrified forts. Though no portions of the stonework are now visible *in situ*, yet such were to be seen within a comparatively recent period.

From Tullyard, the party were conveyed to Drumbo. where they had an opportunity of inspecting the well-known Round Tower.

The repairs of this structure, which have been recently executed, though no doubt calculated to ensure its stability, have not by any means conduced to the pieturesque, the level truncated termination giving the tower a more modern aspect than it presented prior to the execution of the repairs. This tower, of which forty feet now remains, is one of the oldest class of these structures, being built of unwrought stones, the door without tooled dressings or ornaments of any sort, and having a flat lintel.

One mile north-east of Drumbo is Farrell's Fort, which was visited on the way to the celebrated Giant's Ring, near Ballylesson. On the assembling of the whole party in the enclosure of this latter rath, the usual business meeting of the Club was held. The President having taken the chair (on the cromlech), a number of new members were elected, and after an inspection of the rath, the vehicles were put in requisition, and the Ulster Hall reached shortly before sunset. It was remarked on this occasion that though agricultural operations have been much retarded, and the crops not at all in a forward state, yet they present a promising appearance. The flowering of wild plants has also been delayed by the unseasonable weather. As an illustration of this fact it may be mentioned that the President of the Club offered a prize for the first sprig of hawthorn found in flower; but though the hedges were closely scrutinised, not a hawthorn flower was seen, while in 1878 this plant was noted as flowering on 10th May.

On 21st June, to

THE GOBBINS.

The second Field Meeting for the present session was arranged to be held at the Gobbins, on Saturday. the 21st June, and, as might be expected, a considerable amount of interest was excited amongst the members by the contemplated visit to this attractive locality. Saturdays, however, proved unfortunate this season, as respects weather, and this Saturday was no exception. A considerable proportion of those who had intended to avail themselves of this opportunity of becoming somewhat acquainted with the natural history and geology of Islandmagee, assembled at the Northern Counties Terminus shortly after nine o'clock ; but, as the rain descended in torrents, and the weather-wise predicted a bad day, a small number only mustered up courage to carry out the programme. As has so often been the case in the history of the Club, the more hopeful few were rewarded by a much better day than could have been expected. Shortly after mid-day the rain ceased, and soon the sun broke out bright and warm, drying up the damp ground, and sending forth the lark with his cheering carol. The butterflies were soon to be seen in numbers fluttering along the hill-sides and hedge-banks, while busy bees were everywhere extracting the sweets hidden away in fresh and fragrant flowers.

The party were conveyed, as arranged, to Ballycarry station, whence they proceeded on foot to the seashore on the eastern side of Islandmagee. The course lay northward by the shore for a distance of about two miles, over the very rough and broken ground which intervenes between Blackhead and the Gobbins cliffs. Pedestrianism is the only possible means of locomotion over this rugged tract, and progress is not only slow, but laborious; nevertheless, the toil is well repaid by seeing the geological structure of the country laid bare all along the shore, exposing rocks of several geological formations, from the Boulder Clays of the Glacial epoch to the gypsum-bearing marls of the Triassic era. The Cretaceous rocks that crop out along the shore are underlain by the Lias clays, and the slippery character of the latter has caused the superimposed masses to slide down, and thus the sea margin is strewed with great blocks of chalk and greensand, in which are embedded numbers of shells, corals, sponges, &c., once members of the abundant and varied Cretaceous fauna. The vigorous use of the geologist's hammer enabled the party to secure fair specimens of characteristic fossils of several genera, as *Ananchytes, Terebratula, Rhynchonella, Pectin, Belemnites,* &c. The Lias clays of this place are also fossiliferous, but the specimens obtained were badly preserved and not at all numerous. As is well known to most members of the Club, the seas of the Liassic period swarmed with Foraminifera, the calcareous tests of which are found even yet in the rocks of that formation. A small portion of the clay was brought away on this occasion, which yielded those little organisms in profusion. *Marginulina, Rœmeri* and *Polymorphina compressa* were especially abundant, those species having hitherto been but rarely met with in the Antrim Lias.

Geological studies did not entirely engross the attention of the party. The flora of the district, which possesses much attraction, was also attended to, and specimens of much interest were secured. Exceedingly luxuriant examples of some of our most beautiful ferns were met with, especially *Asplenium adiantum-nigrum;* but the best prize of the day consisted of magnificent plants of *Polypodium semilacerum.* Several roots of this fine specimen of the polybody were brought away, in which the fronds were very luxuriant and highly characteristic. Of flowering plants several interesting specimens were collected, though not of special rarity. It was noted that although in the present season the wild plants are much later than usual, yet they are of unusual luxuriance. Specimens of *Carex pilulifera* were gathered twenty inches in height, being twice the average height of this sedge. The magnificent basaltic cliffs of the Gobbins were reached in due time, and were seen to advantage under the bright sunshine of the afternoon. The very fine weather which now prevailed had the effect of sending forth the butterflies in profusion. The unpromising character of the morning had deterred several lepidopterists from attending ; this was unfortunate, as the small blue, *Polyommatus alsus*, so rare in other localities, was seen in abundance, eight examples being observed on the grass within the compass of a square yard. A fine opportunity was also afforded for securing examples of the burnet moth *(Anthoceras filipendula)*; numbers of the cocoons of this species were observed placed on stems of grass and of rushes.

From the Gobbins the party proceeded to Gransha, on the eastern shore of Larne Lough, to inspect an ancient place of sepulture which is locally reported to have been a burial place of the Danes. The interments were discovered when quarrying limestone many years ago, the graves having been made in the soil above the rock. A full description of this interesting relic of an age whose history seems nearly lost, and an account of the various objects contained in the graves, was published in the "Ulster Journal of Archæology." It is fortunate that such is the case, as not a single trace of the interments is now to be found.

From Gransha a smart walk of half an hour brought the party to Ballycarry railway station, whence they returned to Belfast, well pleased with the results of the trip, and only regretting that so many friends were prevented from accompanying them.

On 15th, 16th, and 17th July, to

THE ANTRIM COAST ROAD AND CUSHENDALL.

The third excursion of the Society for the present year was made on 15th, 16th, and 17th July. The locality chosen was the Antrim coast road, with the picturesque village of Cushendall as head-quarters. So attractive is the scenery along this route, and so interesting are the many features presented to the lover of nature by the bold and rugged character of the coast, and the varied geological phenomena which it presents, that on a previous occasion of the Club's visit a feeling was expressed that it should be oftener inserted in the Annual Programme of Excursions. Hence, as on former trips, a fair muster of members and friends assembled at the Northern Counties terminus, in time to start by the 9-30 a.m. train to Larne. After a run of little over an hour, passing on the way the ancient town of Carrickfergus and several points of historic interest, Larne was reached, and all were soon comfortably seated in excellent vehicles. Larne is early mentioned under various names in Irish history; and so far back as the 12th century we read of an expedition by sea, under Aodh O'Neill, attacking it, and burning the greater part of the town. Edward Bruce landed here in 1315, and most probably occupied Olderfleet Castle, the rugged old ruins of which contrast so strongly with the handsome hotels, modern buildings, and improvements that are springing up so rapidly around it.

Leaving Larne, an extended view of the day's route is seen from above Waterloo, headland beyond headland being beautifully shown in diminishing distinctness. Round these, and following the line of the many bays which they enclose, lies our road, which is seldom more than a stone's throw from the sea, and frequently overhanging it. On the shore at this place are perhaps the best sections of the Lias deposits in Ireland, rising as they do to a height of nearly a hundred feet, and stretching beyond low-water mark. Many of the beds are highly fossiliferous, and frequently, after in-blowing gales, good specimens from various zones may be found washed out on the beach. No halt, however, was made till Ballygalley Head was reached, where the same deposit is again seen, and specimens containing lignite, &c., were obtained. Cairncastle, on an insulated outlier of basalt at this point, is a relic of a bygone time of strife and insecurity. Little now remains of it but the foundation walls, and its history is rather obscure. It gives name, however, to the parish, which stretches for several miles along the coast. The bold cliff-line of the coast, which may be said to begin at Knock Dhu—1,262 feet—some distance inland, here gradually approaches the shore, and on nearing Glenarm Bay overhangs the road in a threatening manner, at a height of over 500 feet.

A halt was called at the Deer Park to examine the rugged ground at the base of the cliffs. Here the rocks of various geological formations cover the slopes in the wildest possible confusion. Fossils from Chalk, Greensand, Lias, and Rhætic may be picked up side by side, all having slipped down from the cliffs above. Several of the characteristic fossils were obtained, and materials for microscopic examination brought away. While those of geological tastes were thus employed, others of the party visited the site of the ancient stone-enclosed graves recently discovered in the soil above one of the chalk quarries near Glenarm. A full account of these had been brought before the club at one of the meetings the previous winter, and specimens from them were exhibited at the conversazione.

Passing through Glenarm, with its busy harbour, no further halt is made till Carnlough is reached, where ample justice was done to a substantial luncheon. Cards of admission having been kindly granted to the party to visit the romantic grounds of Garron Tower, a start was again made. Soon the level coast road was left for an uphill winding one, leading to the Castle grounds. The scenery from some of the vantage-points along this road is really magnificent—landward, the densely wooded hillside rises abruptly to a height of several hundred feet, while far below the calm sea may be seen at intervals through the rich verdure. Southward, a grand vista opens of the route along which we have travelled. The sandy beach at Carnlough is followed by the white cliffs beyond, while the richly timbered valley of the Glenarm and Linford Rivers lead temptingly inland. The more distant prospect is well filled in by bold Knock Dhu and the northern extremity of Islandmagee. The Maiden Lighthouses, with the Scotch coast, complete a picture rarely equalled for grandeur and variety of outline and colouring. Garron Tower is an extensive castellated building, built for the most part of the basalt of the district. It is situated on a level piece of ground, about midway between the sea-level and the higher cliff-line, and commands an extensive view of the coast, both north and south. Art has done much to enhance the beauty of the site by forming terraced walks, gardens, and lawns; but to Nature must be accredited the giant share of making the spot so attractive. The point upon which the Castle stands, when viewed on either side from the coast road, shows indisputably that it has at some period—distant, perhaps, even geologically speaking—slipped down from the higher ground above. Leaving the Castle grounds, by a road cut through the rock to the northward, the coastline is again soon reached, and shortly after the wide extent of Glenariffe opens to view. The southern side of this imposing valley is formed by the continuation of the cliffs, which bend round from Garron Point, and run inland for several miles. The northern boundary is a similar range of cliffs, stretching from the bold table-like mountain of Lurigethan— 1,154 feet. The slopes of this valley, up to a considerable elevation, as well as the wide expanse along the comparatively level ground in the centre, are well cultivated, and promise to repay the labour spent upon them. Far up the valley, where the cliffs converge, is seen a fine waterfall, on the main stream of the Glenariffe River, which, after a tortuous course, finds its way into Red Bay, at the village of Waterfoot. A change is here noted in the geology of the district, which up to this point had largely consisted of the white chalk and the dark basalts. At the northern extremity of Red Bay a new colouring is introduced, and dark purple conglomerates and grits form an important feature. On a bluff of this conglomerate, through which the road pierces, stands out prominently the ruins of Red Bay Castle, which, with its little harbour, would form a pretty picture were it not for the unsightly buildings at the base of the cliff. The geological position of these conglo-

B

merates is a point not yet fully settled. They have been considered by some geologists to be New Red; but it may eventually be found that they correspond more nearly with the age of the Dingle and Glengariffe grits of the South-West of Ireland, which they resemble in a remarkable manner, and whose place in the geological system is believed to be lower than Old Red Sandstone

A short drive brought the party to the village of Cushendall, embosomed in trees, and all were soon comfortably attended to by the kind hostess of the Glens of Antrim Hotel. After a hearty tea, the party separated into groups, to follow their own special tastes. One section, bent on archæology, visited the picturesque ruins of Layde Church; another group, armed with hammers and chisels, sallied out to secure specimens of the jasper and porphyry for which the locality is noted; while others, more fatigued by the day's work, were satisfied with a stroll along the beach, or a visit to the remains of an old walled fort, known as " Court Martin," situated above the town. Next morning the more active were up before six o'clock and enjoyed a refreshing bathe, after which, as arranged the previous evening, the ascent of Lurigethan was accomplished. This feat was no joke in the time at disposal, but the view from the summit amply repaid for all the toil, and none of those who were daring enough to venture up are likely to forget the scene which the valley of Glenariffe afforded from the edge of the cliff. More than 1,000 feet below lay the rich valley bathed in warm sunshine, while the morning mists were curling up the hillside in ragged patches. The contrast between the bright valley and the more distant and gloomy hills was very striking. To windward dark clouds were piling themselves up in a very portentous way, and helped to bring into stronger relief the bright scene at our feet. The descent was accomplished more rapidly than the ascent, and on the way a visit was paid to Redbay Castle and Caves, which we had passed the previous evening. After breakfast, the vehicles were again mounted and a start made for

Glendun. The clouds, which earlier in the morning loomed so heavily, now gave us the benefit of their contents in heavy rain, which continued for the greater part of the forenoon. This was rather unfortunate, as it was intended to spend part of the day along the steep sides of Glendun. The load of moisture, however, on the foliage forbade this, and, after a short stop on Glendun viaduct to enable the party to collect specimens of the mountain fern (*Lastrea oreopteris*), the road was again taken to Cushendun, before reaching which the rain had cleared off, and an enjoyable evening was spent examining the caves for which the place is noted. These caves are huge excavations cut by the sea into a cliff of red conglomerate. Unlike that at Redbay, the pebbles here are much larger, ranging from the size of a paving-stone to more than a foot in diameter. They appear to be all dense quartzite, and must have undergone a vast amount of attrition previous to their deposition. The paste which unites them is of a reddish-brown colour, and appears just sufficient to combine all into a solid mass. *Asplenium marinum* and other rock-loving plants were observed here in the crevices of the conglomerates. A few of the party proceeded to visit some archæological remains on the slopes of the hill north of the village. The first, which may be termed a Cashel, is perhaps one of the most perfect of its class in the North of Ireland. It is a circular erection, with an internal diameter of between fifty and sixty feet, and is strongly and regularly built of large stones, no mortar having been used in its construction. The walls are about nine feet thick, by the same in height. There is an entrance to this circle by the eastern side, and there are also the remains of what appear to have been rude steps from the interior of the circle to the top of the wall. At the northern side of the circle and within the enclosure is an opening, about two feet square, which admits to a chamber built within the thickness of the wall. An examination of this shows that it is closed by fallen stones in one direction, but it appears open for some distance in the other. The openings and sharp turnings would, however, scarcely admit of an entrance being made, and it is puzzling to know to what use such chambers, built with evident care and immense toil, could have been put by the long-forgotten people that erected them. A short distance off, on the slope of another hill, are the remains of, apparently, a similar erection, much broken down. The wall seems to have been removed, and the internal chamber is now reached by an opening on top, where one of the covering stones has given way. Two others, more injured than even this last, occur within a short distance. It is surprising, when search is made, how many such remains may still be found scattered over the country. They are, however, fast disappearing, and full descriptions of such as remain should be embodied in some form for future reference.

All being again seated, a sharp drive brought the party back to Cushendall for a late dinner, and the remainder of the evening was spent in the immediate neighbourhood of the village. A few active spirits, having left the vehicle at Glendun viaduct to visit the more distant point of Torr Head, spent a very enjoyable day rambling over the mountains in that neighbourhood. Leaving the main road a short distance north of Loughavemma, and striking northward across the moors, a fine example of a pillar or standing-stone was observed on a slight eminence. A fatiguing scramble, and the top of Carnanmore—1,254 feet—is reached. As indicated by the name, this mountain has on its summit a "great carn," considerable remains of which are still to be seen. It is to be feared, however, that much of it has been erected into very matter-of-fact stone ditches, to mark the boundaries of "my Lord's" estate. The remaining portions are well worthy of examination. The northern side seems to have been partially removed, thus exposing a large chamber of unhewn stones; part of a covering of larger slabs still remains in position, while others lie scattered about. It is probable the carn was erected to commemorate some great victory, or mark the burial place of some powerful chief, whose name and deeds are alike long forgotten. Though the carn is itself a monument of antiquity, one at least of the stones used in its construction belongs to a more distant period still. On its upper surface, but almost defaced by long exposure, are several cuplike depressions, evidently of human workmanship. Were these the only marks upon the stone they might easily have been overlooked; but, on the under side of the slab, which can fortunately be seen by a person entering the chamber above referred to, many more perfect hollows, arranged in something like order, are quite perceptible. The present position of the stone is certainly not that which it occupied when the depressions were cut, as many of those on the under side are now entirely out of reach. An opinion might be conjectured that the carved slab stood convenient to the spot now occupied by the carn, and that the ancient builders utilized it, as to them even at that distant period, it was merely a useful, but meaningless, stone. Similarly marked stones are of frequent occurrence in the South of Ireland, and are supposed to be of pagan origin. The one above referred to is, however, perhaps the first detected in the North, and it was briefly noted by the President of the Club, Mr. William Gray, M.R.I.A., at the meeting of the Royal Historical and Archæological Society of Ireland, held in Belfast early in the present month.

A sharp run was made to the exposed point of Torr Head; time would not, however, allow of more than a short rest here, and the road was again taken for Cushendall. A quarry of beautifully coloured syenite, near Runabay Head, was visited. This stone has all the appearance of durability, and it is surprising that no thorough trial seems to have ever been made of it as an ornamental building stone.

After breakfast next morning the return journey was commenced. The greater portion of the party, desirous to take as much out of the time as possible, halted to examine Ardclinas old church and graveyard, reaching Glenarm about four o'clock, where, after refreshments, a visit was paid to the grounds of Glenarm Castle, the seat of the Earl of Antrim, and afterwards to the interesting museum of Mr. Thompson, of Glenarm, which contains many specimens of the natural history and antiquities of the neighbourhood, as well as some choice productions of foreign countries, all most tastefully arranged. The other section of the party, anxious to reach Belfast by an earlier train, were again attracted to Garron Tower, where the armory, &c., were kindly thrown open to their inspection.

All arrived safely in Belfast, having spent a most enjoyable time, the weather, though not very bright, having been, with the exception of one forenoon, most suitable for an extended excursion.

On 9th August, to

TOOME BRIDGE.

The fourth excursion of the Society took place on Saturday, 9th August, when a small party set out by the 9·45 train for Toome Bridge. The village of Toome, which is unimportant, is situated at the northern end of Lough Neagh, on the Lower Bann, and is noted for the extensive eel fisheries which are in its vicinity. There are several of these at different points on the river, and their management gives employment to many hands during the greater part of the autumn and winter. In construction they are very simple, being V shaped avenues of strong wickerwork erected on poles in the stream. The point where the avenues converge is formed of a strong funnel-shaped net, into which the eels when descending the river find their way. By an arrangement the fish, when past a certain point in the net, cannot return, but are transferred by the fishermen into large floating tanks, from which they are taken and packed for the various markets as required. The fishing is conducted at night, and some idea of the quantities captured may be formed from the fact that it has been estimated over 70,000 eels have been taken in a single night. The principal markets for the produce are London, Manchester, and other large manufacturing towns in England, to which there are regular shipments going on by Belfast and Larne.

Taking boat the party went rapidly down stream, and were soon in Lough Beg, which may be considered an expansion of the Lower Bann. A visit was paid to Church Island, close on the Derry side. In ordinary seasons this is connected with the mainland by an extensive tract of good grazing ground, but this excessive wet season has made it virtually an island, much to the disappointment of the botanists of the party. An hour was spent here examining the old ruined church, with its modern looking spire, which rises so solitary over the low ground. The rag-well, noted in the locality for its healing properties, was also visited. The offerings, in the form of rags, tied to the overhanging thorn, testify to the benefit derived from the application of a few drops of the waters to the "firm believers." The cures have apparently been numerous, and the offerings not extravagant, judging by the bleached and tattered display.

On the return to Toome gatherings were made of the whitish earth through which the "new cut" is made. There is perhaps scarcely a microscopist of any note in Britain whose cabinet does not contain several "slides" of this celebrated Diatomaceous deposit. Under careful manipulation and a high magnifying power this dull-looking earth is resolved into a vast assemblage of diatoms—the silicious remains of an order of extremely minute plants—of the most delicate construction and exquisite beauty. A short visit was afterwards paid to the river bank below the bridge, to search for flint implements, for which the place is also noted, but no success attended the search owing to the very high state of the water. Among the botanical finds were a few of our rarer plants. The gipseywort *(Lycopus europæus)* and the lesser water plantain *(Alisma ranunculoides)* may be mentioned ; the loose-stripe *(Lysimachia vulgaris)*, and *Viola palustris* (or marsh violet) were found on the marshy shores of Lough Beg and the lesser cudweed *(Filago minima)* on the shore of Lough Neagh. Most of the happy hunting ground of the botanist for marsh plants was, however, far out under water, and it will be interesting to note the result on the flora of the long submergence which the ground has suffered from this remarkable season.

A quick run home brought the excursion to a close, the weather having been in every way favourable for field work.

On 23rd August, to

THE BLACK MOUNTAIN.

On Saturday, the 23rd of August, the Society made their fifth excursion for the season, the Black Mountain having been chosen. By arrangement the members met at the principal gate of the Borough Cemetery about half-past two, and proceeded on foot by the Whiterock Road. The weather was everything that could be desired, it being one of those bright, warm, really summer days, which so pleasingly contrast with the more prevalent, gloomy, and wet weather of the present summer. Reaching the quarries recently opened in the chalk at the base of the hill, a search was made for fossils, but with little success. The lower beds, which contain the most fossiliferous zones, have unfortunately been covered up, and it is only by examining stray blocks that have been consigned to the spoil-bank when opening the quarries that fossils can be found. A very fine specimen of Trochus, with examples of several of the more common forms, were thus obtained, after which the party proceeded a short distance northward along the slope of the hill. Here a chasm has been cut by the water, which finds its way from the upper ground, and the various strata are well exposed, from the Keuper Marls to the Basalts. It is notable that the Lias is absent from this section, and from other exposures further south. The glauconitic sands are, however, well represented, and are fossiliferous. After a short time spent here, the road to the top was taken, and soon the breezy heights, purple with heather, were reached, where a halt was called for rest, and to enjoy the landscape spread at our feet. The position of the hill, at an angle where the range which skirts the Antrim coast bends inland, commands a most extensive view of the rich valley of the Lagan and surrounding district. Belfast, comparatively free from factory smoke, with both shores of the bay, looked bright and warm in the evening sunshine, while Strangford Lough and a wide expanse of the County Down, with the Ballynahinch and more distant Mourne Mountains, formed a scene amply repaying the toil of the ascent. A few of the party bent on botany made a rapid circuit of the area between the Black Mountain and Divis. Nothing new, however, was to be expected in a field so near home, and so well worked. The most notable was the curious cryptogam, *Botrychium lunaria*, a species of fern, very sparingly distributed, and most difficult to detect. On the return of the party by the Forth River several of the members visited a standing-stone on the northern slope of the hill, near which are several rude cairns, apparently contemporaneous with it, and which are worthy of a closer examination than time would admit on the present opportunity. A leisurely walk brought the party home about eight o'clock, after having spent a most enjoyable evening.

On 13th September, to

NEWTOWNARDS AND SCRABO MOUNTAIN.

The sixth and last excursion for the season took place on Saturday, 13th September, to Scrabo Hill and the neighbourhood of Newtownards. Starting from the Ulster Hall shortly after noon, and passing through the rapidly improving suburbs of Bloomfield and Knock, no halt was made till reaching Ballyoran, where a short stay was made at the extensive quarries in the Triassic sandstones (new red), close to the roadside. The sandstone here is of a rich, brown colour, thickly bedded, and easily procured in large blocks. Proceeding by the old Newtownards Road a short distance, a second halt was called to allow of a visit to the Kempe Stone, perhaps one of the best examples in the country of those archaic structures known as cromlechs, the covering stone of which is computed to weigh over sixteen tons. Although the Club had visited the place quite recently, yet this striking monument awakened new interest, and several members availed themselves of the opportunity to add a sketch to their albums. The old road to Newtownards is much better to the lover of the picturesque than that now in use. It passes along the crests of the hills, as is almost invariably the case with the earlier made roads, and the traveller to whom time is not a primary object is well repaid for his toil by the extensive view of the surrounding country which he gains. On this occasion, as the day was fine and clear, the ever-changing panorama of hill and dale with the Mourne Mountains as a majestic back-ground was peculiarly pleasing. The old road approaches Scrabo—the sward (scrath or scraw) of the cow (bo) on the north side, and here the party on foot proceeded over rugged dolerite rocks, which are only partially covered by heath, to the tower which crowns the summit of the hill, and which forms a conspicuous landmark seen even far into Antrim. From the summit of the tower the busy town of Newtownards is seen lying almost beneath, and a wide prospect of sea and land, the Isle of Man being visible in the far distance. The walls of the tower were found to be exceeding wet, and it was matter of regret to the visitors that, as it seemed to them, sufficient care was not bestowed on the structure to secure its permanence.

Leaving the hill-top by a path lately constructed, and admirably designed to afford good views of the rich scenery from its convenient resting-places, a visit, under the guidance of Mr. Harbison, was made to the quarries on the southern flank of the hill. Here the junction between the basalt, which forms the higher ground of the hill, and the sandstone in which the quarries are worked, is well seen, and several horizontal intrusions of basalt of older date than that which forms the summit are also well exposed. The large dyke, or filled up fissure, which probably gave vent to the molten material of the later outflows, was also pointed out, as well as its action in altering the sandstone through which it has cut. There is, therefore, in this quarry quite a number of phenomena of igneous rocks to be observed, which, if thoroughly mastered by the geological student, would simplify much that might appear most puzzling. Proceeding towards the opposite end of the hill, all were much surprised at the extent of the quarries in progress. Here again the student will find much to interest him. It is to the geologist an elementary truth that our sandstone rocks are simply the sand deposited on the shores of an ancient world, rendered cohesive by some cementing substance, and hardened by superincumbent pressure. This fundamental truth has been sufficiently established by geological writers; but at Scrabo quarries it is displayed in such a palpable manner that " he who runs may read." A large extent of the quarry floor consists of the rippled surface of an ancient beach, as perfect as when the tide receded from the shore. Thus, the waters in which the new red sandstone was deposited—that is, if an inland sea, as some persons suppose—were at all events sufficiently extensive to have tides like our present oceans. These instructive ripple-marked surfaces were well examined; and also, in close proximity, another phenomenon of similar import—viz., the sun cracks displayed on the same rocks. These are identical in character with the cracks now formed by the heat of the sun in any dried-up pool, and tell of the continuity of the forces of nature, the forces which produce these phenomena at the present day being the same as those which governed the universe in the almost immeasurable past of the Triassic period.

By invitation of Mr. Harbison, the party adjourned to the Model School, where tea had kindly been provided. After tea, the Rev. George Robinson (Tartaraghan) having been moved to the chair, the usual business meeting of the Club was held, and a number of new members were elected; after which, on the motion of the Chairman, seconded by John Ward, Esq., a hearty vote of thanks was passed by acclamation to Mr. and Mrs. Harbison for their kindness in entertaining the Club on their present visit to the district.

All being again seated on the vehicles, a rapid drive brought the party home, after having spent a most profitable and pleasant afternoon, and thus concluded the summer excursions of the Club, which have this year in nearly every case been favoured by good weather, notwithstanding that the season has been one that will long be remembered as calamitous by reason of the heavy and almost continuous rains that prevailed.

WINTER SESSION.

NOTE.—The Authors of the various papers, of which abstracts are here appended, are alone responsible for the views expressed in them.

THE Winter Session was inaugurated by a Conversazione in the Museum, to which the members were invited. The President, William Gray, Esq., M.R.I.A., presided. The following is the report which appeared in the *Belfast News-Letter* :—
" The members of the Belfast Naturalists' Field Club inaugurated their Winter Session on the evening of Friday, 7th November, by a Conversazione at the Museum, College Square North, at which there was a large attendance of the members and their friends, amongst whom were his Worship the Mayor (John Browne, Esq., J.P.), Mrs. Browne, &c., &c. The Museum was tastefully decorated for the occasion with flags, bannerets, shields, wreaths of evergreens, Chinese lanterns, &c., besides flowers and ferns in pots and vases—in the arrangement of the whole the Committee having been largely indebted to the efficient co-operation of the Messrs. Darragh, of the Museum. Largely contributing to the decorative effect of the rooms was the collection of valuable pictures lent by the friends of the Club, amongst the most liberal of whom must, as on many former occasions, be reckoned Dr. James Moore, Hon.

R.H.A., who sent several of his works. Mr. Bell exhibited a large water-colour picture by Hall of a south gale on the beach at Brighton. A number of Continental photographs and original sketches were exhibited by Richard Niven, Esq. Mr. Vinycomb sent several water-colour drawings, executed by himself, including views of Fair Head and the Gobbins, and a little study of rocks in the Mourne Mountains. Mrs. O'Flaherty sent several oil paintings of landscape and still life. Mr. Firth exhibited water-colour sketches of Fair Head, Olderfleet Castle, and drawings of other places in the vicinity. Mr. Lockwood exhibited pen and ink drawings, illustrating the Round Tower and Cathedral of Kildare, and the remarkable sculptured group of the crucifixion over the door of the old church at Maghera, supposed to date from about A.D. 920. He also showed a large drawing of the Grianan of Aileach, near Londonderry, one of the circular stone forts built before the introduction of Christianity into Ireland. But unquestionably the most interesting feature of the pictorial display was a series of photographs, many of large size, contributed by Mr. James Wright. Many of them are the publication of the United States Geological Survey, whilst others are due to the enterprise of Californian photographers, and together they furnish excellent illustrations of the stupendous scenery of the Yosemite Valley, the Sierra Nevada, and Rocky Mountains. A capital collection of sheets of nature-printed ferns was exhibited by Mr. W. H. Phillips. A conspicuous feature in the exhibition was a table devoted to the illustration of lime and limestone in all its branches. Here were specimens of the different limestone formations, from the oldest Primary, through the Carboniferous or mountain limestone, the Magnesian, the Lias, the Oolite, up to the Chalk, each marked by their peculiar and distinctive fossils. There were also many crystalline specimens in the shape of varieties of marble, native and foreign, and masses of coral and other organic forms which are chiefly built up of lime, and which contribute to form limestone. There were also exhibited the microscopic shells of Foraminifera, which are now forming vast beds of limestone, hardly distinguishable from chalk, at the bottom of the Atlantic and Pacific Oceans. Some of the latter, from the Challenger Expedition, were exhibited by Mr. Charles Elcock. Some remarkable fine specimens of stalactite and stalagmite, from limestone caverns were also shown, as well as petrifactions of animals, birds' nests, and other objects, formed by the deposit of carbonate of lime in springs. As usual, a number of the members had their microscopes at work, and exhibited various microscopic specialties. The President, Mr. W. Gray, M.R.I.A., showed several objects multiplied by being seen through the eye of an insect, in which, within a diameter not much larger than a small needle, were seen upwards of four hundred separate representations of the words, God, man, art, &c. Mr. James Wright exhibited in an interesting manner the circulation of sap through the Valisneria, one of our exotic water-plants. The Rev. Canon MacIlwaine, D.D., M.R.I.A., exhibited some slides showing the polarisation of light. Mr. Joseph Wright, F.G.S., showed some recently-discovered sponge spicules from the Carboniferous rocks of Sligo, being the first indication yet found of their existence in the Irish carboniferous formation. Mr. Firth, in conjunction with Mr. I. W. Ward, exhibited some beautifully-mounted diatons and sections of limestone, and Mr. John Pim and Mr. John Browne, M.R.I.A., also exhibited a number of interesting microscopic objects. In addition to his microscope, the President (Mr. W. Gray) exhibited a varied collection of interesting objects. Amongst these was a case of very fine fossil fishes from the Cretaceous rocks of Mount Lebanon, and a fine collection of stone implements from America. He also shewed some bronze and stone weapons recently dredged from the River Bann near Toomebridge. Some Japanese magic mirrors also exhibited by him attracted considerable attention. The Rev. Canon MacIlwaine exhibited a splendid stone war-club, or hatchet, found in the River Bann. He had, besides, an ancient Etruscan lamp and some lachrimatories, or tear bottles, from the catacombs of Rome. A curious tobacco-box, also shown by him, and which was found in the River Lagan, near the old ford, is supposed to have belonged to one of King William's soldiers. Mr. Richard Nevin had a collection of pipes, implements, and pottery from Tumuli on the American prairies. Two fine fossil horns of the Irish elk and red deer, found in a bog in the County Down, were lent by Major Crawford, D.L. Dr. Grainger, D.D., exhibited a number of objects from his collection of great archæologic and scientific interest, and amongst them were noticeable flint implements from Dundrum. An object of no small interest was the leaf of a hymn-book recently picked up on the battlefield of Isandula by Dr. T. Devlin. Mr. John Browne shewed two cases of war medals and clasps, giving a very succinct bird's-eye view of the achievements of the British army. A fine fur cloak of a Zulu chief, and two assegais, exhibited by Miss Lamb, attracted much admiration. Close beside these, and in contrast with them, were two Irish pikes from the rebellion of '98. On a centre table were exhibited the Club's album and a number of other books, the most striking of which was a magnificent volume of some 160 water-colour studies of British flowers, drawn by Worthinglin G. Smith, and exhibited by Mr. John Vinycomb. Some archælogical works, lent by Mr. W. Miller, were also of considerable interest. A number of old maps were exhibited by Mr. G. O'Brien, and a *fac-simile* of a map of Ulster, dated 1600, by Mr. Wm. Millar. Several rare birds lately killed in this locality were exhibited by Mr. Darragh and Mr. Hamilton. In the way of experimental physics a sensitive flame of gas, shown by the President, was the source of no small interest. This flame, whilst unaffected by most sounds, is peculiarly sensitive to those of a particular musical pitch, and much amusement was caused by the discovery that, whilst the loudest clapping or other applause was received by it unmoved, the slightest hiss was sufficient to cause its instantaneous subsidence. The various objects and works of art were continued on view at a small charge during Saturday, when the President and several other members of the club were in attendance to exhibit microscopes, show the sensitive flame, and explain the other objects. A considerable number of visitors availed themselves of the opportunity thus afforded.

PRESIDENT'S ADDRESS.

Mr. GRAY commenced by tracing the history of the establishment of scientific societies and the origin of field clubs, organised mainly for the practical study of natural phenomena in the fields. The hills, and rocks, plants and trees being their books, and their class-room the open country. Probably, the first field club established in Great Britain was " The Berwickshire Naturalists' Club," formed in 1831. The first in Ireland was the Belfast Naturalists' Field Club, established in 1863 ; the next and only other field club in Ireland being the Ballymena Naturalists' Field Club. There are very few places that have such a variety of natural phenomena so readily accessible as we have about Belfast. The physical geography of the surrounding district is diversified in an unusual manner. Mountains and hills of varying heights, glens and valleys of surpassing beauty, a magnificent coast line, and a rare combination of land and water, including one of the largest freshwater lakes in Europe. The geological features of the country include some of the most remarkable of our British rocks, both sedimentary and plutonic—the columnar and other varieties of the trap series; the various granites of the Mourne range, an extensive variety of fossiliferous strata—and all associated with dykes and fissures, dislocations, disturbances, and every phase of metamorphic action, so interesting and instructive to the geological student.

C

Nor are our advantages limited to physical and natural objects of interest. For, over hill and dale—cultivated field and wild waste moorland—are scattered the silent memorials of a long-forgotten ancestry, whose crumbling monuments, rath and fort, cromlech and cairn, remind us of an age moved back by centuries behind the dawn of the Christian era ; and of an ancient race, whose deeds of valour, manly exploits, and tales of love and war, are only whispered in the dying fables of a remote antiquity, or faintly chronicled in the confused legends of mediæval sages. With such a field of interesting inquiry stretching around us in every direction, awaiting our culture and promising a gathering of richest harvest, surely we will not want for workers to assist in securing the promised advantages. In order to explain how the Club should carry on its work, Mr. Gray asked the meeting to accompany him on an imaginary excursion, and said— The programme indicates that our destination is a station on the coast. The secretaries have taken our tickets, allotted us our places ; the whistle sounds, and we are off. We have reached the coast. The sea—that grand old emblem of human life—spreads out before us ; its surface fanned by a breeze just sufficient to give it that expression of motion, without which it loses half its beauty. A bold cliff, bare and rugged, looks seaward, and on its craggy face exposes three well-marked zones, the white Chalk above, and below the Red Sandstone, with an intermediate band of blue and earthy Lias : three representations of distinct and widely-separated ages of geological time. Landward, the crumbling turret of some old Norman tower breaks up still more the outline to the sky, and hardy plants that would perish in the dusty inland hedgerows here delight in wind and spray, and peep forth from nook and cranny to welcome our approach. Just note the distribution of the party, and the different sources of pleasure the same scene is capable of affording. The zoologist has clambered over slimy rocks, and is already peering into the bright pools fringed with purple and crimson algæ, and tenanted by a strange variety of animal life. The antiquarian has reached the floor of the deserted keep to conjure up the scenes of mirth and revelry that made its portals ring in former days. The botanist is at once plunged among ferns and stonecrops, mosses, and marine algæ. The artist has selected his most favoured point of view, and is noting effects for future reference. The geologist is musing on the form and character of the fossil he has extracted from the rock or gathered on the beach, and while the sea breaks against the Red Sandstone of the undercliff and is stained by its marls, he recognises the same processes and continued forces by which the rocky barriers behind him were formerly built up. The mechanic only sees the waves wasting their power upon the beach, and wonders if this agency could not be utilised. The mathematician notes the same power, and strives to express it in some algebraic formula. The poet pensively asks, " What are the wild waves saying?" And the moralist, from a still higher standpoint, whispers, " 'Tis the voice of the great Creator that speaks in that mighty tone." This may be an ideal, but by no means an exaggerated, description of what you may have often seen together, and it faintly illustrates one of the advantages of our organization in affording every student of nature an opportunity of indulging his or her own inclination, and to do so with their fellows for the common good. All the methods of investigating natural phenomena may be divided into three groups—the practical, the artistic, and the moral. The practical or utilitarian, the artistic or æsthetic, and the moral or spiritual. All our effective work must be practical, and all our results must submit to be tested by this standard. Every collector has found this out by experience. Who is it that has collected fossils, or plants, or any other natural object, and has not been asked from time to time—" Well, but of what use are they?" If you are fern-hunting in the country, you will doubtless be followed by some inquisitive rustic who wishes to know "if you want them for a cure?" or, if you show any interest in rocks or stones, you are at once taken for a mining speculator. All this kind of criticism is governed by the utilitarian standard, and is perfectly fair on principle, if the critic would not insist upon endeavouring to put an economic value on everything. Mr. Gray then illustrated how members of our Irish Field Clubs have done good service in collecting and publishing information on such subjects as our industrial resources, &c. He then quoted authorities and referred to examples to prove that the study of natural phenomena was of substantial practical value, and gave illustrations from the history of the Club. He also stated that some of the most flourishing field clubs in England are entirely supported by working men, who have learned the value of a country ramble and to profit by the enjoyment of the pleasures of Nature, that no avarice can monopolise and no oppression can deny. Interested persons may profess to sneer at amateur naturalists and holiday geologists, but the whole history of scientific progress proves that amateur naturalists have been foremost among the leaders of scientific investigation and discovery, assuring us that attention to business, the cares and vicissitudes of commerce, or any other engagement of life is not incompatible with a love for, and correct knowledge of, some branch of natural science, or with successful labour for its advancement; but it is necessary to remember that all really effective study of Nature must be thorough and exhaustive. No fitful glances or transient enthusiasm will add to our store of scientific knowledge, or extend the boundary of the known. In the very effort to master any particular subject, the naturalist learns to estimate the richness of every other department of Nature, and is proportionately impressed by the superior harmony, fitness, and beauty of all Nature's works; and in this manner he acquires a new sense, in a special power of vision, that the untutored observer does not possess. How quickly the trained naturalist will detect a rare plant, an abnormal fern, a characteristic fossil, shell, or insect, that is altogether overlooked by the ordinary observer. Our studies, therefore, not only afford pleasurable and healthy employment for leisure hours, but, rightly conducted, they must have a direct practical result in strengthening our powers of observation, cultivating our reasoning faculties, elevating our conception of what is true, and enabling us to further the advancement of science that has already done so much for the material comfort and the intellectual progress of mankind. Close and accurate observation is the first object of our study as absolutely necessary in our systematic search after truth ; and this habit is most effectually cultivated in the open air. It is by the murmuring stream of some inland valley, or the quiet retreat of the mountain slope, or where the breezes blow freshly across the seaside cliff that the habit of observation is best cultivated. There, with all those healthy and agreeable associations, doubts are dispersed and intellect becomes clear. Fortunately for us all enjoyment of Nature does not depend upon our knowledge, We can enjoy the clear, starry heavens without being able to name a constellation, or trace the Pointers in the Plough. We can enjoy the mountains without any knowledge of their constituent rocks, or be delighted with the woodland scenery, "clad in the golden tints of Autumn," without knowing the difference between one tree and another. Yes, out in the open country, under the exhilarating influence of a pure fresh breeze, when the sun shines out in all its meridian splendour, when the air is vocal with the busy hum of birds and insects, and perfumed with the ascending fragrance of plants and flowers, even common-place scenery is invested with a special charm to enhance the enjoyment of the ordinary observer. And surely if these merely physical sensations are so pleasing, what must be the emotions of the intellectual observer, whose sympathy and love are quickened by his culture, and in his comprehensive survey is enabled to see in the familiar and unpretending, as well as in the grandest, aspects of Nature the fitness of purpose, unity of design, and persistency of laws by which the whole is governed. Reading only, or even collecting specimens can never be effectually substituted for the legitimate work of a Field Naturalist, whose duty it is to court Dame Nature in her own home, and with pick and staff and watchful eye to survey the mountains, explore the valleys, and track out by diligent steps the oft intricate geological phenomenon. It is only in this familiar intercourse that Nature is willing to tell her secrets, and under her influence and inspiration alone can we ever hope to accomplish solid results, and arrive at clear, broad, and thoroughly scientific conclusions. After enforcing the necessity of recording observations, and particularly cultivating a taste for sketching, Mr. Gray continued—The imperfection of all human knowledge, and the limitation of all human experience must involve uncertainty as to special facts, and therefore doubt as to the correctness of general principles. This has been the experience of philosophy during the past history of scientific progress, and must ever remain the heritage of finite man. All we see around us, the broad and beautiful landscape, with its lofty mountains, smoothly-flowing rivers, rocks and trees, birds and flowers, the heavens themselves, with their long retinue of suns and stars, are but the manifested effect of pre-existing *causes*, which recede as the philosopher pushes back the boundary of the known. In the infancy of nations thoughtful men loved to consider the phenomena of the external world under the personification of human forms, but as philosophy became enlightened enough to reason upon the causes of phenomena a strange and mighty power was imputed to antecedent causes. The Indian "sees God in clouds, and hears him in the wind." With the Greeks this ideality pervaded all Nature—each hill and dale, grove and plain, was peopled by their Deities. When the thunder rolled across the heavens the voice of Jove was heard in its rumbling echoes; when the sea was lashed into a storm the roar of its waters was interpreted to be the trumpet of the Tritons, and Neptune showed his anger in the waves. Fauns gambolled in the foam of the torrent as it bounded from the mountain to the sea, and spirits whispered in every breeze. This polytheism of the ancients is certainly more poetic, and probably as rational as the materialism of some modern scientists who solve the problem of Nature by referring them to the inherent vitality of self-acting powers, the vortical movement of nebulous matter, the potential energy of germs, the spontaneous generation of Bathybius, or the fortuitous concourse of atoms. The true Naturalist will not be satisfied merely with the discovery of immediate effects, or antecedent causes, he will not rest satisfied with what science has accomplished for the material welfare of mankind, or is destined to achieve by the endless succession of her wonderful discoveries. He is not satisfied with the contemplation of the beauty and harmony everywhere displayed, or with tracing the varied relations of the elements of matter, or the strange disclosures of time and space. These are simply effects that can only be intelligibly appreciated, and their full value ascertained, by the consideration of the prior causes, each by itself an effect of other causes in the chain that inevitably leads to the Great First Cause of all.

On 9th December—the President (Mr. Wm. Gray, M.R.I.A.) in the chair, a paper—entitled "A Few Words on British War Medals," was read by Mr. John Browne, M.R.I.A.

The essayist commenced by saying that about a couple of sessions ago he had the privilege and pleasure of bringing a paper before the Belfast Naturalists' Field Club on "The Origin and Progress of Coinage," and, as a sort of postscript or continuation of that paper, he proposed that evening to lay before the meeting a few thoughts on British War Medals, a subject which, though therein personally much interested, did not come exactly within the range of this society; yet he hoped it was not altogether out of place. The question might arise in the mind of some one present, what is the attraction in wearing such a decoration? And, in reply, he would only quote a couplet by Sir E. B. Lytton, which appears on the title-page of Carter's work on "Army Medals"—

> "What is a ribbon to a soldier?
> Everything! Glory is priceless."

He then went on to say that in the following paper it would be his object, not to tell over again the many victories which had been won by British arms since medals were first awarded, but simply to notice the medals themselves descriptively, with regard to classification, and according to the following arrangement :—Medals of honorary distinction granted to British soldiers by Charles I. and the Protector—the Peninsular and Waterloo Medals—Medals given for actions and campaigns in India, closing with the Mutiny, 1857-8, including the Honourable East India Company's medals to native troops—the Chinese wars, 1842-1860—the Kaffir and Crimean wars—Medals for long service—Meritorious and distinguished conduct—Regimental medals—and lastly a glance at naval medals. By a look at Carter's work already referred to, you will find that the custom of striking medals to commemorate victories may be traced to the ancients, and the Moguls are believed to have granted them for civil and military service in the twelfth century; but it was only in modern times that they have been issued in order to be worn as personal decorations. Sir Nicholas Harris Nicholas, in his "History of the Order of Knighthood of the British Empire," published in 1842, has given much interesting information regarding many of these decorations, both naval and military, although there has been quite an era in war medals since the publication of his work. After a rapid historical sketch of the early British war medals, Mr. Browne went on to say that he had tried to show that the practice of bestowing honorary distinctions in the many naval and military operations of our country is but of recent date. It is only a few years since that a general order was granted for the distribution of medals to those surviving officers and men of both services who took part in the long-protracted wars between this country and Spain, France, America, and the hostile nations of India—from the declaration of war with France in 1793 to the triumphant entry of Wellington into Toulouse, 12th April, 1814, and the siege and storm of Bhurtpore, January, 1826. This extraordinary delay or unpardonable neglect on the part of those high in authority caused no little disappointment among those who considered that they should be recipients of some distinguished badge or order of merit, to be worn not only in commemoration of the gallant achievement, but as a reward of their faithful and long professional services. It is well known, for much publicity was given to the fact, that the old " Peninsular men," the heroes of Assaye and Laswarie, and the gallant tars who fought at St. Vincent, the Nile, Copenhagen, and Trafalgar had no medals. Every likely opportunity was made use of to stimulate the tardy Government. The accession of William IV., for example, brought forth a plentiful correspondence. It was recommended that "the army and navy should unite, and humbly and respectfully request one of the Royal Dukes to solicit from his Most Gracious Majesty a boon for both services at the beginning of the reign; that he would bestow an order of merit upon all officers and men who have fought the battles of their country." The writer goes on to say—" It is very vexatious to honourable feelings when we go into society at home and abroad to meet foreigners of all nations covered with medals and orders, when we, who have had the pleasure of licking them in every part of the world, have neither orders nor medals." "The seven years of King William's reign passed away; the ranks of those old warriors, the survivors of a hundred fights, gave way before the irresistible march of time; they who had successfully contended with the combined fleets of France and Spain—who had upheld the supremacy of the British arms in the East, and taught Napoleon's marshals so terrible a lesson— had at last to yield to the universal conqueror, with no mark of their glorious services except those honourable scars obtained by their own bravery on the field of battle." Mr. Browne, in bringing his paper to a close with some remarks upon our naval medals, said that the medal for general naval services, 1793-1840, bears on the obverse the diademmed head of the Queen—Victoria Regina, 1848 ; reverse, Britannia seated upon a sea-horse, a trident in her right hand, an olive branch in her left ; ribbon white, with blue edges. This medal was instituted by command of her Majesty by the Lords Commissioners of the Admiralty, by an order dated 1st June, 1847, and conferred upon every surviving officer, seaman, and marine who had taken part in any of the naval actions (for which clasps were awarded) between the years 1793 and 1815. By an after-order dated 7th June, 1848, clasps were granted for Martinique, Guadaloupe, Java, St. Sebastian, Algiers, Navarino, and Syria. There are over two hundred clasps for different actions given with this medal. The clasps vary in number from one to six, which is the largest number on one medal. And, in conclusion, he would say that if any of his friends wished to make themselves up on this subject, he would, among other works, refer them to Carter's book on " British War Medals, and how they were won ;" " The History of the Order of Knighthood," by Sir Nicholas Harris Nicholas ; " Handbook of British War Medals," by J. Harris Gibson ; " The Medallick History of England ;" Simon's " Medals and Coins ;" Sainthill's " *Olla Podrida.*"

On 6th January—the President (Mr. Wm. Gray, M.R.I.A., in the chair)—a paper was read by Mr. M. HARBISON, Newtownards ; subject—"Notes on a Tour through Switzerland, with special reference to the origin of the Swiss valleys."

The reader commenced by giving a brief but graphic sketch of a tour through Switzerland, commencing at Neufchatel, and proceeding through Berne to Lake Thur; thence to Interlaken and the valley of Lauterbrunnen, where the Staubbach waterfall is precipitated over a rock more than 900 feet high ; then over Lake Brienz and the Brunig Pass to Lucerne, where the Righi mountain, 6,000 feet high, was ascended by a railway ; then along the picturesque lake of the Four Cantons, and up the valley of the Reuss, passing Altorf, where William Tell shot the apple on his son's head ; over the celebrated Devil's Bridge to Andermatt, near the commencement of the St. Gothard tunnel; then over the Furca Pass, 8,150 feet above the level of the sea, to the Rhone glacier ; then along the valley of the Rhone to Brie and Martigny ; over Tête Noir Pass to Chamounix, at the foot of Mont Blanc. The reader then described his passage of the Mer-de-Glace, and the route by diligence through the valley of the Arne to Geneva ; thence over the lake of Geneva to the Castle of Chillon, and back to Lausanne. An interesting account was given of the Rhone glacier. Under the influence of the sun the ice was melting rapidly, and the *debris* which came tumbling down when a portion of the ice gave way, resembled in structure our local deposits of boulder clay—earth and stones mixed together, as if it had been tumbled out of a waggon. The infant Rhone issues from a cave in the ice. The delicate ultramarine tint of the ice in the cave renders it a scene of surpassing beauty. The deep, narrow valley of the Rhone, lying between the Bernese Alps on the north and the Pennine Alps on the south, was considered to have been scooped out by a former extension of the Rhone glacier, which must originally have reached the Jura mountains, 120 miles distant. The Lake of Geneva was scooped out by the same glacier. Blocks of granite had been carried from the Alps and deposited on the slope of the Jura, 4,600 feet above the sea level. From this circumstance the original thickness of the ice could be ascertained. Some of these blocks carried down by the ice measure half a million of cubic feet. The Rhone receives in its course 260 muddy streams from glaciers. This mud, deposited in the Lake of Geneva, has already reduced the area of that lake thirty-four square miles. A town situated on the shore of the lake 300 years ago was now a mile inland. Mr. Harbison proceeded to describe the origin and work of glaciers. On the Alps, the height of the snow-line is 8,500 feet. Above this elevation, the heat of Summer is unable to melt the snow that falls during the previous Winter. If there were no means of getting rid of the snow it would in the course of ages be piled up to an enormous height. Some of it is removed by avalanches, which come tumbling down the mountain slopes, but still more by glaciers. Mountains that rise above the snow-line are not covered by a uniform covering of snow. Many of the peaks are so abrupt that the snow does not lie on them. The snow is blown by the wind into hollows, where it accumulates often to the depth of many hundreds of feet. The snow, partly by pressure, which squeezes out the air, and partly by melting and re-freezing, is transformed into ice, which gradually moves down the slope at the rate of about two feet in the day. De Saussure attributed the advance to the pressure exercised on the upper portions by additional masses of snow. Forbes believed that the ice was plastic, and behaved like a sluggish stream. Agassiz maintained that the motion was due to the rains and melted snow and ice, which, falling into the crevasses, get frozen and increase in bulk, and thus force the glacier onward. Tyndall is also of this opinion, which is now generally held. By this theory the motion of a glacier over a ridge may be satisfactorily accounted for. Blocks of stone derived from the cliffs on the margin are scattered over the ice, then falling into the crevasses, yawning gulfs, several hundred feet deep, get stuck in the bottom of the ice, and assist it in grinding the rock beneath. Thus, in the course of ages a deep groove is formed, and when, through change of climate, the glacier retreats to the mountains, a valley is left behind. It is only by studying the effects produced by existing glaciers that one can understand the work done by that ancient sheet of moving ice which once covered our own country, and to which its physical features are mainly due. Blocks of Antrim chalk have been carried to Cork; boulders of granite from the Mourne mountains have been scattered over the central plain; the soil of our plains in many places has been transported by ice. In the neighbourhood of Newtownards the underlying rock is sandstone, but the soil consists mostly of heavy clay, derived partly from the chalk and basalt of Antrim, but chiefly from the hills of Silurian strata, south of Belfast Lough. It is evident that moving ice has scooped out the whole of the Swiss valleys. Without this agent Switzerland would have been one vast snow-clad plateau, without human inhabitants, and wanting that sublime scenery which attracts travellers from the ends of the earth.

The paper, which commanded the close attention of the audience, was followed by an interesting discussion on the various glacial phenomena touched upon by the reader. The election of new members brought the meeting to a close.

On 3rd February—the President (Mr. Wm. Gray, M.R.I.A.) in the chair)—a paper was read by Mr. F. W. LOCKWOOD, Architect, on "The Round Towers: who built them, and for what purpose?"

This paper was a notice of the various contributions towards this question since the publication of the late Dr. Petrie's celebrated work. The conclusions at which Dr. Petrie arrived were shown to be generally sound, though, with the enlarged knowledge now at our command, it turns out that he assigned too early a date for many of the Irish monuments. The leading point which his work attempted to establish, was, that many of the early Irish churches, and the towers, have such a remarkable similarity in their details, that they must have been the work of the same builders. An examination of the additional materials collected in the works of the late Lord Dunraven, Miss Stokes, Mr. Brash, the "Ulster

Journal of Archæology," &c., &c, fully confirms this view, and enables us to fix satisfactorily the order of succession, and approximate to at least some of the principal dates. We have first the pagan stone forts, built without mortar, such as Dun Ængus; then we have early Christian monastic enclosures, such as the one on the Skelligs, very nearly resembling the forts. Often connected with these are the saints' houses, and the small oratories, all built without mortar. Then follow larger churches, in which mortar begins to be introduced, and which show a gradual increase of ornament round the windows, and square-headed doors Then we find the arch gradually introduced, and when fully established, for ornament as well as use, the peculiarities of the native Irish style soon became merged into those of Western Europe. This took place during the eleventh century. The transition from the style of building without, to that with the arch, was taking place throughout the tenth century, and was completed under King Brian Boruma about the year 1000. Amongst other evidence may be adduced the case of the church at Tomgraney, which still remains, and the west door of which has the straight lintel of the earlier style. This church is stated to have been built by Cormac O'Cillen about A.D. 964, and may therefore be about the last of this class. The churches, on the other hand, attributed to Brian Boruma all have arched doorways, though without the richness of decoration found in those known to belong to the later part of the eleventh century. The towers nearly all bear tokens of belonging to this transitional period, for we can see the gradual development of the arch in their details. They belong, therefore, with little doubt, to the tenth century. There are several towers very similar, and apparently about the same age, still remaining in Scotland and the Orkneys; and circular towers, detached or nearly so, have been found on the Continent in connection with churches which date from the same period. Similar towers are also depicted in some of the frescoes and manuscripts from the eighth to the eleventh centuries. The use to which the towers were put is, perhaps, more obscure than their origin, but there is some ground for believing them to be due to the necessity of providing refuge and protection for the ecclesiastics, during the incursions of the Danes or Northmen, which were at their height at this period. There seems to have been a tendency on the part of the builders of the Irish towers, towards the close of the period, to attach them to the churches, and eight or nine instances are known, some attached and some built *on* the church, as at Ireland's Eye and Killossy. It is also probable, had the style been allowed to develop farther, the circular form would have been abandoned, and square attached towers, with well marked stages and panelled decoration, after the manner of Cormac's chapel, Cashel, would have been universally adopted.

The paper was illustrated by a large number of sepia and pen-and ink drawings of towers, churches, details, &c., and an interesting and animated discussion followed, in which many of the members joined.

On 2nd March—the President (Mr. Wm. Gray, M.R.I.A.) in the chair—a paper was read by CHARLES C. RUSSELL, Esq., B.A., Newtownards, on " The Honey Bee and its treatment."

After referring to the antiquity of bee-keeping, as evidenced by the Scriptural allusions to these insects, the essayist proceeded to explain that in every properly constituted hive there should be three forms of bees. First, the queen, the mother of the hive, respected and attended by her retinue; next, the drones or male bees, easily recognised by their size and by the hum or drone which they produce in flying. The drones are not armed with stings, and only live a short time. They are all killed by the worker bees when the hive is preparing to go into winter quarters. The third class constitutes the great bulk of the hive, and are commonly termed "workers." These are undeveloped females, and each is armed with a sting, as some persons before this have experienced. These latter do all the work, as their name implies. They clean up the house, carry out the *debris*, nurse the young, feed the queen, ventilate the hive, secrete the wax, build the comb, gather the honey, and defend the citadel. For a week or so after emerging from their cell they devote themselves to nursing the larvæ, which are hatching out; after which time they proceed to the orchards, fields, and meadows in quest of honey. As there are three kinds of bees, so there are three kinds of cells, in which the queen, drones, and workers are respectively hatched, of which specimens were exhibited to the audience. A singular fact noted was the parthenogenesis of the queen, by which is meant, that in order to lay eggs that will bring forth living bees, it is not necessary that the queen bee should ever become acquainted with a drone; but these eggs invariably hatch out drones. Impregnation is necessary to enable her to produce female eggs, *i.e.*, eggs which will hatch into queens or into workers; but unnecessary as far as drones are concerned. Another curious point referred to was the manner in which the bees can repair the calamity, if by any chance their queen may be lost. This is done by the bees selecting one of the working larvæ and treating it in such a way that instead of it coming out a worker or imperfect bee in twenty-one days, it emerges from its cell a queen or perfect bee in sixteen days. The essayist then proceeded to describe the cruel treatment to which bees are annually subjected in order to obtain their honey. A pit is dug, into which burning coals and sulphur are thrown, and over this the skep of doomed bees is placed; most of the bees are suffocated in from ten to fifteen minutes, but very many of them escape, to wander about with singed wings and legs, until hunger or cold puts an end to their miserable existence. Such a method of treating them cannot give pure honey. Mr. Russell then dwelt upon the humane method of treatment of the honey bee, which consists of employing boxes or glasses called *supers* above the hives, in which the bees are induced to deposit honey uncontaminated by brood; this gives the pure virgin honey, which can be removed at pleasure by the beekeeper, who substitutes empty *supers*. In this way the bees are encouraged to deposit a surplus of honey, which surplus only is taken from them, the honey deposited in the body of the hive being left for the subsistence of the bees during winter. In this way honey absolutely clean and pure can be obtained, in a greater quantity, and of a better quality than under the old system, while the stocks are doubled each year. He then exhibited various glass supers, and the new sectional super, fitted up with Long's foundation comb—that is, an artificial sheet of wax, impressed with indentations corresponding to the size of the cells. This sheet of wax the bees adopt as their own, thankfully, thus saving a considerable amount of time in the honey season, which otherwise they would lose in making a comb. He also illustrated and explained several interesting operations with bees, and concluded by informing the Club, that a few bee-keepers in the North of Ireland, had arranged to have a display of bee manipulation at the next exhibition of the Horticultural Society at Newtownards. These exhibitions would be similar to those which excited so much interest at Kilburn last year, and given annually at the Kensington Museum, and Crystal Palace, London. They intend bringing over the manipulator and the exhibition tent of the British Bee-keepers' Association, and they hope by this means to interest our cottagers and others in humane bee-keeping, and if possible to induce them to abandon the present system of "putting bees down." He considered this was an object which a Naturalists' Club should assist, and felt assured of their countenance and support.

On the 23rd March—the President (Mr. Wm. Gray, M.R.I.A.) in the chair—three papers were read.

In the first paper the PRESIDENT gave an account of "cup

markings" in the North of Ireland. The curious sculpturings in question are of much interest by reason of the obscurity which shrouds their origin, and the absence of any acceptable theory as to their purpose. They are apparently of great antiquity, and consist of shallow cup-shaped hollows rudely cut upon pillar stones, cromlechs, and even upon rocks *in situ*. They usually occur in groups scattered without order over the surfaces. Markings of the same kind are found in the South and West of Ireland, but the examples discovered by Mr. Gray are the first noticed in the North. A fine specimen secured by Mr. Gray has been presented to the Museum,

The second paper was by Mr. WM. GAULT on the " Palæontology of the Irish Cretaceous strata." The author, who has been working for many years at these rocks, gave a short summary of his labours. The discovery of several new species has rewarded the efforts of Mr. Gault, who has in addition detected in our rocks many fossils not previously found in Ireland, but which are known to occur in the equivalent strata of England and the Continent. It results also as a generalisation from these researches that peculiar assemblages of fossils characterise special zones in these rocks, and that these zones may be correlated with recognised subdivisions of the Cretaceous formations elsewhere. Mr. Gault stated that his paper was only preliminary to a more extended account of the Irish beds.

The third paper was by Mr. JOSEPH WRIGHT, F.G.S., on the " Post-tertiary Foraminifera of the North of Ireland." After the reader had briefly explained the nature of Foraminifera, he said that our post-tertiary clays are divided into two groups—Boulder Clay, and Estuarine Clay. The Boulder Clay examined usually contained Foraminifera in greater or less abundance. At Woodburn 48 distinct species were found. *Polystomella arctica*, a truly arctic species, occurred in abundance. It has also been found in other places in our vicinity, thus proving that the climate of the Boulder

Clay period was much colder than at present. The Estuarine Clay of many localities had been carefully examined. At Larne 71 species were found, including *Lagena striata-punctata* in abundance. This is one of the rarest British forms. The Lough Foyle Estuarine beds proved still more interesting. At this place Foraminifera occur in the greatest profusion and variety. Upwards of 10,000 specimens were estimated to be contained in a single grain weight of floatings. Eighty-three species have been met with at this spot, though, as yet, only partially examined. Amongst the rarities found may be mentioned '*Lagena trigona-ornata, aspera, Cassidulina Bradyi, Lingulina carinata, Polymorphina complanata, Discorbina Parisiensis*, and a new *Tinoporus*.

The papers were illustrated by specimens and diagrams, and the meeting concluded with the election of new members.

On 14th April, the Seventeenth Annual Meeting of the Club was held, Mr. WM. GRAY, M.R.I.A., President, in the chair.

Lieutenant-General SMYTHE, F.R.S., M.R.I.A., moved, and Mr. G. O'BRIEN seconded, the adoption of the Secretaries' Report and Treasurer's Statement of Accounts.

The Election of Officers was then proceeded with.

On the motion of Mr. JOSEPH WRIGHT, F.G.S., seconded by Mr. GREER MALCOMSON, Wm. Gray, Esq., M.R.I.A., was re-elected President.

On the motion of Mr. F. W. LOCKWOOD, seconded by Mr. G. O'BRIEN, Lieut.-General Smythe, F.R.S., M.R.I.A., was elected the Vice-President for the ensuing year.

The Treasurer and Secretaries were then elected, and also a Committee of Management.

Mr. Hugh Robinson, late Senior Hon. Sec., having declined to allow himself to be again nominated for election to that office, the following resolution, proposed by Mr. W. F. LOCKWOOD, and seconded by Mr. JOSEPH WRIGHT, F.G.S., was passed by acclamation, and the Secretaries were instructed to convey the same to Mr. Robinson :—

"The members of the Belfast Naturalists' Field Club, whilst acceding with reluctance to Mr. Hugh Robinson's retirement from the post of Honorary Secretary, which he has held for ten years, desire to express their sense of the most efficient manner in which he has discharged the duties of that office. They believe that it is in no small measure due to his exertions that the Club has obtained its present success, and hope that he may be long spared to manifest, in a less burdensome position, the interest which, from the foundation of the Club, he has taken in its work."

The PRESIDENT requested the members present to make suggestions as to places suitable for excursions during the summer, which led to an animated discussion on the merits of various localities, the ultimate decision between the respective claims of each being left to the new committee.

A communication was received from the Rev. H. W. Lett, describing two cinerary urns sent by C. Waddell, Esq., Drumcro House, County Down, by whom they were recently found, near the limestone quarries on his property at Magheralin. They were found fifteen inches below the surface, nearly in the same spot, and in close proximity to where many other larger urns have from time to time been discovered. They had been placed in the ground in the usual way, mouth downwards, on a flat stone, but without any surrounding chamber, and contained calcined bones. The clay for eighteen inches radius all round bore marks of fire, and the bottom of the excavation was strewn with bones similar to those in the urns, and a thin layer of a black substance. The urns are formed of the red clay of the locality, and are only partially burned. One is $3\frac{3}{4}$in. high and 4in. wide, and rudely ornamented with a kind of incised pattern. The other is 2in. high by $3\frac{1}{4}$in., and perfectly plain. This one is almost identical with the smallest urn in the Royal Irish Academy Museum.

A small whinstone celt was found on the 13th March, 1880, in the heart of an ash tree when felled. There was no opening by which it could possibly have got there. It was embedded three feet above the surface; the girth of the tree at the pl?   ·ing ten feet, and its age, as calculated by the concentric rings, was upwards of one hundred and twenty years.

RULES

OF THE

Belfast Naturalists' Field Club.

I.

That the Society be called "THE BELFAST NATURALISTS' FIELD CLUB."

II.

That the objects of the Society be the practical study of Natural Science and Archæology in Ireland.

III.

That the Club shall consist of Ordinary, Corresponding, and Honorary Members. The Ordinary Members to pay annually a subscription of Five Shillings, and that candidates for such Membership shall be proposed and seconded at any Meeting of the Club, by Members present, and elected by a majority of the votes of the Members present.

IV.

That the Honorary and Corresponding Members shall consist of persons of eminence in Natural Science, or who shall have done some special service to the Club; and whose usual residence is not less than twenty miles from Belfast. That such Members may be nominated by any Member of the Club, and on being approved of by the Committee, may be elected at any subsequent Meeting of the Club by a majority of the Votes of the Members present. That Corresponding Members be expected to communicate a Paper once within every two years.

V.

That the Officers of the Club be annnually elected, and consist of a President, Vice-President, Treasurer, Two Secretaries, and Ten Members, who form the Committee. Five to form a quorum. No Member of Committee to be eligible for re-election who has not attended at least one-fourth of the Committee Meetings during his year of office. That the office of President, or that of Vice-President, shall not be held by the same person for more than two years in succession.

VI.

That the Members of the Club shall hold at least Six Field Meetings during the year, in the most interesting localities, for investigating the Natural History and Archæology of Ulster. That the place of meeting be fixed by the Committee, and that five days' notice of each excursion be communicated to Members by the Secretaries.

VII.

That Meetings be held Fortnightly or Monthly, at the discretion of the Committee, for the purpose of reading papers ; such papers, as far as possible, to treat of the Natural History and Archæology of the district. These Meetings to be held during the months from November to April inclusive.

VIII.

That the Committee shall, if they find it advisable, offer for competition Prizes for the best collections of scientific objects of the district ; and the Committee may order the purchase of maps, or other scientific apparatus, and may carry on geological and archæological searches or excavations, if deemed advisable, provided that the entire amount expended under this rule does not exceed the sum of £10 in any one year.

IX.

That the Annual Meeting be held during the month of April, when the Report of the Committee for the past year, and the Treasurer's Financial Statement shall be presented, the Committee and Officers elected, Bye laws made and altered, and any proposed alteration in the general laws, of which a

fortnight's notice shall have been given, in writing, to the Secretary or Secretaries, considered and decided upon. The Secretaries to give the Members due notice of such intended alteration.

X.

That, on the written requisition of twenty-five Members, delivered to the Secretaries, an Extraordinary General Meeting may be called, to consider and decide upon the subjects mentioned in such written requisition.

XI.

That the Committee be empowered to exchange publications and reports, and to extend the privilege of attending the Meetings and Excursions of the Belfast Naturalists' Field Club to members of kindred societies, on similar privileges being accorded to its Members by such other societies.

The following Rules for the Conducting of the Excursions have been arranged by the Committee.

I. The Excursions to be open to all Members, each one to have the privilege of introducing two friends.

II. A Chairman to be elected as at ordinary meetings.

III. One of the Secretaries to act as conductor, or, in the absence of both, a member to be elected for that purpose.

IV. No change to be made in the programme, or extra expenses incurred, except by the consent of the members present.

V. No fees, gratuities, or other expenses to be paid except through the conductor.

VI. Every member or visitor to have the accommodation assigned by the conductor. When the accommodation is limited, consideration will be given to priority of application.

VII. Accommodation cannot be promised unless tickets are obtained before the time mentioned in the special circular.

VIII. Those who attend an excursion without previous notice will be liable to extra charge, if extra charge be incurred thereby.

IX. No intoxicating liquors to be provided at the expense of the Club.

Belfast Naturalists' Field Club.

EIGHTEENTH YEAR.

The Committee offer the following Prizes to be competed for during the Session ending March 31st, 1881 :—

I. For the best Herbarium of Flowering Plants,
   representing not less than 250 Species..........£1 0 0
II. For the best Herbarium of Flowering Plants,
   representing not less than 150 Species.......... 0 10 0
III. Best Collection of Mosses........................... 0 10 0
IV. "   "   Seaweeds........................ 0 10 0
V. "   "   Ferns............................ 0 10 0
VI. "   "   Tertiary and Post Tertiary
                  Fossils......................... 0 10 0
VII. "   "   Cretaceous Fossils.............. 0 10 0
VIII. "   "   Liassic   do. 0 10 0
IX. "   "   Palæozoic do. 0 10 0
X. "   "   Fossil Plants................... 0 10 0
XI. "   "   Marine Shells................... 0 10 0
XII. "   "   Land and Fresh-water Shells.   0 10 0
XIII. "   "   Lepidoptera..................... 0 10 0
XIV. Best Set of 25 Microscopic Slides............... 0 10 0

XV. Best Collection of Archæological Objects £0 10 0
XVI.   "   "   Crustacea 0 10 0
XVII. "   "   Echinodermata 0 10 0
XVIII. "   "   Geological Specimens, illustrative of the Mineral Resources of the Province of Ulster.. 1 0 0
XIX. Best Collection of all or any of the above Objects, collected *at the Excursions* of the Year... 0 10 0
XX. Six best Field Sketches appertaining to Geology, Archæology, or Natural History. 0 10 0

In every case where three or more persons compete for a Prize, a second one, of half its value, will be awarded if the conditions are otherwise complied with.

CONDITIONS.

No Competitor to obtain more than two Prizes in any year.

No Competitor to be awarded the same Prize twice within three years.

All Collections to be made personally during the Session in Ireland. Each Species to be correctly named, and locality stated. The Flowering Plants to be collected when in Flower, and classified according to the Natural System. The Sketches, Drawings, and Microscopic Slides to be the Competitors' own work.

No Prizes will be awarded except to such Collections as shall, in the opinion of the Judges, possess positive merit.

The Prizes to be in books, or suitable scientific objects, at the desire of the successful competitor.

NOTICE.

EXCHANGE OF PROCEEDINGS.

The Committee of the Club acknowledge with thanks the receipt of the following publications which have been received during the past year :—

American Association for the Advancement of Science.
Proceedings of Nashville Meeting, 1877.
,, St. Louis ,, 1878.

Bath Natural History and Antiquarian Field Club.
Proceedings. Vol. IV., Part 3—1880.

Boston (U.S.A.) Society of Natural History.
Proceedings. Vol. XX., Parts 2 and 3—1878-79-80.

Cardiff Naturalists' Society.
Report and Transactions. Vol. XI.—1879.

Dublin—Royal Geological Society of Ireland.
Journal. Vol. V., Part 2, New Series—1878-79.

Dublin—Royal Irish Academy.
Transactions. Vol. XXVI., Science—November, 1879.
" Vol I., Irish Manuscript Series—June, 1880.
" Vol I., Cunningham Memoirs—June, 1880.
Proceedings. Vol. III., Series 2, Part 4, Science.
" Vol II., Series 2, Part 1, Polite Literature and Antiquities.

Eastbourne Natural History Society.
Report and Papers—1879-80.

Edinburgh Geological Society.
Transactions. Vol. III., Part 3—1880.

Glasgow, Natural History Society of.
Proceedings. Vol. IV., Part 1—1878-79.

Leeds Philosophical and Literary Society.
Annual Report—1879-80.

Leeds Geological Association.
Address by B. Holgate, Esq., F.G.S.—October, 1878.

Liverpool Naturalists' Field Club.
Proceedings for 1879-80.

Liverpool Geological Society.
Proceedings. Vol IV., Part 2—1879-80.

Manchester Field Naturalists and Archæologists' Society.
Report and Proceedings—1879.

Norfolk and Norwich Naturalists' Society.
Transactions. Vol. III., Part 1—1879-80.

Pembrokeshire Naturalists' Field Club.
First Annual Report—1880.

U.S.A.—Smithsonian Institution, 1878.
Report on Science.

Warwickshire Naturalists' and Archæologists' Field Club.
Proceedings for 1879.

Watford Natural History Society and Hertfordshire Field Club.
Transactions. Vol. II., Parts 7 and 8—1880.

Wisconsin Natural History Society.
Report—1880.

(From the respective Societies.)

U.S.A.—Department of the Interior.

The Fresh-water Rhizopods of North America—Leidy, being Vol. XII of the Final Reports of the United States Geological Survey of the Territories—1879.

The North American Pinnipeds—a Monograph of the Walruses, Sea-lions, Sea-bears, and Seals of North America, being Miscellaneous Publications, No. 12, of the United States Geological Survey of the Territories—1880.

The United States Geographical Survey of the Territories.
Bulletin. Vol. IV., No. 1, 2, 3, 4—1878.
" Vol V., No. 1, 2, 3, 4—1879-80.

U.S.A.—Geological Survey of the Territories, Idaho and Wyoming.
" " " " Colorado.

(From F. V. Hayden, Esq.)

" **Geological and Natural History Survey of Minnesota.**
Sixth Annual Report—1877.
Seventh " 1878.

(From N. H. Winchell, Esq.)

Æneidea, or Critical, Exegetical, and Æsthetical Remarks on the Æneis. Vol. II. (continued).

(From the Trustees of the late James Henry, Esq., Dalkey.)

BELFAST NATURALISTS' FIELD CLUB.

EIGHTEENTH YEAR—1880-81.

LIST OF OFFICERS AND MEMBERS.

President.
WILLIAM GRAY, M.R.I.A.

Vice-President.
LIEUTENANT-GENERAL SMYTHE, F.R.S., M.R.I.A., &c.

Treasurer.
JOSEPH WRIGHT, F.G.S.

Secretaries.
WILLIAM SWANSTON, F.G.S., | F. W. LOCKWOOD,

Committee.

JOHN BROWNE, M.R.I.A.	GEORGE O'BRIEN.
WILLIAM A. FIRTH.	HUGH ROBINSON.
GREER MALCOMSON.	S. A. STEWART, F.B.S. Edin.
DR. JAMES MOORE, M.R.I.A., *Hon.* R.H.A.	ISAAC W. WARD.
REV. CANON MACILWAINE, D.D., M.R.I.A.	THOMAS WORKMAN.

Members.

Any Changes in the Addresses of Members should be notified to the Secretaries.

Charlton B. Aickin, Murray's Terrace.
Miss Alder, Holywood.
W. J. C. Allen, J.P., Faunoran, Whiteabbey.
Edward Allworthy, Langford Villa.
John Anderson, J.P., F.G.S., Hillbrook, Holywood.
Robt. Anderson, Meadowlands, Balmoral.
W. C. F. Anderson, Springbank, Dunmurry.
Samuel Andrews, Chlorine Place.
Mrs. Andrews, Chlorine Place.
Thomas D. Atkinson, Bangor, Co. Down.

James M. Barkley, Mountpottinger.
Robert Barklie, F.C.S., Carlisle St.
William Batt, Ormeau Road.
E. H. Bell, Knockdara, Strandtown.
Miss Bell, Lucyville, Whitehouse.
George E. Bell, Lombard Street.
James Bennett, Botanic Avenue.
A. W. Blackwell, Wandsworth Villas.
Joseph Boucher, Cliftonville Avenue
W. J. Boucher, Mountpottinger.
Capt. Boulcott, Barracks.
Davys Bowman, University Street.
Charles H. Brett, Laurine, Antrim Road.
Rev. John Bristow, M.A., Cliftonville.
D. H. Brown, Crumlin Terrace.
John Browne, J.P., Ravenhill.
John Browne, M.R.I.A., Drapersfield, Cookstown.
W. J. Browne, M.A., Longford.
W. W. Brydon, Greenisland.
Charles Bulla, Brougham Street.
H. Burden, M.D., College Square North.
J. R. Burnett, Holywood.

John Campbell, Mossley, Carnmoney.
R. G. Campbell, Mossley, Carnmoney.
William Campbell, Argyle House, Donaghadee.

Miss Carruthers, Claremont Street.
E. T. Church, Donegall Place.
J. C. Clarke, Dunedin.
John M. Clelland, Newtownstewart.
William Clibborn, Windsor Terrace.
Foster Coates, Derryvolgie, Windsor.
Sir Edward Coey, J.P., D.L., Merville.
Miss Connery, Mountcharles.
David Corbett, Coolavin.
Thomas H. Corry, M.A., F.B.S.E., Benvue, Windsor.
W. F. C. S. Corry, Chatsworth.
Major J. Sharman Crawford, J.P., D.L., Crawfordsburn.
Elisha Crawford, Fortwilliam Park.
James Creeth, Brookhill Avenue.
William M. Cunningham, Sydenham.

Right Hon. Lord Dufferin and Clandeboye, K.P., Clandeboye (Hon. Mem.)
Thomas Darragh, Museum.
John H. Davies, Glenmore, Lisburn.
Robert Day, F.S.A., Cork.
L. D. Devlin, Ulster Villas.
Thomas P. Devlin, Ulster Villas.
Edw. K. Dixon, University Street.
George Donaldson, Church Street.
Charles Dundee, Carnmoney.

Charles Elcock, Dunluce Street.

William Faren, Mountcharles.
J. George Ffennell, Ardmore, Windsor.
J. H. Ferguson, Antrim Road.
Joseph S. Firth, Whiterock.
William A. Firth, Whiterock.
S. Joseph Flynn, Franklin Place.
T. M. H. Flynn, Bessbrook.
Thomas Fraser, Wellington Park.

R. M. Gilmore, Dunrymond, Monaghan.
W. J. Gilmore, Holywood.
D. Corse Glen, F.G.S., Annfield Place, Glasgow.

George Glen, Durham Street.
G. T. Glover, Holywood.
Major Goldsmid, Hopefield Avenue.
Jas. Goskar, Carlisle Circus.
James Gourley, Derryboy, Killyleagh.
Robert Graham, College Gardens.
Rev. Canon Grainger, M.A., D.D., M.R.I.A., Broughshane (Cor. Mem.)
Rev. James Graves, Inisnaig, Stoneyford, County Kilkenny (Cor. Mem).
William Gray, M.R.I.A., Mountcharles.
Miss Gray, Mountcharles.
Miss Frances Gray, Mountcharles.
Miss Greer, Tarbat Villa, Sydenham.
Edward Gregg, Virginia Street.
H. H. Greenhill, Banbridge.

Joseph Hall, Windsor Avenue.
Hugh Hamilton, University Square.
J. C. Hamilton, University Square.
John Hamilton, Mount Street.
Thomas Hampton, Mountcharles.
L. Hanlon, Heath Cottage, Knock.
Mann Harbison, Model School, Newtownards.
John Harrison, Gardiner's Hill, Cork
W. Harte, C.E., Buncrana (Cor. Mem.)
James Haslett, J.P., Princess Gardens.
H. A. Hawkins, Kin-Edar, Strandtown.
W. D. Henderson, University Square.
Arthur Herdman, College Square North.
J. O. Herdman, College Square North.
F. A. Heron, Greenmount, Craigavad.
Mrs. Heron, Greenmount, Craigavad.
Prof. J. F. Hodges, M.D., F.C.S., Derryvolgie, Malone.
J. Sinclair Holden, M.D., F.G.S., Sudbury, Suffolk (Cor. Mem.)
F. C. Holmes, Belmont.
J. J. Howard, Greenwood, Knock.
Alexander Hunter, Northern Bank.
Miss Hunter, University Street.
Thomas Hunter, Holywood.

James Imrie, Fitzroy Avenue.
Rev. Richard Irvine, A.M., Hampton, Windsor.
R. H. Irwin, Holywood.

John Jaffé, Cambridge Villa, Sydenham.
Mrs. Jaffé, Cambridge Villa, Sydenham.
Hugh Jamison, Duncairn Terrace.
R. M. Jennings, Cork (Cor. Mem.)
James Johnston, West Elmwood.
Miss Johnston, Glenavy.
W. J. Johnston, J.P., Dunesk.

William Kernahan, Antrim Terrace.
Rev. J. A. Kerr, LL.D., Whiteabbey.
George Kidd, Suffolk, Dunmurry.
Henry Knight, Antrim Villa, Weston Super-Mare.
W. J. Knowles, Cullybackey.
Robert Kyle, Richmond.

W. W. Lamb, Divis View.
Miss Lamb, Divis View.
Chas. Lapworth, F.G.S., St. Andrews N.B. (Hon. Mem.)
George D. Leathem, Osborne Park.
F. R. Lepper, Avonmore, Derryvolgie.
Miss R. Lester, Newtownards.
Rev. H. W. Lett, M.A., T.C.D., Ardmore Glebe, Lurgan.
Joseph F. Lewis, Lothair Avenue.
Joseph Lewis, Schomberg Terrace.
Frederick W. Lockwood, Brookhill Avenue.
William Lowry, Oakley, Strandtown.
W. B. Lowson, Chichester Park.
Dr. Heinrich W. Luther, Eiselben, Friars' Bush Road.

John Mackenzie, Balmoral.
Henry Magee, Eglantine Avenue.
S. J. Magowan, Granville Villas.
J. J. Major, Belvoir Hall.
Greer Malcoms on, Shamrock Lodge.
Jas. Malcomson, Rosemount, Knock
Mrs. Malcomson, Rosemount, Knock
Samuel Murphy Malcomson, M.D., Margaretville, Strandtown.
John Marsh, Richmond.
J. C. Marsh, Clifton Park Avenue.

E

Rev. James Martin, Eglintoun.
Mrs. Martin, Eglintoun.
William Miller, Shankhill Road.
William R. Molyneux, Florence Place
James Moore, M.D., M.R.I.A.,
   Hon. R.H.A., Chichester Street.
John Moore, M.D., Carlisle Terrace.
David Morrow, Colin View Terrace.
John Morton, Donegal Terrace.
J. R. T. Mulholland, Northumberland Street.
Robert Mullan, Willowfield.
Jos. J. Murphy, F.G.S., Old Forge, Dunmurry.
J. R. Musgrave, J.P., Drumglass.
John M'Callum, Botanic Avenue.
James M'Clenahan, Tennent Street.
Samuel M'Cloy, Cromwell Road.
Rev. Ed. M'Clure, A.M., M.R.I.A., Lincoln's Inn Fields, London (Cor. Mem.)
Sir Thomas M'Clure, Bart., M.P., Belmont.
W. J. M'Clure, Divis Street.
James M'Connell, Caledonia Terrace.
John M'Connell, North Street.
E. J. M'Ervel, Elmwood Avenue.
Jos. H. M'Ferran, Elmwood Terrace
John M'Hutchinson, Wesley Terrace Cooke Street.
Rev. Canon MacIlwaine, D.D., M.R.I.A., Ulsterville.
Mrs. MacIlwaine, Ulsterville.
John MacIlwaine, Sydenham.
Mrs. MacIlwaine, Sydenham.
J. B. S. MacIlwaine, Stephen's Green, Dublin.
Mrs. MacIlwrath, Dunluce Street.
Daniel M'Kee, Adela Place.
W. S. M'Kee, Fleetwood Street.
Alexander MacLaine, Altmore.
F. P. M'Lean, Huntly Villas.
William MacMillan Sallowmount, Ballinasloe.

Lucien Nepveu, Fitzwilliam Street.
Chas. A. Nicholl, Rathmore, Greenisland.
William Nicholl, Adela Street.
Richard Niven, Chrome Hill, Lisburn.

Thomas Edens Osborne, Marino Cottages

George O'Brien, Botanic Avenue.
Joshua O'Brien, Botanic Avenue.
W. D. O'Brien, Botanic Avenue.
F. H. O'Flaherty, Fitzroy Avenue.
Mrs. O'Flaherty, Fitzroy Avenue.
Dr. O'Flaherty, R.N., Botanic Terrace.
Rev. Jas. O'Laverty, P.P., M.R.I.A., Holywood.
Rev. James O'Neill, M.A., College Square East.

Henry R. Parker, LL.D., Methodist College.
D. C. Patterson, Holywood.
Robt. Lloyd Patterson, Croft House, Holywood.
William H. Patterson, M.R.I.A., Garasard, Strandtown.
James J. Phillips, Granville Terrace.
William H. Phillips, Lemonfield, Holywood.
E. Wakefield Pim, Elmwood Terrace.
John Pim, Bonaven, Antrim Road.
Joshua Pim, Crumlin Terrace.
T. W. Pim, The Lodge, Strandtown.
Chas. D. Purdon, M.D., M.R.I.A., Wellington Place.
Miss Nellie Purdon, Wellington Place.

Jos. Radley, Prospect Hill, Lisburn.
William Rankin, York Street.
John Rea, M.D., Gt. Victoria Street.
James Theodore Richardson, Glenone, Lisburn.
David C. Ritchie, Duncairn Terrace.
Hugh Robinson, Donegall Street.
Mrs. Robinson, Donegall Street.
Rev. George Robinson, A.M., Tartaraghan, Armagh.
James R. Robinson, St. Helen's Terrace.
W. A. Robinson, Crofton, Holywood.
William G. Robinson, Tartaraghan, Armagh.
Richard Ross, M.D., Wellington Place.
Mrs. Rowland, University Street.
Charles C. Russell, Campmer Villa, Newtownards.

Mrs. Scott, Fountainville Terrace
Thomas Shaw, Pakenham Place.
Samuel Smiles, Sydenham.
Charles Smith, F.G.S., Barrow-in-Furness.
Edward Smith, Chichester Terrace.
F. W. Smith, Rugby Road.
George K. Smith, Meadow Bank, Whitehouse.
Rev. George C. Smythe, M.A., Coole Glebe, Carnmoney.
Lieut.-Gen. Smythe, R.A., F.R.S., M.R.I.A., Abbeyville, Whiteabbey.
Rev. J. H. Smythe, Fortwilliam.
Charles Sparkes, Prospect Hill, Lisburn.
Adam Speers, B.Sc., Holywood.
Sir N. A. Staples, Bart., Lissan, Dungannon (Life Mem.)
J. H. Staples, Lissan, Dungannon.
H. Stevenson, Glenfield Place.
J. M'N. Stevenson, Carrickfergus.
Richd. Stevenson, Ashley Avenue.
Peter Stirling, Queen Street.
S. A. Stewart, F.B.S.E., North Street.
Miss Swanston, Annalee Terrace.
William Swanston, F.G.S., Cliftonville Avenue.
Mrs. Swanston, Cliftonville Avenue.
Samuel Symington, Ballyoran House.

Prof. Ralph Tate. F.G.S., A.L.S., University of Adelaide, South Australia (Hon. Mem.)
A. O'D. Taylor, Upper Crescent.
H. F. Thomas, Lower Crescent.
Mrs. Thomas, Lower Crescent.
Henry Thompson, Windsor.
George Thompson, Falls Road.
Prof. Sir C. Wyville Thomson, LL.D., F.R.S., &c., Edinburgh (Hon. Mem.)

Prof. James Thomson, A.M., LL.D., F.R.S., Glasgow (Hon. Mem.)
John Todd, Regent Street.
W. A. Todd, Elgin Terrace.
W. A. Traill, M.A.I., B.E., H.M. Geol. Survey, Ballymena.
James. G. Turtle, Cambridge Terrace.

John Vinycomb, Melrose Terrace.

Herbert C. Waddell, Magheralin.
Thos. R. Walkington, Laurel Lodge, Sydenham.
Isaac W. Ward, Colin View Terrace
John Ward, F.R.G.S., F.G.S., Lennoxvale.
John S. Ward, Lisburn.
Marcus J. Ward, Fernleigh.
Thomas R. Ward, Holywood.
E. H. Watson, Ardmore, Windsor.
Isaac Waugh, Everton Terrace.
Mrs. Waugh, Everton Terrace.
T. K. Wheeler, M.D., Clarendon Place.
William Whitla, M.D., Gt. Victoria Street.
C. Williams, M.R.C.S.E., College Square East.
James Wilson, jun., Albion Place.
James Wilson, Ballybundon, Killinchy.
James F. Wilson, Ventry Street.
John Workman, J.P., Windsor.
Rev. Robt. Workman, A.M., Glastry
Thos. Workman, Westburne, Windsor.
Joseph Wright, F.G.S., Albertville.
Mrs. Wright, Albertville.
S. O. Wylie, College Square North.
William Wylie, Belgrave Terrace.

Robert Young, C.E., Rathvarna.

SPECIAL PRIZES.

XXI. The President offers a Prize of £1 1s for the best set of not less than Three Sketches contributed to the Club's Album. The set to be of uniform size, about 9 x 6 inches, and to be Original Drawings of Ancient Irish Monuments in Ulster. The Judges may award half the prize for two drawings only, or in the event of there being only one Competitor, provided the works submitted possess sufficient merit.

XXII. Mr. William Swanston, F.G.S., offers a Prize of 10s 6d for the best Two Studies, illustrative of Geology, contributed to the Club's Album. The subjects must be from Nature, and may be either in the form of Drawings or Measured Sections. Size not to exceed 15 x 9 inches.

XXIII. A Prize of 10s given by the late Mr. J. W. Murphy, for the best Collection of Recent Sponges, the conditions being the same as those for Prizes I. to XX.

N.B.—The Sketches and Drawings to be Competitors' own work.

EXCURSIONS

ARRANGED FOR THE SESSION
1880-1881.

---

1. DROMORE AND MAGHERALIN   Third week in May.
2. CULTRA........................   First   "   June.
3. CHARLEMONT ....   Fourth   "   June.
4. GREYABBEY..................   Second   "   July.
5. SOUTH DONEGAL..............   First   "   August.
6. BALLYCLARE AND LARNE.....   First   "   September.

Due notice will be given to the Members as to the day and object of each Excursion; and the Members are invited to avail themselves of the arrangements to be made at each for giving information to inquirers.

WM. SWANSTON, F.G.S.,
50, King Street,
F. W. LOCKWOOD,
5, Corn Market,
} Hon. Secs.

BELFAST, *10th May, 1880.*

Presented
11. FEB. 86

www.ingramcontent.com/pod-product-compliance
Lightning Source LLC
Chambersburg PA
CBHW051844300426
44117CB00006B/266